Elements of
a Two-Process
Theory of Learning

Elements of
a Two-Process
Theory of Learning

J. A. GRAY
Department of Experimental Psychology,
University of Oxford, South Parks Road,
Oxford

1975

Academic Press
London New York San Francisco
A Subsidiary of Harcourt Brace Jovanovich, Publishers

ACADEMIC PRESS INC. (LONDON) LTD.
24-28 Oval Road,
London NW1

United States Edition published by
ACADEMIC PRESS INC.
111 Fifth Avenue,
New York, New York 10003

Library of Congress Catalog Card Number: 74-5677
ISBN: 0-12-296850-6

PRINTED IN GREAT BRITAIN BY
WILLIAM CLOWES & SONS LIMITED
LONDON, COLCHESTER AND BECCLES

Preface

The main purpose of this book is not to present a fully-fledged theory of learning, or even a review of the theories of learning proposed by others. Rather, it is to give students of this difficult topic some guidance in the mysterious ways learning theorists think. Since their thinking is, in fact, sometimes muddled, I hope that en route I may be able to cast some light in dusty corners, and make a marginal contribution to the solution of the problems with which learning theory deals. But my major aim will have been achieved if this book is found useful by undergraduates, or by scientists coming into psychology from other disciplines, who need to find out what sorts of questions learning theorists ask and what sorts of evidence are relevant to their questions. Some of these questions are particularly knotty. These, moreover, tend to be the fundamental ones, which need some clarity of perception before one is even in a position to approach the remaining problems in the field. It is these, in particular, with which I shall attempt to deal. If the student is once able to see clearly these questions, and the kind of evidence that bears on them, he will, I believe, find that the methods of thought for which they call will be equally valuable in dealing with many other issues in the theory of learning which we must ignore here.

I shall not, however, use these didactic purposes as an excuse for coming to no conclusions about the issues with which I deal. In some cases, I believe a conclusion on some of these issues is possible (though never uncontroversial, still less certain). By the end of the book, the general approach to the theory of learning which I favour will have become clear; and, indeed, we shall be in possession of a kind of mini-theory of learning which can at least serve as a guide to further thinking on these matters. For the initiated, it can be said that this mini-theory will look most like Mowrer's (1960) "two-process" theory. I hope, however, that it will be possible to reject my conclusions at every point, and the mini-theory with them, and yet still learn from this book how to think about learning theory.

A second function I hope this book will serve is that of acting as a kind of scaffolding for a theory of the physiological basis of personality. As I have suggested elsewhere (Gray, 1972a), learning theory has had a pivotal role to play in the development of physiologically based causal theories of personality. Theories of this nature—as exemplified by Pavlov's typology (Teplov, 1964), Eysenck's (1967) theory of extraversion and neuroticism, or my own similar theory (Gray, 1970a, 1973)—attempt to account for individual differences in

v

behaviour by reference to variation in the sensitivity or reactivity of particular components in the system (the "conceptual nervous system") which controls behaviour. Viewed in this way, learning theory is the attempt to describe the general structure of this system, i.e., the structure which is common to all members of the species in which the individual differences are observed. Some knowledge of this general structure is clearly a prerequisite to any investigation of individual differences in the functioning of parts of the structure. It is in this sense that learning theory is a scaffolding for a theory of the physiological basis of personality.

More particularly, in order to facilitate an experimental and theoretical attack on the problem of the physiological basis of personality, we need some idea of the number and kind of separate sub-systems or "components" which go together to make up the general structure. Armed with such information, it is possible to make reasonable guesses as to the kind of individual differences in process which underlie the observed individual differences in behaviour. With this end in mind, therefore, I have devoted much attention in this book to distinguishing between different processes which look alike, or to identifying as the same processes which look different, whenever either of these strategies has seemed possible. The outcome of this approach is summarized in the concluding chapter of the book. However, there is no reason why this aim should obtrude upon the reader whose interest is confined to the theory of learning itself; nor, I believe, has it affected the conclusions I have reached.

Most of the points which will come up arose first in tutorials with undergraduates reading psychology at Oxford University. They have contributed much, and not only as sounding boards: I hope they will accept a collective acknowledgement for their help.

JEFFREY GRAY,
*Department of
Experimental Psychology,
Oxford*

For Venus

Contents

1. Habituation and Expectancy

Two of the issues which come up repeatedly in learning theory concern "expectancy" and "inhibition". The first of these suffers from never having been defined, and the second from having been defined many hundreds of contradictory times, usually with a modifying adjective to indicate the brand of inhibition we are supposedly dealing with. It turns out that the study of what is probably the simplest kind of learning—the waning of response which occurs when a stimulus is repeatedly presented: "habituation"— contains clues which not only enable us to gain a clear perspective on what is meant by these terms, but also allows us to decide that there are probably real processes to which they correspond.

We have just defined "habituation" by using the two most primitive terms in the psychological vocabulary—"stimulus" and "response". How, in turn, do we define these? This is a matter to which we must devote some preliminary attention.

Operational Definitions: "Stimulus" and "Response"

The universe of discourse of the psychologist may be divided into (1) his experimental operations, (2) his observations and (3) the theories he constructs to account for the way in which his observations vary according to his operations. The most important aspect of this tripartite division is the gulf which separates (1) and (2) from (3). It is the clear segregation of method (1) and data (2), on the one hand, from theory (3), on the other, which marks off the natural sciences from other kinds of intellectual endeavour. Conversely, it is the failure of such activities as psychonanalysis or existential analysis to preserve this distinction which renders them different sorts of games altogether to the scientific one. Though it is in better shape than these subjects, experimental psychology, too, has often had difficulty in preserving the necessary distinctions. In coping with this difficulty, it has often sought aid in the "operational" definition of the words in its vocabulary, i.e. a definition in terms of experimental operations and observations. However, such definitions present their own problems. Both the problems and the virtues of operational definitions are well illustrated by "stimulus" and "response".

At face value the term "stimulus" refers to something that the subject observes and "response" to something that the subject does. However, it is precisely information about what the subject observes and does which we lack. Indeed, many of the psychologist's experiments are concerned to supply just this missing information. Thus, if we defined "stimulus" and "response" in this way, we would be using them as *theory*-words, making hypotheses, in effect, as to the nature of the processes which we are attempting to discover. It is, however, sufficient to glance at any paper picked at random from the psychological literature to see that this is not how these words are in fact used. On the contrary, they very obviously form part of the psychologist's operation and observation-vocabulary: the word "stimulus" describes, not what the subject observes, but what the experimenter does; and the word "response" describes, not what the subject does, but what the experimenter observes. And it is in this sense that these terms (and their corresponding symbols, S and R) will be used in this book.

However, the difficulties caused by "stimulus" and "response" do not stop here. Not everything the experimenter does can count as a stimulus; and not all descriptions of observations made on an animal's behaviour can count as descriptions of a response. This became evident early on in the history of behaviourist psychology. Thus the early attempts to define "stimulus" and "response" sought for strictly independent definitions based on the physical characteristics of the experimenter's apparatus and measuring devices. A stimulus, for example, would be defined as a physical energy change taking place at a particular location in time and space; and a response as a set of contractions in a specified set of muscle fibres as recorded, say, on an electromyograph. But the physical energy change does not necessarily cause any alterations in the subject's behaviour (e.g. it may not have been noticed), and if it fails to do this it cannot be regarded as a stimulus. Similarly, it can readily be shown that whatever else an animal learns to do, it is not usually to contract a specific set of muscle fibres. A classic demonstration of the latter point is the experiment by MacFarlane (1930), who trained rats to walk down a maze for a food reward and then flooded the maze; the animals promptly swam to the goalbox, choosing the correct path but, of course, using a totally different set of muscle contractions. In fact, as we shall see when we come to deal with "instrumental" or "goal-directed" learning, it is perfectly clear that what animals learn to do under such conditions is to produce a particular kind of change in their own environment—i.e., they learn to produce a stimulus.

To define "stimulus" and "response" in terms of what the animal observes and does, then, is to use theory-words as though they were operational and observational words; and to define them in terms of what the experimenter does and observes risks using them trivially. It turns out that the only useful way out of this impasse is to define them interdependently, by saying, roughly: a stimulus is something that evokes a response and a response is something that is evoked by a stimulus. On the face of it, this is a tautology of the most empty kind, and it has frequently been taken as a cause for scandal that it should be so.

However, the interdependence of "stimulus" and "response" need offer no cause for scandal. The word "stimulus" is, in effect, the psychologist's widest term for any operation which has a rather immediate effect on an experimental subject; and the word "response" is his widest term for any observation of the behaviour of an experimental subject which may be given a reasonably precise placement in time. And it turns out that there is a general inter-dependence between a scientist's operations and his observations of which the interdependence between stimulus and response is but one parochial example.

This interdependence flows, in the first instance, from the essential scientific demand for public replicability of experimental observations. If a scientist describes a phenomenon P observed when he carried out operation O, this claim is only given full credit if other scientists are able to repeat operation O and observe the same phenomenon P. Only those operations which, upon repetition, produce a repeatable observation can be regarded as useful; and only observations which can be made whenever the same operations are repeated can be regarded as reliable.

A second feature of the scientific endeavour which gives rise to the interdependence between operations and observations is the search for regular functional relationships between the two. This search involves a "bootstrap" progression which takes the following form: operations are repeatedly refined and re-defined to produce observations which show a lawful or systematic relation to them; and, simultaneously, observations are refined and re-defined to the same end. The outcome, necessarily, is a procedural and logical interdependence between operation and observation of just the kind which concerns us (though, to be sure, psychology has a long way to go before this process of refinement and redefinition has been completed with respect to its own special terms).

With this preamble, let us pass on to the business of defining "stimulus" (S) and "response" (R) for our own purposes. A stimulus, then, is any change produced by the experimenter in the subject's environment which can be shown to be related to a subsequent change in the subject's behaviour; and a response is any change in the subject's behaviour which can be shown to be related to a prior change in the subject's environment. According to this definition, one ought not to use response for changes in behaviour which can be observed, but not related to antecedent stimuli. For some purposes of discussion, it is useful to have a separate term for such a form of behaviour; and the term behaviour change might do. However, particularly in the study of instrumental learning, it is such common practice to refer to behaviour emitted by the subject as a response in the absence of knowledge of antecedent stimuli, assuming even that these always exist, that it would be difficult to depart from it. We shall therefore use response and its symbol R, to refer both to responses as defined strictly, above, and to behaviour changes *per se*.

A distinction which may now be made is between the "distal" stimulus, i.e. the environmental change as made by the experimenter, and the "proximal" stimulus, i.e. the effective stimulus as perceived by the subject and as it controls the subject's behaviour. Similarly, on the response side, one can ask what the response learned by the animal consists of (which, by analogy, one might term the "proximal response"), as distinct from the behaviour which is recorded on the experimenter's apparatus (or "distal response"); and the study of transfer of learning, for example, attempts to discover this. Now "proximal" stimuli and responses as so defined, are hypothetical or theory-words; though in principle, enough experimentation should eventually give us a very good idea as to what the proximal stimuli and responses actually are in any given situation. Usually, however, we shall be in a good deal of ignorance about them. But lack of knowledge of the actual proximal stimulus or response need not inhibit us in our use of "stimulus" and "response": for, in the first instance, these terms refer to operations carried out by the experimenter and the observations with which these are correlated, and these can be perfectly accurately specified in any experimental situation. In this book, we shall need on occasion to consider the nature of the proximal stimulus and response, particularly when we come to deal with the distinction between classical and instrumental conditioning in Chapter 2. However, for many purposes, this issue can be ignored, so that, except when otherwise indicated, "S" and "R" will refer (as already indicated) to what the experimenter does and observes rather than to what the animal observes and does.

Habituation or Orienting Responses

Having practised these elementary distinctions of operational thinking on "stimuli" and "responses", we can now turn to the study of habituation and put them to work.

The waning of response which occurs when the stimulus which elicits it is repeatedly presented is a very common phenomenon, observed throughout the animal kingdom. It is this process which is termed "habituation". This term is applied, however, only when the stimulus which elicits the response does so innately, that is without any special learning involved. Such a stimulus was called by Pavlov an "unconditioned stimulus" (UCS). (The waning of response which is observed under various conditions of repetition of a stimulus which did not at first innately elicit its correlated response, but came to do so only as a result of special training procedures, is dealt with separately in later chapters.) Many examples of habituating responses, and a detailed discussion of the variables which affect habituation, can be found in a number of sources (Thorpe, 1963; Horn and Hinde, 1970). Since our purpose here is to use the phenomenon of habituation to illustrate certain central issues in the theory of learning, rather than to consider the phenomenon in its own right, we shall make no attempt to duplicate or even summarize these reviews. Instead, we shall concentrate on the major features of one class of habituating responses, the "orienting responses". These have been studied in detail by Sokolov (1960, 1963a; see also Lynn, 1966), as well as by a number of authors who contributed to the symposium edited by Horn and Hinde (1970).

It is customary, but it can be misleading, to describe orienting responses by listing them. Such a list is peculiarly heterogeneous. It includes, among other things, the turning of head and eyes towards the source of the stimulus, a change in the wave pattern recorded in the electroencephalograph (EEG) known as "alpha-blocking" or "desynchronization", a constriction of the blood vessels in the limbs coupled with a dilation of the blood vessels in the temples, changes in respiration and heart rate, and a fall in the electrical resistance of the skin on the palm of the hand and the sole of the foot which is known as the "galvanic skin response (GSR)". Details of these various responses can be found in the sources quoted above. It is sometimes suggested that the adaptive value of all of these responses is to increase the capacity of the organism to process sensory information. Although this is plausible for such responses as head-and eye-turning, it is quite unclear at the present time that the EEG changes, the GSR, or many other orienting responses, have this, or indeed any other, adaptive function. Certainly, it would be impossible to compile such a list of responses by picking the ones which do have such a function. Thus there must be some other principle by which the list has been compiled.

This principle is, in fact, a perfectly clear one. It is again an operational one. The rule which was adopted by the Soviet investigators who, under Sokolov's direction, pioneered the investigation of the orienting responses in the 1950s (though Pavlov had first pointed out their importance much earlier) was as follows: if any response is elicited by (1) novel stimuli, which (2) may belong to any modality, and if (3) the response habituates upon repetition of the stimulus, then this response is an orienting response (OR). It will be clear that (1) and (3) in this formulation come to the same thing, since, if habituation failed to occur, it could not be the case that the OR was elicited only by novel stimuli. Thus we may define ORs as *that class of habituating responses, the stimuli for which are modality nonspecific.* More generally, one could say that the ORs are reactions elicited by novelty of any kind.

Armed with this definition, we may carry out the operations it specifies, that is to say, we may observe what an animal or a human subject does when we present it with novel stimuli of a multitude of kinds, and any responses we observe which follow these rules will be appropriately called ORs. It is in this way that the list of ORs was in fact compiled. And if at some future time a scientist claims that some new response—say twitching the left little toe—is an OR, we can be sure what it is that the scientist is claiming and we can easily verify for ourselves whether it is in fact so. Whereas neither of these things would be true if, for example, an OR was defined in terms of some putative adaptive function.

This is not to say, of course, that questions about adaptive function are unimportant: quite the contrary. But they are questions which inevitably involve theory and this theory will need to be put to the test of experiment. It will not be possible to carry out such experiments in a sufficiently rigorous manner without an objective vocabulary with which to describe what we do and what we see. And it is such a vocabulary which an operational definition is able to give us.

There remains one last point of terminology to clarify. It is commonly assumed that the various orienting responses are all aspects of a single process or mechanism in the brain. This process is termed the "orienting reaction" or "orienting reflex". For our present purposes it is unimportant whether or not this assumption is correct; though the general covariation between the particular ORs makes it at least likely. By the term "*the* OR", therefore, we shall mean either this single process, assuming it exists, or the collective behaviour of the particular ORs.

Now that we know what the OR is, let us consider the problems raised by its habituation. At this point we pass beyond the ground-clearing procedures which are involved in the formulation of operations, observations and their corresponding vocabulary and enter the realm of theory. Two theoretical issues are raised by the data on habituation of the OR. The first concerns the notion of "expectancy". The question we shall need to consider in this connection may be put as follows: do the data on habituation of the OR require us to postulate a process whereby the organism is able to predict, on the basis of the stimuli to which it has recently been exposed, what stimuli are likely to be presented in the future? The second issue concerns the notion of "inhibition". Here our question is: do these same data require us to postulate a process which actively suppresses a response which would otherwise be elicited by a stimulus? Both of these questions are entwined in the controversy which Lynn (1966), in a lucid review of data and theory in this field, has termed that between "one-stage" and "two-stage" models of habituation of the OR. One-stage models deny the need for either expectancies or inhibition ("inhibition" meaning a response-suppression process of the kind indicated, and nothing else). One particular two-stage model—that of Sokolov (1960, 1963a)—asserts the need for both.

The data which form the battle-ground for this controversy are reasonably clear: it is their interpretation which is in doubt. Let us summarize the major features of these data and then consider how they bear on the controversy.

In a typical experiment of Sokolov's, a simple stimulus—e.g., a tone of specified pitch, loudness, duration etc.—is presented to the subject (usually human) and one or a number of the ORs—say the EEG changes and the GSR—are measured. The stimulus is presented repeatedly, either at fixed or varying intervals, until the ORs are no longer observed. At this point a number of variations may be introduced into the basic experimental situation, and these have led to the following findings (Sokolov, 1960, 1963a; Lynn, 1966).

(1) Change along any one of the dimensions by which the stimulus may be characterized (pitch, loudness, duration etc.) is sufficient to re-instate the habituated OR. The degree of change which is effective is usually very small compared to the results obtained with other methods used to evaluate an animal's ability to discriminate between two closely similar stimuli (e.g. differential conditioning of a positive response to one stimulus and a negative response to the other). Repetition of the changed stimulus leads to a second process of habituation, which usually proceeds faster than habituation to the initial stimulus.

(2) If a period of time is allowed to elapse after habituation without presentation of the habituated stimulus (this period being long relative to the inter-stimulus interval used during initial habituation: say 24 hours compared to several minutes), there is a return of the OR when the stimulus is re-presented after this period. This phenomenon is similar to the "spontaneous recovery" described by Pavlov (1927, 1928) as affecting extinguished conditioned reflexes (CRs), which also recover their strength over a period of time during

which the extinguished conditioned stimulus (CS) is not presented. The spontaneously recovered OR (again like the CR) is smaller than the initial OR and, upon further presentation of the stimulus, it re-habituates at a faster rate than during the initial habituation. If this process is repeated sufficiently often, lapse of time no longer gives rise to a recurrence of the OR, and the OR is said to be "chronically" habituated, in distinction to the "acute" habituation observed in a single testing session. This distinction, too, is paralleled by the distinction between "acute" and "chronic" extinction of CRs.

(3) Presentation of a second novel stimulus (the "extra stimulus" or ES) just before presentation of the habituated ex-novel stimulus leads to a recurrence of ORs to the habituated stimulus both on this trial and on a few following trials, even though on the latter trials the ES is not presented again. After two or three repetitions of this process the ES loses its effect and habituation to the original stimulus is undisturbed. This phenomenon is known as "de-habituation" and it is reminiscent of "disinhibition" of CRs (see Chapter 3).

(4) If, after habituation is complete in one particular session, the habituated stimulus continues to be repeatedly presented, the following sequence of events is observed. The subject (human) becomes drowsy, as shown by the appearance of the EEG which is being recorded throughout. It is then observed (after perhaps 80–100 repeated presentations) that there is a sudden return of ORs to the previously habituated stimulus, and the returned ORs last for many more trials before being habituated a second time, by which time the subject is properly asleep. The phase of return of the previously habituated ORs is termed "overhabituation", the final disappearance of the ORs being called "secondary habituation". At the time of overhabituation, Sokolov has also reported that any strong arousing stimulus, such as an ES, or any treatments which re-alert the subject, such as the administration of caffeine (a stimulant drug), cause the prompt disappearance of the overhabituated ORs, the EEG at the same time showing a return to patterns of wakefulness.

Note that this last phenomenon contains an odd kind of reversal of effects: whereas, against a background of primary habituation of the OR, the presentation of an ES causes de-habituation of the OR to the habituated stimulus (see 3, above), against a background of recurrence of an over-habituated OR, the ES leads once more to the disappearance of this OR. It is as though the principle upon which the system works is, "given a new novel stimulus, cancel the last instruction for ORs: if the OR to a previously habituated stimulus is currently being suppressed, release it; if such an OR is currently being elicited once more, suppress it." Incidentally, the phenomenon of overhabituation of the OR is one which you will probably have encountered frequently in your own experience, when the ticking of a clock, to which you have beome thoroughly habituated, suddenly achieves deafening loudness just as you are falling asleep.

One-Stage and Two-Stage Models for Habituation: Evidence for Expectancies

Given these findings, the next job is to attempt to explain them. Explanations in pyschology, as in other fields, can take various forms. In the theory of learning, the usual form of explanations which is sought is, in effect, a description of a system which could produce the observed phenomena, given the same programme of experimental stimuli. We may call such a system, following Hebb (1955), a "conceptual nervous system (CNS)": it is conceptual, because it is based, not on data about the real nervous system (RNS), but on purely behavioural data; but it is a nervous system, nonetheless, because, if it is correct—i.e., if it correctly describes the way the real organism is constructed and operates—then it is the construction and the operation of the RNS which it describes.

We shall, whenever possible, present such theories in this book in the form of black-box diagrams of the proposed system, rather than as verbal descriptions; for such diagrams are an invaluable aid to clarity of thought.

One of the interests of Sokolov's work on habituation of the OR is that it illustrates very clearly the difference between the search for a successful CNS and the search for mechanisms in the RNS to explain the same behavioural data. What Sokolov did, in effect—and in my view this tends in general to be a very effective strategy in the behavioural sciences—was to conduct his investigation of the way the brain handles habituation of the OR in two phases. In phase 1, he developed a CNS which appeared to handle the behavioural data; then, in phase 2, he began to investigate the brain directly to see if he could find structures and neural elements which operated in the way that would be expected if his CNS was correct. We shall follow him through both these phases.

Sokolov's CNS, or "model", for habituation of the OR is a two-stage one. As the name implies, this has more machinery in it than a one-stage model. Following the well-known principle of parsimony in scientific explanation, therefore, we shall only want to accept a two-stage model if a one-stage model is unable to do the job. Let us begin, then, by outlining, in very general terms, the one-stage model and then look to see whether there are data which it cannot handle.

One-stage models for habituation of the OR all have in common the principle that there is one and only one set of what I shall call "elements" (which, in the RNS, would be neurons, but in a CNS may remain more abstract) intervening between the S and the R which the S elicits, and that it is change in some portion of these elements which leads to habituation. Two-stage models, in contrast, postulate one set of elements to mediate the initial elicitation of the R by the S, and a second set of elements, which come to be operated by the S after repeated presentation and which are responsible for the eventual habituation of the OR. These two models are presented as black-box diagrams in Fig. 1.1. We need not concern ourselves in detail with the nature of the change which is supposed to occur with repeated presentation of the S, according to one-stage models, and which leads eventually to unresponsiveness in the chain of elements. At the neurophysiological level, a number of different processes have been proposed, e.g. depression in the size of the synaptic potential or in transmitter release at the synapse (Horn, 1970). For the arguments we are going to deploy, the nature of the proposed process is irrelevant. Furthermore, we may also regard the proposals that habituation of the OR is due to adaptation in sensory receptors or fatigue in effector organs as special cases of the general one-stage model, in which the critical changing elements are close to the input or output side of the system respectively. There are, in fact, as we shall now see, special arguments which can be used to show that these last proposals are insufficient to account for the data, but they are also refuted by any arguments which can infirm one-stage models in general.

Clearly, one way to invalidate the one-stage model would be to show that, at the time the habituated OR is no longer being elicited,

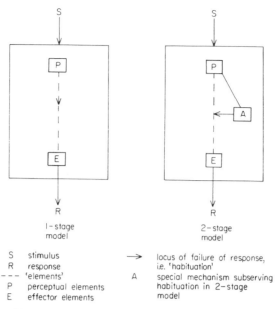

S   stimulus   →   locus of failure of response,
R   response   i.e. 'habituation'
– – – 'elements'   A   special mechanism subserving
P   perceptual elements   habituation in 2-stage
E   effector elements   model

FIG. 1.1. One and Two Stage Models for Habituation.

nonetheless the pathway between stimulus and response is still open. This can easily be shown in such a way as to eliminate unresponsiveness in the receptors or effectors themselves. At the time when the S is no longer eliciting an OR, it is quite likely to continue to elicit other responses: e.g., the continued presentation of an electric shock, which initially elicited an OR in the form of vasodilation in the temples, will, after habituation of this OR, come to elicit vasoconstriction in the same location, this being part of the defensive reaction to shock (Sokolov, 1960, 1963a). Similarly, there can be no question of effector fatigue, because, as we have seen, upon change of any one of the parameters of the stimulus, the OR is at once re-elicited. Thus, if a one-stage model is to be correct, the elements which develop unresponsiveness must be elements lying between the receptors and the effectors. By "receptors and effectors", in this context, we mean the initial central processing of the stimulus which is involved in perception, as well as changes in the peripheral receptor organs; and also the motor commands which lead to the contraction of muscles or to the secretion of glands, as well as the latter events themselves.

What evidence is there, then, that the pathway between receptors and effectors remains open even after habituation of the OR? Clearly facts such as spontaneous recovery and dehabituation do no more than show that the unresponsiveness, if it has developed, is not permanent, but dissipates with time and may be affected by other variables as well. And, indeed, one-stage theorists (e.g., Thompson and Spencer, 1966; Horn, 1970) have no difficulty in arranging their models for such data. But there are four kinds of experiments which have been claimed to infirm one-stage models in general. All of them involve in some way reducing or weakening the stimulus after habituation has been achieved and showing that such stimulus reduction leads to a re-appearance of the OR in exactly the same way that any other change in the stimulus parameters has this consequence.

The notion behind this kind of experiment is as follows. If the reason that the habituated OR is no longer being elicited is due to a blockage of the pathway between S and R, then, on a one-stage model, any change in the stimulus parameters which re-elicits an OR must normally be regarded as stimulating either different receptor elements or different elements on the pathway between S and R. To counter this view, therefore, one seeks for changes in the stimulus parameters which cannot easily be understood in this way. Such changes may be produced by altering either stimulus intensity or stimulus duration. Alterations of this kind are rather naturally regarded as leaving the stimulated elements unchanged, but changing the degree to which they are stimulated (though, as we shall see, this view is open to challenge). It is therefore felt that reductions in stimulus intensity or duration are of more interest than increases in these parameters. It is as though there is a road-block on the route from S to R which is sufficiently strong to block the passage of an S of the original strength: if we increase the strength of the S, and the road-block is broken, this is hardly surprising; but, if we *decrease* its strength, we would not expect a weaker stimulus to break through a road-block powerful enough to stop a stronger one. Thus, if we can show a re-elicited OR after decreasing stimulus strength (i.e., intensity or duration), this is *prima facie* evidence against a one-stage model.

The first version of this experiment consists in habituating the OR to a stimulus of intensity I, and then reducing its intensity, while changing nothing else, and showing a return of the OR. The facts are not in dispute: this certainly occurs (Lynn, 1966). Can a one-stage model explain them? The notion that a one-stage model *cannot* explain them seems to be based on our understanding of the way the real nervous system works. It is known that, in general, the intensity of a stimulus is coded, *along the pathways from the receptor organs to the primary sensory areas in the neocortex*, by the *rate* of firing (the higher the intensity, the higher the firing rate) of the neurons which carry the information about the other aspects of the stimulus, not by the firing of *different* neurons for different intensities, as is the case, say, for different locations of points of light in space. It is argued, therefore, that, if some of the elements along the pathway from stimulus to response have developed unresponsiveness, it might be reasonable to expect this to be broken down by the higher firing rate which is a consequence of an *increase* in stimulus intensity, but not by the lower firing rate which is a consequence of a decrease in stimulus intensity. However, there is a flaw in the argument.

Even though it appears to be the case that stimulus intensity is coded by firing rate during the initial stages of the processing of sensory information by the nervous system, there is no guarantee that this continues to be the case all along the pathway from S to R. It is quite conceivable that, at some stage along this pathway, signals of different strength, as coded up to that point by firing rate, are shunted off into different pathways as a result of some internal process of analysis. This is shown diagrammatically in Fig. 1.2. This would allow elements on the original S–R pathway to develop the unresponsiveness which is shown by habituation of the OR, leaving, however, fresh elements to respond either to stimulus intensity increase or to stimulus intensity decrease.

It might be asked why, in the face of evidence about the way the RNS actually codes stimulus intensity, we should imagine a CNS which does it differently. To this there are two answers. In the first place we are still very ignorant of the way the RNS works, and it is perfectly possible that what seems like solid knowledge today will appear very insubstantial tomorrow. Indeed, there are already indications (Goldberg and Greenwood, 1966) that neurons in the cat's auditory pathway respond best at particular stimulus intensities. In the second place, if we set our standards a little higher and find evidence which *no conceivable* one-stage model could handle, then

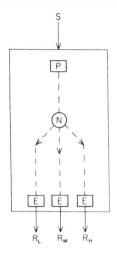

FIG 1.2. One-stage Model for Dishabituation to Stimulus Intensity Reduction. R_L, R_M, R_H: responses to stimuli (S) of, respectively, low, medium and high intensity, as sorted out by element N on the basis of firing rate of elements from P to N. Remaining conventions as for Fig. 1.1.

not only do our conclusions stand unshakeable by future physio-logical findings, but furthermore they can act as useful constraints on the directions in which to seek such findings. Let us therefore see if we can find other evidence of a more durable nature than that provided by the stimulus intensity reduction experiment.

The second experiment is a stimulus *duration* reduction. Again, the facts are not in dispute (Lynn, 1966). If the OR is habituated to a stimulus of duration t sec, then either increasing or decreasing t, while making no other alterations, is sufficient to re-elicit the OR. The argument against the one-stage model from this finding is strong. Since any interval less than t sec is contained by an interval of exactly t, it must follow that any road-block which is effective against a stimulus of t sec duration has already demonstrated its effectiveness against a stimulus of less than t sec duration. However, we must not underestimate the tenacity of the one-stage model.

Again we call on physiological knowledge, but this time to defend the one-stage model. It is known that the nervous system responds equally well to the turning off of a stimulus as to its turning on. We may presume, therefore, that when the OR has habituated to a stimulus of t sec duration, among the parameters of the stimulus to which habituation has taken place is the offset of the stimulus. All we need suppose in addition to this is that the nervous system possesses a clock which is initiated by the onset of the stimulus and which counts the passage of time from stimulus onset in some units or other (let us say seconds for convenience). (Any theory, including a two-stage model, must of course make some such assumption as this in order to account for the fact that stimulus duration is an effective parameter of the stimulus in the first place. And, in any case, the evidence that animals possess such timing mechanisms is very strong.) The one-stage defender can now argue as follows. The stimulus to which the OR was habituated was in fact "stimulus offset plus a count of t sec". The stimulus which re-elicits the OR is a stimulus made up of "stimulus offset plus a count of t' sec", where t' is less than t. We have to show that it is possible for this second kind of stimulus to affect different elements, at some stage on the pathway from S to R, from those affected by the first stimulus. As we shall see, this problem can be regarded as a special case of the "compound stimulus" experiment. We shall therefore consider the latter experiment before returning to the stimulus duration reduction experiment.

If we continue to reduce stimulus intensity or stimulus duration without limit, the outcome is to omit the stimulus entirely. The problem is to do this and let our subject know by some other means that we have done it: if we can do this, and if our efforts are rewarded by the re-elicitation of a previously habituated OR, it is going to be extremely difficult to see how a *non*-stimulus can get through a road-block of any kind. One way of letting our subject know that a non-stimulus has just occurred is to present stimulus A usually accompanied by stimulus B (that is to say, a "compound" stimulus, e.g. a tone with a light) and then present stimulus A alone. This procedure is sufficient to re-elicit a habituated OR (Lynn, 1966). Surely our one-stage Houdini cannot wriggle out of this one?

In fact, it is very easy to get out of the compound stimulus experiment. In principle, what Houdini must do is to treat the compound stimulus as more than the sum of its components. He can then argue that stimulus A on its own is a *different* stimulus from stimulus A in compound with stimulus B, i.e. it will traverse different elements on its route to the OR and so find no road-block. The possibility that a compound stimulus may be more than the sum of its parts is, in fact, sufficiently respectable among learning theorists for Hull (1932) to have hallowed it as his postulate of "afferent stimulus interaction", so we must clearly take this suggestion seriously. Furthermore, Horn (1970) has suggested detailed machinery to do the job, as set out in Fig. 1.3.

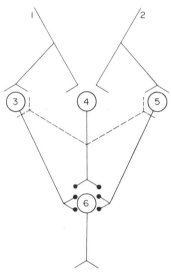

FIG. 1.3. Horn's One-stage Model for Dishabituation in the Compound Stimulus Experiment. Cell 6 executes the orienting reflex and inputs 1 and 2 transduce the two stimuli which make up the compound stimulus. Filled circles represent habituating terminals, i.e. points at which repeated stimulation results in a failure of conduction. Other terminals are non-habituating. Excitatory connections are shown as continuous lines, inhibitory ones as broken lines. Cell 4 is activated if inputs 1 and 2 are simultaneously operative, but not by one alone. When Cell 4 is active it inhibits cells 3 and 5. Thus habituation to the compound stimulus occurs at the terminals from 4 to 6. If input 1 now occurs without input 2, cell 4 does not fire, leaving cell 3 free to respond and thus excite cell 6 at terminals which have not yet habituated. (From Horn, 1970.)

The proposal set forth in Fig. 1.3 is very simple; yet it certainly seems to do the job for which Horn intended it—it allows the return of an habituated response after omission of one element in a compound stimulus, while relying only on one-stage principles. It can also cope with the stimulus duration reduction experiment, if we simply suppose that inputs 1 and 2 in Fig. 1.3 are "stimulus offset" and "count of t sec" respectively. After habituation has taken place to this special stimulus compound, we present a stimulus of t' sec, where t' is less than t as before (in fact, the same argument exactly can be applied to the case where t' is greater than t, but this is of less significance for the controversy between one- and two-stage models of habituation). Input 1 in Fig. 1.3 is "stimulus offset" as before, but, in place of the former input 2, we must suppose some new input, 3, representing a count of t' sec. Dishabituation of the response to stimulus offset can thus take place as in any other compound stimulus experiment, according to the model shown in Fig. 1.3. We must suppose some further set of elements along the same lines as those shown in this Figure to allow habituation to take place to the new stimulus of duration t' sec, and so on for every change in stimulus duration to which the subject can selectively habituate; as well as the clock which measures stimulus duration. But the nervous system contains many neurons, and a two-stage model has to postulate at least as much machinery.

Three times, then, we have tried to infirm the one-stage model by a stimulus reduction experiment, and three times we have failed. The fourth time, however, I think we can succeed. Our fourth and last attempt is another way of presenting a non-stimulus and letting the subject know about it: the stimulus omission experiment. In this, we present a stimulus at regular intervals (say t sec between successive stimulus onsets) and then, after habituation of the OR, we simply omit the stimulus on the next occasion when, had we continued the previous sequence, it would have been presented. This experiment, like all the others discussed, is due to Sokolov (1960), and it too succeeds: the OR is re-elicited. An example of the results of such an experiment, conducted by Churcher and Hughes in Oxford, is shown in Fig. 1.4.

This time we have got Houdini trapped, even when this formidable escapist takes on the likeness of Gabriel Horn. In every other case the one-stage modelist has had the advantage, in converting what looks like one stimulus into two, that some stimulus event or other *occurs*: the stimulus whose intensity is reduced is presented to the subject, as is the offset of the stimulus whose duration has been reduced, and as is one stimulus in the compound when the other is not. Thus, in each case, he has been able to argue that the stimulus event which does occur sets up stimulation in a chain of elements which is not fully coincident with the chain of elements stimulated hitherto. In the pure stimulus omission experiment, however, there is *no* stimulus event: nothing happens, and yet the subject responds. How can this be, unless the subject has stored a representation of past events and

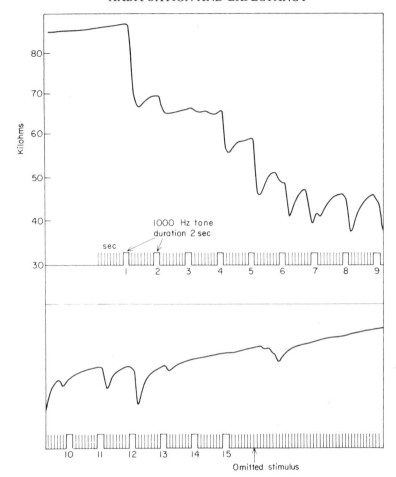

FIG. 1.4. Dishabituation of the OR in a Stimulus Omission Experiment. Shown in the graph is skin resistance recorded from the palm of a man seated in a quiet room. Once every 10 sec a 2 sec tone is sounded. This elicits an OR in the form of the galvanic skin response or GSR (i.e., a brief fall in skin resistance). By the thirteenth presentation of the tone, this response has disappeared, "habituation" having taken place. At the time when the sixteenth presentation might have been expected to occur, no tone was sounded: this results in a GSR, i.e. an OR to stimulus omission. (Results obtained by M. Hughes and J. Churcher in Oxford.)

extrapolated from this stored representation to the likely future? That is to say: how can this be if the subject does not have an *expectancy*?

And yet, have we got Houdini trapped? Horn (1967) has proposed a way out. His proposal is set out in Fig. 1.5. The circuit shown in this figure has the following essential features:

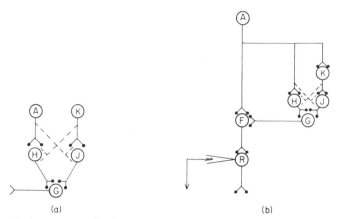

(a)   (b)

FIG. 1.5. Horn's One-stage Model for Dishabituation to Stimulus Omission. Excitatory connections indicated by continuous lines, inhibitory ones by broken lines. (a) A difference detecting circuit in which the activity in cell G is equal to the difference between the activity in cells A and K. (b) An assembly of "neurons" incorporating the difference detecting circuit in which cell R commands the execution of the orienting reflex and cell A receives an exteroceptive stimulus. Cell K is an "extrapolatory neuron", i.e. if a stimulus is repeatedly presented at intervals of t sec, cell K comes to fire at the time when, given a continuation of this regular sequence of events, the next stimulus presentation should occur. Since cell K forms part of the difference detecting circuit, cell G (and hence cell R) will fire either if A fires and K does not (i.e., if the exteroceptive stimulus is novel) or if K fires and A does not (i.e., if the exteroceptive stimulus in a recurring sequence is omitted). (From Horn, 1967.)

(i) Habituation to the repeated stimulus takes place at the terminals between "neuron" A and neuron F—i.e., at a point on the pathway which actually mediates the OR (executed by neuron R) in the first place.

(ii) Dishabituation, when the repeated stimulus is omitted, is the result of excitation of neuron F at the terminals from neuron G—i.e. the excitation producing the re-elicited OR has travelled a different pathway from that producing the initial OR.

(iii) Excitation is able to travel along this second pathway in response to stimulus omission because of two special properties of the circuit lying between neuron A and neuron G: (a) neuron K is an "extrapolatory" neuron sensitive to temporal repetition (this is explained below); and (b) the reciprocal connections between neurons H and J form a "comparator" (also explained below) able to detect differences between the messages coming from neurons A and K.

If the reader studies Fig. 1.5 carefully, he will see that it does indeed do the job Horn requires of it: it responds to the omission of a stimulus in a temporally regular sequence. The question is, however, whether the circuit it depicts is truly a one-stage model for habituation.

Before considering this question, we must anticipate a later part of this chapter, in which we examine the work of Sokolov and his colleague Vinogradova (see Figs 1.7 and 1.8). These workers have described cells in the brain which commence firing only after a particular stimulus has been repeated regularly at a particular interval, and which then fire at the time when the next presentation of the stimulus would occur, assuming that the the regularity of the preceding sequence had been maintained. They call these cells "extrapolatory neurons". As we have seen, neuron K in Horn's model for the stimulus omission experiment (Fig. 1.5) is meant to be such a cell. Sokolov (1963b) also proposed the existence of "comparator" neurons, which do essentially the same job as the reciprocal links between neurons H and J in Horn's model: they receive inputs from both the extrapolatory neurons and from the neurons signalling the occurrence of the actual sensory input to which the extrapolatory neurons are linked, and they fire if one of these inputs occurs without the other.

Now, as we shall see, Sokolov regarded his model for the stimulus omission experiment as a *two*-stage one and yet Horn, in his apparently one-stage account of it, has taken over two features of the Sokolovian model: extrapolatory neurons and a comparator for detecting sameness/difference as between the outputs from the extrapolatory neurons and the sensory neurons to which they are linked. We must be careful, therefore, that Horn is not offering us a two-stage model in one-stage clothing.

Earlier in this chapter, I characterized the difference between one and two-stage models (see Fig. 1.1) as follows:

(1) One-stage models have in common the principle that (a) there is one and only one set of "elements" intervening between the S and the R which the S elicits; and (b) it is change in some portion of these elements which leads to habituation.

(2) Two-stage models, in contrast, postulate one set of elements to mediate the initial elicitation of the R by the S, and a second set of elements which (a) come to be operated by the S after repeated presentation, and (b) are responsible for the eventual habituation of the OR.

Now, if we examine Horn's proposal (Fig. 1.5) in the light of this analysis, we see that it is in a kind of half-way house between the two kinds of model just distinguished. It is a one-stage model insofar as habituation itself occurs at a point in the chain of elements lying between the S and the R initially elicited by the S. But it is a two-stage model in that the second set of elements it postulates as underlying dishabituation is not merely a set of elements set into operation by a new kind of stimulus; operation of these elements depends critically on acceptance of the two-stage principle described in (2a) above—storage of an extrapolation from a series of past events. Examined in this way, we see that Horn's proposal differs from the specification of a two-stage model which I have given above only in that the two-stage principle is called in to account for *dis*habituation, rather than for habituation (see Fig. 1.6). While this is an important problem for the detailed specification of a two-stage model, we need not wait upon its resolution before coming to an even more important general conclusion: the data on habituation and dishabituation of the OR require us to postulate some mechanism which stores and extrapolates from past regularities—i.e., a mechanism for forming expectations. And this conclusion does not depend on the details of Horn's particular proposal: it depends on

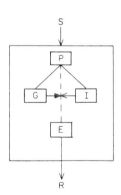

FIG. 1.6. Alternative Two-stage Models of Horn and Sokolov. Both G and I are versions of "A", the special mechanism in Fig. 1.1 which subserves habituation in a 2-stage model. G actively excites (→) the chain of elements resulting in R, the orienting response. It is the same as "neuron" G in Fig. 1.5, and P contains the circuitry (extrapolatory neuron plus comparator circuit) lying between "neurons" A and G in that figure. Thus the left-hand side of the figure above depicts Horn's *dis*habituation version of a 2-stage model as applied to the stimulus omission experiment. I, in contrast, inhibits the elements between P and E and is the locus of habituation (→) in Sokolov's original 2-stage proposal (right-hand side of figure).

the fact that in the stimulus omission experiment, there is *no external input* at the time of stimulus omission able to specify *which* stimulus has not occurred.

Sokolov's Two-Stage Model: Evidence for Inhibition of the OR

The one-stage model, in short, can only be defended at the cost of such great concessions that it becomes indistinguishable from a two-stage model. Let us, then, abandon it, and consider the most detailed proposal for a two-stage model of habituation yet worked out: Eugene Sokolov's.

Sokolov's (1960) two-stage model for habituation of the OR postulates not only that habituation is the result of the building up of stored representations of repeated stimuli and their matching with current stimuli, but also that, when the result of this matching process is the outcome "familiar", the OR is prevented from occurring by an active process of inhibition or response-suppression. This notion is contained in the right-hand diagram of Fig. 1.1. Clearly, the evidence we have regarded as rendering a one-stage model untenable does not by itself entail the conclusion that the operation of a two-stage model includes an active process of inhibition. However, there is rather good evidence for the existence of such a process.

It will be evident that the most direct evidence for the existence of an inhibitory mechanism of the kind depicted in Fig. 1.1 would be to inactivate this mechanism, and show that the OR is no longer susceptible to habituation. Such experiments have been done, the technique used being that of ablation of the neocortex. Two experiments of this kind were done in Pavlov's laboratories in the 1930s, one with dogs and one with pigeons. In both cases, according to Vinogradova's (1961) review of the literature, the result of the operation was that motor orienting responses (head and eye turning towards the source of a novel stimulus, etc.) became completely resistant to habituation. A Western report to the same effect has come from Jouvet and Michel (1959), who recorded that EEG changes to novelty from the subcortex after removal of the neo-cortex in cats: these changes showed no sign of habituation after as many as 800 repetitions. The inhibitory role of the cortex came out particularly clearly in the latter experiments, for Jouvet also reports that, if only a small island of cortex was left intact, habituation was attained. It seems, then, that not only can we conclude that normal habituation of the OR is due to the activity of a special response-suppression mechanism, but also that this mechanism is located in part or in whole in the neocortex.

Based on this kind of data, then, indicating both the need for a mechanism which builds up stored representations of past experience to serve as models against which to match incoming stimuli and the need for a response-suppression process, Sokolov (1960) proposed the model for habituation of the OR which is shown in Fig. 1.7.

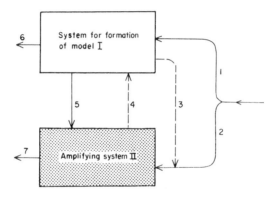

FIG. 1.7. Sokolov's Model for the Orienting Reflex, I. Modelling system. II. Amplifying system ·1. Specific pathway from sense organs to cortical level of modelling system. 2. Collateral to reticular formation (represented here as amplifying device). 3. Negative feedback from modelling system to synaptic connections between collaterals from specific pathway and reticular formation (RF) to block input in the case of habituated stimuli. 4. Ascending activating influences from the RF to the modelling system (cortex). 5. Pathway from modelling system to amplifying system (this is the pathway through which the impulses signifying non-concordance between input and existing neuronal models are transmitted from cortex to RF). 6. To specific responses caused by coincidence between the external stimulus and the neuronal model (habitual responses). 7. To the vegetative and somatic components arising from the stimulation of the RF. (From Sokolov, 1960.)

According to this theory, when a stimulus of a given set of parameters (modality, quality, intensity, duration, inter-stimulus intervals, etc.) is repeatedly presented, the "system for formation of the model" builds up a "neuronal model" which codes for and stores all the parameters, change in which is shown to re-elicit a previously habituated OR. The OR is itself produced by the "amplifying system", which receives direct inputs from all stimuli, unless it is inhibited from so doing by a message from the system for formation of the model. Such an inhibitory message is sent if incoming stimuli match any existing neuronal model. If there is a mismatch, either because an incoming stimulus fails to find an existing neuronal model to match it, or because a neuronal model fires but without any incoming stimulus to match *it*, then an OR occurs. In the former case, this is because the incoming stimulus reaches the amplifying system, and this does not also receive an inhibitory signal from the model-forming system. In the latter case, the model-forming system itself sends an excitatory signal to the amplifying system, so producing an OR.

The latter method of production of the OR is, of course, needed to account for the results of the stimulus omission experiment we have discussed above. It is supposed that, when the previously experienced regular inter-stimulus interval has passed, the appropriate neuronal model commences to fire. If on this occasion the stimulus is in fact omitted, mismatch is declared, and an excitatory signal is passed to the amplifying system. It is clear that, if the action taken by the model-forming system under such conditions were merely that of not sending an inhibitory signal to the amplifying system, there would be no OR, since there would be no stimulus at all for the latter.

Having constructed this CNS for habituation of the OR, Sokolov's group now went one stage further and considered what might correspond to it in the RNS. This they have done in two ways. One is at a "micro-physiological" level: what gross brain structures might match the major blocks in the model shown in Fig. 1.7? The other is at a "micro-physiological" level: what neuronal mechanisms might be involved in these gross brain structures?

As would be expected, in the light of the data on decorticate dogs, pigeons and cats discussed above, Sokolov (1960) suggests that the model-forming system is located in the neocortex. However, data gathered subsequently to test Sokolov's micro-physiological ideas, as we shall see, suggest strongly that structures in the limbic system, and especially the hippocampus, are also involved. It is quite possible, in fact, that the experiments on decortication also involved damage to underlying limbic structures, and these experiments require repetition to control carefully for this point. With regard to the location of the amplifying system, Sokolov suggests that this is located in the midbrain reticular formation (RF). The chief argument in favour of this suggestion is that experiments involving electrical stimulation of this structure have shown that virtually all the particular ORs may be elicited in this way (Vinogradova, 1961). In particular, the EEG changes which form part of the OR are well known to depend critically on the midbrain reticular formation (Magoun, 1963).

One important feature of this proposal is that it is believed that nerve fibres reach the RF from all sensory tracts (Fig. 1.8), thus providing the putative amplifying system with the direct input from

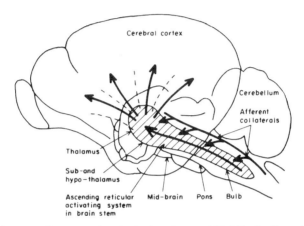

FIG. 1.8. The Ascending Reticular Activating System (ARAS). Outline of a cat's brain showing the distribution* of sensory information to the reticular system in the brain stem. In Sokolov's model the ARAS is held responsible for execution of the orienting reflex. (From Starzl *et al.*, 1951.)

any incoming stimulus which is required by the model shown in Fig. 1.7. Furthermore, the time-course of conduction from the sense-organs to the sensory analysing areas of the neocortex, and from there to the RF, is thought to be sufficiently rapid for impulses to reach the RF by this route before the arrival of the slower impulses which travel to the RF from the sense-organs along other, multi-synaptic pathways (Sokolov, 1960). Thus there is time, in the case of a match being declared in the model-forming system for an inhi-bitory impulse to reach the amplifying system in the RF before this has executed an OR.

* According to the original conception of the ARAS, fibres travelling in each of the sensory pathways gave off collaterals ("afferent collaterals" in Fig. 1.8) to the reticular formation. More recent evidence (Brodal, 1969) has failed to confirm this view for all sensory systems. Nonetheless, it is clear that the reticular formation receives information concerning sensory inputs in all modalities, if not by afferent collaterals, then by other routes.

Sokolov has applied this model to the odd phenomenon of overhabituation (see above). As we have seen, he holds that habituation is a consequence of an active inhibitory process for which the neocortex is responsible. Now, overhabituation occurs at a time when the EEG recording the electrical activity of the neocortex through the scalp displays a pattern associated with drowsiness. Furthermore, overhabituation can be removed by treatments (a highly arousing stimulus, caffeine, etc.) which remove these EEG signs and restore alertness. It is a natural step, therefore, for Sokolov to suggest that overhabituation arises because the neocortex itself falls into a state of lowered functioning (i.e., drowsiness) and cannot any longer exercise its active inhibitory function. This explanation is plausible enough, as far as it goes; but it should be noted that it leaves unexplained the eventual occurrence of secondary habituation, at which time, of course, the EEG is still showing signs of drowsiness, and, indeed, these are more pronounced than during the stage of overhabituation. At this stage, some other mechanism must take over the role of inhibiting the OR, if we assume that Sokolov's account is in general on the right lines. But, if such a second mechanism exists, there then arises the question why it cannot carry out the job of habituation of ORs in decorticate animals. Conceivably, it can only be brought into play when the neocortical mechanism has first done its job.

In order to approach the *micro-physiological* level of analysis, Sokolov (1963b) had first to draw up a "micro-CNS" (Fig. 1.9) for the likely neuronal mechanisms involved in the making of a neuronal model. His hypothesis proposes the existence of three types of neurons: (1) "afferent" neurons, which fire whenever the appropriate form of sensory input is received; (2) "extrapolatory" neurons, which are connected to afferent neurons, and commence firing only when they have received the same input on a number of occasions from these; and (3) "comparator" neurons, which receive inputs from both afferent neurons and the corresponding extrapolatory neurons and fire if they receive an input from one of these, but not both. As it can be seen, the comparator neurons, according to this hypothesis, report "mismatch" either when an incoming stimulus does not encounter a neuronal model (i.e., firing in an appropriate set of extrapolatory neurons) or when the extrapolatory neurons fire and there is no incoming stimulus. In either event, the

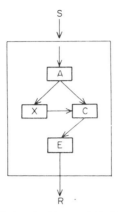

FIG. 1.9. Sokolov's "Micro-CNS" for the Neuronal Model of the Stimulus. A: "afferent" neuron, which fires whenever the appropriate stimulus occurs. X: "extrapolatory" neuron, which fires when it has received the same input from its afferent neuron on a number of occasions. C: "comparator" neuron, which fires (1) if A fires, but not X, or (2) if X fires, but not A, and does not fire (3) if neither A nor X or (4) if both A and X do fire. E: "executive" neuron for production of the OR, i.e. the "amplifying system" of Fig. 1.7.

comparator neurons send an excitatory input to the amplifying system, and an OR results. In order to account for the results of the stimulus omission experiment, it is necessary to suppose that extrapolatory neurons are sensitive to the regularity with which they are caused to fire by the receipt of impulses from afferent neurons. If they have received such impulses every t sec on a number of occasions, they have the property that they commence firing spontaneously at subsequent intervals of t sec.

At the time when this hypothesis was proposed, afferent neurons were, of course, known to exist in many parts of the nervous system, especially the sensory areas of the cortex and the sensory relay nuclei of the thalamus. Comparator neurons, in the shape of neurons which fire to novel stimuli irrespective of the exact qualities of the stimulus and cease firing upon repetition of the stimulus, had also been reported by Lettvin et al. (1961); and they have been reported many times since in diverse areas of the brain (Horn and Hinde, 1970). Extrapolatory neurons however, had not been reported; and these, of course are critical to the whole endeavour, and, furthermore, would provide direct evidence of expectancies at the neuronal level. The announcement, therefore, that extrapolatory neurons had been found in the hippocampus of the cat (Sokolov, 1966; Vinogradova and Sokolov, 1966; Vinogradova, 1970) was of great importance.

These neurons, as Sokolov's hypothesis proposed, have been found to fire only when the same stimulus has been repeated on a number of occasions. Furthermore, some of them have been found to extrapolate from regular inter-stimulus intervals and to commence firing in slight anticipation of the next stimulus in the regular train: that is to say, they can do all that is required for a two-stage explanation of the stimulus omission experiment.

The excursion made by Sokolov and Vinogradova into the RNS to verify the accuracy of their map of the CNS, then, has paid handsome dividends. Not only do we have good evidence for the validity of a two-stage model for habituation of the OR involving both expectancy and inhibition, but there are also good indications of the structures in the brain which mediate these functions and of the neuronal mechanisms by which they do it.

The notions of expectancy and inhibition are of great importance in many issues encountered in the theory of learning. Thus the demonstration that they are well-founded in the comparatively simple form of learning which is habituation has a quite general significance, and will make us more willing to use these notions to deal with other dilemmas. However, we must not think that, because we have won some ground in the controversy over the explanation of habituation, we shall have no need to cover this same ground again. We cannot be sure that, because expectancies and inhibition are involved in habituation, the same mechanisms are also involved in other forms of learning; even though these may seem more complex and even more in need of them. It is perfectly possible that the nervous system reserves the mechanisms we have uncovered to deal *only* with the problem of habituation, i.e. the analysis of familiarity/ novelty. An example from another field of psychology will make this clear.

Julesz (1964) developed an ingenious method for studying binocular depth perception. The subject is presented with two patterns, one to each eye, in the familiar stereoscope. The novel feature of Julesz's method consists in the nature of the patterns used. These are 100 x 100 matrices of square cells, each one of which is randomly either filled in black or left white (Fig. 1.10). The two patterns presented to the eye are randomly generated independently from each other, with the exception of a small region, composing the "figure", which consists of identical cells in both patterns, but shifted

FIG. 1.10. A Random-dot Stereogram as Used by Julesz (1964). See text for explanation.

laterally a few elements in one pattern relative to the other. Each pattern by itself presents a completely random texture, but when they are viewed together in the stereoscope the figure is readily seen in depth, displaced either forward or backward away from the rest of the background (seen as a blur) depending on the direction of displacement of the appropriate regions in the two patterns. Thus, when the two patterns are presented simultaneously in a stereoscope, the brain is in some way able to match the 10 000 cells of the left-hand pattern with the 10 000 cells of the right-hand one in a sufficiently large number of alternative ways to be able to detect the one way which yields an area of identity, and this is then seen as a figure appropriately placed in depth against a background. Furthermore, this extraordinary feat is accomplished in less than 100 msec, as Julesz showed by experiments in which the duration of presentation of the pairs of stereograms was varied. But—and here is the important point for our present purpose—if the two patterns are placed side by side and regarded with both eyes in the normal manner, the subject is *unable to detect the identical region which they have in common.* In other words, the incredibly efficient and complex machinery which is able to perform the feat of scanning and matching just described is brought into play *only* for the job of binocular fusion; under other conditions, we are simply unable to call on it.

We have no guarantee that the same is not true of Sokolov's neuronal models: they may be used to analyse only novelty/familiarity. Thus we shall have to establish our right to talk of expectancies, or of inhibition, afresh in the case of each type of learning which appears to call for them.

2. Classical and Instrumental Conditioning

The question whether classical and instrumental conditioning are essentially the same process or fundamentally different from each other has been a central issue in learning theory for several decades now, and it has certainly not been finally resolved. Nevertheless, I think there is sufficient evidence to conclude that, in all likelihood, they are two distinct forms of learning.

The distinction between classical and instrumental conditioning is, in the first analysis, an operational one. In the classical conditioning paradigm the experimenter regularly presents to the animal two stimuli which follow each other in time, i.e. $S_1 \rightarrow S_2$, where S_1 is termed the "conditioned stimulus (CS)", S_2 is an "unconditioned stimulus (UCS)" and the arrow indicates sequence in time. The animal's behaviour has no effect on the occurrence or otherwise of the UCS. The changes in the animal's behaviour which are taken to indicate that classical conditioning has occurred are observed in the interval of time between the onset of the CS and the onset of the UCS. In the instrumental conditioning paradigm, on the other hand, the experimenter arranges that the presentation of a stimulus, known as a "reinforcing stimulus (S^R)", occurs if and only if the animal emits a particular response (R), that is, $R \rightarrow S^R$. The changes in the animal's behaviour which are taken to indicate that instrumental learning has taken place are alterations in the probability or frequency of emission of the reinforced response. If this probability goes up when a particular S is made to follow the R, the S is an "S^{R+}" or "positive reinforcer" and the operation involved is one of "reward". If the probability of response goes up when the response is followed by the termination or omission of a particular stimulus, the S is an "S^{R-}" or "negative reinforcer" and the two kinds of learning involved are known as "escape" (based on termination of an S^{R-}) or "avoidance" (based on its omission). (These, and other, ways of altering response probability are considered in more detail in later chapters.)

Our problem, then, is to decide whether these two different sets of operations and observations, one for classical conditioning and the other for instrumental learning, correspond to differences in the processes of learning involved. And, closely related to this problem, is that of determining the nature of the processes actually involved in each form of learning, whether these are the same or different. Resolution of these problems, however, is considerably hampered by the fact that it is extremely difficult to observe in the laboratory a pure case of either kind of conditioning uncontaminated by the other.

In fact, it is almost impossible to observe a pure case of instrumental conditioning without the necessary occurrence also of some form of classical conditioning. The presentation of the S^R necessarily occurs in some kind of environment which acts as a source of stimuli to the experimental animal. Furthermore, the animal's response, on which presentation of the S^R is made contingent, must itself provide a set of stimuli which regularly precede presentation of the S^R. It must then follow that stimuli from the environment, and even more likely response-produced stimulus feedback, will be in a position to become CSs in relation to the UCS provided by the S^R.

Classical Conditioning Uncontaminated by Instrumental Effects

We shall see later in this chapter that, formidable as these difficulties are, they appear to have been surmounted by experiments on the deafferented monkey (Taub and Berman, 1966). But we shall first consider attempts (of which there have been rather more) to arrange the other kind of pure case: classical conditioning uncontaminated by instrumental learning. The problem here is that the occurrence of the behavioural changes which constitute the conditioned response (CR) may modify the *effects* of the UCS on the experimental animal, even though they do not alter the experimenter's actual presentation of the UCS. (This is the problem of distinguishing between the distal and proximal stimulus to which we referred in Chapter 1.) It is entirely possible that such a modification of the effects of a UCS can act as an S^R and alter the probability of emission of the response (i.e. of the apparent CR) which regularly precedes such an S^R. In other words, what appears to be an S → S procedure applied by the experimenter may become an R → S procedure in part controlled by the subject of the experiment.

An example may help to make this clear. In a standard Pavlovian classical conditioning experiment using aversive stimuli, acid is regularly deposited in the animal's mouth following the presentation of, say, a tone. A salivary response comes to occur in the interval between tone onset and presentation of the acid, and this is regarded as a CR. But, although presentation of the acid is independent of the animal's behaviour, including the salivary response, the animal's *perception* of the acid may well be altered by its flow of saliva. Thus it is possible that the *effective* stimulus to the animal's mucous membranes is contingent upon the occurrence of salivation, and that what looks like a conditioned response of the classical kind is in fact an instrumental response (IR); or indeed that the salivary response observed is a mixture of a CR and an IR.

However, although it is difficult to arrange a pure classical conditioning experiment, it is not impossible, and indeed several attempts to achieve this goal have probably been successful. Two examples of such attempts will be described.

Gormezano (1965) and his associates have made use of the rabbit's response of closing the nictitating membrane in response to a puff of air (the UCS) delivered to the cornea. The nictitating membrane (or "third eyelid") consists of "a fold of conjunctiva supported by a triangular sheet of cartilage which moves from the inner canthus of the eye laterally across the surface of the cornea. Although the mechanism of movement of the membrane is not clearly understood, it is reliably extended by a corneal air puff or shock with a latency of about 25 to 50 msec. Furthermore, the membrane when activated rarely extends past the midline of the pupil, thus leaving a portion of the receptor surface of the cornea exposed. This property of the response thus appears to provide the investigator with a high degree of control over the sensory consequences of a corneal air puff. By presenting the air puff to the temporal region of the cornea, anticipatory extensions (i.e. CRs) do not appear to modify its sensory effects" (Gormezano, 1965, p. 54). This method, then, appears to offer the experimenter a chance to set up a classical CR which is unlikely to be contaminated by instrumental learning effects. Using it, Gormezano's group has been able to obtain reliable conditioning of the nictitating membrane response to a tone CS.

A second way in which it appears to be possible to obtain classical conditioning uncontaminated by instrumental learning involves the use of the paralysing drug, curare. For example, Black (1965) describes a series of experiments using this drug with dogs to which the classical conditioning sequence of stimuli, tone-shock, is repeatedly applied. Observations of the animal's heart rate showed that this sequence was sufficient to produce a conditioned response (heart rate acceleration) to the tone. It is very difficult to see how a completely paralysed animal (and the degree of paralysis was verified in Black's experiments by means of an electromyogram) can alter the sensory effects of shock, nor how the conditioned change in the heart rate itself have such an effect. Again, therefore, we appear to have an example of classical conditioning which is effective when all possible contingencies between the animal's behaviour and the effects of the UCS have been eliminated.

A determined supporter of the view that what appears to be classical conditioning is in fact always instrumental learning could, of course, contend, in the face of Gormezano's or Black's experiments, that closure of the nictitating membrane or changes in heart rate *might* alter the sensory consequences of the UCS. Presumably, any suggestion of this kind would have to suppose that the alteration involved would consist in a *reduction* in the felt intensity of the air-puff (in Gormezano's experiments) or the electric shock (in Black's). For, if either of these stimuli act as instrumental reinforcers for the apparent CR in these experiments, it can only be as a *negative* reinforcer, since they are both known to be in general aversive stimuli. Thus it would be necessary to suppose, e.g., that closure of the nictitating membrane in some way reduced the intensity of the corneal air-puff, even though the nictitating membrane itself did not stretch as far as the point of impact. One might propose, for example, that the making of the CR activates a reflex pathway through the central nervous system which results in centrifugal inhibition of afferent signals from the whole of the cornea; such centrifugal inhibitory mechanisms are known to exist from physiological evidence (e.g., Granit, 1955). Arguments of this nature are very difficult to test; and the temptation is to seek physiological evidence either to confirm or reject them. However, there are ways to answer this type of objection by carrying out purely behavioural experiments.

An example of such an experiment is described in a paper by Soltysik and Jaworska (1962). This paper is particularly important for its introduction of an empirical test of the presence or absence of instrumental learning effects in an apparently classical conditioning situation. This test is applicable only to cases in which the UCS is aversive; that is to say, cases in which, were the apparent UCS in fact functioning as an S^R, it would be as an S^{R-}, whose termination, omission or reduction in intensity would increase response probability (including the probability of occurrence of the presumed CR).

In the Soltysik and Jaworska experiment, the animals used were dogs, the UCS was shock to the forepaw, and the response observed both as UCR to the shock and in response to the buzzer CS was paw-flexion. (This is a standard classical conditioning situation, introduced by Pavlov himself.) After the flexion response was occurring reliably to the CS, test trials were introduced in which, upon presentation of the CS, the UCS was omitted. The purpose of these test trials was as follows. If the flexion response was being performed, not simply in consequence of the CS-UCS sequence presumably involved in classical conditioning, but because of some reduction in the aversive effects of shock, then the non-delivery of the shock would be still *bigger* instrumental reinforcement and, on the next trial, the flexion response should be stronger or, at the least, not weaker. On the other hand, if the flexion response was maintained by the CS-UCS sequence of classical conditioning, then omission of the UCS should *weaken* the flexion response on the next trial. The results of the test trials showed that omission of the UCS weakened the flexion response (increasing its latency), thus suggesting that it was a true CR. Conversely, other test trials in which the duration of the UCS was increased resulted in a shortening of the latency of the response on the next trial, as would be expected on a classical conditioning model (since this would be an increase in UCS intensity), not a weakening of the response as would be expected if the animal was in fact performing an instrumental response designed in some way to lessen the sensory effects of shock.

The same sort of experiment has also been reported by Kimble *et al.* (1955), using an eyelid conditioning procedure with human subjects. They began their subjects either on a classical conditioning schedule, in which the CS (a light) was always followed by an air puff, or on an instrumental avoidance schedule, in which an eyelid closure in the interval between light onset and the programmed air-puff onset avoided the air puff. After sixty trials, half of each group was switched to the alternative schedule and half continued on the one on which they had begun. As can be seen from their results (Fig. 2.1) the classical conditioning procedure produced more

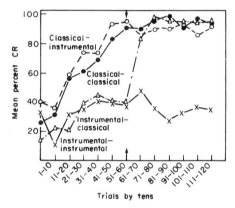

Trials by tens

FIG. 2.1. Effect of Shifting from Classical to Instrumental Conditioning or Vice Versa on Conditioned Eyeblink. Arrow indicates shift from classical to instrumental conditioning or vice versa. (From Kimble *et al.*, 1955.)

efficient learning of the eyelid response initially; furthermore, the switch from the instrumental to the classical schedule produced a large and rapid increase in performance, whereas the switch from the classical to the instrumental schedule produced a small, but statistically significant decline in performance. Now we may argue, as in the Soltysik and Jaworska experiment, that, if in the group initially given apparent classical conditioning the response was "really" maintained by a reduction in the sensory consequences of the UCS, then the performance of this group should have improved when their eyelid response was given the even bigger instrumental reinforcement of total avoidance of the air puff. Conversly, the group switched from avoidance learning to the classical conditioning paradigm should have done worse. But, as we have seen, in both cases the reverse occurred, showing that in this experiment, too, the major control over the learnt response was exerted according to the classical conditioning S → S relationship, not according to the instrumental learning R → S relationship.

Soltysik and Jaworska's test of instrumental effects buried in the classical conditioning procedure is applicable, as already stated, only to the case in which the UCS is aversive, i.e., a potential S^{R-}. For, if it were a potential S^{R+}, the expectation from both the classical conditioning and the instrumental learning model would be that its omission should give rise to extinction of the previously acquired response. Recently, however, a phenomenon has been observed which appears to do for an S^{R+}/UCS what the Soltysik and Jaworska experiment does for an S^{R-}/UCS*. This is the phenomenon of "autoshaping".

Autoshaping was first demonstrated by Brown and Jenkins in 1968, in a study of the prototypical instrumental response (or "operant", as it is commonly called): key-pecking for food in a hungry pigeon. A substantial proportion of the operant conditioning literature has been generated by investigations of this response. It came, therefore, as something of a shock when Brown and Jenkins showed that reliable keypecking can be produced without any kind of R → S contingency in operation at all. Usually, this contingency takes the form that a peck at a lighted disc (the key) set into one wall of the experimental chamber is followed by the delivery of food. The latter is arranged by the raising of a food hopper, containing grain, from which the pigeon is allowed to eat for a few seconds before it becomes inaccessible again. What Brown and Jenkins demonstrated was that keypecking can be generated by simply pairing illumination of the key with the delivery of food *independently* of the pigeon's response, i.e. according to an S → S contingency. The key is repeatedly lit up for a period of say, six seconds, at the end of which grain is automatically delivered and the light on the key goes out again. The pigeon need do nothing at all. But, in fact, it comes to peck at the lighted key during the six seconds for which it is alight (and not during the inter-trial intervals), and it does so at a substantial rate: this is "autoshaping".

This observation raises considerable doubts as to whether the

---

* I shall use the notation "S^{R+}/UCS" to indicate a stimulus capable of acting in the given experimental situation either an an instrumental positive reinforcer or as a classical UCS or as both; the symbol "S^{R-}/UCS" will similarly indicate a stimulus capable of serving as either an S^{R-} or a UCS or both.

prototypical operant is an operant at all. It has been strongly urged by Moore (1973), in particular, that "it seems parsimonious to interpret the pigeon's simple instrumental peck as a Pavlovian conditioned response". Moore further suggests that the response which is classically conditioned in this way is the pigeon's consummatory response to grain: that is to say, the pigeon pecks at the lighted key as though it were eating a piece of grain. In support of this suggestion, he cites experiments by Jenkins and Moore in which pigeons were autoshaped using either food or water as the UCS/S^{R+}. As Moore says: "Obviously the Pavlovian process should cause water-reinforced birds to drink rather than peck, the key; and this is precisely what happens. Jenkins and Moore (1973) made films of key responses auto-shaped with food and with water reinforcement. Student judges were able to distinguish between filmed food and water reactions with 87% accuracy. 'Blind' procedures were of course used, and the food and water reactions were screened in random order. The judges characterized the food responses as sharp, vigorous pecks, whereas the birds auto-shaped with water were said to make slower, more sustained contact with the key, often accompanied by swallowing movements. With water reinforcement, the bird's beak is typically closed, or almost so. With food reinforcement, however, the beak typically springs open just before contact with the key" (Moore, 1973, p. 161).

The question of what it is that gets conditioned in an autoshaping experiment is one to which we shall return (see Capter 5); as is also the question whether instrumental learning can in general be treated as classical conditioning in disguise, as claimed by Moore for the pigeon's keypecking response. For the moment, however, the aspect of the autoshaping experiments which most concerns us is that they appear to demonstrate, with an S^{R+}/UCS, classical conditioning under conditions in which the operation of an R → S contingency is excluded.

This cannot be asserted on the basis of the experiments described so far. For, even though the pecking behaviour is established in consequence of a purely S → S contingency, once the first keypeck occurs it is the case that it is regularly followed by food or water delivery, so that all the usual difficulties in distinguishing between classical and instrumental effects remain. However, a critical experiment has been performed by Williams and Williams (1969) which eliminates the instrumental contingency beyond any plausible doubt. Williams and Williams describe their procedure as "autoshaping with a negative response contingency". Trials consisted of a six-second illumination of the key, after which the key light was turned off and the food hopper was presented for 4 sec—provided the pigeon did *not* peck at the key during the 6 sec for which it was lit up. If the pigeon did peck at the lighted key, the light was turned off and the grain hopper was not presented. Keypecks had no further consequences—the next trial commenced at the scheduled time with the same contingencies in operation as before. Clearly, the R → S contingency in operation (given that we know food for a hungry pigeon is normally an S^{R+}) should result in the pigeon's *refraining* from pecking. Yet, as Williams and Williams report, their birds all came to peck at the key with a very high probability—so high, in fact, that they typically prevented themselves from receiving more than about 10–40% of the programmed food deliveries*. Thus a result was obtained, in consequence of the application of an S → S pairing procedure, which was the *opposite* of what might be expected to occur were an R → S contingency affecting the behaviour.

Results such as Williams and Williams', then, demonstrate probable† classical conditioning effects under conditions in which an R → S^{R+} contingency is ruled out; just as results such as Soltysik and Jaworska's demonstrate classical conditioning effects under conditions which rule out an R → S^{R-} contingency. A further test of instrumental effects hidden in the classical conditioning procedure— one which is applicable to either positive or negative instrumental reinforcers—has been developed by Doty and Giurgea (1961).

* It is worth noting that, when this experiment is done with rats, which also display the basic autoshaping phenomenon, members of this species very rapidly adjust to the R → S contingency and refrain from responding (Leslie and Ridgers, in preparation). This result is consistent with a number of other findings considered later which suggest that mammals are much more sensitive to R → S contingencies than birds.

† It should be noted, however, that there are two difficulties in the way of considering autoshaping as a straightforward classical conditioning phenomenon. One, pointed out by Brown and Jenkins (1968) and Williams and Williams (1969), is more apparent than real. It consists in the fact that the CR is *directed towards* the CS. However, we shall see in Chapter 5, in which this aspect of autoshaping is given further attention, that this is quite a common feature of other classical conditioned effects. The other is that, normally, classical conditioning is severely disrupted by partial reinforcement, as is discussed at the end of the present chapter. Yet in the Williams and Williams (1969) experiment, as we have seen, the pigeons in the autoshaping procedure with a negative response contingency received food on only 10–40% of trials, but nonetheless persisted in responding.

These workers were following up the earlier observations of Giurgea and Raiciulesco (1959) that it is possible to use as the UCS in a classical conditioning experiment electrical stimulation of the motor cortex, of a kind which elicits movement of a limb in the experimental animal. In some, though not all, cases pairing of a CS with this stimulation has the result that the CS too comes to elicit a similar limb movement. Doty and Giurgea (1961), having successfully performed experiments of this sort, wished to eliminate the possibility that what seemed like a classical conditioning effect was in some way due to an instrumental reinforcing effect of the stimulation of the motor cortex which had served as UCS. They therefore trained their subjects (dogs) to press a lever for a food reward according to an instrumental paradigm. They then made stimulation of the motor cortex (as applied in the classical conditioning experiment) also contingent upon lever-pressing. Now, if the stimulation had positive reinforcing effects, these should have shown up as an increase in the rate of lever-pressing; conversely, if it had negative reinforcing effects, these should have shown up as a decrease in the rate of lever-pressing. (We defined an S^{R-} above as a stimulus whose termination or omission increases the rate of a response on which such termination or omission is made contingent. However, stimuli which pass this test for negative reinforcement normally pass a "punishment" test for negative reinforcement as well—i.e. responses on which their *presentation* is contingent show a *decrease* in rate. The equivalence of the two definitions of negative reinforcement is taken up in later chapters.) The results of Doty and Giurgea's experiment were clearcut: in spite of successful use of the cortical stimulation as a UCS in the classical conditioning experiments, the same stimuli applied to the same animals in the lever-pressing situation had no effect on response rate.

The experiments conducted by Soltysik and Jaworska (1962), Kimble *et al.* (1955), Williams and Williams (1969) and Doty and Giurgea (1961), then, appear to demonstrate classical conditioning in circumstances which rule out the possibility that the apparent CR is in fact maintained by direct instrumental reinforcement by the UCS, whether this reinforcement is positive or negative in sign. However, there is a more subtle way in which a defender of the view that all conditioning is "really" instrumental learning could approach this kind of experiment. It could be maintained that the CR *prepares* the animal to receive the UCS in such a way that the arrival of the UCS is more beneficial or less aversive than it would be if this kind of preparatory response were not made (e.g. Perkins, 1968). Thus, the instrumental reinforcement (changed consequences of the UCS given that the CR has occurred) would be forthcoming *only if the UCS is in fact delivered.* It could then be argued, in the case of experiments such as Soltysik and Jaworska's, that performance of the CR falls off when the UCS is no longer presented because the instrumentally reinforcing alteration in the effects of the UCS cannot occur once the UCS is no longer there for its effects to be altered.

An example of this kind of argument, with experimental observations to back it up, is due to Wagner *et al.* (1967a). The argument is applied to the kind of experiment we have just considered, in which the UCS consists of direct electrical stimulation of the motor cortex. Specifically, the authors of this paper suggest that the subject of an experiment employing cortically-elicited limb-movement as the UCS, "upon receiving the CS, could adopt a postural adjustment which served to minimize the abruptness or forcefulness of the UCR, and to partially mitigate any noxiousness that might be associated with that response". Note that such a postural adjustment would be of use to the animal only if the UCS was in fact delivered. Thus, in such a case, it might be possible for Soltysik and Jaworska's test to indicate classical conditioning, in spite of the presence of this "preparatory" kind of instrumental conditioning.

Wagner *et al.* (1967a) went on to justify their suggestion by performing an experiment which gave their animals (again dogs) the choice between making an unsignalled UCR (limb-movement elicited by stimulation of the motor cortex as before) or a CS-signalled UCR. According to their hypothesis, the latter would allow them to make postural adjustments of the kind described above. The dogs were trained to press either one of two panels for instrumental food reinforcement. After this, they were given stimulation of the motor cortex (eliciting limb-movement) contingent upon presses to both panels. In the case of one panel, this UCS was preceded by a CS, commencing one second before UCS onset; presses of the other panel resulted in delivery of the UCS alone at a one-second delay. The dogs showed a clear preference for the panel, presses to which gave rise to the CS → UCS pairing. From this finding, Wagner *et al.* conclude that: (a) there are instrumental contingencies at work in the apparent

CR based on stimulation of the motor cortex as UCS; and (b) these contingencies probably result from the possibility the animal has, given the CS, of modifying its posture to reduce the aversiveness of the UCS.

While these arguments and the experiment on which they are based are undoubtedly cogent, there are several reasons why they need not be taken as invalidating the conclusion we have already drawn that classical conditioning can be obtained in the absence of instrumental contingencies.

In the first place, evidence that a CS → UCS pair is instrumentally reinforcing (relative to an unsignalled UCS) by the Wagner et al. preference test is logically independent of the question whether the CR is itself formed according to instrumental contingencies. It could for instance be instrumentally reinforcing to the dog to be informed of the imminent arrival of the UCS, whether or not the conditioned response to the CS modifies the effects of the UCS.

In the second place, the hypothesis that the apparent CR in the motor-cortex experiments is maintained by instrumental contingencies occurred to Wagner and his co-workers because of a certain feature of this CR which distinguishes it from more normal CRs: very great variability. As Wagner et al. conclude, both from their own studies and from those of other workers: "Some subjects have not shown any CRs, while others have evidenced behaviours to the CS which were descriptively unrelated to the UCR. Furthermore, in some subjects the nature of the CR has been reported to change drastically during conditioning, for no apparent reason, as from right foreleg flexion to left foreleg flexion." This variability could arise from the animals' efforts to find an instrumentally effective posture or from a conflict between a true classical conditioned response and an instrumental response of the kind Wagner et al. postulate. However, CRs arising in more normal classical conditioning experiments do not manifest this kind of variability, so that, while the conclusions of Wagner et al. may be correct so far as they go, there is no compelling reason to apply them to classical conditioning experiments in general.

Finally, the preparatory response argument has no natural application to the Williams and Williams (1969) result, in which the keypecking response prevented the delivery of the UCS/S^{R+} (auto-shaping with a negative response contingency). For how can a response be instrumentally reinforced by preparation for a stimulus by which it is never followed?

Thus, although the experiments and arguments of Wagner *et al.* (1967a) must leave us a little uneasy, they do not succeed in overthrowing the conclusion we have reached on the basis of the other experiments described earlier in this chapter: namely, stimulus–stimulus relations of the kind explicitly programmed in classical conditioning procedures probably do determine the behaviour changes observed in response to such procedures; and they do this independently of any response–stimulus relationships of the kind which are explicitly programmed in instrumental learning procedures but which may covertly enter into the classical conditioning paradigm.

Instrumental Learning which cannot be Classical Conditioning

Now, as we have seen, it is extremly difficult to arrange a pure case of instrumental learning to complement the apparently pure cases of classical conditioning which we have been considering. But, given the evidence that classical conditioning can determine a learning process which is independent of instrumental contingencies, suppose we demonstrate that, when instrumental contingencies are *explicitly* programmed, the animal's behaviour changes in ways which cannot be predicted from knowledge of the classical conditioning contingencies also involved. Then it will become clear that a second process of learning, besides that of classical conditioning, also exists. Such a demonstration is easily arranged.

This demonstration is best introduced with respect to the notion that classical conditioning is a process of "stimulus substitution". According to this view, the result of classical conditioning is that the CS comes to elicit the same responses as were initially elicited by the UCS. It has been known for years that, stated thus baldly, this view is wrong: as has been frequently pointed out, if the flash of a light bulb is made regularly to precede the delivery to a hungry dog of a morsel of food, the dog does *not* usually attempt to eat the light bulb (though, as we have seen, the auto-shaped pigeon does appear to "eat" the key at which it pecks). However, a more restricted and more precisely stated version of this general point of view probably does represent the truth (with rare exceptions which will be discussed in Chapter 8).

Suppose we list the response components which go to make up the total reaction of the animal to the UCS as a vector of changes with the directions of change noted (see Fig. 3.2). And suppose we do the same for the total reaction, after conditioning, to the CS. Then it is in general the case that, if we exclude responses evoked by the CS before conditioning has begun, any component which exists in the CS vector also exists in the UCS vector and with the same direction

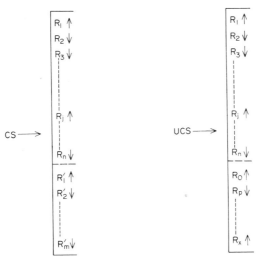

FIG. 2.2. Modified Stimulus Substitution Rule for Classical Conditioning. All responses $(R_1 \ldots R_n)$ evoked after conditioning by the CS figure among the responses evoked by the UCS and with the same direction of change, increase ($\uparrow$) or decrease ($\downarrow$), except those responses $(R'_1 \ldots R'_m)$ already evoked by the CS before conditioning commences. However, some responses $(R_0 \ldots R_x)$ exist in the UCS $\rightarrow$ UCR vector without appearing in the CS $\rightarrow$ CR vector.

of change (but not necessarily with the same degree of change). The converse, however, is not usually the case, that is to say, there will usually be components in the UCS vector which do not figure in the CS vector. (A more detailed discussion of this "modified stimulus substitution rule" for classical conditioning is given in Chapter 5.)

It is clear that this statement places considerable restrictions upon the type of response change which may be obtained, using the procedures of classical conditioning, with any given UCS. Such restrictions do not appear to exist in the case of instrumental conditioning procedures: there need, in general, be no relationship between the series of response components elicited by an S^R and the responses whose probability of occurrence is altered as a result of pairing them, according to an instrumental contingency, with this S^R. As a result, it is possible, by using the same stimulus as a UCS and as an S^R in parallel experiments and observing the same responding system in both, to obtain response changes by means of an instrumental paradigm which cannot be obtained by means of a classical conditioning paradigm. In this way it can be demonstrated that there is a second process of learning, over and above that of classical conditioning, and that this appears to be determined by instrumental contingencies.

An example will make this argument clearer. Such an example is easier to provide now than it would have been a decade ago, as a result of the extensive work which has been carried out on instrumental learning of responses mediated by the autonomic nervous system (Miller, 1969); for it is these responses which have previously provided the bulk of our information about the process of classical conditioning. Let us take an experiment carried out by Lisina (1958) in Moscow (though many other examples can be culled from the work reviewed by Miller, 1969). In this experiment, the UCS and the S^R are both provided by an electric shock delivered to the fingers of human subjects. The response system observed consists of vascular changes in the fingers. Now the UCR to shock in the fingers is vasoconstriction. As we would expect, therefore, the CR to a CS paired with shock according to a classical conditioning procedure is also vasoconstriction; under these conditions, conditioned vasodilation is not observed. In experiments using instrumental procedures, however, Lisina made the omission of shock contingent upon the occurrence of vasodilation in an avoidance conditioning paradigm. That is to say, shock was not presented if vasodilation occurred, but presented if vasodilation did not occur. This led to an increase in the probability of vasodilation (the opposite of the change seen during classical conditioning).

Given this result, and the many similar ones observed in other "bidirectional conditioning" experiments like it (Miller, 1969), it is not possible to claim that there is only one form of learning and that this conforms to the classical conditioning pattern; for a result was obtained using the instrumental learning paradigm which cannot be obtained with this UCS by a stimulus–stimulus pairing. It would be possible to argue, if we restrict our attention to this type of experiment alone, that there is one process of learning, and that this is an instrumental learning one: for one could claim that vaso-constriction is obtained with the classical conditioning paradigm because this response reduces the felt intensity of shock; although, of course, not as much as does actual avoidance of the shock when the instrumental paradigm is explicitly in effect. But, given the arguments already adduced to show that there are *some* experiments where instrumental learning cannot be the correct account of the behaviour changes observed, the only valid conclusion must be that there are *two* separate learning processes: *both* classical conditioning, in which stimulus–stimulus relationships alter the nature of the response elicited by the CS, *and* instrumental learning, in which response–stimulus relationships alter the probability of occurrence of the response followed by the reinforcing stimulus.

It is worth noting that the Williams and Williams (1969) experiment on autoshaping with a negative response contingency is essentially the same in design as the bidirectional conditioning experiment; with the difference, of course, that the outcome of their experiment indicated the essential absence of instrumental effects in the auto-shaped keypecking response. That is to say, the instru-mental contingency which was imposed was one which should have encouraged the pigeon to refrain from pecking, and yet it pecked. The question therefore arises as to which response–reinforcer combinations will permit bidirectional effects to be obtained and which will not. This is a question to which we shall return when we look at the experiments of Turner and Solomon (1962) below.

There is a second, and very different, kind of approach which appears to have established beyond any plausible doubt the efficiency of $R \rightarrow S$ contingencies in the control of behaviour. This approach uses surgical means to attain the goal of establishing instrumental conditioning uncontaminated by $S \rightarrow S$ contingencies. The experiment in question (which is described in further detail in Chapter 10) is due to Taub and Berman (1968). These workers used rhesus monkeys which were trained to avoid shock by flexion of one limb. The responding limb was first surgically deafferented by section of the appropriate dorsal roots in the spinal cord. This operation eliminates the proprioceptive feedback which would normally in-dicate to the brain that a limb has been moved. View of the limb was impeded, thus precluding visual feedback as well. The S^{R-} was an electric shock which was delivered after a warning signal (a click) if the animal did not make the avoidance response. The warning signal was of fixed duration, and so brief that there was no question of its apparently being terminated by the avoidance response. On non-avoidance trials, an interval elapsed between the termination of this click and the delivery of the shock. Thus, the only S → S contingency available for the animal to learn was that which connected the click, on non-avoidance trials, to the shock occurring some seconds later. The effect of successful avoidance responses was to weaken that contingency, since shock did not follow the click on those trials. As far as the avoidance response itself was concerned, since all stimulus feedback from movement of the limb had been eliminated, the only association the animal could made was between the *central motor command to flex the limb* and the non-occurrence of the shock which otherwise followed the click. This, of course, is an R → S contingency; indeed, it is a highly purified R → S contingency, since the "R" is merely the central command to make the response. Under these circumstances, it would be reasonable to doubt whether monkeys could learn to avoid shock at all: but Taub and Berman's monkeys did. And, in so doing, they demonstrated a capacity for R → S learning of an exceptionally pure kind. The implications of these remarkable findings are considered further in Chapter 10.

There is one further line of evidence which urges the reality of the distinction between classical and instrumental learning. This too, like the Taub and Berman experiments, utilizes surgical procedures, but this time to eliminate instrumental rather than classical conditioning. The procedure used is that of removal of the neocortex.

There are a large number of studies which show that classical conditioning is unimpaired after total decortication (e.g. Oakley and Russell, 1972). In contrast, instrumental learning is severely impaired following both destruction of neocortical tissue (Pinto-Hamuy *et al.* 1963; Saavedra *et al.,* 1963) and chemical disruption of the functioning of the neocortex (Plotkin and Russell, 1969; Russell *et al.,* 1970). It is tempting, therefore, to conclude that the neocortex forms part of the mechanism subserving instrumental, but not classical, conditioning (Russell, 1966). Before this conclusion can be regarded as firm, however, it is necessary to control for all the many extraneous differences (besides that of learning paradigm *per se*) which almost invariably distinguish the two kinds of experiment (type of response, stimuli, etc). Fortunately, there is one study which appears effectively to do this.

This experiment is due to Di Cara *et al.* (1970). It makes use of the discovery (Miller, 1969) that autonomic responses, which have long been the basic material for classical conditioning, are also susceptible to instrumental conditioning. It thereby becomes possible to subject an animal to classical and instrumental conditioning of the identical response to the identical stimulus. One can then see whether the effects of decortication depend on the learning paradigm when this is the *only* difference involved.

Di Cara *et al.*'s experiment was carried out on rats immobilized by means of the paralysing drug, curare. For all conditions the stimuli used were a tone (as CS or S^D * in the classical and instrumental paradigms, respectively) and an electric shock to the tail (as UCS or S^{R-}). In the classical conditioning procedure the UCS was presented 5 sec after the onset of the CS. In the instrumental learning procedure the UCS was presented 5 sec after the onset of the S^D unless the criterion response was made during that period. The criterion response reinforced in this way was an increase in heart rate for one group and a decrease in heart rate for a second group. (Note the use of bidirectional conditioning to ensure that it was indeed instrumental learning that was going on.) The response measured in the classical conditioning case was similarly heart rate, which might be expected to decrease (but not increase) when the CS was presented. The results were clearcut: normal rats showed both instrumental and classical conditioning of heart rate, decorticate rats only classical. In a second experiment essentially the same procedures were applied, but using intestinal contraction or relaxation as the instrumental avoidance response and intestinal contraction as the classical conditioned response, shock again serving as the UCS/S^{R-}. Again decortication abolished instrumental learning, but left classical conditioning intact. Thus, depending only on the contingency in operation, S → S or R → S, decortication had quite different effects—even in the cases (heart rate decrease and intestinal contraction) in which not only the CS/S^D and the UCS/S^{R-} were identical in the two paradigms, but also the

---

* "S^D" stands for "discriminative stimulus". This must be carefully distinguished from "conditioned stimulus (CS)". "CS" applies only to classical conditioning procedures. "S^D" is a stimulus in the presence of which an instrumental response is followed by an S^R, the S^R not being delivered if the response is made in the absence of the S^D.

direction of learned response change. It is difficult, in the light of this evidence, to escape the conclusion that classical and instrumental conditioning employ fundamentally distinct mechanisms, only the instrumental one including circuits in the neocortex*.

Contiguity and Contingency in Classical Conditioning

Having concluded that there are two processes of learning, one governed by stimulus–stimulus relationships and the other by response–stimulus relationships, one may now go on to ask what the nature of these relationships is. The most common answer has been that the effective stimulus–stimulus relationship involved in classical conditioning is one of "temporal contiguity", and the effective response–stimulus relationship involved in instrumental learning is one of "contingency".

By "temporal contiguity" is meant the following: given two events, E_1 and E_2, E_1 either precedes and overlaps the onset of E_2 or it precedes the onset of E_2 by only a short interval (usually taken to be of the order of seconds, and certainly not greater than the order of minutes). In the case of classical conditioning, E_1 is of course the CS and E_2 the UCS. However, in instrumental conditioning there is also a relationship of temporal contiguity, the R acting as E_1 and the S^R as E_2. The "contingency" includes temporal contiguity, but also something more: the relationship symbolized by logicians as ↔, i.e., if and only if E_1, then E_2. In the case of instrumental conditioning the R is again E_1 and the S^R E_2. However, a contingency of the same kind is normally also involved in classical conditioning, for the UCS is usually presented if and only if the CS is first presented. Thus there is no obvious reason why it should be thought that temporal contiguity is the critical relationship for classical conditioning and contingency for instrumental learning. Indeed, so long as we keep to simple 100% or "continuous" reinforcement (CRF) schedules, in which every CS and nothing but a CS is followed by the UCS (or every R and nothing but an R by an

---

* A recent report by Huston and Borbely (1973) claims to have obtained instrumental learning for positive reinforcement in the neodecorticate rat. The learning observed is somewhat strange, however, in that it is not subject to extinction—upon removal of the S^{R+} (stimulation of the hypothalamus via implanted electrodes) the response (movement of the head or tail) does not decline in probability. But, even if instrumental learning of a kind can be seen in the decorticate rat, the force of the demonstration Di Cara *et al.* that different mechanisms were at work in the particular case they studied is not weakened.

S^R), there is no way of distinguishing between temporal contiguity and contingency.

Once we begin to depart from CRF schedules, however, the distinction can be made. Such a departure can be made either by allowing UCSs or S^Rs to occur without a preceding CS or R (a procedure known as "free reinforcement"); or by allowing CSs or Rs to occur without a following UCS or S^R ("partial reinforcement", PRF). To see what these two procedures do to the full contingency (*iff* E_1 then E_2*) we must first realize that this contingency necessarily implies its mirror image, *iff E_2, then E_1*. By analogy with the terms "forward" and "backward" as applied to classical conditioning (a topic we deal with below), we may call the former contingency the "forward" one and its mirror image a "backward" contingency. Now, the forward and backward contingencies are logically equivalent to each other when both are absolute. But as soon as we take a more probabilistic approach, for example by adding some proportion of free reinforcements or adopting a partial reinforcement schedule, it is possible for the two contingencies to vary independently of each other. Thus the addition of some proportion of free reinforcements directly reduces the forward contingency (E_2 sometimes occurs without a preceding E_1), while a partial reinforcement schedule directly reduces the backward contingency (E_1 sometimes occurs without a following E_2). Furthermore, the former change may be accomplished while leaving the backward contingency intact (E_1 never occurs without a following E_2, as when every CS is followed by a UCS, in spite of the fact that additional UCSs are also presented); and the latter change may similarly be accomplished while leaving the forward contingency intact (E_2 never occurs without a preceding E_1, as when every UCS is preceded by a CS, even though additional CSs are also presented).

It can now be seen that the chief difference between temporal contiguity and contingency is that the former is an event occurring at a point in time, albeit an event which may be frequently repeated; whereas the latter is a property of a *series* of events. For it is only possible to conclude that "E_2 occurs iff E_1 has preceded it" by evaluating what happens both when E_1 does occur and when it does not and comparing the probabilities of E_2's occurring under the two conditions; and similarly, to decide that "E_1 occurs iff E_2 follows", it is necessary to evaluate what happens both when E_2 occurs and

* i.e. if and only if.

when it does not and to compare the probabilities of E_1's having occurred under the two conditions.

More formally, let us define the conditional probability that E_2 (UCS or S^R) will occur in a particular unit of time, given that E_1 (CS or R) has occurred in that time unit, as $p(E_2/E_1)$, and the conditional probability that E_2 will occur in a particular unit of time, given that E_1 has *not* occurred in that time unit, as $p(E_2/\bar{E}_1)$. The forward contingency, now viewed as a continuous variable, may then be measured as some relation between these two probabilities, perhaps as the arithmetic difference or as a ratio. In the absence of further empirical or theoretical considerations a decision on the exact statistic to use is arbitrary and, in any case, it does not affect the arguments pursued here. Whatever statistic is used, there is a positive forward contingency when $p(E_2/E_1) > p(E_2/\bar{E}_1)$ and a negative forward contingency when $p(E_2/E_1) < p(E_2/\bar{E}_1)$. Similar definitions may be offered for the backward contingency; but it is the forward one which will principally occupy us in the next few pages. (The contingencies are often also talked about in terms of *correlations* between E_1 and E_2. It should be noted that, if in fact the degree of CS–UCS or R–S^R contingency is evaluated by a correlation coefficient, this statistic is sensitive to both forward and backward contingencies.)

Now, as indicated above, since both temporal contiguity and forward contingency occur in both the standard classical and the standard instrumental conditioning situations, it is by no means clear why one should assume that temporal contiguity is of the essence in the classical case and the contingency in the instrumental one. In fact, it turns out that, with regard to classical conditioning, temporal contiguity is neither necessary nor sufficient for conditioning to take place; and also that a contingency is neither necessary nor sufficient for instrumental learning. Instead, the experimental evidence suggests that the key feature of the classical conditioning procedure is the *contingency* it involves, while the key feature of the instrumental learning situation consists in temporal *contiguity*, plus something else. We shall leave discussion of the instrumental case till Chapter 6, in which we examine David Premack's theory of reinforcement. In the present chapter, we shall confine our attention to the experimental evidence regarding contiguity and contingency in the classical conditioning situation.

The view that classical conditioning is a consequence of temporal contiguity between CS and UCS was Pavlov's, and it has been a hardy one. However, in spite of the fact that, under many common experimental conditions, the critical dependence of classical conditioning on the exact temporal relationship between CS and UCS has been frequently demonstrated, this view is open to serious objections. The complexities attaching to the notion of temporal contiguity as applied to classical conditioning come out clearly in the elegant experiments of Rescorla and LoLordo (1965) and Rescorla (1967).

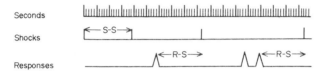

FIG. 2.3. A Diagrammatic Representation of the Sidman Avoidance Schedule. The animal is given a punishment (e.g. electric shock) at regular intervals (the "shock–shock" or "S–S" interval), and each response (e.g. pressing a lever or jumping from one side to the other of a "shuttlebox") postpones the next shock by a specified amount of time (the "response-shock" or "R–S' interval). By responding sufficiently frequently the animal can avoid shock altogether. (From Gray, 1971a.)

These workers used as their test of conditioning the ability of a CS to alter the level of fear displayed by dogs in a continuous ("Sidman") avoidance situation. (We shall leave to a later chapter explanation of the concept of "fear".) In a Sidman avoidance situation (Fig. 2.3) programmed electric shock is postponed for a period of t sec when the subject makes a designated instrumental response (which, in this instance, consisted of jumping from one side to the other of a two-compartment "shuttlebox"). Once a stable rate of response is established in this way, the effects of a presumed fear or fear-inhibiting stimulus can be evaluated by presenting such a stimulus to the animal while it is performing the Sidman avoidance response. Increases in fear in response to an applied stimulus are shown by a rise in the rate at which the avoidance response is performed, and decreases in fear by a fall in this response rate.

The classical conditioning part of Rescorla and LoLordo's experiment was performed separately from this test of the nature of the conditioning which had been produced. For our present purposes,

Rescorla and LoLordo's key conditions were: (1) positive conditioning, in which a shock UCS invariably followed an initially neutral CS; (2) negative (or "explicitly unpaired") conditioning, in which a similar stimulus was never followed by the shock UCS, which otherwise occurred randomly throughout the session; and (3) "truly random" pairing, in which the neutral stimulus and the UCS each occurred in random association with each other, so that on some occasions, the shock did in fact follow this stimulus. Now, if simple temporal contiguity were the key factor in producing classical conditioning, the expected outcome of the experiment would have been for positive conditioning to produce considerable conditioning of fear (most pairings with temporal contiguity); for random pairing to produce some conditioning of fear (some pairings with temporal contiguity); and for negative conditioning to produce no change in the neutrality of the stimulus (no pairings with temporal contiguity).

The actual outcome of the experiment, however, was different. Condition (1), positive conditioning, did indeed have the consequence that the originally neutral stimulus came to elicit a high level of fear, as indexed by an increase in the rate of avoidance responding in the test phase of the experiment. Condition (3), random pairing, led to no change in the neutrality of the stimulus, which had no effect at all when presented to the animals when they were performing the avoidance response. And condition (2), negative conditioning, made of the initially neutral stimulus one which, when presented during avoidance responding, actually *lowered* the rate at which this response was made. Now we shall consider the significance of this latter finding in at least two other contexts in this book: with regard to the concept of inhibition in the next chapter, and with regard to the concept of expectancy in Chapter 10. For the moment, however, it is its significance with regard to the relationship which governs classical conditioning which concerns us. And, from this point of view, Rescorla and Wagner (1972, p. 87) conclude from the results of this experiment and of others like it that: "The organism appears to evaluate the probability with which shocks occur both in the presence and in the absence of the CS, and it is the relation between these two probabilities which determines the amount of fear conditioning observed to the CS. The organism is apparently behaving as a relatively complex probability comparator".

Subsequent work has tended to confirm Rescorla and LoLordo's

(1965) results, while, however, revealing further complexities. Among these complexities are a number of reports (e.g., Kremer, 1971; Kremer and Kamin, 1971) of the production of CSs with excitatory (i.e., fear-inducing) properties by means of the "truly random" procedure. This finding, of course, is in accord with the view that temporal contiguity is sufficient for classical conditioning and at variance with the view that it is degree of contingency that matters. An analysis of the conditions under which such results have been obtained, carried out by Benedict and Ayres (1972), suggests that the critical variable is the relationship between presentations of the CS and of the UCS on the earliest trials on which the animal is exposed to either.

This conclusion is supported by the results of an experiment performed by these authors themselves. In this experiment, groups of rats were exposed to a number of different sequences of presentation of UCS (shock) and CS (tone), all of which were computer-generated so as to be "truly random"—i.e. $p(UCS \mid CS) = p(UCS \mid \overline{CS})$—by the end of the sequence. However, as luck would have it, the sequences to which some groups of rats were exposed involved a relatively large positive degree of contingency during the initial part of the sequence, while, for other groups, this was not so, the degree of contingency even being initially negative (i.e. the probability of occurrence of the UCS was lower given the CS than in its absence). Figure 2.4 shows the actual time course of the degree of CS–UCS contingency calculated cumulatively over the conditioning sessions for the different groups used by Benedict and Ayres. It can be seen that for two of the six groups this statistic was initially large and positive: only these two groups showed in a subsequent behavioural test that the CS had acquired fear-inducing properties. This result appeared, moreover, in spite of the fact that, as is visible in Fig. 2.4, by the end of the sequence of conditioning trials the degree of CS–UCS contingency had been zero for the last three quarters of training for these two groups, as well as for all the others. Thus a critical importance attaches to the first few pairings to which the animal is exposed. This is a phenomenon we shall meet again.

Now, as Benedict and Ayres (1972) point out, their results are neutral with respect to the question whether the effects of these first few pairings are to be attributed to temporal contiguity or to contingency. However, if they are taken in conjunction with other

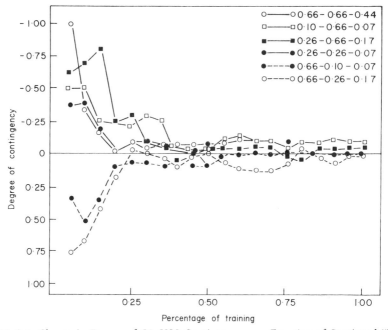

FIG. 2.4. Change in Degree of CS–UCS Contingency as a Function of Continued "Truly Random" Pairing in Six Experimental Groups. Each curve is for a different group given the treatment indicated by the numbers in the top right corner: the first number specifies the probability of the CS; the second, the probability of the UCS; and the third (their product), the probability of a chance pairing of CS and UCS. The ordinate shows the actual contingencies which, by chance, operated at different stages of training in the six groups. Not until a quarter of the way through training did the intended "truly random" pairing become an actual zero contingency for all groups. (From Benedict and Ayres, 1972.)

evidence, there is a strong presumption that the operative variable is indeed contingency. Consider for example an experiment reported by Kremer (1971).

This experiment follows essentially the same lines as that of Rescorla and LoLordo (1965), in that there is a classical conditioning phase of the experiment, whose object is to condition fear-inducing or fear-reducing properties to initially neutral stimuli. It differs from the Rescorla and LoLordo experiment in the technique used to measure fear. Kremer's technique (which was also used in the Benedict and Ayres experiment just described) was developed in 1941 by Estes and Skinner; it is known as "conditioned suppression" or the "conditioned emotional response (CER)". In the simplest form* in which this technique is used, CS–UCS pairings are first

* The form described is a so-called "off the baseline" or "transfer of control" experiment: the classical conditioning phase of the experiment is explicitly separated from the "baseline" instrumental response, and the effects of the CS are subsequently tested by

carried out in the usual way, the UCS typically being electric shock. The CS is then presented to the animal while it is performing an instrumental response (e.g. pressing a bar) for positive reinforcement. The fear-inducing effect of the CS (and thus the effect of the prior classical conditioning) is measured as a decrement in the rate of the instrumental response (see Fig. 2.5).

Kremer (1971) used this procedure to compare two groups of rats, one of which received a truly random pairing of CS and UCS, the other (the "explicitly unpaired" group) being treated in exactly the same way except that any UCSs which were programmed to occur together with the CS were cancelled. The CS employed was a 2 min period of noise, which came on four times at random during a 2 h daily session. The UCS was a 0.5 sec electric shock, also programmed randomly, and independently of the CS, to occur four times during each daily session. There were twenty consecutive sessions of this kind in all. During this time, four of the 80 programmed shocks happened to occur during periods when the CS was on. These four shocks were cancelled for the explicitly unpaired group, which thus received only 76 shocks over the twenty days. At the end of this phase of the experiment, both groups were given further CS–UCS pairings with a new CS, a light. As a result, barpressing for food was suppressed during presentation of the light stimulus, the degree of suppression being total and the same in both groups.

The critical test of the differences between the two groups in their reaction to the noise stimulus now followed. The animals were presented with a compound stimulus, consisting of the noise plus the light, while they were barpressing for food. The results of this part of the experiment are presented in Fig. 2.6, which shows the suppression ratios produced by the noise–light compound in the two groups. As the figure shows, there is a substantial (and statistically significant) difference in the degree of suppression produced by the compound stimulus in the two groups: suppression is much less in the explicitly unpaired group.

Now, in interpreting this difference between the two groups, we must bear in mind two points. First, the light on its own produced

---

seeing whether it alters the rate of performance of this response. In an "on the baseline" experiment (which was Estes and Skinner's original design, as shown in Fig. 2.5) the CS–UCS pairings are conducted while the animal performs the instrumental response and assessment of the effects of the CS is carried out at the same time.

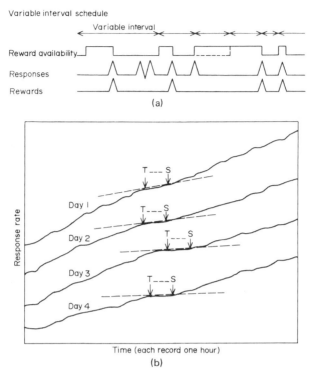

FIG. 2.5. The "Conditioned Emotional Response (CER)" or "Conditioned Suppression". (a) Diagrammatic representation of the "variable interval (VI)" schedule on which the animal is initially trained to respond (e.g., by pressing a lever) to obtain reward (e.g., food). Rewards become available (provided the animal then responds) at intervals which are randomly distributed round some mean value (which specifies the particular VI schedule used). Responses which occur before the next reward availability has been reached are not rewarded. If two reward availabilities are reached without the animal having responded during the first (as indicated by the dashed line), the next response produces only one reward. Thus, if response rate drops too low, the animal does not get all the rewards it could. The VI schedule typically generates a rather stable response rate. (From Gray, 1971a.) (b) The Estes Skinner technique for measuring the intensity of fear. The animal is first trained on a VI schedule. It is then repeatedly presented with a warning signal (here a tone, marked "T") followed by an electric shock ("S"). It is found that responding become much less during the warning signal. The example shown is for a group of six rats over four consecutive days. The degree of response suppression may be expressed as a ratio of response rate during the warning signal to response rate in its absence and thus provides a quantitative index of the intensity of the fear elicited by the signal. (From Estes and Skinner 1941.)

complete suppression in both groups; therefore, the noise has acquired fear-inhibitory properties in the explicitly unpaired group, as in the same group in Rescorla and LoLordo's (1965) original report. Second, as is clear from other results reported in Kremer's

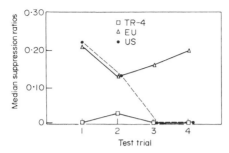

FIG. 2.6. Inhibition of Fear by Stimulus Negatively Correlated with Occurrence of Shock. Median suppression ratios (0 = total suppression, 0.5 = no suppression) in summation test. All groups tested with light (CS+)—noise compound. Light on its own (not shown) produced total suppression all groups. TR-4: "truly random" control group. EU: "explicitly unpaired" group. US: a group not previously exposed to the noise stimulus. Results show that the noise, by being "explicitly unpaired" with shock, had acquired the capacity in the EU group to reduce the conditioned suppression produced by the light alone. (From Kremer, 1971.)

(1971) paper, the truly random procedure left the noise stimulus functionally neutral, its effects being neither to increase nor to decrease the barpressing rate in the truly random group: thus the difference between the two groups in the effects of the compound stimulus on barpressing rate can be attributed entirely to the inhibitory properties of the noise in the explicitly unpaired group. The question then is, where do these inhibitory properties come from? What is it about the explicitly unpaired procedure, as compared to the truly random procedure, which allowed these properties to accrue to the CS? And, owing to the design of Kremer's experiment, it is possible to give a fairly precise answer to this question: the difference between the two groups consisted in four shocks which were *cancelled* in the case of the explicitly unpaired group, but allowed to occur during the CS in the case of the truly random group. (Remember that, besides the four shocks which differentiated the two groups, there were also 76 shocks occurring outside CS periods which they had in common.) Now, since the positive effect accounting for the difference between the two groups is the inhibitory influence of the noise stimulus in the explicitly unpaired group, we must suppose that the critical events are, not the occurrence of the four additional shocks in the truly random group, but their *non*-occurrence in the explicitly unpaired group. But, since the occurrence of shocks in both groups was random with respect to time, the *non*-occurrence of shocks *lacks any definable locus in time.*

And it is very difficult to see how temporal contiguity can act when one of the events entering into this relationship has no definite temporal locus. Thus it is much more natural to take the contingency view: that is, to suppose along with Rescorla and Wagner (1972) that the animal computes the probability of shock in the presence of the CS and the probability of shock in its absence, evaluates the difference between them (to a remarkably high degree of accuracy), and acquires different sorts of response tendencies to the CS (and its absence) accordingly. (We shall come across very similar findings when we consider Herrnstein's experiments on avoidance learning, discussed in Chapter 10. And the notion of non-occurrence of an expected event, which we first encountered in Chapter 1, is one we shall meet again in several further contexts.)

These experiments, then, go far to establishing that it is the CS–UCS contingency, rather than pure temporal contiguity, which is most important in determining the outcome of a classical conditioning procedure. A second way in which it is necessary to complicate the view of classical conditioning as depending on temporal contiguity concerns the actual time intervals involved. This is a matter which must concern us whether or not CS–UCS contingency is the important variable; for the contingency, as we have seen, also involves temporal contiguity, even though this is only part of a more complex relationship. Now "contiguity" ought to mean, and usually does mean, that the CS either overlaps with the onset of the UCS or terminates only very briefly before it. It is true that this appears to be the best arrangement for securing good and speedy conditioning. But even in Pavlov's day there were known cases in which the CS–UCS interval could be quite long. More recently, instances have come to light of apparent classical conditioning over very long intervals indeed, in the so-called "bait-shyness" phenomenon.

"Bait shyness" is the rejection by an animal of poisoned baits to which it has previously been exposed, and from which it has suffered sickness, but has survived. It has been known for a long time that one experience of such poisoning is sufficient for subsequent rejection of the bait, even though the symptoms of sickness do not normally ensue for some hours after it is eaten. It is always possible, however, to imagine that there is some immediate stimulus consequence of bait-consumption which can serve as UCS and thus to preserve a traditional view of temporal contiguity operating in the classical conditioning S–S relationship. However, some ingenious experiments pioneered by Garcia *et al.* (1955; see Revusky and Garcia, 1970, for review) dispose of this possibility.

The key feature of these experiments is that the animal is fed a perfectly harmless (but distinctively flavoured) substance and then, several hours later, it is exposed to some independent treatment which produces a gastro-intestinal disturbance. The independent treatment most frequently used has been exposure to X-rays, producing mild radiation sickness. Revusky (1968), for example, offered food deprived rats sucrose for five minutes and then subjected them to X-irradiation 4, 8, 16, 24, or 32 h later. Irradiated controls were given rat chow instead of sucrose, and sham-irradiated controls were given sucrose but no X-rays. The results of the experiment are presented in Fig. 2.7. This shows preference for sucrose, as against milk, five days after the single learning trial described above. It is clear that, with a four-hour interval between ingestion of sucrose and subsequent irradiation, there is a considerable depression of the rat's normal preference for sucrose. Many other similar results have been reported; and there can be little doubt that, in the bait-shyness phenomenon, we have an example of conditioning* spanning a time interval which it is difficult to comprehend under the label of temporal contiguity.

A further phenomenon which is in sharp contrast to the view that temporal contiguity, with the CS just preceding the UCS, is necessary

* It is not entirely clear that it is correct to treat bait shyness as a case of *classical* conditioning. Like a number of other procedures, it is ambiguous with respect to the classical/instrumental dichotomy. This arises in part because it is effectively a one-trial learning phenomenon, so that it is difficult to analyse it into S → S and/or R → S components. In the absence of such an analysis, it is possible to regard the poisoned food (or rather its taste, smell etc.) as a CS and to treat the phenomenon as a case of classical conditioning. Alternatively, one could regard the act of eating the food as a response which is punished by the subsequent symptoms of illness, thus treating it as a case of instrumental conditioning. There are two reasons why it seems best to regard the classical conditioning interpretation as at least nearer the truth. The first is that analysis of the effective stimuli controlling the subsequent rejection of once-poisoned baits shows very clearly that these depend critically on the nature of the cues received by the animal at the time of approach to and ingestion of the poisoned substance, rather than on the kind of response performed by the animal: in particular, gustatory and olfactory stimuli are very much more powerful in the control of the phenomenon than any other source of stimuli (Garcia *et al.*, 1972). The second is that bait shyness appears, in fact, to be an instance of what, in Chapter 8, I shall call "behavioural inhibition". And I shall argue in that Chapter that, although behavioural inhibition appears to be a case of instrumental learning (viz., the variety termed "punishment"), it is in fact in its essentials dependent on a classical conditioning process.

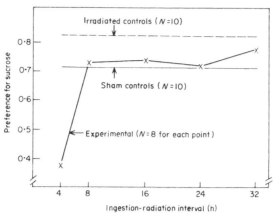

FIG. 2.7. Preference for Sucrose relative to Milk as a Function of the Time between Consumption of Sucrose and X-Irradiation. See text for explanation. (From Revusky and Garcia, 1970.)

for classical conditioning is that of "backward conditioning". Razran (1971) reviews the chequered history of this phenomenon, which has now been claimed to be impossible and now to be definitely established. Razran himself, on the basis of his review of over eighty experiments, is certain that the latter conclusion is correct. In other words, it is possible for the pairing $S_1 \rightarrow S_2$ to have the result that S_2 (i.e., the UCS in the more usual case) comes to elicit a response appropriate to S_1 (the CS in the more usual case). A very good example of backward conditioning (though it also includes the more usual "forward" conditioning in a complex design called "two-way" conditioning) is given by Asratian (1965), describing an experiment conducted by Varga and Pressman.

Varga and Pressman, using dogs, paired passive lifting of the animals' legs with puffs of air into the eyes, evoking a blinking reflex. Both responses, lifting of the leg and blinking, were recorded. The two stimuli—passive lifting and air puff—were paired in some experiments in the sequence, puff-lift, and in others in the sequence, lift-puff. The results are shown in Fig. 2.8. It is clear that when the sequence puff-lift was applied, a conditioned lift of the leg occurred to the puff (forward conditioning), but also an eyeblink occurred in response to the passive lift (backward conditioning). The reverse pairing, lift-puff, produced the same sort of result. Good evidence of backward conditioning has also been presented recently by Rescorla (1972).

a

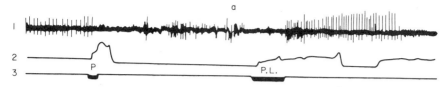

b

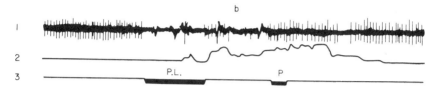

FIG. 2.8. Simultaneous Forward and Backward ("Two-way") Classical Conditioning. A "two-way" connection resulting from the pairing of a passive lifting of the leg with application of air puffs to the eye. (a) Conditioned motor reflex appearing when paired stimuli are applied in the stereotyped sequence "air puffs–passive lifting". In response to air puffs P the dog blinks and lifts the leg, as indicated by the disappearance of action potentials in the gastrocnemius muscle. The lifting of the leg P.L. is again accompanied by blinking, which indicates a reverse connection. (b) A conditioned eyelid reflex appearing when the paired stimuli are applied in the stereotyped sequence "passive lifting–air puffs". In response to the passive lifting of the leg P.L. the dog blinks. After air puffs into the eye P there is observed, along with the blinking, the disappearance of action potentials in the gastrocnemius muscle, which indicates a reverse connection. 1, electromyogram of the gastrocnemius muscle; 2, eyelid movement; 3, stimulation. (From Asratian, 1965.)

It appears, then, that neither temporal contiguity nor the temporal sequence, CS → UCS, are *necessary* conditions for classical conditioning to occur. It is also the case that, under certain circumstances, temporal contiguity and a CS–UCS sequence of the usually effective kind are not *sufficient* conditions for classical conditioning to take place, even though the stimuli used as the would-be CS and UCS are fully effective in that capacity under other conditions. We have already seen experimental support for this conclusion in the experiments on the CS–UCS contingency described earlier in this chapter. It emerges even more strongly, however, from Kamin's (1968, 1969) experiments on the so-called "blocking" phenomenon.

In these experiments, Kamin used the conditioned emotional response (CER) technique described earlier in this chapter. Essentially what he showed is this. If a CER is first established using CS_1 (e.g., a tone) and if CS_1 is then joined to CS_2 (e.g. a light) in the sequence $CS_1 + CS_2 → UCS$, then CS_2, when subsequently tested on its own, turns out to have acquired virtually no capacity to produce conditioned suppression of an instrumental response (though CS_2 would have been an effective substitute for CS_1 had it initially been paired with the UCS by itself). Conditioning of the emotional response to CS_2, in short, appears to be "blocked" because conditioning to CS_1 has already taken place and because CS_2 is paired with the UCS only in the further presence of CS_1. This phenomenon has attracted considerable notice because of its significance for "attention" theory (Sutherland and Mackintosh, 1971; Rescorla and Wagner, 1972). For our present purposes, however, it is sufficient to point out that it is a clearcut case in which two stimuli (CS_2 and the UCS) stand in the relationship of temporal contiguity (and, indeed, in the relationship of S → S contingency) to each other, yet nonetheless classical conditioning does not take place.

Kamin has also shown that this blocking of conditioning can itself be prevented from occurring if, during the compound conditioning trials ($CS_1 + CS_2$ → UCS), some change is made in the UCS. From this "deblocking" effect, together with the original observation of blocking, Kamin concludes, reasonably enough, that in addition to temporal contiguity and a CS → UCS sequence with normally effective CS and UCS it is necessary, if classical conditioning is to take place, for the CS to convey some new *information* to the subject—i.e., the UCS should not be already fully predictable from other CSs to which the animal is simultaneously exposed. However, there is an important question as to the nature of the new information which is adequate to overcome the blocking effect.

The two UCS parameters which Kamin (1969) changed on the compound trials to produce deblocking were intensity and number of shocks. In one experiment, shock intensity was increased from 1 mA to 4 mA and in the other the usual 0.5 sec 1 mA shock was followed, 5 sec later, by a second shock of the same kind. Clearly, both of these changes may be regarded as increases in the effective intensity of the UCS (although Kamin advances arguments to discount this possibility in the case of the change from one to two shocks). Furthermore, we already know of one other change in UCS intensity—reduction to zero—which, far from producing a "deblocking" effect, results in the CS_2 acquiring conditioned inhibitory properties and *reducing* the CER (see Kremer's 1971 experiment, described above). The question therefore arises as to whether the change on compound conditioning trials which is necessary for CS_2

to acquire excitatory properties is not *an increase in effective UCS intensity.*

This proposition has been tested by Rescorla (1972). His interest in the problem derived from the theory of classical conditioning advanced by Rescorla and Wagner (1972; Wagner and Rescorla, 1972) which we consider briefly below. This theory accounts for the blocking and deblocking effects in terms of the discrepancy between the CR already conditioned to the stimuli presented to the animal and the maximum CR the given UCS is capable of sustaining (represented in the theory by the parameter λ: see below). In consequence, it predicts that deblocking should only be produced by changes which increase the magnitude of the conditioning which the UCS can sustain, that is to say, changes which increase effective UCS intensity. In his test of this prediction, therefore, Rescorla (1972) changed the UCS on the compound trials in such a way as to keep effective UCS intensity unaltered. He did this by using two combinations of UCS current intensity and duration (0.5 mA x 2 sec and 2 mA x 0.5 sec) which had been shown not to differ from each other with regard to the rate of conditioning and asymptotic magnitude of the CER they produced as UCSs in identical experiments. Using these two UCSs Rescorla compared (1) the degree of blocking produced when the UCS was the same during the compound trials as during initial conditioning to CS_1 with (2) the degree of blocking produced when the UCS was changed to the other shock stimulus on the compound trials. The degree of blocking was identical in the two cases. It seems, then, that for deblocking to occur the change made in the UCS during the compound conditioning trials must take the form of an increase in effective UCS intensity.

It appears, then, that we have to allow for a rather complex process going on in a classical conditioning experiment. This process apparently enables the organism to compute the probability of the UCS following the CS at a number of different intervals of time following CS onset, and to compare this with the probability of the UCS occurring without the CS preceding it by the interval in question. If the probability of the UCS occurring at a specified interval after CS onset is greater than it would be without the CS having occurred at that time, the CS acquires a positive conditioned significance. If the two probabilities are alike, the significance of the "CS" remains neutral. If the probability of the UCS occurring at the specified interval after CS onset is actually *lower* than if the CS had not occurred at that time, then the stimulus becomes a negative or inhibitory CS (what this means, we shall consider in more detail in Chapter 3). Furthermore, Asratian's experiments on backward conditioning mean that these statements have to be expanded to take account of changes in the response to the second of two stimuli following each other in time depending on the nature of the first of the two stimuli; and Kamin's experiments on blocking mean that it is only if the predictability of effective UCS intensity is increased by taking account of the occurrence of the CS that conditioning takes place.

The Rescorla–Wagner Theory of Classical Conditioning

In the preceding paragraph, and at several earlier points in this chapter, I have talked of animals "computing the probability of the UCS"; and we have seen that the results of experiments on the role of contingencies in classical conditioning make such talk rather natural. However, this kind of notion is repugnant to many psychologists brought up in the Behaviourist tradition—it smacks too much of "mentalism". In fact, especially since the advent of the electronic computer, there is no particular difficulty in designing machinery to compute probabilities or, say, to calculate a running correlation between occurrences of CSs and occurrences of UCSs. Nonetheless, reluctance to admit this kind of process in animals goes so deep that Rescorla and Wagner (1972; Wagner and Rescorla, 1972; Rescorla, 1972), whose experiments and early theorizing did much to establish the importance of contingencies, have recently proposed an important new theory of classical conditioning in a bold attempt to avoid the necessity of doing so. Among other things, this theory succeeds in deducing most of the critical experimental findings on the role of contingencies from what are essentially principles of temporal contiguity. Although it is not possible to do justice to it in the present compass, our discussion would certainly be incomplete without a brief look at the approach advocated by these workers.

Rescorla (1972, p. 11) has outlined the theory in simple terms as follows:

> The basic intuitive notion of the theory is that anticipated reinforcements have consequences different from those of unanticipated reinforcements. The effect of a reinforcement in conditioning depends not upon that

reinforcement itself but upon the relationship between that reinforcement and the reinforcement that the organism anticipated. The very same reinforcing event may vary from being highly effective to being totally ineffective in producing conditioning, depending upon the degree to which the organism anticipated that reinforcement. Similarly, the consequences of nonreinforcement vary according to the events the organism anticipated. Furthermore, if an organism correctly anticipates the US based upon learning with one CS, then the reinforcing effects of the US are modified not only for that CS but for all other simultaneously present CSs.

Rescorla and Wagner (1972) have incorporated this intuition into a somewhat more precise statement. Consider a situation in which a compound stimulus, AX, is followed by a given reinforcer, US_1. The equations below describe the theoretical change in conditioning to the component stimuli, A and X, as a result of a single such trial. V_A represents the associative strength, or amount of conditioning to A, and is presumed to be monotonically related to such dependent measures as probability of response or latency of response.

$$\Delta V_A = \alpha_A \beta_1 (\lambda_1 - V_{AX})$$
$$\Delta V_X = \alpha_X \beta_1 (\lambda_1 - V_{AX})$$

The parameter λ_1 represents the asymptote of conditioning supported by the applied US_1: it is US-dependent and is subscripted to indicate that. The α and β are learning-rate parameters dependent respectively upon the qualities of the CS and the US. Although we will have little occasion to refer to them here, they are present to allow for the obvious possibility that different CSs and different USs will yield different rates of conditioning.

The fundamental expression determining changes in associative strength is $(\lambda_1 - V_{AX})$, the difference between the current associative strength of the compound and the asymptote appropriate to the applied US. Some proportion of that difference, depending upon the α and β parameter values, goes into changing V_A and V_X on each trial. So the amount of change in the associative strength of an element depends upon the current associative strength of the *compound*, not simply the associative strength of the element itself. To relate this formal model to the intuition with which we began, V_{AX} represents the degree to which the organism anticipates the US_1 following the AX, whereas λ_1 represents the potency of the US_1. So it is the relationship between the potency of the US received and the degree to which it was anticipated that determines conditioning.

Rescorla (1972, p. 13) goes on to apply this theory to two of the phenomena we have considered above (as well as to a number of other findings): the Kamin blocking effect and the effect of degree of CS–UCS contingency on conditioning.

Consider first Kamin's finding that if an AX compound is followed by reinforcement, the prior conditioning history of A determines the amount of conditioning to X. Within the present model, the pretreatment of A with a given reinforcement results in a V_A which is close to the appropriate λ. When AX is then followed by the same US, the expression determining the changes in V_X and V_A is $(\lambda - V_{AX})$. Because V_A is close to λ, then $V_{AX} = V_A + V_X$ is close to λ, so $(\lambda - V_{AX})$ is close to zero. Since it is this expression which determines the increment to V_X on those trials, this means that prior conditioning of A severely restricts the possible conditioning to X by that reinforcer. The anticipated reinforcer is ineffective. Hence, the simple blocking effect follows easily from the model.

Rescorla then goes on to show that the available data on "deblocking" (by increasing UCS intensity during AX trials: see above) can also be derived from the model, as well as to discuss a number of other aspects of the blocking phenomenon.

In his treatment of the effects of CS–UCS contingency or "correlation" on conditioning, Rescorla applies essentially the same strategy as to the Kamin blocking effect. But, to do so, he finds it necessary to treat "background stimuli", i.e. constant features of the experimental environment in which the CS and the UCS are presented, as the equivalent of stimulus A in the account of the blocking effect. His account is centred around the experiment whose results are presented in Fig. 2.9. In this experiment, animals received shocks at different rates in the presence and absence of a 2 min. CS, and the level of conditioning (as indicated by the extent of conditioned suppression produced subsequently) reflected the relationship between those shock rates as shown in the figure.

Consider the following analysis of that experiment. Whenever the animal is in the experimental chamber, it is exposed to stimuli from the apparatus. Although these stimuli are not under explicit exper-imental control, they may be expected to influence the organism. If we label these background stimuli as A, one way to conceptualize the presentation of a CS, X, is as the conversion of A into AX, background plus CS. The treatment of the various groups then involves differential shock rates for A and AX.

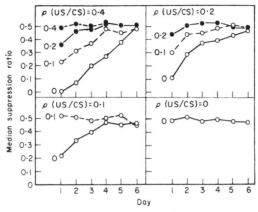

FIG. 2.9. Conditioned Suppression as a Function of Shock Probability in Presence and Absence of CS. Median suppression ratio for each group over six extinction test sessions. The suppression ratio is calculated so that 0.5 = no suppression and 0 = total suppression. Within each panel, all groups had the same probability of shock during the CS; the parameter alongside each curve within each panel is the probability of shock in the absence of the CS. (From Rescorla, 1968.)

Rescorla and Wagner (1972) present a more detailed application of the present theory using this approach. For purposes of applying the theory, the session may be conceptually divided into time units the length of the CS. The session can then be represented as a sequence of background (A) and background plus CS (AX) trials, each reinforced the appropriate percentage of the time. The equations appropriate to reinforcement and nonreinforcement may be applied to such a sequence of "trials"and learning curves plotted for V_X. Fig. 2.10 shows the result of one such simulated application of the model, for various US probabilities in the presence and absence of the CS. For this particular simulation, the CS was assumed to be present one-fifth of the time and to have a salience five times that of the background ($\alpha_A = 0.1$, $\alpha_X = 0.5$); the rate parameter associated with reinforcement was assumed to be twice that associated with non-reinforcement ($\beta_1 = 0.1$, $\beta_2 = 0.05$), while the λ's associated with reinforcement and nonreinforcement were taken to be 1 and 0. The first number after each curve indicates shock probability during the CS; the second, shock probability in the absence of the CS.

The asymptotic values for V_X shown in Fig. 2.10 are clearly in agreement with a correlational notion and with much of the data shown in Fig. 2.9. Positive V values are associated with positive correlations, negative values with negative correlations, and zero values with the absence of a correlation. Furthermore, the greater the magnitude of the correlation, the stronger the deviation of V_X from zero (Rescorla, 1972, pp. 19-21).

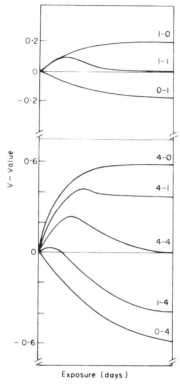

FIG. 2.10. Associative Strength of Stimuli Receiving Various Correlational Procedures, as Predicted by the Rescorla–Wagner Theory. For explanation see text. (From Rescorla, 1972.)

Brief as they are, it is hoped that these extracts from Rescorla's (1972) paper will be sufficient to indicate to the reader how he and Wagner are able to deduce many of the key phenomena which apparently stand in the way of a contiguity approach to classical conditioning from contiguity principles. These principles, moreover, are essentially similar to those used by other theorists before them, with one major exception. This exception is described by Wagner and Rescorla (1972) thus:

The most direct way to approach the model is by way of comparison with those familiar theories (e.g. Hull, 1943; Estes and Burke, 1953; Bush and Mosteller, 1955; Spence, 1956) all of which have commonly assumed that successive CS–US pairings lead to a negatively accelerated growth in some associative tendency. If we adopt a common notational system which ignores certain differences in the nature of the associative variable, each of the theories assumes that when a particular CS, A, is repeatedly paired with a US, the associative strength of that CS, V_A, will eventually approach some value λ, with the increments in V_A on each trial being $\Delta V_A = \phi(\lambda - V_A)$. That is, the increments in V_A are taken to be a decreasing linear function of the difference between V_A and the fixed-point value towards which it may grow as a consequence of such trials. It is generally assumed that the latter value, λ, is greater the greater the intensity of the US involved (e.g. Hull, 1943) so that one may account both for different asymptotic levels of responding with different US values, and for changes in conditioned responding when US values are increased or decreased.

Now, an interesting option is presented to such a theory when not just a single CS, but several CSs are concurrently present on a trial. That is, suppose that two cues A and B are presented in compound and followed by a US. Should we assume that the associative value of the components will be modified until each individually reaches λ? Or should we assume that the associative values will be modified only until the collective value of the compound reaches λ? There is nothing intrinsic to the theories we have mentioned which necessarily implies either possibility, but all have none the less followed the former option. And what basically sets our model apart is that we have chosen to follow the latter alternative.

It is striking how an apparently minor change of this kind can generate a host of new predictions, many of which are at first sight totally at variance with any kind of trial-by-trial contiguity principle. The interested reader would do well to consult the original papers by Rescorla and Wagner to appreciate the full scope of their theory. For out present purposes, their work must stand as a warning not to abandon a simple contiguity principle too lightly. Let us therefore consider again the question whether it is necessary to suppose that rats, dogs and other such nonverbal mammals can calculate running correlations between events.

A recent experiment by Mackintosh (1973) prompts once more the answer "yes" to this question. Mackintosh, in an elegantly designed experiment, demonstrates that the rat can learn a zero correlation between two events; and it will be clear from the passage cited from Rescorla (1972) above that this is one kind of correlation that the Rescorla–Wagner theory cannot have the rat learn, since a CS which has zero correlation with the UCS on that theory ends up neutral (see Fig. 2.10).

The design of Mackintosh's experiment is shown in Table 2.1. The subjects used were thirsty rats and the apparatus consisted of a small chamber equipped with a water tube, a grid floor to which shock could be delivered, and a loudspeaker through which the animal could be exposed to a tone CS. In Phase 1 of the experiment, the different groups were treated as in Table 2.1. They were exposed to presentations of tone alone, of water alone or just left in the apparatus ("control" group) as three control treatments. The two

TABLE 2.1.   Design of Mackintosh's (1973) experiment

Conditioning to water		Conditioning to shock	
Phase 1	Phase 2	Phase 1	Phase 2
Control		Control	
Tone only		Tone only	
Water only	Tone → Water	Shock only	Tone → Shock
Tone/Water		Tone/Shock	
Tone/Shock		Tone/Water	

→ indicates S → S pairing.
/ indicates "truly random" relationship.

experimental treatments consisted of random and uncorrelated presentations of both tone and water ("tone/water" group) or of both tone and shock ("tone/shock" group). In Phase 2 of the experiment half of each group was given tone → water pairings according to a standard classical conditioning procedure, the conditioned response being measured as an increase in licking at the tube in the first five seconds of the CS (before water itself was delivered) compared to licking in the 5 sec preceding the CS. The other half of each group was given tone → shock pairings, conditioning now being measured as suppression of licking during the 20 sec presentation of each tone compared to a 20 sec period preceding CS presentation.

The results of the experiment are shown in Figs 2.11 and 2.12. Statistical analysis confirmed the impression given by this figure: the tone/water group was slower than every other group to acquire a conditioned licking response, but was not impaired in the acquisition

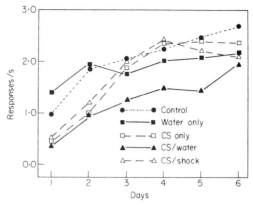

FIG. 2.11. Results of Tone-Water Conditioning in Phase 2 of Mackintosh's (1973) Experiment. Acquisition of conditioned licking following different treatments in Phase 1 of the experiment (see Table 2.1). The graph shows group means of the number of responses per sec during the CS minus the number of responses per sec in the 5 sec preceding each CS. (From Mackintosh, 1973.)

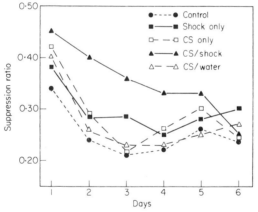

FIG. 2.12. Results of Tone-Shock Conditioning in Phase 2 of Mackintosh's (1973) Experiment. Acquisition of conditioned suppression following different treatments in Phase 1 of the experiment (see Table 2.1). The graph shows group mean suppression ratios; 0.5 = no suppression, 0 = total suppression.

of conditioned suppression; and the tone/shock group was slower than every other group to acquire conditioned suppression, but was unimpaired in the acquisition of the conditioned licking response. In other words, the rats appear to have learnt in Phase 1 quite specifically that there was a random relationship either between tone and water (in the tone/water group) or between tone and shock (in the tone/shock group). As Mackintosh says, "this seems to imply that there is more to be said for a contingency view of conditioning than has recently been thought". Certainly, it is difficult to see how any contiguity theory, even one as sophisticated as Rescorla and Wagner's, can handle Mackintosh's findings.

The Responses Amenable to Classical and Instrumental

It will be evident that our discussion in this chapter of the differences between classical and instrumental conditioning has so far been quite neutral with respect to the type of response which is amenable to the two types of learning. In the past, there have been numerous attempts (Kimble, 1961, p. 100) to link classical conditioning to responses mediated by the autonomic nervous system and instrumental learning to those mediated by the skeletal nervous system. It is now quite clear that such attempts have failed: both types of learning can occur with either class of response. As far as responses mediated by the skeletal nervous system are concerned, these of course have furnished the bulk of responses which have been instrumentally conditioned in the laboratory. From the start of experimental work on classical conditioning, however, there was also one skeletally innervated response which was frequently shown to respond to this learning paradigm—the paw-flexion response to electric shock. Furthermore, given the Soltysik and Jaworska (1962) experiment described earlier in this chapter, it is clear that the learning which is observed in such experiments is genuinely classical conditioning and not a disguised case of instrumental learning. As far as concerns reponses mediated by the autonomic nervous system— the major source of responses for classical conditioning experiments —the work of Miller (1969) and his associates, as well as numerous other investigators in recent years, has removed all doubts that these are also amenable to instrumental conditioning.

In a major review of work on instrumental autonomic conditioning, Miller (1969) describes a number of important experiments from his own laboratory in support of this conclusion. The argument which carries most weight is drawn from bidirectional conditioning experiments of the kind discussed earlier in this chapter. As the reader will recall, if one uses a given stimulus as UCS in a classical conditioning paradigm, the responses eventually elicited by the CS will normally have figured in the vector of responses elicited by the US, and with the same direction of change (the modified stimulus substitution rule: Fig. 2.2). Even though there are exceptions to this rule (Chapter 8), it remains the case that the kind of response change it is possible to observe with a purely classical conditioning paradigm is severely limited; and it is certainly not possible to obtain a response-change in *two opposite* directions using one UCS. In the instrumental conditioning paradigm, however, it is in principle (though not always in practice: Hinde and Stevenson-Hinde, 1973) possible to alter a response in either direction simply by changing the $R \rightarrow S$ contingency from one that reinforces increases to one that reinforces decreases or *vice versa*. Thus, if a response-system can be shown to change in both directions when the appropriate $R \rightarrow S$ contingency is applied, it is difficult to maintain that the observed changes are due to a covert process of classical conditioning. Miller (1969) and his associates have been able to demonstrate such bidirectional changes for salivation, heart rate, intestinal relaxation and contraction, the rate of urine formation in the kidney, changes in the blood supply of the stomach, and vasomotor changes of opposite sign in the two ears simultaneously. These experiments were mostly performed in the curarized rat, removing the possibility (which has been suggested as an explanation of such findings) that the autonomic changes observed are secondary to a response controlled by the skeletal nervous system, and that it is the latter which has "really" been instrumentally trained.

It seems, then, that classical conditioning and instrumental learning are different processes which, as far as we know, can be applied to all responses in the organism's repertoire. However, even though there is apparently no distinction between the absolute response classes available for classical and instrumental conditioning, there does appear to be a differential ease of conditioning depending on the relationship between the stimulus used as the UCS or the S^R, on the one hand, and the response which the experimenter attempts to classically or instrumentally condition, on the other. This conclusion emerges from the experiments of Turner and Solomon (1962) and from their review of earlier experiments.

These workers suggest that, if the degree of "reflexiveness" of the response to the UCS/S^R is high (i.e. if the probability of the response to the UCS/S^R is high and its latency low) then it is comparatively easy to subject this response to classical conditioning and comparatively difficult to subject it to instrumental avoidance conditioning; conversely, responses of low reflexiveness (low probability, high-latency responses to the UCS/S^R) are difficult to obtain as classically conditioned responses to a CS, but easily subjected to instrumental avoidance conditioning. They also report that there is a critical latency of response to the UCS, of approximately 700 msec (which, of course, probably depends on the properties of the response system—limb movement—and the subjects—human—which they were using), below which the learning of this reaction as an instrumental avoidance reponse was very difficult. Thus these results point to some feature of the interaction between the central mechanisms which process the UCS/S^R and the UCR elicited by this stimulus as being critical in the determination of the ease with which such responses will become classically or instrumentally conditioned.

Further support for this view comes from a study by Warren and Bolles (1967). These workers trained three groups of rats to run in a running wheel in order to avoid electric shock. The shock could be avoided by making the running response sufficiently promptly between the onset of a signal warning of the shock and the onset of shock itself. The three groups differed with respect to the delivery of the shock on trials on which the animal failed to make the avoidance response: the shock was delivered either to the hind paws, or to the forepaws. Now the reflex response to shock on the hind paws is a lurch forward, i.e., a response very similar to the running designated as the avoidance response. In contrast, the reflex response to shock to the forepaws is a lurch backward, i.e., a response which is directly incompatible with the designated avoidance response. Thus, on Turner and Solomon's view, the case in which shock was delivered to the hind paws should be the most difficult circumstance for the learning of an instrumental avoidance response consisting of running forward; for, in this case, the designated avoidance response is closest to the reflex response to the UCS/S^{R-}. The results of Warren and Bolles' experiment came out in just this way: animals shocked on the hind paws learnt the avoidance response less well than animals shocked on the forepaws. Note that this result is rather surprising on a common sense basis: one would have thought that it would be far easier for the rat to build up the probability of the response that it gives as a reflexive response to the shock in any case. Apparently, however, this is not so.

A recent experiment by Schwartz and Williams (1972) suggests that something of the same sort may be going on in the phenomenon of autoshaping. It will be recalled that, in this procedure, the lighting up of a key is followed by the automatic delivery of food (or water) to the pigeon, and that, under this purely $S \rightarrow S$ contingency, the animal comes to peck at the lighted key. Furthermore, it does so even if this response cancels the programmed delivery of food (Williams and Williams, 1969); and, if the UCS is food, the auto-shaped keypeck resembles the animal's consummatory response to grain, while, if the UCS is water, the keypeck resembles the consummatory response to water (Moore, 1973). These findings strongly suggest, as we have already seen, that the autoshaped keypeck is a classically conditioned reflex. Now, if Turner and Solomon's (1962) analysis is correct, it is precisely the consummatory (i.e. reflex) response to the UCS which should be easy to classically condition and hard to turn into an instrumental response. One possibility, therefore, most strongly urged by Moore (1973), is that the pigeon's apparently instrumental keypecking response, which has generated an enormous volume of research in "operant conditioning" laboratories, is in fact a Pavlovian conditioned reflex in disguise. A second possibility, however, is that there are two kinds of keypecking response, one of which is a classically conditioned antici-patory consummatory reflex, and the other an instrumental response under the control of $R \rightarrow S$ contingencies. The latter possibility is rendered more plausible by the findings of Schwartz and Williams (1972).

These workers used the procedure of Williams and Williams (1969), in which pecks prevent the delivery of food which is otherwise programmed to occur following the lighting up of the key. They measured the duration of the keypeck auto-shaped in this way, and found it almost invariably to be very short, less than 20 msec. They also measured the duration of keypecks omitted under the control of $R \rightarrow S$ contingencies, in particular, fixed-ratio (FR) and fixed-interval (FI) schedules. (In the former of these, an S^{R+} is delivered after a fixed number of responses, in the latter for the first response after the lapse of a specified period of time.) The duration of the keypeck under these conditions was typically 2–5 times longer than that of the auto-shaped response. The frequency with which the pigeon emitted short-duration keypecks was unaffected by alterations in R → S contingencies, while the frequency of long-duration responses altered in an appropriate manner as these contingencies changed. Not unnaturally, Schwartz and Williams suggest that "short-duration pecks arise from the pigeon's normal feeding pattern and are directly enhanced by food presentation, while long-duration pecks are controlled by the contingent effects of food presentation." If this suggestion is correct (and it seems plausible), the autoshaping data would fit Turner and Solomon's analysis very nicely: the reflex, short-duration peck elicited by grain is readily classically conditioned to the lighted key in the autoshaping procedure, but is insensitive to R → S contingencies; conversely, the long-duration peck, which is not elicited by grain, is readily affected by R → S contingencies, but not classically conditioned. However, before this conclusion can be regarded as firm, it will be necessary to take careful measurements of the duration of unconditioned pecks elicited by grain.

Another case in which Turner and Solomon's principle may be at work is in the conditioning of salivary responses. Salivation is, of course, a reflex response to food in the mouth and, with food as the UCS, the conditioned salivary response has been the most common subject of research in Pavlovian laboratories. Water, in contrast, does not have any pronounced unconditioned effect on salivation (Miller and Carmona, 1967). Thus, on Turner and Solomon's view, one might expect salivation to be more readily susceptible to instrumental training with water as S^{R+} than with food. It is in accord with this view that Sheffield (1965) failed to instrumentally condition dogs to refrain from salivating to obtain a food S^{R+} (using essentially the same design as the Williams and Williams "autoshaping with a negative response contingency" and obtaining essentially the same result); whereas Miller and Carmona (1967) were able to train dogs both to increase and decrease their rate of salivation using a water S^{R+} in a bidirectional instrumental conditioning design.

Coda: Partial Reinforcement, Evolution

One of the difficulties in the way of recognizing the fundamental difference between instrumental and classical conditioning has always been the existence of an overwhelming number of similarities in the laws which appear to apply to both kinds of learning—e.g., those of stimulus generalization, discrimination learning, extinction, spontaneous recovery, etc. As we shall argue in later chapters these similarities may readily be understood on the view that instrumental learning is normally based on an accompanying process of classical conditioning. Nevertheless, their existence clearly renders more difficult the task of one who would claim that classical and instrumental conditioning are fundamentally different processes. For this reason it becomes particularly necessary to pick out those features of classical and instrumental conditioning which do appear to be different. At present, it seems that only one kind of item can be entered on such a list with any degree of certainty. This kind of item concerns some of the effects of what, in the instrumental case, is called "frustrative nonreward", i.e., the non-delivery of an expected S^{R+}. This is a topic with which we deal in detail in Chapter 9. There we shall see that, if two groups of animals are given the same number of trials on an instrumental response, but one group is rewarded on every trial (the continuous reinforcement or CRF group) and the other on only a randomly chosen proportion of trials (the partial reinforcement or PRF group), the PRF animals often perform the response at asymptote more vigorously and almost invariably display much greater resistance to subsequent extinction than do the CRF animals (Lewis, 1960; Robbins, 1971). Neither of these effects seem to occur with any regularity in classical conditioning. Pavlov (1927, 1928) himself reported that partial reinforcement reduced the magnitude of the CR and lowered resistance to extinction, and this has been supported by more recent work (Berger *et al.*, 1965; Gonzalez *et al.*, 1962; Longo *et al.*, 1962; Thomas and Wagner, 1964; Vardaris and Fitzgerald, 1969; Wagner *et al.*, 1967b). There have been occasional reports of increased resistance to extinction after partial reinforcement training in classical conditioning situations, but (with the exception of a study by Holmes and Gormezano, 1970) only when number of reinforcements rather than number of trials (as in the instrumental studies) has been equated (Fitzgerald, 1966; Fitzgerald *et al.*, 1966; Hilton, 1969; Gonzalez *et al.*, 1963) or under other rather special conditions (Wagner *et al.*, 1967b; Spence, 1966). At the very least, it is clear that the effects of partial reinforcement are quantitatively very different in the two kinds of learning, and there is a strong possibility that they are qualitatively different*.

It remains to consider one last point in favour of the distinction between classical and instrumental conditioning, one which, if correct, is particularly telling. Razran (1971) has reviewed an extensive literature from both Soviet and Western sources on the evolution of the capacity for different forms of learning. He concludes that classical conditioning is already possible at a level (lower invertebrates, e.g., earthworms) at which instrumental learning with positive reinforcement is not. It is, of course, always dangerous to place too much reliance on a negative: improved techniques may well establish a clearcut case of instrumental appetitive learning in the earthworm tomorrow. But, if this conclusion stands the test of time, it is of major importance, both for the issue which has occupied us in this chapter, and for the general problem of the evolution of learning.

It is even possible that Razran's conclusion concerning the absence of instrumental learning lower down the phylogenetic scale is too conservative. The recent discovery of autoshaping has driven home rather dramatically the point that what looks like instrumental learning may on occasion be purely classical conditioning in disguise. This is especially so when the apparently instrumental response bears a close resemblance to a consummatory response elicited by the stimulus used as the S^R, as in the case of the pigeon's pecking response. Although I have not attempted any general survey of the literature on operant conditioning in fish, reptiles and birds, it is my impression that the response conditioned in such experiments is almost always part of the natural consummatory response-pattern of the species concerned. Thus the only convincing evidence that the $R \rightarrow S$ contingency apparently operative in such experiments truly controls the behaviour observed would come from a bidirectional conditioning experiment of the kind reviewed by Miller (1969) and described earlier in this chapter. As far as I am aware, all the experiments using the bidirectional technique have employed mammalian subjects. The possibility remains open, therefore, that

---

* Given the fact that partial reinforcement constitutes a weakening of the contingency relationship, the different effects it exerts on the two kinds of learning may derive from the importance of contingencies in classical conditioning (this chapter) and their lack of importance in instrumental conditioning (Chapter 6).

only with the advent of mammals, and perhaps birds, does a true instrumental learning capacity emerge.

There is one line of evidence in support of this view. As we have just seen, the effects of partial reinforcement appear to differ quite considerably between classical and instrumental conditioning. We shall consider some of the effects of partial reinforcement and other forms of frustrative nonreward in Chapter 9. But it is worth noting at this point that a number of experiments have shown that the special effects of frustrative nonreward which are commonly observed in instrumental learning experiments with mammals are absent in similar experiments conducted with fish and amphibia (Pert and Bitterman, 1970). Experiments conducted with members of these classes have revealed behaviour in partial reinforcement situations and other situations involving frustrative nonreward which is essentially the same as that observed in classical conditioning experiments with mammals. This pattern of results might be expected if fully-fledged instrumental conditioning is absent at these phylogenetic levels.

This brings to a close our survey of the differences between classical and instrumental conditioning. (There are a number of other differences which turn on the relationship between drive and reinforcement; but since we deal with this relationship *in extenso* in Chapter 4, we shall postpone consideration of these differences till then.) We have come down firmly for the view that classical and instrumental conditioning involve fundamentally different processes. By no means every authority agrees with this conclusion (Miller, 1969; Black, 1971); but it is an essential basis for the construction of a "two-process" theory of learning of the kind presented in this book.

3. Inhibition

We saw in Chapter 1 that it is possible to give the much-maligned term "inhibition" a quite precise meaning, in the sense of an active process of response–suppression performed by a mechanism specialized for this task, and that the data on habituation of orienting responses strongly suggest that such a process does in fact occur. However, it is in other contexts that the star of inhibition has shone most brightly. We shall delay consideration of "behavioural inhibition" in instrumental learning until Chapters 8 and 9; in the present chapter we consider principally Pavlov's use of the term "inhibition" as applied to classical conditioning.

Pavlov's Classification of Inhibitory Processes

It is in Pavlov, in fact, that the most luxuriant growth of inhibitory constructs is found, each genus and species being given its own name. The classification he used (Table 3.1), though it under-went a large number of confusing vicissitudes, finally took on a tidy and logically convenient shape (Pavlov, 1956). According to this final classification, there are two genera of inhibition: "external" and "internal". The items classified beneath these headings are all instances of response decrement: that is to say, cases in which an existing conditioned reflex is in some way or other reduced in

TABLE 3.1.   Pavlov's Classification of Types of Inhibition

Genus	External or unconditioned	Internal or conditioned
Species	external inhibition transmarginal inhibition of intensity transmarginal inhibition of repetition disinhibition	extinctive inhibition differential inhibition conditioned inhibition inhibition of delay

magnitude or caused to disappear. The principle of classification can be variously stated.

"External inhibition" covers those cases where the response decrement is maximal on the first occasion when it occurs, and subsequently may decline as the appropriate experimental conditions are repeated; that is to say, no learning is involved in the production of the response decrement, though some might be involved in its disappearance. "Internal inhibition" by contrast, covers those cases in which the response decrement grows gradually over time with repetition of the changed experimental conditions which give rise to it; that is to say, learning may well be involved in the production of the response decrement. This difference between external and internal inhibition gives rise to a pair of synonyms for the two genera: "unconditioned inhibition" (i.e., external) or "conditioned inhibition" (i.e., internal).

The difference between external and internal inhibition can also be considered, not from the point of view of the temporal course followed by the response decrement, as above, but from the point of view of the stimuli which give rise to the response decrement. Response decrements of the external inhibitory kind arise when the experimental conditions are changed in ways which do not alter the basic S → S contingency which is used in establishing and maintaining the appropriate CR; response decrements of the internal inhibitory kind arise when the change in the experimental conditions does involve a change in this basic S → S contingency. This second distinction is a natural bedfellow to the first, which, as we have seen, stresses the learning apparently involved in the production of internal inhibition, and its lack in the production of external inhibition; for, in internal inhibition, it is the actual contingency governing learning in classical conditioning (see Chapter 2) which is changed.

Within each genus of inhibition, there are a number of species. External inhibition comes in four varieties: external inhibition proper, transmarginal inhibition of intensity, transmarginal inhibition of repetition, and (a very odd species, this) disinhibition. Similarly, internal inhibition has four species: extinctive inhibition, differential inhibition, conditioned inhibition proper (to be distinguished from the same term as the name of the genus), and inhibition of delay. A brief description of each of these eight species of inhibition will make clear the distinction between the two genera.

External inhibition proper is observed in the following experimental paradigm. Just before, or simultaneously with, presentation of the CS for an established CR, a novel stimulus of any modality (NS) is also presented to the animal. It is observed that the CR is smaller in magnitude than usual, and may even be totally absent. Upon further repetition of the same sequence, the response decrement produced in this way by the NS gradually disappears until the CR returns to its original magnitude.

Transmarginal inhibition (also known as "protective" inhibition) of intensity occurs when a CS of very great intensity is used. In order to understand it, we must first consider another of Pavlov's discoveries: the "law of strength".

This law describes the relationship which Pavlov found to hold between the intensity of the CS and the magnitude of the corresponding CR: the greater the former, the greater the latter (Gray, 1964b, 1965a). This relationship has been found to hold in instrumental learning situations as well. For example, in an experiment of my own (Gray, 1965b), rats were rewarded on a variable interval (VI) schedule (see Fig. 2.5) for pressing a bar in the presence of white noise, but not in its absence: the barpressing rate was then found to be a positive function of the intensity of the noise (Fig. 3.1).

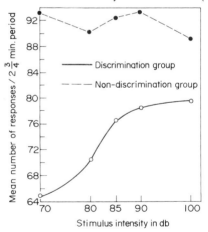

FIG. 3.1. Relation between Instrumental Response Rate and Intensity of Discriminative Stimulus: Stimulus Intensity Dynamism. The response studied was lever-pressing for a food reward on a variable interval (VI) schedule (Fig. 2.5). Each curve is the mean for a group of four rats. In the discrimination group the VI schedule was only operative in the presence of the discriminative stimulus (noise) whose intensity was varied (abscissa). In the non-discrimination group the availability of reward was uncorrelated with the presence or absence of noise. (From Gray, 1965b.)

Note that, in this experiment as in the classical conditioning experiments, the intensity of the discriminative stimulus (S^D), i.e., the white noise, or of the classical CS is not explicitly correlated with the magnitude of the reinforcement (S^{R+} or UCS), so that it appears to be genuinely the *intensity* of the S^D/CS which causes an increment in the response. However, it has been suggested by Perkins (1953; see also Logan, 1954 and Gray, 1965a) that, in classical conditioning necessarily and in instrumental learning whenever a discrimination procedure is used (as in the Gray, 1965b, experiment just described), the law of strength (or "stimulus intensity dynamism", as Hull, 1952, has called the equivalent relationship in instrumental learning) results from a *covert* correlation between CS/S^D intensity and reinforcement. This relationship arises because *non*reinforcement occurs in the *absence* of the CS/S^D, and this absence can be regarded as a stimulus of zero intensity. The greater response rate found during 90 dB noise than in 60 dB in the experiment shown in Fig. 3.1, might, therefore, arise simply because 90 dB is more discriminable from zero dB than is 60 dB. It is in agreement with this view that stimulus intensity dynamism does not appear if a non-discriminative stimulus is used, e.g., when the noise in Gray's (1965b) experiment was uncorrelated with the availability of reinforcement (Fig. 3.1).

It has proved very difficult to infirm Perkins' (1953) hypothesis and demonstrate a true effect of the intensity of a discriminative stimulus (Gray, 1965a). However, in a recent experiment MacMillan *et al.* (1973) have succeeded in doing this. The situation was a complex one in which rats were required to form a discrimination between two contrasting patterns of sound interspersed with silence. Time was divided up into 3 sec lengths, themselves consisting of two segments of 2.2 and 0.8 sec. One of the stimuli to which the rat was exposed had the longer segment filled with noise and the shorter with silence; the other had the longer segment allotted to silence and the shorter to noise (Fig. 3.2). Half the rats were trained with the former stimulus as S^D, i.e., correlated with the availability of a food reward for barpressing on a variable interval schedule, and the latter acting as negative stimulus (or S^Δ), i.e. correlated with unavailability of reinforcement. For the other rats, the significance of the stimuli was reversed. In both cases, response rate was higher during the segment of time for which noise was present than during the silent

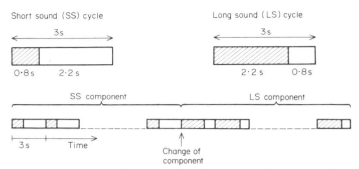

FIG. 3.2. Stimuli used by MacMillan *et al.*, 1973. Two groups of rats were studied. One had the short-sound (SS) stimulus positive (i.e. correlated with the availability of reward for bar-pressing), the other had the long-sound stimulus (LS) positive. Each stimulus was repeated for the duration of a "component" (usually 3 min), and then replaced by the other component. Both groups responded at a higher rate during the sound segment of both repeating stimuli than during the silence segment. (From MacMillan *et al.*, 1973.)

segment. Thus, even in the case in which longer periods of *silence* were associated with reinforcement, there was an invigorating ("dynamogenic") effect of *sound*, as compared to silence, on response rate. This experiment, then, appears to establish the phenomenon of stimulus intensity dynamism under conditions in which Perkins' (1953) hypothesis cannot hold.

Having convinced ourselves that Pavlov's law of strength (or Hull's equivalent stimulus intensity dynamism) is a real phenomenon, we may now return to transmarginal inhibition of intensity. The relationship between CS intensity and CR magnitude breaks down at very high stimulus intensities (Fig. 3.3), though this does not occur in all individuals (indeed, the occurrence or otherwise of trans-marginal inhibition has been used by Pavlov and his followers as a test of personality: Gray, 1964a). Above this point, response magnitude may cease to increase further with increases in stimulus intensity or it may actually fall. It is this fall which is termed "transmarginal inhibition of intensity". Notice that, tested in this way, transmarginal inhibition is not a response decrement observed on a particular occasion: rather, it is a breakdown in a lawful relationship obtaining over a series of observations. It is possible also to observe a decrement in response magnitude if CS intensity is increased after the CR has been established to a CS of lower intensity; but it is impossible to distinguish this kind of decrement from external inhibition proper, since an increase in intensity is a novel stimulus.

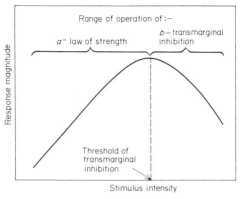

FIG. 3.3. The law of strength and transmarginal inhibition in Pavlovian theory. See text for explanation. (From Gray, 1964a.)

Transmarginal inhibition of *repetition* occurs when a CR is elicited at unusually short inter-trial intervals. A CR is first established and its average magnitude measured with tolerably long intervals between CS presentations (of the order of several minutes). It is then repeatedly elicited at much shorter intervals (under a minute) and it is found that its magnitude decreases (Pavlov called this "extinction with reinforcement"). If a return is made to the longer inter-trial intervals, CR magnitude is restored to its previous level. This phenomenon, too, does not occur in all individuals and has been used as a test of individual differences in a quite broad personality trait (Gray, 1964a). Pavlov called both this phenomenon and the breakdown in the law of strength at high stimulus intensities by the same name of transmarginal inhibition, because he believed that shortening the inter-stimulus interval in the extinction with reinforcement procedure leads to an effective increment in stimulus intensity as a result of summation of excitation (Fig. 3.4).

The fourth kind of external inhibition, disinhibition, will be discussed after we have considered the four kinds of internal inhibition.

As already indicated, internal inhibition involves a response decrement arising from a disruption of existing CS–UCS contingencies.

Extinctive inhibition refers to the decrement which occurs when the UCS is no longer presented after the CS (a procedure known, of course, as "extinction"), and the CR gradually decreases in magnitude with repeated presentations of the CS alone.

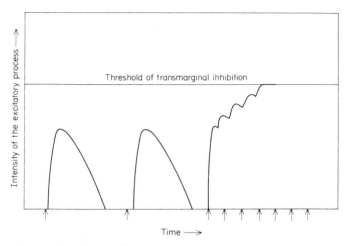

FIG. 3.4. Theoretical mechanism for transmarginal inhibition of repetition. With repeated elicitations of the CR (arrows on the abscissa) at sufficiently short intervals there is a build-up in the intensity of the resulting "excitatory process' until the threshold of transmarginal inhibition is reached, at which point there is a decrease in the magnitude of the response elicited by further presentations of the CS.

Differential inhibition, in a similar way, refers to the response decrement which gradually occurs when (with a CS already established as eliciting a particular CR) a second stimulus, the "differential stimulus" (DS), is introduced and followed by nothing in repeated presentations: that is, pairings of the form CS → UCS, are contrasted with pairings of the form, DS → no UCS. The result of this procedure (known as "differentiation") is that, first, the DS fails to elicit a CR and may even inhibit the CR elicited by the existing CS (a phase of external inhibition proper); then the DS (often, but not always) does elicit a CR, even though it is never in fact followed by the UCS, a phenomenon termed "generalization"; and finally, with further repeated presentations, the CR to the DS declines in magnitude and disappears. It is this final phase which is regarded as showing differential inhibition.

The experimental paradigm involved in the third species of internal inhibition–conditioned inhibition proper–is to contrast pairings of the form, CS → UCS with the pairings of the form, S_2 + CS → no UCS; S_2 being termed a "conditioned inhibitor" (CI). Usually, the CI is presented just before the CS, but it may also be presented after it (Soltysik, 1960). Again, the sequence of events which is observed is: first, the CI, since it is a novel stimulus, acts as an external inhibitor; then generalization from CS alone to the combination CI + CS occurs, so that this combination too elicits the CR; and finally, with repeated non-reinforcement of the combination by the UCS, the gradual response decrement indicative of internal inhibition is seen.

The final species of internal inhibition is inhibition of delay. Here conditioning is first established with a fairly short CS-UCS interval (of the order of seconds), and then the CS-UCS interval is lengthened till it is measured in minutes. It is found that, whereas immediately after the lengthening of the CS-UCS interval the onset of the CR continues to be observed a few seconds after the onset of the CS and just prior to the previous onset of the UCS, the temporal pattern of the CR gradually changes with repeated presentation of the new CS-UCS interval until eventually onset of the CR is delayed until a point in time relatively close to the new time of onset of the UCS. This occurs whether the CS fills the interval between CS onset and UCS onset ("delayed conditioning") or whether CS termination occurs some time before UCS onset ("trace conditioning").

Returning now to the final species of external inhibition, dis-inhibition, this is of particular importance in that its occurrence against a background of any one of the four kinds of internal inhibition is one of the key reasons given by Pavlov for regarding the latter as all instances of one general process. The experimental procedure employed is like that involved in external inhibition proper. A novel stimulus (NS) is presented, in conjunction, not with a CS as in external inhibition proper, but with one of the four kinds of internal inhibitory stimulus. Provided the internal inhibitory stimulus produces a response decrement which is already reasonably strong, but not of extremely long standing in the animal's experimental history, the NS, surprisingly, produces a recurrence of the internally inhibited CR. With repeated presentation of the NS, as in the case of external inhibition proper, the phenomenon of dis-inhibition disappears. It will be clear from this description why Pavlov called this phenomenon "external inhibition of internal inhibition": the experimental procedure and the time course of the response change produced by the NS is identical to that involved in external inhibition proper, but it is the inhibitory effect of the internal inhibitory stimulus, not the CR itself, which is disturbed.

Having completed this survey of Pavlov's classification of the kinds of response decrement which are seen in response to different experimental procedures in a classical conditioning situation, there are a number of questions one is prompted to ask about it. Does the division between external and internal inhibitory response decrements correspond to a real difference between two kinds of underlying process? Do the various species of external inhibition truly belong together in that they all involve the same underlying process? And, similarly, do the various species of internal inhibition belong together? If so, what is the nature of the central process uniting the four forms of external inhibition and of the central process uniting the four forms of internal inhibition? And, returning to the issues which occupied us in Chapter 1, do these processes in any way involve an active response–suppression mechanism of the kind which deserves to be called "inhibitory" in the fullest sense?

The first question—the reality of the difference between external inhibitory response decrements and internal inhibitory response decrements—is the most easily dealt with: the conditions which give rise to each of these and the time course followed by each, on which the Pavlovian classification is based, seem so diametrically opposed to each other that it is difficult to see how a single mechanism could be responsible for both. The phenomenon of disinhibition, in particular, in which an external inhibitory procedure is sufficient to cause the disappearance of an internal inhibitory response decrement, is an immense obstacle to any theory which wished to claim a fundamental similarity between the two Pavlovian genera of inhibition.

What is harder to establish is that the separate species of each of these genera are truly united by a single process. This is particularly so for external inhibition.

External Inhibition, the Orienting Reflex and Arousal

If Chapter 1 was successful in teaching the reader to use the operational definition given there for the orienting reflex, he may by now have noticed something odd about both external inhibition proper and disinhibition. Both these phenomena conform completely to this definition: that is to say, they are elicited by novel stimuli, of any modality, and decline with repeated presentation. Furthermore, as Pavlov noted, they are accompanied by other responses (e.g. head- and eye-turning towards the source of the stimulus) which are known to be ORs. The fact that the function of external inhibition and even more of disinhibition is more obscure to us than is head- and eye-turning should be no deterrent to including these phenomena quite simply among the list of the ORs; for, as we have seen, this list is compiled purely according to the operational definition, and it already contains a number of other obscure phenomena. Some writers prefer to speak of the OR *causing* external inhibition (and disinhibition) of CRs; but, until we have a theory of how the mechanisms involved actually work, such a description is premature.

Disinhibition, in particular, is a strange phenomenon, both from the functional point of view and from the point of view of possible mechanism. Functionally, it is as though the system works according to the principle, "when something new (and therefore potentially dangerous) occurs, stop whatever activity is the most recently acquired in this environment and go back to the one before that": if the most recent activity acquired is that of responding with a CR, the CR is inhibited (external inhibition proper); if the most recent activity acquired is that of internally inhibiting the CR, the internal inhibition is itself removed, and the old CR re-established (disinhibition). In terms of mechanism, if only to make disinhibition seem a little less mysterious, a simple system which appears to be capable of doing the job (proposed by A. Tribe and E. Webb, of University College, Oxford) is shown in Fig. 3.5.

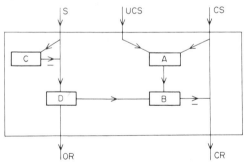

FIG. 3.5. The Tribe–Webb Model for External Inhibition and Disinhibition. The model assumes an existing CS → CR link (right-hand side). Box A records CS → UCS pairings and activates Box B to an increasing degree the more CSs occur without UCSs. Box B, when sufficiently excited, inhibits the CS → CR link. Thus Boxes A and B mediate "internal inhibition", e.g., during extinction. A novel stimulus (S, on the left-hand side) acts via Box D to produce the OR unless it is inhibited via Box C. Box C is Sokolov's "neuronal model of the stimulus" (Figs 1.6 and 1.7) and inhibits the OR after repeated presentation of S (habituation). Box B acts as an "exclusive-or" gate. That is, it responds (inhibiting the CR) if it receives an input *either* from Box A (internal inhibition) *or* from Box D (external inhibition) but not both (disinhibition). excites inhibits

If both external inhibition proper and disinhibition appear to be ORs, the same does not seem to be true of the other two species of external inhibition: transmarginal inhibition of intensity and of repetition. Neither of these two phenomena depend critically on the novelty of the experimental conditions in which they are observed. However, it is possible that all four forms of external inhibition do have in common a rise in the level of arousal.

The term "arousal" (or its synonym "activation") started out in life outside the bounds of learning theory, being used principally by students of the physiological correlates of performance under a variety of stressful and non-stressful conditions (e.g., Freeman, 1948; Duffy, 1951, 1957), and it has come into its own largely through the discovery in the brain of the ascending reticular activating system (ARAS: Moruzzi and Magoun, 1949). However, very similar concepts existed in both Pavlov's and Hull's theories of learning: Pavlov's "intensity of the excitatory process" and Hull's "general drive". (We deal with general drive more completely in Chapter 8.) These various terms all have in common that they are used to refer to variation in the *intensity* of behaviour as distinct from variation in the *direction* of behaviour. Roughly speaking, they refer to a dimension of behaviour varying from sluggishness or drowsiness, at the low arousal end, to great alertness, vigour or excitement, at the high arousal end.

I have analysed the uses to which various writers have put the term "arousal" in some detail elsewhere (Gray, 1964b, p. 290), so here I shall simply summarize my earlier conclusions. First, we must be clear about the status of the term. As used by all, "arousal" refers to a state of the *organism*: level of arousal is dependent on antecedent and concurrent stimulus conditions, and it affects concurrent and subsequent responses, but it can be identified with neither. Thus it is clearly a theory-word, not an operational or observational term. The links between this hypothetical state of the organism, on the one hand, and stimuli (operations) and responses (observations) on the other (as far as I can deduce these links from various writers' uses of "arousal", "activation" and "arousal level") are set out in Fig. 3.6.

It will be seen that, in this figure, observations are divided into two kinds: "determinates" of arousal level and "indices" of arousal level. The reason for this division is that, as is generally agreed, arousal level is related to performance variables of the kind listed to the right of Fig. 3.6 by an inverted-U function: efficiency is low at both low and high levels of arousal and is greatest at intermediate levels. It follows that performance variables of this kind cannot be used to measure level of arousal directly. (It is as though I.Q. tests could not be used to measure intelligence because individuals with both high and low intelligence did badly on them.) In the hope of getting round this problem, arousal theorists have assumed that certain kinds of physiological measures (EEG, GSR, muscle-tension etc.) may provide direct, monotonic indices of level of arousal (as shown in the middle column of Fig. 3.6), though it is by no means certain that this assumption is justified.

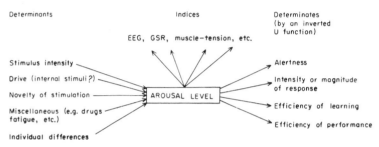

FIG. 3.6. Determinants, Indices and Determinates of Arousal Level. See text for explanation. (From Gray, 1964b.)

One important thing to note about Fig. 3.6 is that the operations which are regarded as leading to an increase in level of arousal include both stimulus novelty (which, as we have seen, is the key variable involved in the production of external inhibition proper and disinhibition, two of the four species of external inhibition) and stimulus intensity (the key variable in transmarginal inhibition of intensity and possibly also in transmarginal inhibition of repetition— see Fig. 3.4—the other two species of external inhibition). The other important thing to note is that most workers in this field have attributed control of level of arousal to the brain-stem reticular formation (RF). This, as we saw in Chapter 1, is thought by Sokolov (on good grounds) also to control the orienting reflex; and both external inhibition proper and disinhibition are part of the orienting reflex. It seems possible, therefore, that the unity which Pavlov saw between the four species of external inhibition is real, and that it depends on an increase in level of arousal brought about when either novel or intense stimuli act on the RF (see Fig. 1.8). In terms of Sokolov's model for habituation of the OR—see Fig 1.7—the RF is the "amplifying system"; and in terms of the Tribe-Webb model for disinhibition—Fig. 3.5—it is box D. We shall reconsider this general kind of system for external inhibition in Chapters 8 and 9 (though under the new title of "behavioural inhibition").

Internal Inhibition and Habituation of the Orienting Reflex

By now it has become clear that our reasons for holding that all four species of external inhibition belong to the same genus are far from strong. Nor are we better off when we come to consider the same question with respect to internal inhibition. About the best reason for concluding that the four species of this kind of inhibition belong together is that they are all susceptible to disinhibition. Though this is hardly conclusive, evidence against the view that they belong together is even scantier; and in view of the general similarities between them, we may conclude, cautiously, that it is best for the moment to accept Pavlov's classificatory scheme.

If internal inhibitory response decrements are truly the result of a single underlying process, what is the nature of this process?

One possibility is that, just as external inhibition appears to be linked to the production of orienting responses, internal inhibition is linked to their habituation. At any rate, there are a number of similarities between habituation of the OR and internal inhibition of CRs which cannot fail to attract our attention. Both habituated ORs and internally inhibited CRs show spontaneous recovery and the distinction between acute and chronic habituation or extinction (see Chapter 1). Disinhibition of CRs bears undoubted resemblances to de-habituation of ORs, since, in both cases, application of a novel stimulus causes the re-appearance of the previously habituated or inhibited response to a different stimulus. Both habituation and internal inhibition are rendered more difficult to attain by stimulant drugs, such as caffeine or amphetamine (Hilgard and Marquis, 1940; Lynn, 1966).

Another possible similarity between internal inhibition and habituation of the OR concerns the over-habituated OR (see Chapter 1) and the "hypnotic" phases of conditioning described by Pavlov.

The latter involve, first, oddities in the law of strength and trans-marginal inhibition of intensity and, second, oddities in internal inhibition. The former oddities appear in the so-called "equalization" and "paradoxical" phases of conditioning and the latter in the "ultra-paradoxical" phase. It is the latter, in particular, which resemble overhabituation.

All the hypnotic phases were observed in dogs which had served in the same experimental situation for many months or even years and, according to Pavlov, the three phases follow each other in the order listed. The equalization phase involves a distortion of the law of strength such that, whereas there has previously been observed a stable relationship between CS intensity and CR magnitude, this is replaced by constant CR magnitude, irrespective of the CS used. In the paradoxical phase, which follows if conditioning is continued, CSs which previously evoked weak CRs come to evoke strong ones and, conversely, stimuli which previously elicited strong CRs now elicit weak ones: i.e. there is a reversal of the usual law of strength. Finally, in the ultra-paradoxical phase, the animal ceases altogether to respond to positive CSs, but gives a CR to stimuli which were previously internal inhibitors (extinguished CSs, differential stimuli etc.), even though, as before, these continue not to be reinforced. As in the case of overhabituation, these oddities can be overcome if the animal is restored to full alertness.

Sokolov's account of overhabituation (Chapter 1) can be applied quite naturally to some of the observations made in the ultra-paradoxical phase of conditioning, if we assume that internal inhibition, like habituation, is a function of the neocortex. This phase occurs only after many months of conditioning, when the monotony of the experimental situation has had the consequence that the dog shows signs of drowsiness very rapidly after the experimental session commences. If it is not possible for the cortex under such conditions to exercise its inhibitory role, there would be the observed restoration of the previously internally inhibited CRs. However, although this account makes sense of the restoration of the previously inhibited CRs, it does not explain why the previously elicited CRs should simultaneously disappear. Nor does it explain the distortions of the law of strength through which the animal passes before entering the ultra-paradoxical phase. So the mysteries of the hypnotic phases of conditioning remain very mysterious.

Is Internal Inhibition an Active Process of Response Suppression?

Intriguing as these parallels between the habituated OR and the inhibited CR may be, then, it is clear that the arguments for a similarity of underlying mechanism between habituation and internal inhibition are less than compelling. And, indeed, a direct examination of the hypothesis that they are identical by Reiss and Wagner (1972) has produced discouraging results. Before we consider this experiment, however, let us look at the results of experiments which have attempted to establish the nature of the process actually involved in internal inhibition. In particular, let us address ourselves to the question whether there is any evidence that this is indeed a true inhibitory process: does internal inhibition involve a mechanism for the active suppression of a response which, in the absence of that mechanism, would occur?

Let us approach this problem with as few preconceptions as possible. What evidence is there, in the first place, for the notion that an internal inhibitor (which we shall denote CS−, in distinction to the positive or excitatory CS+) exerts any active influence at all? Why should one not conclude that a stimulus which did not initially elicit a CR, and then for a while did, has now simply reverted to its original status as a neutral stimulus? If all that we observe is the *absence* of response both in the initial neutral phase and in the final "internally inhibitory" phase, surely no other conclusion is warranted?

There are a number of good reasons not to accept this "*status quo ante*" view (in spite of its forceful advocacy by Skinner, 1938). The first is the phenomenon of disinhibition. A novel stimulus presented together with a neutral stimulus does not elicit the CR: this only occurs when the novel stimulus is presented together with an internal inhibitor. A similar argument can be drawn from the phenomenon of positive induction. If an internal inhibitory stimulus is presented just before (usually within about 30 sec) a positive CS for a CR, then Pavlov (1927) reports that the magnitude of the CR is significantly greater than upon presentation of the positive CS on its own; and again the same effect is not obtained by a neutral stimulus which, if novel, might *reduce* the magnitude of the CR, but would not increase it.

An internal inhibitor, then, does something special to the organism; but is this something the activation of a response-suppression mechanism? Certainly, the phenomenon of disinhibition suggests an active inhibitory process which is disrupted by the novel stimulus; and the Tribe-Webb model (Fig. 3.5) makes explicit one mechanism whereby this could occur. And the phenomenon of positive induction might perhaps suggest that the internal inhibitor simultaneously elicits a tendency to respond and blocks expression of this response; and that the following positive CS simultaneously elicits its own response tendency and removes the block on expression of the response tendency already elicited by the internal inhibitor. But such suggestions fall well short of proof.

The kinds of experimental proof which have been offered for the active response-suppression powers of internal inhibitors in the classical conditioning paradigm have recently been reviewed by Rescorla (1969). Very stimilar arguments have been proposed by Hearst *et al.* (1970) in the case of stimuli which, in an instrumental learning situation, are correlated with the non-delivery of positive reinforcement for a response which, in the presence of other stimuli, does obtain reinforcement. Such "negative discriminative" stimuli as these (symbolized as S^Δ or $S-$, in contrast to the S^D or $S+$ which is correlated with the availability of instrumental reinforcement), like internal inhibitors, apparently suppress the unreinforced response. They also, however, possess other properties which we shall consider in detail in Chapter 9. For the moment, therefore, we shall continue to concentrate on internal inhibition, with only a brief glance at the active suppressive powers of negative discriminative stimuli.

Four classes of experiment which offer evidence for response suppression may be distinguished: "summation" or "combined-cue" tests; "retardation" or "resistance to reinforcement" tests; the construction of an "inhibitory generalization gradient"; and the demonstration of a "reaction of the reverse sign" (a phenomenon reported by a number of Soviet workers, but which has so far received little explicit attention in Western research). We shall consider each of these in turn.

In a summation test for response suppression, some positive CS (CS_2) is presented which is known to elicit a response of given amplitude, measured, say, as the number of drops of saliva in a classical salivary conditioning situation. Paired with it is the putative internal inhibitor ($CS-$) under test. The $CS-$ will have been previously paired with non-reinforcement in conjunction with some other positive stimulus (CS_1). For example, if the $CS-$ is a conditioned inhibitor, it will have been presented previously to the animal according to the paradigm, $CS_1 \to UCS$, $CS- + CS_1 \to No$ UCS. The UCS for both CS_1 and CS_2 is normally the same (though not always—a point we take up below). Then, on the critical test, the $CS-$ is paired for the first time with CS_2. The expectation is that, if the $CS-$ has a general response-suppressive capacity, it will suppress the response to CS_2, even though the animal has never been exposed to the sequence, $CS- + CS_2 \to No$ UCS. Suitable controls have to be instituted for the effects of exposing the animal to a novel sequence of stimuli *per se* (e.g. by examining the effects of the stimulus pair $S_3 + CS_2$ on the response to CS_2, where S_3 is a novel stimulus). Experiments of this kind have been conducted on numerous occasions, both in Pavlov's (1927) original work and more recently (Konorski, 1948; Rescorla, 1969), and there can now be little doubt that the response-suppressive capacity of an internal inhibitor set up with one positive stimulus does transfer to others. (We shall leave till later the question whether this happens in the case of all four kinds of stimuli treated by Pavlov as internal inhibitors.)

A similar experimental design in an instrumental learning context has been reported by Brown and Jenkins (1967). This experiment consisted of three phases. During the first phase, pigeons were trained to peck at the right-hand side of a key (for food reward) when the key was red (S_1^D) and at the left-hand side when the key was green (S_2^D). In the second phase of the experiment the key was always red and a tone (S^Δ) was sometimes present and sometimes absent. Pecking at the key was never reinforced with food when the tone was present, and, when it was absent, still only pecks at the right half of the key were rewarded. In the final test phase of the experiment, the key was made green and pecking, as before in the presence of green, was reinforced only when it was directed to the left side of the key. The tone was now presented to the pigeon and it duly suppressed pecking under the control of the green stimulus to the left side of the key, even though it had never been presented in this context before. Thus, if the red S_1^D is equated to the training CS+, the tone S^Δ to a conditioned inhibitor, and the green S_2^D to the test CS+ in an equivalent classical conditioning experiment, the outcome is the same: the S^Δ suppressed responding to the test S^D in the same way that a conditioned inhibitor suppresses responding to a test CS+.

A rather direct indication of the response-suppresive capacity of an internal inhibitor using a modified version of the summation test has been reported by Thomas (1972). Thomas's experimental design depended on presenting the CS− in combination with the UCS for the appropriate response (rather than a CS+, as in the examples we have considered so far). Experiments of this nature have been conducted on a number of occasions, with varying results (Rescorla, 1969). The special feature of Thomas's (1972) experiment was the nature of the UCS: direct electrical stimulation of the brain (in cats) via permanently implanted electrodes. The electrodes were located in the hypothalamus, at sites where stimulation elicited signs either of rage or fear. The UCS was preceded by a CS+ in the usual way, and the CR was measured as the amplitude of movement occurring in response to the CS. The CS− was established by differentiation: i.e. CS+ → UCS, CS− → No UCS. At various times during conditioning "threshold probe" tests were conducted. In these, the threshold hypothalamic current able to elicit the uncon-ditioned rage or fear response on about 50% of occasions was applied to the animal with and without prior presentation of the CS+ and the CS−.

The results obtained differed according to the kind of stimulus which had been used as the CS−. If the CS− and the CS+ were quite similar to each other (i.e. two tones of different pitches), so that there had initially been a great deal of generalized responding to the CS− before the establishment of the differentiation, the CS− actually *increased* the probability of hypothalamic elicitation of the UCR (as did the CS+). Only if the CS− was very different from the CS+ (i.e. a light versus a tone) and had never elicited any generalized responding did its presentation *decrease* the probability of hypo-thalamic elicitation of the UCR, showing a true response-suppressive capacity. The results of this experiment (both the course of con-ditioning of the two kinds of CS− and the outcome of the threshold probe tests) are presented in Fig. 3.7. It can be seen that, even at the end of conditioning, when neither kind of CS− any longer elicits any response, there is a clearcut difference between them in the threshold probe test: the CS− belonging to a different stimulus modality from the CS+ exerts a definite response-suppressive effect and the CS− belonging to the same modality is equally definitely excitatory by this test. Thus, the results of the Thomas experiment, while they

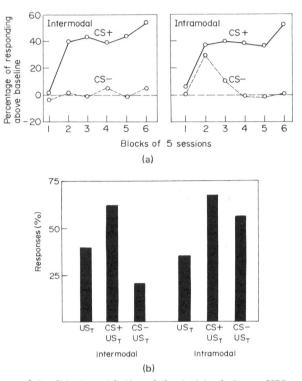

FIG 3.7. Course of Conditioning with Hypothalamic Stimulation as UCS and Results of "Threshold Probe" Tests in Thomas's (1972) Experiment. (a) Progress of conditioning with CS+ and CS− belonging to same (intramodal: right) or different (intermodal: left) modalities. (b) Percentage of CRs elicited by threshold UCS (stimulation of hypothalamus: US_T) with or without CS+ or CS− in intramodal and intermodal conditions. (From Thomas, 1972.)

demonstrate that a true inhibitory capacity can accrue to a differential stimulus, also make it clear that one cannot assume such a capacity merely from the absence of a conditioned response to the CS−.

In a retardation test for response-suppression, the attempt is made to turn the putative internal inhibitor into an excitatory CS: the assumption is that, if the internal inhibitor suppresses the response which is now being positively conditioned, conditioning will be retarded in comparison to the conditioning of stimuli which have not previously served as CS−. Retardation tests have been applied extensively by Konorski (1967), especially for the assay of differential stimuli in experiments in which the UCS is either shock or food. In both cases, results from his laboratory have been clearcut in demonstrating great difficulty in the conversion of such a differential CS— into a CS+ for the same UCS as was used during the initial establishment of the stimulus as a CS—.

An example of the retardation test applied to instrumental learning has been reported by Hearst, Besley and Farthing (1970). This experiment also demonstrates the construction of an "inhibitory generalization gradient" as evidence for active response suppression, so that it is worth describing in some detail.

Pigeons were trained to peck at a key for a food reward when the key was white; responses made when the white key was bisected by a thin black line (the S^Δ) were not reinforced. For some pigeons, this line was vertical, for others it was at an angle of 30 degrees. When the animal had thoroughly learnt this discrimination (only 4% of its responses or less being made in the presence of S^Δ), the attempt was made to convert the S^Δ into an S^D by now reinforcing responses made to it. For this purpose, the animal was presented, in random order, with seven different orientations of line, including the old S^Δ, on the white key, all pecks at the key being reinforced on a variable interval schedule (see Fig. 2.5), as were responses to the white key in the first part of the experiment. The critical data consisted of the number of pecks occurring in the presence of each of the orientations of line. A response-suppressive effect of the erstwhile S^Δ should show up as a reduced number of responses made in its presence as compared to responses in the presence of other angles of orientation. As can be seen from Fig. 3.8, this was the finding made, the retarding effect of the previous training with a particular angle of orientation lasting on average three sessions, each nearly an hour in duration.

Another feature of the results shown in Fig. 3.8 is the orderly way in which response rate rises as the angle of orientation of the line stimulus becomes more unlike the angle used as the S^Δ in initial training: this is the "inhibitory generalization gradient". It is the obverse of the "excitatory generalization gradient" which is a familiar feature of both classical and instrumental conditioning (see Fig. 3.9). In this, the magnitude of the response falls off systematically as the stimulus changes along some dimension or other (e.g. hue, pitch or angular orientation) from the value used as the CS+ or S^D.

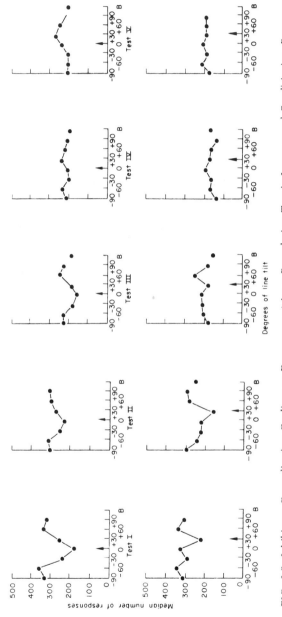

FIG. 3.8. Inhibitory Generalization Gradient as Demonstrated by a Retardation Test in Instrumental Conditioning. Response rates in presence of lines of different angles of orientation projected on the key, pecking at which produced occasional rewards for the pigeon subjects of the experiment. The pigeons had previously been exposed to only one angular orientation (0° for the upper panels, +30° for the lower ones), in the presence of which responding had not been reinforced. Upper panels: mean results over five successive days for group of 9 pigeons. Lower panels: same for different group of 8. The point "B" on the right of the abscissa shows response rate to the blank key, in the presence of which responding had always been reinforced. (From Hearst et al., 1970.)

An important feature of the procedure used by Hearst, Besley and Farthing (1970) is that the dimension along which the inhibitory gradient is measured (angular orientation) is *orthogonal* to the difference which distinguishes the S^Δ from the S^D. That is to say, there is no reason to suppose that any particular orientation of line is further away from, or closer to, a white key with no line on it at all

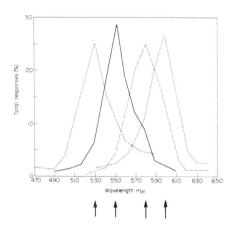

FIG. 3.9. Stimulus Generalization. The phenomenon of stimulus generalization appears to be a very general property of learnt responses. In the case illustrated, four groups of pigeons were rewarded for pecking at a disc on to which light of the four different wavelengths indicated by the arrows was projected. When the wavelength of light was changed, there was an orderly decline in the pigeons' rates of response: the greater the stimulus change, the greater was the decline. (From Guttman and Kalish, 1956.)

than is any other orientation of line. (Though Hearst *et al.* themselves point out a number of reasons why such an assumption might in particular cases be wrong.) The value of such an orthogonal dimension procedure is that it separates the generalization of inhibitory effects to stimuli adjacent to the S^Δ from the generalization of excitatory effects to stimuli adjacent to the S^D. Suppose, for example, that one carries out an "intra-dimensional" discrimination training experiment in which the S^D is a vertical line and the S^Δ a horizontal one. If response rate is then measured to a line oriented at 45° and found to be midway between the rates observed in the presence of the training S^D and S^Δ, this could either be because of the generalization of excitation from the S^D or because of the generalization of inhibition from the S^Δ or both. The orthogonal procedure eliminates this difficulty. Thus, results such as those obtained by Hearst *et al.* (and there are a number of similar findings) are good evidence for the existence of a response-suppressive property of an S^Δ which generalizes in a systematic manner to other stimuli as a function of their degree of similarity to the S^Δ.

The final class of experiments which offer proof of a response-suppression mechanism at work in internal inhibition consists of investigations of the "reaction of the reverse sign". This phenomenon, which has been reported by a number of Soviet workers, consists in a response elicited by an internal inhibitor which is opposite in direction to the response elicited by the positive CS. Bunyatyan and his colleagues, for example, reported that, when a conditioned rise in blood-sugar level was extinguished, presentation of the extinguished CS eventually led to a fall in blood-sugar; conversely, as a result of the extinction of a conditioned decrease in the level of blood-sugar, presentation of the extinguished CS resulted in a rise in blood-sugar level (Bunyatyan, 1952; Bunyatyan *et al.*, 1952). Ilina (1959) has reported similar phenomena during extinction and differentiation of the "photochemical conditioned reflex". In this CR, an initially neutral stimulus is paired with a UCS consisting of a flash of light shone in the dark-adapted eyes of a human subject and comes, as a CS+, to elicit a rise in the absolute visual threshold. The reaction of the reverse sign, described by Ilina as occurring to an extinguished or differentiated CS, consists in a *fall* in the absolute visual threshold.

There have also been some Western observations of "reactions of the reverse sign", though they have not been given this name. In the experiment by Rescorla and LoLordo (1965), which we considered in some detail in the previous chapter (see Fig. 2.3), the effects of Pavlovian conditioning were evaluated by looking at changes produced by CSs, previously paired with presence or absence of shock, in the rate of Sidman avoidance responding in a shuttlebox. As the reader will recall, the effect of a CS+, previously paired with the UCS of shock, is to increase the rate of avoidance responding in this situation, an effect which is said to indicate that such a CS has acquired "fear-inducing" properties (see Chapters 8 and 10). The effect of a CS−, previously paired with the absence of the shock UCS according to a number of different designs (differentiation, conditioned inhibition, etc.), was exactly the reverse: it reduced the rate of avoidance responding (an effect which can be attributed to a "reduction in fear": Chapter 10). Essentially, therefore, there is, in Russian terms, a reaction of the reverse sign.

A similar phenomenon has been demonstrated by Terrace (1972a) in an instrumental learning situation with human subjects. The subject was financially rewarded on a variable interval schedule for pushing a joy-stick to the right when an S^D (a particular kind of computer generated random-dot pattern) was projected onto a screen. When the S^Δ (a different kind of pattern) was projected on the screen, responding was never rewarded. The joy-stick could not be pulled to the left beyond its central resting place, but force exerted on the joy-stick in that direction could be measured (though the subjects of the experiment were unaware of this fact). During conventional discrimination training a very large number of such left-going responses occurred during presentation of S^Δ—that is to say, there were again (as in the classical conditioning experiments) "reactions of the reverse sign" or "antagonistic" responses as Terrace calls them.

Having considered these four kinds of test of response-suppression, it remains to ask which of the four kinds of Pavlovian internal inhibitors (extinguished CSs, differential stimuli, conditioned inhibitors and delayed or trace CSs in the early part of the delay interval) pass these tests. Rescorla (1969) has recently reviewed the evidence bearing on this question, and we shall follow his treatment.

With regard to an extinguished CS+, Rescorla concludes that the contention that such a stimulus acquires actual inhibitory properties (rather than simply losing its erstwhile excitatory properties) is very weak. There are no satisfactory reports of summation tests, with positive outcomes, and, with regard to the retardation test, it is well known that, far from it being especially difficult to re-condition a CR to an extinguished CS+, it is particularly easy to do so (Pavlov, 1927; Konorski, 1967). Against these conclusions, however, there stand the observations of Bunyatyan (1952) and Ilina (1959), described above, on reactions of the reverse sign occurring during extinction of metabolic and "photochemical" conditioned reflexes. This problem, then, stands in need of further investigation before definite conclusions are reached. Two possibilities which should be considered in such an investigation are: (1) that the paradoxical results of retardation tests with extinguished stimuli are due to the increased "attention" (Sutherland and Mackintosh, 1971; and see below) which an animal pays to an erstwhile CS+, compared to a control neutral stimulus; and (2) that the reaction of the reverse sign found in Ilina's and Bunyatyan's research was due to the practice, common in Soviet and Eastern European experiments (Rescorla, 1969), of continuing to reinforce other CSs while extinguishing one particular CS+, so that the latter may serve as a differential stimulus, as well as an extinguished one.

The evidence for response-suppressive properties accruing to differential stimuli is much better than for extinguished stimuli. Positive outcomes have been reported from summation tests using both a CS+ and direct electrical stimulation of the brain as the excitatory stimuli with which the CS− is combined (Konorski, 1967; Rescorla, 1969; Thomas, 1972). There have also been a number of positive reports of response-suppression using the retardation test (Konorski, 1967; Rescorla, 1969). Finally, both inhibitory generalization gradients (Pavlov, 1927) and reactions of the reverse sign (Ilina, 1959; Rescorla and LoLordo, 1965) have been observed after differentiation. However, as noted above in the description of Thomas's (1972) experiment, the evidence does not always show that a differential CS−, even when it elicits a zero response, is acting in an inhibitory manner.

Conditioned inhibitors have been less extensively investigated than differential stimuli. However, there is evidence both from the summation test with a CS+ (Pavlov, 1927) and from the reaction of the reverse sign (Rescorla and LoLordo, 1965) for a response-suppressive capacity accruing to such stimuli.

Least evidence is available for inhibition of delay. However, an elegant experiment reported by Rodnick (1937) demonstrated the reality of this kind of inhibition by means of a summation test. At the same time this experiment demonstrates the important point that internal inhibition is not necessarily limited to reactions which are based on the same UCS as that whose absence the CS− has signalled during the establishment of its inhibitory properties. For this reason, we describe this experiment in some detail.

The experiment was performed with human subjects, in which two classical conditioned reflexes were established. One of these was an eyeblink CR to a vibratory stimulus applied to the skin as CS and a puff of air on the cornea as UCS. This was set up first, with a brief (0.5 sec) interval between CS and UCS onsets. In a second session a galvanic skin reflex (GSR) was conditioned to a light CS with electric shock as the UCS. For this reflex, the interval between CS onset and UCS onset was set at 20 sec, and the light remained on until the UCS occurred (i.e. a "delayed" conditioning procedure was used). When this reflex was fully established and the mean latency between CS onset and the onset of the conditioned fall in skin resistance had lengthened from an initial value of 5 sec to a value of 10 sec, the critical test trials were conducted. The logic of the argument which guided these test trials is set out in Fig. 3.10.

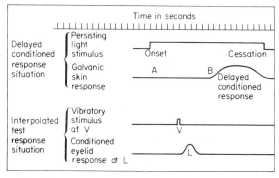

FIG. 3.10. Design of Rodnick's (1937) Experiment on Inhibition of Delay. For explanation see text. (From Rodnick, 1937.)

As this figure shows, Rodnick's design was to present the CS for the eyeblink response after the CS for the delayed GSR and in the period of 10 sec during which (on the grounds that the conditioned GSR had not yet begun to appear) inhibition of delay could be presumed to be operating. The expectation was that, on test trials such as these, the amplitude of the conditioned eyelid response would be reduced (owing to summation with inhibition of delay) as compared to control trials on which the conditioned eyelid response was measured in the absence of the CS for the GSR. In the same way, it could be predicted that the latency of the conditioned eyeblink response might be increased on the test trials. Both these expectations were satisfied at a high degree of confidence. Results from a representative sequence of pre-test, test and post-test trials are shown in Fig. 3.11, taken from Rodnick's paper. Various control

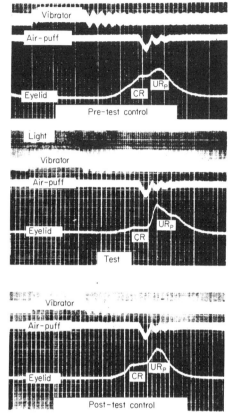

FIG. 3.11. Results of Representative Sequence of Pre-Test, Test and Post-Test Trials in Rodnick's (1937) Experiment. Specimen photographic records of a complete test cycle. The test record shown in the centre was taken during the interval of delay of a delayed conditioned response, 5 sec after the onset of the light stimulus. The pre-test control was taken 85 sec prior to and the post-test record 45 sec following this test situation. It is seen that the conditioned response (CR) occurs before the unconditioned response (URp) and is considerably smaller in magnitude. Horizontal lines measure amplitude in mm. The fine vertical time lines are 20 msec and the heavy lines 100 msec apart. By comparing the test conditioned lid response with the mean of the controls the effect of the interval of delay may be determined. In this figure, the persisting light stimulus depresses the amplitude of the test-response to an extent of 71%. The increment in latency is 9%. (From Rodnick, 1937.)

experiments established rather clearly that the reduction in the size of the conditioned eyeblink response on the test trials was due to the association of the light stimulus with the delayed conditioning of the GSR, and not to some other feature of this stimulus or of its experimental history.

This experiment, then, demonstrates that, on a summation test, the stimulus for a delayed CR possesses true response-suppressive powers. A similar demonstration has been provided by Rescorla (1967, 1968) using both delayed conditioning and trace conditioning procedures for the conditioning of fear-inducing properties to a CS followed by the UCS of shock. When such CSs were subsequently presented to animals in a Sidman avoidance situation, the rate of avoidance responding was reduced just after presentation of the delay or trace CS and then grew gradually throughout the CS–UCS interval until it exceeded the baseline rate, i.e. the rate obtaining in the absence of any additional exteroceptive stimulation. Thus, in these experiments, the summation test disclosed both the inhibitory capacity of a delayed or trace CS just after its onset and its excitatory properties as the time of expected UCS onset approaches.

An important aspect of Rodnick's experiment, as already pointed out, is that it shows that the transferability of the response-suppressive capacity of an internal inhibitor is not necessarily limited to responses based on the same UCS; though experimental investigations of internal inhibition have only rarely departed from the custom of using the same UCS for the establishment of an internal inhibitor and for the test of its inhibitory powers. However, the transferability of internal inhibition across classes of UCS is not without limit. Indeed, some experiments of Konorski's (1967, p. 335) using the retardation test show that under certain conditions it is easier to turn an erstwhile CS– into a CS+ for a new CR (based on a different kind of UCS) than to turn the old CS+ for the previous UCS into a CS+ for the new CR. The conditions under which this phenomenon occurs involve two UCSs of which one is an instrumental positive reinforcer and the other an instrumental negative reinforcer.

In Konorski's experiments, dogs were trained on two CRs, one using food as the UCS and salivation as the measured response, the other using electric shock as the UCS and paw-flexion as the response. Both CRs underwent differentiation, so that the dog initially learned about four stimuli: $CS+_{food}$, $CS-_{food}$, $CS+_{shock}$, $CS-_{shock}$. At the end of this phase of the experiment, the attempt was made to transform the significance of the stimuli in the following ways: $CS+_{food}$ into $CS+_{shock}$; $CS-_{food}$ into $CS+_{shock}$;

$CS+_{shock}$ into $CS+_{food}$; and $CS-_{shock}$ into $CS+_{food}$. Konorski's results indicated that the conversion of the $CS+_{food}$ into a positive CS for shock was extremely difficult, whereas the conversion of the $CS-_{food}$ into a $CS+_{shock}$ proceeded very rapidly and efficiently. Similarly, it was very difficult to convert the $CS+_{shock}$ into a postive CS for food, but quite easy to turn the $CS-_{shock}$ into a $CS+_{food}$.

The key difference between these results and those obtained by Rodnick (1937) probably lies in the fact that Rodnick's two UCSs (an airpuff to the cornea and electric shock to the wrist), although different in quality, were both aversive. Taken together, the two experiments suggest the following generalization: within the class of aversive (or appetitive) UCSs—i.e., those which can serve as an instrumental S^{R-} or S^{R+} respectively—an internal inhibitor is transferable (Rodnick's result); but across the boundary between these two classes, transfer is *negative*—i.e., results such as Konorski's are obtained, transfer being easier if the sign of the CS is reversed. This generalization obviously stands in need of extensive experimental testing before it can be accepted as more than a hypothesis; but, if correct, it would fit very well with a number of findings which have been made in other contexts and which we shall review in Chapters 9 and 10.

Internal Inhibition and Habituation Revisited

We are now in a position to return to a question which we addressed earlier in the chapter: the possibility that habituation of the orienting reflex and internal inhibition employ the same fundamental inhibitory mechanism. This question has been the object of an experimental attack by Reiss and Wagner (1972). In effect, their experiment consists in a comparison between the summation and retardation tests of active response-supression as applied to a stimulus, the orienting reflex to which is first strongly habituated. The rationale for such a comparison is set out by Rescorla (1969), in his review of procedures for the assay of internal inhibition.

In setting out this rationale, Rescorla is concerned to distinguish inhibitory effects from those which arise because of diminished "attention" to the stimulus. The concept of "attention" has been given extensive analysis by a number of learning theorists in recent years (see the thorough review by Sutherland and Mackintosh,

1971). For our present purposes, however, it is sufficient to treat diminished attention as the equivalent of a reduced tendency for a stimulus to elicit the orienting reflex. The use of combined retardation and summation tests in distinguishing between the effects of diminished attention and internal inhibition is explained by Rescorla (1969, p. 85) as follows:

> It seems reasonable that a stimulus to which the organism does not attend will be retarded in the acquisition of an excitatory CR but will produce little effect in the summation procedure. On the other hand, a stimulus which attracts attention might be expected to produce decrements in the summation testing procedure but to lead to facilitated acquisition of an excitatory CR. Thus if a stimulus affects the attention of the organism it should not behave like a conditioned inhibitor in *both* the summation and retardation-of-acquisition test procedures. For this reason, when attentional accounts seem plausible, it may be valuable to have information from both of these procedures for a stimulus thought to be a conditioned inhibitor.

Now, it has been known for some time that, if a stimulus is repeatedly presented to an animal for many trials without reinforcement before the animal is exposed to any conditioning procedure, it is extremely difficult to turn it subsequently into a CS+, a phenomenon termed "latent inhibition" by Lubow and Moore (1959). That is to say, such a stimulus (which, in effect, is one to which the orienting reflex has been habituated) passes the retardation test of inhibition. But it is at least as plausible to regard a "latent inhibitory" stimulus as one which the animal learns to disregard (since no important consequences are associated with it). Thus, it is possible that excitatory conditioning is retarded, not because of any response-suppressive capacity attached to the stimulus, but simply because the animal fails to attend to it. Following Rescorla's analysis, then, the key test is summation: if a latent inhibitory stimulus is one to which the animal does not attend it should not disrupt the response to an existing CS+, while, if it has genuine response-suppressive powers, it should reduce the magnitude of such a response.

In an experimental examination of this deduction, Reiss and Wagner (1972), therefore, presented one stimulus (stimulus A) 1380 times to rabbits without reinforcement. A second stimulus (B) was presented in the same way for only 12 times. A third stimulus (C) was then used as the CS+ in the usual way to establish a conditioned nictitating membrane response. Finally, the attempt was made to condition the same response to stimuli A and B, respectively. The data of interest in this part of their report consist of the difference between stimulus A (the putative latent inhibitor) and stimulus B (the control) in ease of conditioning. As in the case of previous experiment using this design, their results (Fig. 3.12) showed the latent inhibition phenomenon: that is to say, conditioning was significantly slower to stimulus A than to stimulus B. In a second experiment, exactly the same procedure was followed up to the conditioning of the CR to stimulus C as the CS+. At this point, instead of a

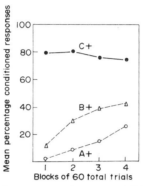

FIG. 3.12. Results of Retardation Test of Latent Inhibition Conducted by Reiss and Wagner (1972). Mean percentage conditioned eyelid responses displayed by rabbits to already conditioned CS(C) and to two stimuli previously presented for 1380 (A) or 12 (B) times without reinforcement before any conditioning had begun. All three stimuli were reinforced during the period in which the data illustrated were obtained. (From Reiss and Wagner, 1972.)

retardation test as in the first experiment, a summation test was carried out. That is to say, stimulus C was presented either alone, as before, or in conjunction with stimuli A and B. This test was carried out under two conditions: with continued reinforcement for all three stimuli (C alone, and the AC and BC compounds), or with reinforcement for C alone and no reinforcement for either the AC or the BC compounds. Now, if the repeated initial presentation of stimulus A had reduced attention to it, one would expect that responding to the AC compound would not be very different from responding to C alone, whereas, if stimulus A possessed true response-suppressive properties, the AC compound would be expected to elicit a much lower response than that elicited by C on its own. The compound BC acted as the control for the effects of combining any stimulus with C. The results clearly supported the diminished attention hypothesis: both when the two compounds were reinforced and when they were not, the AC compound produced a *greater* response than did the BC compound (see Fig. 3.13). The different between the two compounds probably reflects the greater *external* inhibitory effect of stimulus B (previously presented to the animal only 12 times) as compared to stimulus A.

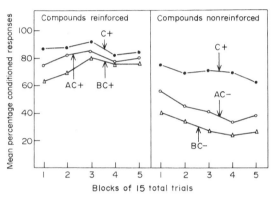

FIG. 3.13. Results of Summation Test of Latent Inhibition Conducted by Reiss and Wagner (1972). The graphs show mean percentage conditioned eyelid responses displayed by rabbits to training CS (C) alone or in compound with stimuli A or B. Stimulus A had previously been presented 1380 times without reinforcement before any conditioning had begun; stimulus B had been presented in the same way only 12 times. Left-hand panel: results when compounds were reinforced. Right-hand panel: results when compounds were not reinforced. (From Reiss and Wagner, 1972.)

This experiment, then, discounts the possibility that habituation of the OR produces a stimulus with exactly the same kind of properties as belong to an internal inhibitor. Note, however, that it does *not* show that habituation of the OR does not involve *any* inhibitory process, a conclusion which would be the opposite of the one we reached in Chapter 1. The term "inhibition" must always be understood as inhibition of something specific. In the case of a habituated stimulus, it is the OR which is inhibited (if we accept the evidence and arguments adduced in favour of this conclusion in Chapter 1); in internal inhibition it is some specific kind of CR which is inhibited. The Reiss and Wagner (1972) experiment succeeds in showing that a habituated stimulus does not inhibit the specific CR which they investigated. But then indeed, why should it? At the time that the rabbit was presented with stimulus A over and over again without further consequence, it had not yet been exposed to any kind of conditioning in the experimental situation. It could not tell what was round the corner—conditioning with food as the UCS, with shock, with water or cold, or indeed conditioning of any kind at all. So that, if the habituated stimulus *had* turned out to have inhibitory properties in Reiss and Wagner's summation test, it would have been necessary to suppose that habituation allows the habituated stimulus to inhibit *any* CR which is subsequently acquired by the experimental animal. While such an outcome is not beyond the bounds of imagination, it has a low *a priori* probability, and it is difficult to see what function such a process could serve.

The point is driven home by a consideration of the experiment by Mackintosh (1973) which was described in some detail in Chapter 2 (see Figs 2.11 and 2.12). In this experiment, it will be recalled, rats first exposed to random presentations of tone and shock subsequently showed impaired acquisition of conditioned suppression with tone → shock pairings, but normal acquisition of a conditioned licking response with water as UCS and the tone as CS; while, conversely, rats first exposed to random presentations of tone and water subsequently showed impaired acquisition of the conditioned licking response to the tone, but normal acquisition of conditioned suppression to it. Thus the Mackintosh experiment shows that, under the right conditions, an animal can learn specifically that S1 and S2 are uncorrelated, as distinct either from learning that S1 is in general not worth his attention or from developing a tendency to inhibit all and any CRs in its presence.

Note, however, that Mackintosh's result does not on its own give us license to speak of "inhibition". Indeed, in the light of Rescorla's experiments with the "truly random" control procedure (which is, of course, what Mackintosh's rats were exposed to in the first phase of his experiment), it is likely that the tone would not have been found to possess inhibitory properties by a summation test. It seems, then, that there are still other possibilities than those of internal inhibition and diminished-attention-in-general considered by Rescorla. As illustrated by Mackintosh's experiment, specific learning of a zero correlation between two stimuli appears to be one of them.

Returning to the question whether habituation of the OR and internal inhibition involve the same processes, the Reiss and Wagner

(1972) experiment leaves open the possibility that, although habituation leads to inhibition of the OR and internal inhibition to inhibition of a specific CR, the inhibitory mechanism is the same in the two cases. However, as we have already seen, there is little reason to suppose at present that the same inhibitory mechanism *is* involved. Thus the safest conclusion, for the moment, is that habituation of the OR and internal inhibition of CRs involve two separate response-suppressive mechanisms. The difference in the conditions which give rise to habituation of the OR, on the one hand, or internal inhibition of a CR, on the other, appears to reside in this: simple habituation takes place when a stimulus is followed by nothing; internal inhibition is set up, in contrast, when the stimulus is followed by the non-occurrence of a particular second stimulus (the UCS) which might reasonably be expected to occur in the experimental situation.

This discussion of the differences between habituation and internal inhibition, then, brings out rather clearly certain features of the latter process which have been implicit throughout our treatment of it. Internal inhibition appears to arise when: (a) there is some reasonable expectation that a particular UCS will occur, this expectation deriving from stimuli to which the organism is currently exposed; (b) this expectation is not fulfilled; and (c) the non-fulfilment of the expectation can be associated with some specific stimulus in the animal's environment (a stimulus which, as in the case of inhibition of delay, may be temporal). Furthermore, as shown most clearly in the experiments on the reaction of the reverse sign, the effect of internal inhibition is to restrain the particular response tendency which is elicited by the CS+ for the omitted UCS. These conclusions are in essential agreement with the arguments we have advanced concerning expectations in Chapter 1 and 2 (see especially the discussion in Chapter 2 of Kremer's experiment on the role of contingencies in the S → S relationship of classical conditioning). They also agree with the fundamental postulates of the elegant mathematical theory of classical conditioning advanced by Wagner and Rescorla (1972; and Rescorla and Wagner, 1972) which we looked at briefly in the previous chapter.

4. Drive and Reinforcement

It is often difficult to tell, in the disputes of learning theorists, where the boundary lies between purely conceptual and terminological issues and issues which can be settled by appeal to experiment. Nowhere is this more true than in the tangled knot which binds together the concepts of "drive" and "reinforcement". Before we can even begin on the task of seeing how these two concepts fit together, and the empirical issues raised by this fit, we must first see exactly what has been meant by each concept taken on its own. This task is especially difficult, since each term has been used with more than one meaning. As we shall see, which issues turn out to be purely logical and which empirical depends critically on (1) which pairs of meanings one chooses to consider together, and (2) the kind of experiment in respect of which one so considers them.

Meanings of "Drive": Drive$_{TV}$

Let us start by considering the uses to which the term "drive" has been put.

It is clear that "drive" is a theoretical term: it refers to some unobservable state or other in the CNS. The need for such a theory-word arises in the first instance, quite simply, because behaviour in a perfectly constant environment is not constant: therefore something must be changing within the experimental subject. Suppose we are observing a rat in an environment which has a constant supply of food, water, nesting material, other rats of the opposite sex, and so on, and that we simply record the animal's behaviour over time. We see that at some times the animal is particularly busy eating, at other times drinking, at other times copulating, at still other times nest-building, and so on. If (*per impossible*) our graph of behaviour over time were to show complete covariation between the curves describing these various classes of behaviour, the probabilities of all of them rising and falling simultaneously, one might wish to postulate one global "drive" state which varies in strength in an appropriate manner over time. This, of course, is not what we observe (though the notion of "general drive" has been introduced into learning theory on other grounds). Instead we see that the curves for each of these separate classes of behaviour follow rather separate courses (Fig. 4.1). Thus we are led to postulate

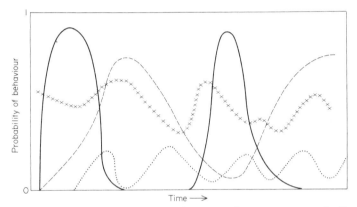

FIG. 4.1. The Temporal Variation Concept of Drive. Each curve represents the fluctuation over time in the probability of observation of behaviour patterns of a separable class of behaviour. See text for further explanation.

one separate "specific" drive for each class of behaviour we are able to distinguish: a "hunger" drive, "thirst" drive, "sex" drive, and so on. Let us call this sense of "drive" the "temporal variation" sense, or "drive$_{T\ V}$" for short.

So far I have been deliberately vague in my use of the phrase "class of behaviour", implying that it is intuitively obvious how we ought to split up an animal's overall behaviour into separate classes, such as eating, drinking, and so on. However, it is very dangerous to take anything in the theory of learning as being intuitively obvious: Martians might well make a much better job of studying behaviour on our planet than we do—they would start off with fewer intuitively obvious misconceptions. Consider, for instance, the fact that "sleeping" is almost never treated as a specific drive. Yet this form of behaviour (still speaking vaguely) is no less regular in its variation over time than is, say, eating behaviour, and by the same token it deserves its own "sleep drive". The reason why sleep nonetheless fails to figure in the list of specific drives usually found in the textbooks is probably that this list has been infiltrated by another sense of drive, the notion that drive is an "energizer" of behaviour; and, of course, sleep is a noticeably unenergetic activity. This is an example of the way in which learning theorists have been tempted by their intuitions about the *nature* of drives away from the task of systematically splitting behaviour up into rationally based classes of activity, each explicitly chosen on the same criteria.

How, then, should we go about this task? There are two natural places to start: we could have regard to the nature of the motor patterns which the animal displays, or we could have regard to the stimuli in the environment to which these patterns are related. In view of what was said in Chapter 1 about the necessary inter-dependence between the definitions of stimulus and response, it will come as no surprise that the only useful way to carry out our classification is in fact to employ *both* the nature of the animal's motor activity *and* the stimuli to which this motor activity is related.

Our first move would be to record in some detail the animal's motor patterns, making a much more fine-grained analysis of the total observed behaviour than is implied by the kind of division I have been making so far, into eating, drinking and so on. We would record, for example, such easily recognizable and virtually invariant units of behaviour as "gnawing", "licking", "scratching the head", "intromission", "lying down curled up", etc. In principle, units such as this can be defined, without reference to particular environmental stimuli, sufficiently objectively for good inter-observer agreement to be obtained and for accurate recording to be carried out. In contrast, terms such as "eating", "drinking", etc, contain necessary reference to classes of *stimuli* and also (which is the dangerous element) hidden implications as to the *goal-directed* nature of the class of behaviour distinguished; and, as we shall see, the notion of goal-direction is contained in yet another sense of drive, so that the chances of intuitive misconception are further increased.

Having distinguished in this way the elements of the animal's motor behaviour, the next task is to consider the transitional probabilities between each of them: that is to say, if element A has just occurred, what is the probability that the next element will be B, C, D, ... X? If this is done, it will be discovered that such transitional probabilities are not randomly distributed: that is to say, the probabilities of some elements will be high and of others low after the occurrence of element A, and after the occurrence of element B a different set of elements will have, respectively, high and low probabilities. Then, by drawing a boundary at some moderately high probability value, one could objectively class together a set of elements linked together by high transitional probabilities (e.g. "picking object up in teeth", "chewing", "swallowing") and distinguish it from other sets of elements also linked to one other, but not so closely linked to elements of the first set. In this way, we might obtain a first approximation to, say, a definition of eating behaviour*.

However, the results of this first move would be *only* an approximation. In order to turn it into something more, we have to take into account the relationship of these sets of motor elements to *classes of stimuli*. Remember that, so far, our analysis has been carried out in an unchanging environment: we have simply been sitting, say, behind a one-way vision screen watching a rat get on the with the business of living. We now make our first intervention into this environment: we take away the solid pellets of food which have been there so far, substitute a bowl of wet mash, and go back behind our one-way vision screen to start observing again. If we have been truly objective and have stuck to recording motor units of behaviour, we shall see that the animal's behaviour has changed: at points in time when the probability of "picking up object in teeth" and "chewing" should be high, from extrapolating the previously recorded graph, we now see instead "lowering snout" and "lapping". Of course, if we had been recording what is generally regarded as "eating", we would see no difference in the graph; but we would have departed from the objectivity guaranteed by recording only motor units of behaviour.

This example makes it clear that transitional probabilities between motor units of behaviour are not enough. It is necessary to broaden our approach and seek for *temporal covariation between sets of motor units and classes of stimuli related to these sets*. If we change the nature of the stimuli in the animal's environment, we may change the pattern of motor behaviour in which it engages; but this change

---

* The problems encountered in practice by this kind of approach (and they are formidable) are well illustrated by Blurton–Jones' (1968) monograph on the "threat displays of the Great Tit".

will take the form that some new motor unit (or set of such units) will take over the transitional probabilities previously possessed by a different motor unit, and substitution of the new motor unit for the old one will leave the graph of behaviour against time essentially unchanged.

This complication in our task of splitting behaviour up into classes means that we now have two further tasks: we must establish the limits within which we may vary (1) the environmental stimuli and (2) the observed motor units of behaviour without altering our graph of temporal variation. For example, if we were Martians rather than Earthmen, it would not be intuitively obvious that, among the materials which animals ingest, the one with the chemical formula H_2O is somehow special. We would discover this by observing that, if we substituted water for wet mash in a continuation of the experiment we started above, the resulting lapping behaviour would *not* be an extrapolation of the previously observed graph of the time-course of ingestion of solid pellets or wet mash: in this case the Earthman's intuition that drinking is separate from eating would turn out to be correct.

In case this example should appear to be excessively trivial, it might be as well to describe an experiment by Miller (1961) which made use of precisely this form of argument to establish a very important point about the nature of the behaviour elicited by electrical stimulation of the lateral hypothalamus, a part of the brain which is concerned with the control of eating and drinking behaviour. Miller had observed, as have many others, that stimulation of this kind is capable of causing a food-satiated animal to eat. The question then arises whether this is *merely* a particular motor unit of behaviour (e.g. "chewing") which is being elicited, or whether the electrodes are activating a "hunger drive". The full answer to this question can only come when we have considered other senses of "drive". For the moment, however, we should note one of the tests to which Miller subjected his animals to show that it was indeed a hunger drive which was being elicited. Miller offered his rats solid food pellets, milk and water on different occasions when stimulating them. He observed that they chewed the pellets, and that they lapped the milk but not the water. Thus, the electrodes were not stimulating a motor unit: they were activating one of a set of possible motor units depending on the nature of the stimuli in the animal's environment. Clearly, the particular relationships between motor units and environmental stimuli observed justify the conclusion that it was hunger, and not thirst, which was being elicited.

So far, our interventions in the animal's environment have been minimal, confined to an alteration of the stimuli available in a particular location so as to define the limits of the class of stimuli which are appropriate for a particular specific drive, in the sense in which we have so far used the term "drive". As a result, we are in a position to define a *specific drive* in this sense as follows. Drive X consists of a hypothetical internal state of the organism unifying and underlying that set of motor units of behaviour, R_x, with high transitional probabilities connecting the members of the set, which show in an unchanging environment a particular course of temporal variation, and which are related to a particular class of stimuli, S_x. The corresponding class of stimuli, S_x, can be defined as that class, the substitution of members of which one for the other leaves unchanged the course of temporal variation of drive X, although not necessarily the members of the set of motor units of behaviour R_x. These definitions are inter-dependent, in the way that we encountered when discussing the definition of stimulus and response in Chapter 1, but they are not circular.

If we now increase our degree of intervention in the experimental situation, we come to new senses of "drive". We may make such interventions in one of two ways: we can interfere with the temporal structure of the animal's environment, leaving unchanged the disposition of stimuli in space; or we can interfere with the spatial lay-out of the environment, and in particular alter the animal's means of access to the classes of stimuli which are appropriate to each of the specific drives. Corresponding to the first of these interventions, we come across the notion of drive as involving a *deprivation function*; and, corresponding to the second of these interventions, we come across the notion of drive as involving *goal-direction*.

Meanings of "Drive": Drive$_{DEP}$

In a typical experiment of the first sort, we would consult a graph of the kind shown in Fig. 4.1 and from this we would extrapolate forward in time to the next moment when the probability of, say, eating or copulation is likely to be high. We would then remove from the animal's environment the stimuli which relate to these two specific drives (food and a sexually receptive member of the opposite sex, respectively) at the time of high probability of the corresponding behaviour. Next, we re-introduce these stimuli at some later time, say a time when, had the next bout of eating or copulation been allowed to take place normally, the probability of eating or copulation would have been extremely low. What would be our expectation for the outcome of such an experiment?

Clearly, in order to answer such a question, we need more than the notion that, corresponding to each of the specific drives we have been able to isolate, there is some internal state or other: we need to have some idea of the properties of this state. The idea which has lain behind experiments on deprivation, whether in the work of learning theorists such as Hull (1952) or in the work of ethologists such as Lorenz (1950), has been that, corresponding to the build-up of the probability that behaviour appropriate to specific drive X will occur, there is a build-up in the CNS of a kind of "motivational energy" (this is the notion of drive as an "energizer" to which I have referred earlier). If this energy is not allowed an outlet, owing to the experimental deprivation of the appropriate class of stimuli, S_x, it will not only continue in being until it is allowed an outlet, but will actually increase in magnitude with the further passage of time. Thus, when the appropriate class of stimuli is returned to the experimental space, the expectation would be that behaviour appropriate to specific drive X will occur with even greater probability and even greater vigour than at the time when, had there been no experimental intervention at all, maximum probability would have been attained on the graph of temporal variation.

There are two things to notice about this idea. The first is that the facts of temporal variation which have led to the formulation of drive$_{T V}$ in no way require this new notion of drive. The second is that there is no guarantee that all specific drives are going to be organized in the same way: had this second point been realized earlier, much sterile controversy would have been avoided.

In fact, it turns out, for example, that, if we do this experiment with female rats, we obtain quite different results for eating behaviour and sexual behaviour. Both eating and sexual behaviour, of course, give perfectly stable graphs of temporal variation; indeed, the estrous cycle in the female rat, which is sexually receptive for one day in every four or five, is one of the best examples of temporal variation available. Now, if we deprive the animal of food and then present food some hours later, we obtain exactly the results predicted by the "deprivation" notion of drive: the animal eats with a high degree of probability and ingests more food than it would have done had it not been deprived at all. But if we deprive the female rat of a male with which to copulate at the point of maximum receptivity in the estrous cycle, and then offer her a male two days later, when the uninterrupted cycle would be at a low point of probability of sexual behaviour, that low point is quite unaffected. Furthermore, if we wait till the next point of maximum receptivity, we observe exactly the same degree of sexual behaviour as would have been observed in any case. The sexual behaviour of the female rat, in other words, while showing perfectly stable temporal variation, is completely insensitive to deprivation of the stimuli to which the behaviour relates.

The difference between the results obtained for eating and sexual behaviour in the female rat, then, makes it clear that, empirically as well as logically, it is an open question whether drive in the sense of responding to deprivation with increased behavioural vigour—let us call this "$drive_{DEP}$" for short—and $drive_{TV}$ go together: they may or they may not, depending on the behaviour investigated.

The sexual behaviour of the female rat is an example of $drive_{TV}$ without $drive_{DEP}$. What about the reverse case: can one find an example of $drive_{DEP}$ without $drive_{TV}$? That is to say, are there forms of behaviour which do not show any regular variation over time in an unchanging environment, but which show a great increase in vigour if deprivation of the appropriate stimulus is imposed? One rather obvious example is breathing: this certainly shows a strong response to deprivation (shown in the ensuing hyperventilation), but no temporal variation (except in the trivial sense of the inspiration/ expiration cycle). Thus the split between $drive_{TV}$ and $drive_{DEP}$ can operate in both directions.

Meanings of "Drive": $Drive_{GD}$

Having interfered with the temporal structure of the animal's environment in the deprivation experiment, we can now carry out the second kind of intervention, which is to vary the spatial lay-out of the environment. The simplest version of such an experiment would be simply to alter the spatial locations of the various stimuli contained in the environment: we might, for example, take the water which had hitherto been in the north-west corner of the experimental space and interchange it with the food which had been in the south-east corner. We could then return behind our one-way vision screen and carry on observing. A more complex intervention would be, say, to interpose a lever or a wheel between the animal and its food and require that a press of the lever or a turn of the wheel be executed for a pellet of food to be delivered into the food-receptacle. If we do this, we shall see that the animal varies its behaviour from that obtaining before the experimental change was introduced in such a way that it continues to achieve access to food or water with the same course of temporal variation as before. This kind of behaviour, which compensates for disturbances in the environment so that the same end-point is always reached (in this case, approximation in space to members of the class of stimuli, "food"), is known as "goal-directed". (Goal-direction has sometimes been seen by philosophers—e.g. Taylor, 1964—as mysterious and requiring the attribution of "intentions" to the organism displaying goal-direction. If this is so, guided missiles, among many other automatic devices, have intentions, because they undoubtedly display goal-directed behaviour.) In the language of drive, the temptation is to say that the animal has a "drive for food". The question then is: is this goal-direction sense of drive—"$drive_{GD}$"—necessarily linked to the first two senses of drive we have distinguished?

Logically, there would seem to be no reason why either temporal variation or reactivity to deprivation should entail goal-direction. Empirically, there is also reason to doubt that $drive_{GD}$ necessarily goes with $drive_{TV}$ or $drive_{DEP}$.

With regard to the link between $drive_{GD}$ and $drive_{TV}$, the behaviour of the estrous female again serves as a probable counter-example. Bolles et al. (1968) recorded running speeds of female rats in a straight alley. In one condition the goalbox contained a male rat able and eager to copulate; in a second condition it contained a castrated male rat with no interest in this activity. The females were run in the alley under these two conditions both during estrus and when sexually unreceptive. They ran faster during estrus under both conditions, but neither during estrus nor when sexually unreceptive did their running speeds differ according to the potency of the male they ran towards. Thus there was evidence of some kind of generally energizing effect of estrus on running speeds, but none that the estrous female regards a copulating rat as a more desirable goal than a non-copulating one.

As pointed out by Drewett (1972), however, this experiment is not entirely convincing. Only eight trials were run for each rat, and all groups were running rapidly by the last trial, whether to a potent or an impotent male; thus the lack of a difference in running speeds to the two kinds of male may simply be due to a ceiling effect. More convincing would be a choice response, in which the female would be required to perform one response to gain access to a potent male and a different one for an impotent male. Drewett (1973) carried out such a study, in a T-maze in which one goalbox contained a potent male and the other an impotent one. He obtained clear-cut evidence that the estrous female rat learns to go to the arm containing the potent male. Furthermore, when the arms containing the potent and impotent males were interchanged, the female's choice behaviour also reversed direction in an appropriate manner (Fig. 4.2).

Drewett's experiment, then, seems to demonstrate that the female rat has a $drive_{G D}$ for a sexually potent, as compared to a castrated, male. But it cannot be the case that this $drive_{G D}$ is the same as the $drive_{T V}$ displayed in the spontaneous estrous cycle. For, when Drewett tested his rats out of estrus, they continued to choose the arm containing the potent male with the same frequency as when in estrus (Fig. 4.2). It is not possible, therefore, that there is only one internal state in the female rat controlling *both* the copulatory behaviour she displays during estrus *and* the goal-directed behaviour which gains her access to a potent male*.

These results leave us, it seems, two options. The first is to declare that the female rat's goal-direction for potent males is not a *sex*

* French *et al.* (1972) have recently reported that female rats, allowed to press one of two bars to secure the release of one of two potent males, exhibited clear preferences for one of the males (pressing the bar more often for him than for his rival) when in estrus, but not during di-estrus. Thus, the state of estrus appears to control choice of mating partner. However, scrutiny of their results reveals that the effect of estrus consisted as often in a *drop* of bar-pressing rate for the *non*-preferred partner as in a *rise* in barpressing rate for the *preferred* partner. Thus this experiment cannot be held to indicate the existence of a $drive_{G D}$ for mating closely correlated with the estrous cycle (which is what we are seeking). It could equally well indicate an aversive effect of mating which is mitigated by some aspect of the preferred sexual partner.

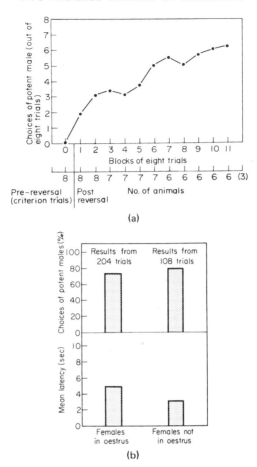

FIG. 4.2. Choice of a Potent or Impotent Male in the Female Rat. (a) The course of learning when the position of the potent and impotent males was reversed after initial learning. The results from any one animal are only included up to the point at which it attained the learning criterion (8 consecutive choices of the potent male). (b) Effects of estrus on choice and running speed. (From Drewett, 1972.)

drive$_{GD}$ at all (since it does not co-vary with actual copulatory behaviour), but some other kind of drive$_{GD}$, as yet unknown. The second is to say that the female rat has both a sex drive$_{TV}$ and a sex drive$_{GD}$, the former reflected in copulatory behaviour and the latter in potent-male-seeking behaviour, but that they are independent of each other. Either way, it is clear that in this case drive$_{GD}$ is as empirically distinct from drive$_{TV}$ as it is distinct logically.

What of the reverse case: are there instances of $drive_{GD}$ without $drive_{TV}$? Breathing is again a useful example. There is no doubt that there is a drive, in the sense of goal-direction, for air or oxygen. Broadhurst (1957) has in fact used access to air after varying periods of deprivation of air as the reward for rats in an underwater swimming task, with very successful results. On the other hand, as already pointed out, there is nothing resembling a $drive_{TV}$ shown in the animal's spontaneous breathing behaviour.

Another possible example is exploratory behaviour. It has been shown in a large number of experiments that rats, monkeys and a number of other animals will perform a response which is followed by access to novel stimuli or to an environment containing novel stimuli. Thus they show goal-directed behaviour for which the goal is "novelty" or "stimulus-change" (Fowler, 1967, 1971). It has not been shown that, corresponding to this $drive_{GD}$, there is a $drive_{TV}$, i.e. that behaviour directed towards novelty varies in probability in a systematic manner over time. This may merely reflect the technical difficulty of showing a $drive_{TV}$ for *novelty* in an *unchanging* environment (which is the necessary experimental condition in which a drive in this sense has to be demonstrated). Presumably, for the purpose of demonstrating such a $drive_{TV}$, one would need to construct an environment with a constant availability of novel stimulation in one part of it, corresponding to the constant availability of food, water, etc. in other parts. While not impossible, this difficult feat has not been attempted, let alone achieved. It may be of some significance, however, that, in the hundreds of experiments which have been performed in this area (Berlyne, 1960; Fowler, 1967, 1971), there appears to be no suggestion that novelty-directed behaviour is easier to observe at some times rather than others; and my own intuitions lead me to doubt that such a $drive_{TV}$ exists. Thus, taken together with the breathing example, the experiments on behaviour for novelty give rise to the conclusion that, not only can one find $drive_{TV}$ without $drive_{GD}$ (as in the female rat's sexual behaviour), but also $drive_{GD}$ without $drive_{TV}$.

With regard to the connection between $drive_{GD}$ and $drive_{DEP}$, the most relevant data again appear to be those from studies of responding for novelty. Two responses which have been widely used in such studies are barpressing to turn lights or sounds on or off and running down an alley in which the startbox and the runway are one brightness and the goalbox a different one (Fowler, 1967). The question which concerns us is whether the animal's behaviour in such experiments depends on prior deprivation of the stimulus which is contingent on barpressing or alley-running. There are certainly some reports of such a dependence. For example, Butler (1957) and Fox (1962) have shown that the rates at which monkeys respond for the opportunity to look through a window or for light-onset are an increasing function of the number of hours they have previously been deprived of such visual incentives. In other experiments, however, and particularly with rats, responding of this nature has been barely affected, if at all, by similar deprivation. And, for our purposes, it will be sufficient if there are some well-established instances of responding for stimulus change independently of prior deprivation of the stimulus concerned; it is not necessary that all such responding be independent of deprivation.

There are, in fact, a number of apparently reliable reports of novelty-seeking behaviour which is independent of prior stimulus deprivation (e.g. Charlesworth and Thompson, 1957; Montgomery and Zimbardo, 1957; Ehrlich, 1959; Premack and Collier, 1962; Haude and Ray, 1967). Since, however, it is difficult to base a case purely on negative findings, it is more instructive to consider in detail an experiment in which, it is claimed, a positive effect of deprivation was found. Such an experiment has been reported by Fowler (1967).

Fowler's basic situation consisted of an alley with a black (or white) startbox and runway and a white, grey or black goalbox. Rats in this apparatus showed stable acquisition and performance of a running response which was faster, the greater the degree of stimulus change (e.g. black to white vs black to grey) encountered in the goalbox. Now, Fowler argues, deprivation of the stimulus to which the running response is directed can be regarded with respect to this experimental situation in two ways. On the one hand, one can consider the length of time for which the animal is exposed to the startbox conditions before it is allowed to commence the running response which will take it to the goalbox. Alternatively, one can consider the stimulus conditions to which the animal is exposed in its home cage, between experimental sessions: these could be the same as or different from the stimuli found in the startbox and goalbox. Let us call the first kind of deprivation "immediate" and second "maintenance".

With regard to immediate deprivation (of, e.g. white) Fowler's results (Fig. 4.3) show consistently that the rat's running speed is greater, the longer it is confined in the startbox (over the range 1–7 min). The problem, however, is whether startbox confinement time can truly be regarded as a deprivation operation, corresponding, say, to hours of deprivation of food. Consider that the effective goal for the running response in this experiment appears to be stimulus change: how is it possible to define stimulus change independently of the length of time for which the subject is exposed to the stimulus from which the change is being made? The amount of food placed in

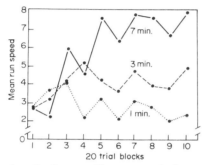

FIG. 4.3. Effects of Startbox Confinement Time on Speed of Running to Stimulus Change. Each curve is for a group of rats detained in the startbox for the period indicated. (From Fowler, 1967.)

the goalbox can be specified without reference to the number of hours since the animal was last fed, and conversely: but the degree to which white is a change from black is not equally independent of the time for which the animal is exposed to black. To take an example, suppose an animal was kept in a white environment, which then changed to black for 0.1 sec before reverting to white: could the change back to white reasonably be described as a "stimulus change"?

A better way of looking at Fowler's results is in the context of a suggestion made by Premack (1965). Premack proposes that goal-directed behaviour depends on the degree to which the subject's access to the goal is restricted in the actual experimental situation, as distinct from the period before it is placed in the experimental situation. This distinction obviously corresponds closely to the one in Fowler's experiments between "immediate" and "maintenance" deprivation. We shall examine Premack's analysis of restricted access to the goal more fully in Chapter 6, and we shall return to Fowler's experiments at that time. To anticipate, however, we might predict that, if startbox confinement time were affecting running speeds by altering the degree to which the animal's access to the goal was restricted in the actual experimental situation, it would do so only in interaction with the time the animal was allowed to remain in contact with the goal; whereas, if startbox confinement time were truly analogous to a deprivation operation, it would determine running speeds directly and independently. Fowler's results, obtained in an experiment in which he jointly varied startbox and goalbox confinement time, clearly support the former view (Fig. 4.4):

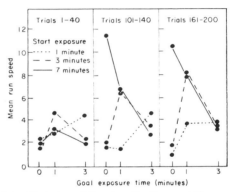

FIG. 4.4. Effects of Joint Variation of Startbox Confinement Time and Goalbox Exposure Time on Speed of Running to Stimulus Change. Mean run speeds at various stages of training for groups detained in startbox for 1, 3 or 7 min as a function of goalbox exposure time. (From Fowler, 1967.)

running speed was determined by a complex interaction between the durations of exposure to these two parts of the apparatus. Certainly they do not suggest any simple effect of startbox confinement time which might be analogous to the effects of food or water-deprivation, as Fowler claims.

Turning to the effects of "maintenance deprivation" in Fowler's experiments, the results of the relevant experiment are displayed in Fig. 4.5. In this experiment, rats were maintained from the age of 30 days to 80 days in a specially painted cage which was either black, white, grey, or "composite" (one wall of each of these colours, the fourth wall being a hardware cloth front). On the 81st day of life (when training in the runway began) half the rats in the black and white cages had their colours reversed, the remainder continuing as before. All the rats were then trained to run from a black-startbox and runway into a white goalbox (half of each group) or from a white startbox and runway into a black goalbox (the other half of each group). There was one trial per day for trials 1–10, two per day for trials 11–20, and three per day thereafter. As shown in Fig. 4.5, all groups learned quite well to run into the goalbox for the resulting stimulus change. The effect of maintenance conditions during the training period is shown by the fact that two groups which had the same colour in their home cage as in the startbox (and therefore the opposite home-cage colour to that in the goalbox), i.e. those labelled "S" and "DS" in Fig. 4.5, ran significantly faster by the end of the training than the two groups which had the opposite colour in their

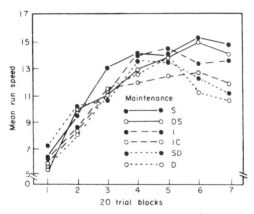

FIG. 4.5. Effects of "Maintenance Deprivation" on Speed of Running to Stimulus Change. For explanation see text. (From Fowler, 1967.)

home cage to that in the startbox (and therefore the same home-cage colour as that in the goalbox), i.e. those labelled "D" and "SD". The groups with a grey composite home cage (the curves labelled "I" and "IC", respectively) achieved intermediate speeds by the end of training.

These results are said by Fowler to show that responding for stimulus change, like responding for food, is greater, the more the animal has been deprived of the stimulus for which it is responding. But there are several features of his results which make one reluctant to accept this interpretation. Consider the rats in group D. These had lived for fifty days before the experiment began in an environment of one colour and continued to live there between their one or two daily trials in the runway. They were placed on each trial for a mere three minutes in a startbox of a different colour and, at the end of this time, they could return to a box of the same colour as that in which they normally lived. On what grounds, one wonders, is it the *goalbox* which offers these animals "stimulus change" at all: should it not rather be the startbox? Why do they bother to run at all to get back into the colour in which they spend all their time anyway? Yet, not only did they run, for one hundred trials (i.e. until the fifth trial block: Fig. 4.5), they ran as fast as the rats in group S—for which the one minute in the goalbox was the *only* time they were exposed to the goalbox colour. Only after this do the curves for the two groups diverge, and even then this is apparently not because of a greater effect of "deprivation" in the S group (whose curve continues to rise much as before and then flattens out), but because of an actual *drop* in running speed on the part of the D group. If this is "deprivation" at work, it works very differently from food deprivation, and with very small effects.

All in all, then, it seems that responding for stimulus change is goal-directed, but pretty independent of the degree to which the subject has been exposed outside the experimental situation to the stimulus for which it is responding: that is, it is a case of $drive_{G\ D}$ without $drive_{D\ E\ P}$.

What about the reverse possibility: are there cases of $drive_{D\ E\ P}$ which are not also cases of $drive_{G\ D}$? If there are, I cannot think of them, and it does not seem easy to construct such a case. Although the notion of responding to deprivation with increased behavioural vigour and that of goal-direction are logically distinct, it is difficult to imagine the former without the latter. On evolutionary grounds, as well, one might suppose that any function sufficiently important to evolve a special reactivity to deprivation would also evolve goal-direction. But, of course, arguments of this kind are of only limited validity. At an empirical level, one might derive some support for the notion that $drive_{D\ E\ P}$ necessarily also involves $drive_{G\ D}$ from the fact that the sexual behaviour of the female rat, which is a classic case of $drive_{T\ V}$, is *neither* a $drive_{D\ E\ P}$ *nor* (probably) a $drive_{G\ D}$.

Of the six pairs of senses which can be combined from $drive_{T\ V}$, $drive_{D\ E\ P}$ and $drive_{G\ D}$, then, there appear to be both logical and empirical arguments for holding that each can be split from the other

TABLE 4.1.   Empirical separations between three senses of drive

		Present		
		Drive$_{TV}$	Drive$_{DEP}$	Drive$_{GD}$
	Drive$_{TV}$	–	Breathing	Breathing; Response for stimulus-change
Absent	Drive$_{DEP}$	Female sexual behaviour (rat)	–	Response for stimulus-change
	Drive$_{GD}$	Female sexual behaviour (rat)	?	–

in every case but one: it is possible that drive$_{DEP}$ never in fact occurs (though logically it could occur) without the behaviour in question also showing goal-direction. The arguments which have brought us to this point are summarized in Table 4.1.

Meanings of "Reinforcement"

After this long consideration of drive taken on its own, it is time to look at the connections between the various senses of drive and the concept of reinforcement. However, this concept too comes in at least three varieties: positive or appetitive instrumental reinforcement (S^{R+}); negative or aversive instrumental reinforcement (S^{S-}); and reinforcement in classical conditioning (UCS). Since the problems raised by classical conditioning are somewhat different from those posed by instrumental reinforcers, we shall leave the relations between drive and the effects of a UCS until the end of the chapter, considering instumental reinforcement first.

We have already come across the operational definition of an instrumental reinforcer in Chapter 2. If presentation of a stimulus following a response ($R \rightarrow S$) has the consequence that the probability of future emission of that response is altered, then the S is an S^R or reinforcing stimulus. If the change in probability takes the form of an increase, the stimulus is an S^{R+} or positive ("appetitive") reinforcer, and the operation carried out is one of reward. If it takes the form of a decrease, the stimulus is an S^{R-} or negative ("aversive") reinforcer, this operation (presentation of an S^{R-}) being termed "punishment". As we shall see in later chapters, it also turns out to be the case that responses followed by the termination or omission of an S^{R+} go down in probability (the appropriate operations being termed "time-out" and "extinction", respectively), and that responses followed by the termination or omission of an S^{R-} go up in probability, this pair of operations being "escape" and "active avoidance", respectively.

Historically an S^{R-} was originally defined by Skinner (1938) in terms of the avoidance operation. However, there do not appear to be any recorded cases in which an S^{R}_- defined in this way is not also effective in a punishment operation. Furthermore, if such a case were to be discovered, it is not certain that we would continue to regard the stimulus involved as a negative reinforcer*. Consider the parallel case of an S^{R+}. This is initially defined in terms of the reward operation; but I know of no case (in an intact animal†) in which the probability of a response has gone up when an S^{R+} is made contingent upon it without falling again when extinction is in force. Furthermore, if such a case turned up, it is unlikely that we would consider that we had a normal S^{R+} on our hands. More likely, we would conclude that we had failed to isolate the truly effective S^{R+} maintaining the behaviour. In any event, until new facts arise which force us to do otherwise, it is probably safe to employ the terms S^{R+} and S^{R-} without differentiating between the establishment of the propriety of their use by, on the one hand, the operation of presentation (reward and punishment) and, on the other, the operations of termination (time-out and escape) or omission (extinction and active avoidance). In the same vein, one can argue that, for the time being at any rate, there is no need to distinguish between the establishment of positive and negative reinforcers by the operation of termination and by that of omission. Again, I know of no facts which would force such a distinction of terminology upon us.

* See Chapter 6 for a further discussion of this point.

† Huston and Borbely (1973) have reported apparent instrumental learning for positive reinforcement, which then failed to extinguish upon removal of the S^{R+}, in rats surgically deprived of the neocortex, hippocampus and part of the corpus striatum. The S^{R+} was electrical stimulation of the hypothalamus and the response, movement of the head or tail. Even though extinction had no effect on the maintenance of these responses, it was possible to alter the direction of an already acquired response by making the S^{R+} contingent upon the reverse response (e.g. movement of the tail down rather than up). Thus the bidirectional conditioning test for instrumental learning (Chapter 2) was passed. Whether or not this result should cause us to recast our definition of an S^{R+} for the *intact* animal is a moot point.

This classification of positive and negative reinforcers, and of the operations by which they are each capable of being established, is set out in Table 4.2.

There is another distinction which should be made with regard to reinforcement, besides those listed in Table 4.2. We have defined a reinforcer as a stimulus which, if presented following a response,

TABLE 4.2. Instrumental reinforcing procedures with unconditioned reinforcing events

OUTCOME

PROCEDURE	$p(R)\uparrow$	$p(R)\downarrow$
Presentation	Rew (approach)	Pun (passive avoidance)
Termination	Pun! (escape)	Rew! (time-out)
Omission	Pun (active avoidance)	Rew (extinction)

S^{R+}

S^{R-}

The abbreviations and symbols are as defined by the intersection of row (procedure) and column (outcome). $p(R)\uparrow$: outcome is an increase in the probability of the response on which the reinforcing event is made contingent. $p(R)\downarrow$: outcome is a decrease in the probability of this response. Crosshatching indicates those procedures-plus-outcomes which define a stimulus as an S^{R+} or an S^{R-}, respectively. Bracketed phrases refer to typical learning situations in which the various reinforcing procedures are employed. Rew: reward; Pun: Punishment; !: termination; —: omission.

"has the consequence that the probability of future emission of that response is altered". Now there is a good deal of ambiguity in the words "future emission". How far in the future must the alteration in response probability be for the stimulus which produced it to qualify as an S^R? Depending on the answer we give to this question, we may emphasize two rather different aspects of the notion of reinforcement which are often confused. I shall call these the "performance" and the "learning" aspects of reinforcement.

The aspect most strongly suggested by the definition of reinforcement just given is probably the learning one. A positive reinforcer, according to this view, is a stimulus which, if presented following a *new* response, causes the animal to emit that response with greater probability *on some future occasion* when it is once more placed in the same set of environmental circumstances (both external and internal); and a negative reinforcer, similarly, is one which, if terminated or omitted following a new response, has the same consequence. Furthermore, on the later occasion, when the newly acquired response is emitted again, it is not necessary that the S^R be actually part of the animal's environment at the time of emission. There is no need, in other words, for the response to be directed towards or away from a physically present S^R. It is this "learning" sense which has been to the fore in most of the controversies about the nature of reinforcement.

However, many of the actual experiments which are concerned with reinforcement focus on something rather different: namely the degree to which a stimulus can arouse behaviour directed *immediately towards (or away from) itself*.

Consider, for example, an experiment in which a rat is able, by licking at a tube, to obtain a drop of water or sucrose. It is not obvious that one should regard the act of licking at a tube for liquid "reinforcement" as a newly learnt response. Even if one does so regard it the first time it occurs, it would be strange to treat the animal as learning a new response every time the experimenter varies the quantity of the quality of the liquid with which a lick is "reinforced", as he might in an investigation of the relative "reinforcing effects" of different sucrose solutions. Experiments on electrical self-stimulation of the brain (see below) illustrate the same point. It is typical in such experiments to compare different current intensities, frequencies or durations with regard to the rate of barpressing they are able to maintain. The barpress itself is learnt once and once only; and the process of acquisition of this response is rarely even mentioned in the experimental report. Thereafter, the experimenter is concerned merely to use the rate of occurrence of the barpressing response as an assay for the reinforcing effect of the stimulus which is presented to the animal as an immediate consequence of this response. With regard to negative reinforcers, imagine an experiment in which a rat is first trained to run down an alley for a food reward; the experimenter then sounds a very loud noise in the goalbox and measures the reduction in speed of running to the goalbox which ensues. Or consider an experiment in which the experimenter electrifies the startbox and runway of a similar alley, and measures the speed with which a rat runs to the unelectrified goalbox as a function of shock intensity. In all these cases, it is the *performance* aspect of reinforcement which is foremost: i.e. the degree to which a stimulus arouses behaviour directed to *its own immediate production* (in the case of an S^{R+}); or the degree to which a stimulus arouses behaviour directed to its own immediate termination or reduction (in the case of an S^{R-}).

Most of the arguments we shall pursue in this and later chapters are unaffected by the distinction between the learning and the performance aspects of reinforcement (with the important exception of the discussion of positive feedback in Chapter 5). We shall therefore refer to this distinction only when it is of direct relevance. It is, however, an important distinction, and should not be forgotten.

The Relations between Drive and Reinforcement

Given the three senses of drive (Table 4.1) and the various operations by which positive and negative instrumental reinforcers are established (Table 4.2), we can at last address the question of the connection between drive and reinforcement. Two influential claims have been made about this connection: the first is that drive is necessary for reinforcement, and the second (associated closely with the names of Clark Hull and Neal Miller) is that reinforcement consists in the reduction of drive. Clearly, the second claim entails the first: one could not reduce a drive without its being there, so, if reinforcement consists in drive reduction, drive must be necessary for reinforcement to take place. The first claim, however, does not entail the second: drive might be necessary for reinforcement for some other reason than that reinforcement depended on drive reduction. Let us, therefore, consider each of these claims in turn, confining our attention in the first instance to the operation of reward: presentation of an S^{R+} contingent upon some response.

The first point to notice is that the operational definition of an S^{R+} is *identical* to the definition of drive in the goal-direction sense; but looked at, as it were, from the standpoint of the S rather than from that of the R. As we have seen, $drive_{GD}$ is detected by showing that, when we vary the means of access to the members of a particular class of stimuli, the animal varies its behaviour in such a way that it achieves the same end-point, i.e. approximation in space to the particular stimulus used. It must follow, therefore, that this stimulus increases the probability of emission of the behaviour which has this result. Therefore, the same relationship, $R \rightarrow S^{R+}$, is involved in defining both the goal-directed behaviour, of which R is an element, and the positive reinforcer, S^{R+}. Thus, if we use "drive" in the goal-direction sense, it is *logically* necessary that positive reinforcement can only occur if there is a drive. But, of course, if this connection is logically necessary (as a consequence of our definitions of terms), it is empirically empty.

The interesting empirical questions, then, cannot concern the relation between $drive_{GD}$ and the presentation of an S^{R+}. They must concern the relations between, on the one hand, goal-direction plus positive reinforcement ($R \rightarrow S^{R+}$) and, on the other, the temporal variation and deprivation senses of drive. But these we have already discussed, in considering the relations between $drive_{GD}$, on the one hand, and $drive_{TV}$ and $drive_{DEP}$, on the other (see Table 4.1). And we concluded that $drive_{GD}$ can occur in the absence either of $drive_{TV}$ (as in breathing and responding for stimulus change) or $drive_{DEP}$ (as in responding for stimulus change). So, in sum, drive appears to be necessary for reinforcement only in the trivial case where it is logically defined as being so.

In case these conclusions seem excessively obvious, it is worth recounting the main lines of the controversy which occupied the 1950s concerning light-contingent barpressing and similar examples of "sensory" reinforcement or exploratory behaviour. As already mentioned, the key discovery here is that rats and other animals will work to turn on lights or sounds of moderate intensities. When this discovery was made, it was said by some writers (e.g. Hurwitz, 1956) to disprove the assertion that drive is necessary for reinforcement. It was claimed by others, on the contrary, that it showed the existence of a hitherto unnoticed "curiosity" drive (e.g. Berlyne, 1950), which was elicited by the novel stimuli to which the resulting exploratory behaviour was directed. Still others (e.g. Myers and Miller, 1954; Fowler, 1967) posited a different kind of drive as underlying the phenomenon of sensory reinforcement: a boredom drive which was aroused by prolonged exposure to a monotonous environment and which could be reduced by exposure to novel stimulation. Given the widely differing senses in which the term "drive" has been used in psychology, each of these positions has some justification. The view that drive is inessential for sensory reinforcement can be maintained by pointing to its lack of anything resembling temporal variation (drive$_{TV}$) and its insensitivity to deprivation (drive$_{DEP}$). The view that a new "curiosity" drive had been demonstrated could be sustained by reference to the goal direction sense of drive. Both these views in effect, were take-over bids for exclusive rights to use of the word "drive". If goal-direction is the main criterion, there is a "curiosity" drive but there may be no sex drive in the female rat; if the criterion is regular temporal variation, the converse is true. The third reaction to the data on sensory reinforcement—the hypothesis of a boredom drive—was a brave attempt at a more substantive solution to the problem. It supposed that at least two senses of "drive"—drive$_{GD}$ and drive$_{DEP}$—necessarily go together in the empirical world. However, as we have seen, the evidence tends not to support this position: sensory reinforcement appears not to be susceptible to the usual kinds of deprivation operations.

The Drive–Reduction Hypothesis of Reinforcement

To anyone familiar with the major issues which have occupied learning theorists in the last three decades this chapter must so far seem like a production of "Hamlet" without the Prince: the drive-reduction hypothesis of reinforcement. But the stage is at last properly set for the Prince to enter.

As we have seen, the definition of a reinforcer is purely operational, and thus it tells us nothing about the nature of reinforcing stimuli—it merely tells us which stimuli we are allowed to term "reinforcers", under given experimental conditions and for a given species. That is why Thorndike's so-called "Law of Effect" (according to which responses followed by positive reinforcers are strengthened and those followed by negative reinforcers are weakened) is no law at all, but a tautology*. Thus at some point we need to ask what it is about reinforcing stimuli that makes them reinforcing. It might be the case, of course, that different types of reward act in different ways, and that the only way forward is to take first one and then another and analyse the way they work. But one would naturally hope to find some property which all reinforcers (or at least all positive reinforcers) have in common. Discovery of such a property would have two important consequences. In the first place, by giving us an independent criterion of a reinforcer, it would elevate the Law of Effect from the status of a tautology to that of a truly empirical law. And, secondly, it would offer us an important clue as to the mechanism (located, presumably, in the brain) by which reinforcers exert their reinforcing effects. Hull's need-reduction hypothesis of reinforcement and Miller's drive-reduction emendation of it represent an attempt—and indeed, the most important and sustained attempt yet made—to discover such a universal property of reinforcing stimuli and thereby construct a truly explanatory theory of reinforcement.

According to the initial need-reduction hypothesis, states of deprivation lead to tissue-changes which signal imminent physiological damage by sending appropriate messages to the CNS. The CNS then initiates action to lead the organism to stimuli in the environment which will reverse the state of deprivation. Only stimuli which do have this effect (i.e. which reduce a need) are (it is held) reinforcers; and their reinforcing effect consists precisely in their reduction of a need. Thus the need-reduction hypothesis contains the notions of susceptibility to deprivation and goal-directed behaviour which we have seen to be central to two meanings of "drive". In addition, however, it contains the notion that drives are initiated by states involving tissue-damage or the danger of tissue-damage and can

---

* Concerning this point, R. F. Drewett (personal communication) has made the following important comment. "As it is phrased, the Law of Effect is a tautology certainly. But the way out, I think, is simply to recognize that it is an existential, rather than a conditional; what it asserts is that the set of rewards is not empty. This is certainly a straight empirical claim; it is logically possible that, given the standard definition of a reward, there should be *no* stimuli that act as rewards. It is, indeed, perhaps empirically true that to the *Diptera* (but not, say, the *Hymenoptera*) there are in fact no rewards (Yeatman and Hirsch, 1971); put another way, they have no operant behaviour". To which I would add that, given the discovery that much of what has passed for operant or instrumental behaviour in the pigeon appears to be classical conditioning in disguise (the autoshaping phenomenon, discussed in Chapter 2), there may be more species than we think for which there are no rewards.

only be directed towards stimuli which can reverse such states. This was soon seen to be insufficient. There is no tissue damage which arises from lack of sexual outlets*, nor does copulatory behaviour reverse any such state of affairs; and, while we may have legitimate doubts about the involvement of drive and reinforcement in the sexual behaviour of female mammals, we need have no such doubt about sexual behaviour in males, which shows typical reinforcement and (with some complications) deprivation effects. Furthermore, even when we may reasonably regard deprivation of a particular class of stimuli (e.g. those making up "food") as leading to tissue-damage, it was shown by Sheffield and his co-workers that this kind of deprivation can result in goal-directed behaviour towards stimuli which do not reverse this state.

Some of the critical experiments of Sheffield's (Sheffield and Roby, 1950; Sheffield, Roby and Campbell, 1954) involved showing that animals would learn to run in mazes for the reward of saccharin, a substance which, though sweet, has no nutritive value. However, though this kind of experiment helped to demolish the need-reduction hypothesis, even more important was the way in which it forced the development of a clear *drive*-reduction hypothesis. This development was due to Miller (1951), who, by introducing an explicit objective test of drive-reduction, clarified the meaning of this hypothesis.

As we have seen, if we take drive in the goal-direction sense, it is logically necessary that reinforcement involves drive. It might seem, therefore, that a drive-reduction hypothesis of reinforcement, if allied to this sense of drive, would be similarly tautological. In fact, however, as Miller's test shows, it is not: although reinforcement must (logically) involve drive$_{GD}$, it need not logically involve *reduction* in drive$_{GD}$. Thus one may ask whether empirically it does in fact involve reduction in drive$_{GD}$. Now, if drive is being taken in the sense of a class of behaviour directed towards gaining access to a class of stimuli, it is clear that reduction in drive will appear as a reduction in the incidence of such behaviour. In other words, it will appear as *satiation* of the behaviour as a function of the degree to which it is successful in attaining the appropriate stimuli. This is not logically involved in the notion of goal-direction: there is no logical

---

* The fact that sexual behaviour is necessary for the survival of the *species* does not entail a need within the *individual*.

reason why, the environment permitting, goal-directed behaviour should not continue indefinitely at peak intensity. The drive-reduction hypothesis proposes, in effect, this slogan: no reinforcement without satiation; for it holds that reinforcement consists in drive reduction.

The way, then, to test for drive-reduction is to look for satiation. This is what Miller (1955) did: he showed that, after eating saccharin, rats not only ate less of a further offering of the same substance, but also less dextrose, milk or solid food. Notice, by the way, that, as well as illustrating the satiation test of drive-reduction, this experiment involves the same problem of defining the class of stimuli appropriate to a drive$_{GD}$ which we encountered earlier in connection with drive$_{TV}$. What we might call the "cross-satiation" test—showing that saccharin satiates for sugar, milk and other kinds of food—is evidence that these stimuli belong to the same class.

Miller's experiment may be said, then, to involve "class-satiation": the satiation is observed, not during the performance of the behaviour reinforced by one member of the appropriate class of stimuli, but subsequently when the animal is offered another member of the class. An even simpler test of satiation is "self-satiation", i.e. the observation that the reinforced behaviour itself declines as a function of successful access to the reinforcer (also involved in the saccharin experiments). The strongest evidence *against* the drive-reduction hypothesis comes from experiments in which goal-directed behaviour has been observed, but with no sign of self-satiation.

This phenomenon appears most dramatically in the self-stimulation experiments poineered by Olds. As is now well-known, if a rat is implanted with electrodes in certain parts of the brain, it will work, for example by pressing a bar, to cause the passage of a small electrical current through the tissue around the electrode. When the electrodes are in the lateral hypothalamus or the medial forebrain bundle, the reinforcing effects of such stimulation are so strong that the animal will work for hours at a time with no sign of stopping: that is to say, the self-satiation test for the drive-reduction hypothesis is not passed.

It could of course be argued that the drive-reduction hypothesis was meant to apply only to intact animals, and that data from self-stimulation experiments are irrelevant. Such a view would, in effect, claim that the drive-reduction hypothesis concerns the systematic nature of the way in which the organismic machine behaves, not the way in which the machine is put together. While weaker than Hull probably intended his theory to be, such a view would be intellectually respectable. However, there is also evidence that a failure of self-satiation can occur in experiments involving peripheral reinforcement. Hendry and Rasche (1961), for example, discovered what they called "a new non-nutritive reinforcer": the opportunity to lick at a stream of air. This opportunity is found reinforcing by rats, if and only if they are water deprived. The resulting behaviour is of interest on several counts.

First, it is an excellent refutation of the *need*-reduction hypothesis, because, far from reducing the water-deficit which is a necessary condition for animals to engage in this form of behaviour, it actually *increases* water-loss as a result of evaporation from the tongue (Hendry and Rasche, 1961).

Secondly, although the reinforcing effects of air-drinking are extremely strong, its self-satiating effects are very slight and very short-lasting. Fig. 4.6, for example, shows results obtained by Oatley and Dickinson (1970). Consider the behaviour of the group of rats rewarded for licking with 0.1 sec of a low-pressure (0.05 lb/in^2) air stream after 48 h deprivation of water. These rats produced on average nearly 14 000 licking responses in the 1 h testing session (far more than the number of licks emitted by the animals rewarded with water) and their rate of licking barely declined at all from the start of the session to the end. There is some degree of self-satiation produced by air-licking, to be sure. Williams *et al.* (1964) examined the effects of varying periods of free access to a continuous air stream on the subsequent barpressing rate for a further 3 sec of air per response, and also the effects of varying periods of delay between a 2 h free-access session and the subsequent barpressing session, obtaining the results shown in Fig. 4.7. A 2 h period of free air-drinking significantly reduced the subsequent barpressing rate for air, but this effect disappeared within 30 min of the end of the free air-drinking session. The satiating effects of water on subsequent water-ingestion are, of course, much stronger than this. At the very least, therefore, one can conclude that the self-satiating effects of air-drinking are much weaker than those produced by water, and yet the reinforcing effects are certainly no less; whereas, if reinforcement

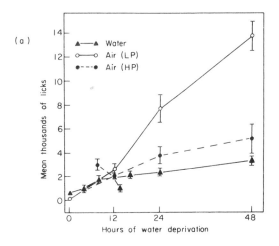

(a)

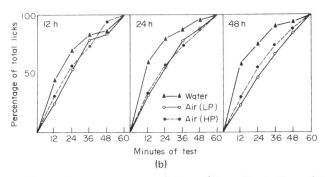

(b)

FIG. 4.6. Rate of Air Licking as a Function of Hours of Water Deprivation and Duration of Test Period. A. Mean number of licks for water or for low-pressure (LP) or high-pressure (HP) air-puff following different degrees of water deprivation. B. Mean cumulative percentage of total licks over a 1 hour test period after different degrees of water deprivation.

consists in drive-reduction, the degree of reinforcement ought surely to be proportional to the magnitude of the drive-reduction. Further-more, even such self-satiating effects of air-drinking as have been shown to occur may well be causally unrelated to the reinforcing effect of air-drinking. The latter is almost certainly due to direct effects of air on the tongue and mouth. The satiation effects, on the other hand, may be at least partly due to the air which is swallowed and reaches the stomach, as pointed out by Oatley and Dickinson (1970), who showed that there was about 10 ml of air in the

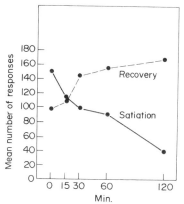

FIG. 4.7. Satiation and Recovery from Satiation of Air Drinking. Ordinate: mean number of barpresses for 3 seconds of air. Abscissa: duration of either preceding period of free access to continuous air stream (for "satiation" curve) *or* interval between two-hour free-access session and barpressing session (for "recovery" curve). (From Williams, Treichler and Thomas, 1964.)

stomachs of rats which had taken part in a 1 h air-drinking session. If this could be prevented in some way from occurring, it is possible that air-drinking might display reinforcing effects in the complete absence of self-satiation, as does electrical self-stimulation of the brain.

The third point of interest concerning air-drinking behaviour is that, even though it shows little if any self-satiation, it does result in a substantial amount of class-satiation, in the sense that it reduces the amount of *water* subsequently ingested. Hendry and Rasche (1961) showed that, after a 1 h air-drinking session, there was a 20% reduction in the amount of water drunk immediately after the session, and still a 15% reduction in the amount drunk one hour after the session (Fig. 4.8). If this result is compared with the curve labelled "recovery" in Fig. 4.7, it will be seen that a 1 h air-drinking session is apparently capable of reducing subsequent water ingestion for considerably longer than the time for which a 2 h air-drinking session can reduce subsequent air-drinking. Intuitively, one might have expected class-satiation to be a less robust effect of reinforcement than self-satiation, but, in the air-drinking experiments at any rate, the reverse is apparently the case.

Again it might be objected that air-licking is a very odd sort of behaviour, but once one is alerted to the possibility of reinforcement which does not produce satiation, it is not difficult to think of perfectly normal forms of behaviour which are likely to fit the same pattern. If air were made available for breathing only when a button were pressed, it seems implausible that button-pressing would fall off over time as a function of the attainment of air. The fact is that learning theorists have tended to think of behaviour around one of two models: hunting for food or avoiding shock. The hunting-for-food model has dominated views of drive and reinforcement, and hence the concentration on deprivation, tissue-damage, and satiation.

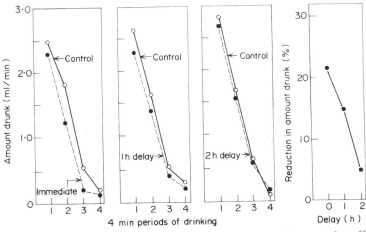

FIG. 4.8. Reduction of Water Intake by Prior Air Drinking. First three graphs: effects of one-hour air-drinking session on water intake immediately, 1 hour or 2 hours after. Right-hand graph: the effect of delaying the drinking test on average reduction in water consumption expressed as a percentage of control consumption. (From Hendry and Rasche, 1961.)

But, to reiterate a warning sounded earlier in this chapter, there is no guarantee that all behaviour classes are going to be organized by mechanisms of an identical kind: natural selection has bred into many species mechanisms to do many jobs, and the nature of the specific job may well dictate the way the particular mechanism has been put together.

But the final blow to the drive-reduction hypothesis has come from the self-stimulation experiments. Not only are these, from the point of view of drive-reduction theory, anomalous in showing no self-satiation, they push refutation to the point of scandal and suggest that it is actually drive-*induction** which is reinforcing. The

* But see Chapter 6, where this possibility is explored further.

key observation here is what happens when the experimenter delivers current through the same electrodes which, if given the opportunity, the animal will use to self-stimulate. In an early experiment of this kind, Hoebel and Teitelbaum (1962) showed that, with electrodes in the lateral hypothalamus (a focal point for the self-stimulation phenomenon), and with the animal previously sated for food, experimenter-applied stimulation caused the animal to eat for as long as the stimulation was applied. This finding is, of course, totally at variance with drive-reduction theory, which would rather lead us to expect that reinforcing stimulation would reduce eating. Furthermore, stimulation of the adjacent medial hypothalamus, which *does* reduce eating, apparently by operating a mechanism which is responsible for the termination of eating when satiation has been achieved under normal conditions (Grossman, 1967; Sclafani and Grossman, 1970), is not only *not* rewarding, as it should be on the drive-reduction hypothesis, it is often (Olds and Olds, 1965), though not always (Ball, 1972), found actually to be punishing—i.e. the animal will work to turn it off.

The case against the drive-reduction hypothesis from this kind of experiment is all the stronger, given the evidence that it is indeed a hunger drive which is being activated by stimulation of the lateral hypothalamus. We have already seen some of this evidence, in Miller's (1961) observation that, though it will cause the stimulated rat to chew solid food and lap milk, it will not cause it to lap water (though stimulation of other points in the hypothalamus is capable of producing the latter effect). In addition, it can be shown that stimulation of this kind will cause an animal to perform a previously learnt instrumental response which is rewarded by food (even though the subject of the experiment has recently been fed to satiation) and to learn a new response to the same end (Grossman, 1967). In short, by all the tests appropriate to drive in the sense of goal-direction, stimulation of the lateral hypothalamus is able to turn on a hunger drive. Yet this same stimulation is found to be reinforcing. Thus, rather than reduction of the hunger drive being reinforcing, it is apparently *induction* of the hunger drive which has this property. Furthermore, these results can be generalized to a variety of other points in the brain involving a variety of other drives$_{GD}$ (Glickman and Schiff, 1967).

Notice that it is not only Hull who has taken a beating from these experiments: so has common sense. Hull's theory, after all, is only common sense writ large: we all *know* that we eat or go to restaurants to reduce hunger; how can it be said that we behave in such a way as to *make ourselves feel hungry*? And yet this is exactly what the data suggest.

Of course, if our intuitive model had been that of sexual behaviour rather than hunger, we would be much less surprised by the outcome: a great deal of civilized life appears to be concerned with making ourselves feel *sexy*. And, indeed, once you begin to think about it, it is possible to find similar kinds of things going on in the case of eating behaviour. That excellent custom, the pre-dinner apéritif, has as its express purpose sharpening the appetite. Hebb (1949) has similarly pointed to the "salted-nut phenomenon": you may be quite lacking in appetite for nuts until you have eaten your first one, but then you become avid for them. All of which goes to show the dangers inherent in intuitive knowledge: a Martian might start with fewer hypotheses, but also with fewer signposts pointing in the wrong direction.

It is, of course, entirely possible that the data which appear to indicate a reinforcing effect of centrally elicited drive$_{GD}$ will eventually prove to demand quite a different explanation. There already exist data which are difficult to reconcile with the view that the anatomical covariation of points in the brain from which drives$_{GD}$ can be elicited and points which sustain self-stimulation is a consequence of an actual functional identity between the drive-inducing and the reinforcing effects of brain stimulation (Deutsch, 1964a; Ball and Adams, 1965; Ball, 1972). But though we cannot conclude that reinforcement consists in drive-*induction* (a problem to which we return in Chapter 6), it is certainly clear that the self-stimulation experiments are an insuperable obstacle to the drive-*reduction* hypothesis of reinforcement. But, if this is so, we obviously need some supplementary account of the fact, that, where normal eating, drinking, sexual behaviour, etc., are concerned, both self- and class- satiation do in fact occur. Such an account will be even more necessary should it turn out that reinforcing stimuli are stimuli which actually increase the drive directed towards their attainment. For this latter process, left to itself, would leave the animal locked permanently into whichever rewarding activity it started first (as apparently happens when this activity is that of directly stimulating the lateral hypothalamus).

Here we must distinguish between two views of the association between reinforcement and drive-reduction. The one we have been considering so far holds that reinforcement *consists* in drive-reduction: the latter is both a necessary and a sufficient condition for the former. A much weaker view would be that, in the case of some rewarding activities, and especially those concerned with the homeostatic maintenance of the internal milieu (most typically, eating and drinking), reinforcing stimuli exercise two *parallel but independent* effects, one reinforcing and the other satiating or drive-reducing. If the latter view were correct, the strong drive-reduction hypothesis of Hull and Miller would have arisen because the regular co-existence of reinforcing and satiating effects in normal eating and drinking (the most studied behaviour in the laboratory) suggested a causal connection between the two which does not in fact exist. McFarland (1969) has conducted an experiment which suggests that in an absolutely paradigm case for the drive-reduction hypothesis—drinking behaviour in the Barbary dove—just this is the case: the reinforcing and satiating effects of drinking are causally independent of each other.

McFarland prepared doves with chronic oesophageal fistulae so that water could be placed directly into the gut, bypassing the usual stimulation of oral receptors which accompanies the act of drinking. He then compared the reinforcing effect of water delivered in this way with that of water delivered in the normal manner, and similarly compared the satiating effects of water delivered in the two ways. In the reinforcement test, the doves were first trained to peck at a key for a reward of water delivered orally. When this behaviour was firmly established, they were tested to see if they would transfer from pecking at this key (now rendered ineffective in the attainment of water) to a second key. In one condition, pecking the second key was also rewarded with water delivered orally; in a second condition, it was rewarded with water delivered directly into the fistula. Transfer took place readily under the first condition, but there was no sign of transfer when water was delivered to the fistula. Thus, in the conditions of this part of McFarland's experiment, the reinforcing effects of water were entirely produced by oral factors. In the satiation test, each key press delivered water simultaneously via the usual oral route and also directly to the fistula. Three conditions were compared: 0.05 cc to the fistula plus 0.05 cc orally; 0.1 cc to the fistula plus 0.1 cc orally; and 0.1 cc orally only. The data recorded consisted simply of the total amount of water drunk, via both routes together, before the animal stopped pecking at the key. The results were very clear-cut: satiation as measured in this way was determined by the total amount drunk (which was identical in all three conditions) irrespective of the route of delivery. Since water delivered orally *also* reached the stomach, if there were an oral contribution to satiation, we would expect water delivered via this route to be more satiating than water placed directly into the stomach. Thus the simplest interpretation of the results of this part of McFarland's experiment is that satiation is determined by alimentary factors only. Overall, then, McFarland's results appear to permit the conclusion that, in the Barbary dove, the reinforcing effects of drinking are due to purely oral factors and the satiating effects of drinking to purely alimentary factors. In normal drinking, of course, these two factors co-vary perfectly, but, causally, they are quite independent.

If this independence of reinforcing and satiating effect is generally the case (though in the rat and other mammals they may not separate out so neatly into oral and gastric factors as in McFarland's dove experiment: e.g. Miller and Kessen, 1952), we can see a simple basis for understanding the failure of satiation to occur with self-stimulation of the lateral hypothalamus at points whose stimulation by the experimenter produces eating and a hunger drive$_{GD}$. All we need to suppose is that the electrodes are at a point in the CNS which collects the reinforcing signals (e.g. signals of appropriate oral stimulation) of food, but which is not on the route by which the independent satiating signals are transmitted.

Earlier in this chapter we set ourselves to address two questions with respect to the operation of an S^{R+}: is drive necessary for reinforcement and does reinforcement consist in drive-reduction? The answer to both questions appears to be "No". This answer, naturally, forces us to go on to ask other questions, concerning the properties possessed by an S^{R+} (if any) apart from the sheer capacity to act as a positive reinforcer; concerning the mechanism by which an S^{R+} exerts its reinforcing effects; and concerning the means by which drive$_{DEP}$ or drive$_{TV}$ alter the effectiveness of positive reinforcement under those conditions in which this does occur. We shall postpone consideration of these questions until Chapters 5 and 6. In the remainder of the present chapter we shall trace the fate of the concepts of drive and reinforcement when they are applied to instrumental *negative* reinforcement and to *classical* conditioning.

"Drive" as Applied to Escape and Avoidance

It is much easier to consider the application of "drive" and "drive-reduction" to behaviour reinforced by the termination or omission of an S^{R-} than it has been to apply these concepts to positive instrumental reinforcement. The reason for this is simple: there is nothing about negatively reinforced behaviour which corresponds to $drive_{TV}$ or $drive_{DEP}$ and nothing corresponding to satiation (i.e., drive-reduction). It is just as well therefore that we have had to abandon any hope of accounting for the effects of positive instrumental reinforcement by reference to drive and drive-reduction: had this venture succeeded, it would have been at the expense of any chance of an integrated theory of instrumental reinforcement.

In justification of the claim that instrumental negative reinforcement does not partake of anything resembling $drive_{TV}$, $drive_{DEP}$ or drive-reduction, consider the kind of experiment in which an animal performs some response or other in order to escape from (i.e. terminate) or avoid an electric shock. This is typical goal-directed behaviour, the goal being the minimization of shock. But where would one look for drive in any sense other than $drive_{GD}$? There is no known temporal variation in the willingness of a rat to avoid or escape from an electric shock. Nor is it possible to "deprive" an animal of electric shock. One could perhaps say that a shocked animal is "deprived of nonshock", and that such "deprivation" increases with the duration of imposed shock. But it is hard to see how this could be anything more than playing with words; and, in any case, it is possible to obtain extremely stable avoidance behaviour which is so successful that the animal is hardly ever shocked any more, though he nonetheless continues to perform the avoidance response (see Chapter 10). Thus all we are left with is the goal-direction sense of drive, in which, as we already know, there is a logical connection between drive and reinforcement. In the case of aversive reinforcement, this logical connection takes the following form: (1) a $drive_{GD}$ away from punishment (or towards non-punishment) is shown by variation of behaviour with variation of the means of terminating or avoiding punishment in such a way that the termination or avoidance of punishment continues to be attained; and (2) that a given stimulus is indeed a punishment or negative reinforcer is shown by a decreased probability of behaviour leading to its presentation or an increased probability of behaviour leading to its termination or omission. Thus, to say that $drive_{G\,D}$ is necessary for reinforcement is as tautological in the case of an $S^{R\,-}$ as it is in the case of an $S^{R\,+}$. Furthermore, since $drive_{G\,D}$ is the only drive we've got, it follows that there are *no* empirical discoveries to be made about the connection of drive and reinforcement in the case of negative reinforcement.

There is not even any value, in the case of aversive reinforcement, in Miller's empirical test of the drive-reduction hypothesis of reinforcement. As applied to, say, escape behaviour, this would lead us to expect that the behaviour of escaping from punishment (e.g., an electric shock) declines in probability as a function of the amount of non-punishment the behaviour succeeds in attaining. This is definitely not the case: escape behaviour is extremely persistent. (The difficulties which active avoidance behaviour, as distinct from escape behaviour, has posed for reinforcement theory in general, and drive-reduction theory in particular, have been even more acute; but we shall delay consideration of these until Chapter 10.) In short, there is no case for applying the vocabularly of drive—except as a synonym for goal-directed behaviour—and drive-reduction to behaviour determined by negative reinforcement.

It might again be thought that this conclusion is so trivial that we need not have bothered to derive it. However, a perusal of learning theory texts of the 1940s and 1950s shows that the example of escape learning was often given to substantiate the view that reinforcement is based on drive and subsequent drive-reduction. It was said that the application of an electric shock set up a drive, and that behaviour which led to the termination of the shock was learned because it was followed by reduction of the shock-induced drive. But this is clearly just another way of saying that behaviour which is followed by the termination of the shock itself is learned; and this is what requires explanation.

"Drive" in Classical Conditioning

Finally, we consider the application of the drive vocabulary to classical conditioning. Once more, we lose one of our senses of drive, but this time it is the goal-direction one: this is obviously inappropriate to an experimental situation in which the experimenter follows one stimulus by another irrespective of the animal's behaviour (Chapter 2).

One important consequence of this is that, in the case of classical conditioning, we do not have to divide up our discussion by means of the appetitive/aversive distinction. This distinction arises purely in the instrumental case, being based on the *direction* of a drive$_{GD}$ (towards or away from the reinforcing stimulus); that is, on whether presentation of the S^R following a response increases or decreases the subsequent probability of emission of the response. If we did not already know that acid and food in the mouth were, respectively, aversive and appetitive according to tests of their instrumental reinforcing powers, there is nothing about their effects as UCSs in a classical salivary conditioning experiment which could make that distinction for us. (The chemical constitution of the saliva making up the two CRs, the one based on an acid UCS and the other on food, differs in the two cases, it is true: but the chemical constitution of saliva carries no lable saying "appetitive" or "aversive"!) The laws of classical conditioning, as far as is known, are equally applicable to aversive and appetitive stimuli and, indeed, to stimuli which have no known instrumental reinforcing powers. The lack of an appetitive/ aversive distinction in classical conditioning is, therefore, an important addition to the list of differences between this and instrumental learning which we drew up in Chapter 2.

A second consequence of the loss of the goal-direction sense of drive in the case of classical conditioning is that we do not have to consider the drive-reduction hypothesis as applied to this kind of learning; for, as we have seen, the drive-reduction hypothesis of reinforcement is tied to the goal-direction sense of drive.

The questions, then, to which we need to address ourselves as regards the relations between drive and the effects of a UCS in a classical conditioning procedure are: (1) Is classical conditioning possible only when the animal is in a state of drive$_{TV}$ with respect to the UCS? (2) Is classical conditioning possible only when the animal is in a state of drive$_{DEP}$ with respect to the UCS?

The first question is easily dealt with, since it is possible to obtain classical conditioning in situations which apparently do not involve any temporal variation. For example, the Russians have made great use of a method of conditioning which results in a "photochemical conditioned reflex (PCR)" (Gray, 1964a). This reflex is established as follows. The subject (human) sits in a dark room until dark adaptation is complete. The absolute visual threshold is measured in the dark and after presentation of a flash of light (the UCS), which, of course, leads to a temporary rise in the visual threshold. This flash of light is regularly preceded by an originally neutral stimulus (i.e., one which has no effect itself on the visual threshold, e.g. a tone) according to a normal classical conditioning paradigm. As a result of such pairing, it is found that the tone CS on its own elicits a rise in the visual threshold. This is the PCR. Now, there is absolutely nothing analogous in this situation to the kind of temporal variation seen, say, in food-seeking behaviour or sexual behaviour. Once the subject is dark-adapted we have no reason to suppose that there are going to be any changes over time in the visual threshold. There are many other situations one could describe to which the same would apply. Thus the notion of temporal variation seems inappropriate to classical conditioning.

What about deprivation? Certainly, Pavlov used regularly to deprive his dogs of food for salivary conditioning experiments, and it is clear that such conditioning is easier when the dog is so deprived. More recently, DeBold *et al.* (1965) have conducted an experiment using rats and water as UCS in which, when the animals were totally satiated, classical conditioning was impossible to obtain. However, it seems highly unlikely that this result can be of general significance. There is, for example, no need to deprive a dog of anything when acid is used as the UCS for a salivary conditioning experiment. Or consider an experiment in which vasomotor changes are conditioned. The subject starts out with the hand at room temperature. We can now obtain either conditioned vasodilation to a tone CS if we follow the tone by *hot* water or conditioned vasoconstriction to the same tone if we follow it by *cold* water. If we say that we managed to get conditioned vasodilation in the first experiment because the subject was "deprived" of heat, then how shall we account for the results of the second experiment? Or vice versa. In the face of experiments such as these, it is clearly impossible to maintain that deprivation is *necessary* for reinforcement in classical conditioning.

How shall we account, then, for the effects of drive on classical conditioning in those experiments in which such effects have been found? Let us take the DeBold *et al.* (1965) experiment mentioned above. These workers used rats which had had a fistula inserted into the snout through which water could be poured directly into the mouth. The response measured was licking at the bottom of the fistula. Water poured into the fistula served as UCS. Rats given conditioning trials when water-deprived and subsequently tested when water-deprived showed a good conditioned licking response to an initially neutral CS paired according to the usual classical conditioning paradigm with the UCS. Other rats were given their conditioning trials satiated for water (they were given free access to water for one hour immediately before the conditioning session). A special group was given conditioning trials in a "supersatiated" condition: after the same free access to water for one hour as in the satiation group, a further quantity of water was poured into their mouths via the fistula. "In most cases", as the authors write, "subjects in the supersatiated group eliminated much of the water by making expulsion movements with the tongue". Rats in both the satiation and the supersatiation groups showed no sign of acquisition of the conditioned licking response even when subsequently tested under water-deprivation.

Clearly, this result could be taken to indicate that, at least when the response is one which does relate to a drive$_{DEP}$, drive is necessary for classical conditioning to occur. There is, however, an equally plausible interpretation which has the advantage of being consistent with the data on responses which do not have any natural relation to a drive$_{DEP}$. As we saw in Chapter 2, it is not normally the case that a response becomes conditioned to a CS unless a response in the same direction is also elicited by the UCS (the modified stimulus substitution rule). It is very likely that in the case of the supersatiation technique (which was devised to ensure that drive really would be reduced to zero), licking ceased to be a response to the UCS: for, as mentioned above, the rats exposed to this procedure made actual "expulsion movements with the tongue". Thus we have no reason to suppose that classical conditioning should result in the CS acquiring the power to elicit conditioned licking. The satiation procedure might also alter the nature of the UCR to water; though the authors of the paper provide no indication on this point. Until this possibility is eliminated, however, the most reasonable conclusion is that, when drive$_{DEP}$ does affect classical conditioning, it does so *by altering the nature or intensity of the to-be-conditioned UCR.*

Earlier we dismissed the possibility that goal-direction, as such, could be involved in classical conditioning; and this, of course, follows from the conclusion we reached in Chapter 2 that classical conditioning can be differentiated from instrumental learning and is governed by $S \rightarrow S$ contingencies. There is one way, however, in which one could approach the question of the relationship between drive$_{GD}$ and classical conditioning: this is to enquire whether stimuli which can be used as UCSs in classical conditioning experiments would necessarily be found positively or negatively reinforcing in an instrumental conditioning paradigm. Clearly, many if not most of the stimuli actually used as UCSs in classical conditioning experiments are capable of serving as S^Rs: food, acid, electric shock, etc. However, it is by no means obvious that *all* UCSs would fit this description. Take, for example, the "thought" experiment we just discussed, in which, by use of heat and cold as UCSs, we conditioned vasodilation or vasoconstriction, respectively. It seems implausible, *a priori*, that, no matter what baseline of room temperature we started from, changes in temperature in the direction of both increases and decreases would always be found either positively or negatively reinforcing by an instrumental test. At some point, we would expect to find a relatively neutral range of temperature (Budgell, 1971). Assuming that, nonetheless, changes over this range could still act as UCSs to produce vasodilation or vasoconstriction, the question would then be, can these be successfully used in a classical conditioning experiment?

As far as I know, only one experiment of this kind has been carried out. We discussed this experiment, by Doty and Giurgea (1961), in Chapter 2, in connection with the distinction between classical and instrumental conditioning. Doty and Giurgea successfully used direct electrical stimulation of the motor cortex as the UCS in classical conditioning experiments with dogs. They then made the same stimulation of the motor cortex contingent upon lever-pressing, and failed to produce either increases or decreases in response rate in this manner. Thus they were able to obtain classical conditioning with a UCS which lacked the capacity to evoke goal-directed behaviour, whether appetitive or aversive, as tested by instrumental conditioning. Notice, by the way, the odd situation we would be in if the outcome of experiments such as Doty and Giurgea's were to be the reverse of what these investigators actually found. This would presumably suggest that the laws of classical conditioning took cognizance of whether or not a stimulus was instrumentally reinforcing, but not of the direction (positive or negative) of the reinforcing effect it produced. It seems, however, that the actual situation is simpler: classical conditioning is quite unaffected by goal-direction (though, as we shall see in later chapters, goal-direction is certainly not unaffected by classical conditioning).

This brings to a close our treatment of the relations between drive and reinforcement. The doubt we have cast on the drive-reduction hypothesis of reinforcement, and indeed on the explanatory force of the notion of drive itself, has raised more questions than it has answered. Among them, is the one which is central to any theory of learning: how do reinforcers work, i.e. how does an animal find its way to those parts of its spatio-temporal environment in which its needs are satisfied and away from those parts in which danger threatens? The rest of this book can be regarded as an attempt to set out the lines of one kind of answer to this question: the answer offered by "two-process theory".

5. Secondary Reinforcement and Incentive

The failure of the drive-reduction theory of positive reinforcement leaves us with a number of unanswered questions. In particular:

(1) What properties (other than the sheer fact that they are reinforcing) *can* we ascribe to positively reinforcing stimuli?

(2) What is the mechanism by which an S^{R+} produces its reinforcing effects? (The answers to questions 1 and 2 may or may not be essentially the same: it was a virtue of the need- and drive-reduction hypotheses that they attempted to answer them both simultaneously.)

(3) By what means do $drive_{TV}$ and $drive_{DEP}$ alter $drive_{GD}$, i.e. the effectiveness of an S^{R+}? Although we concentrated in the previous chapter on the evidence that drive is of no *essential* consequence for reinforcement, there are of course great quantities of data to show that under many conditions $drive_{TV}$ and $drive_{DEP}$ do affect the reinforcement operation to a considerable degree. The drive-reduction hypothesis was able to offer an explanation for this fact—yet another of its virtues. But virtue, no matter how great, is no substitute for success.

Similar questions can be raised with respect to negative reinforcers; but we shall leave these till later chapters. We shall also postpone further consideration of Question 1 above until the next chapter, in which Premack's theory of reinforcement is examined. In the present chapter we concentrate on the second question: how do positive reinforcers work?

Positive Feedback

The answer to this question may be relatively simple: as the signals for a positive feedback mechanism. "Positive feedback" is a term taken from engineering control theory. McFarland, in an introductory text on the application of control theory to animal behaviour, puts the matter thus:

> When the value of a dependent variable Y is determined uniquely by an independent variable X, the behaviour of Y may be said to be "controlled" by X. When the value of Y in no way influences the value of X, the control can be said to be "open-loop", in contrast to "closed-loop" control in which some influence does occur.

Diagrams of simple open- and closed-loop control configurations are shown in Fig 5.1 Positive feedback is one kind of closed-loop system:

> "Positive feedback" exists when the consequences of the monitored output tend to accentuate further output. In a linear system the feedback is added to the input and the controlled device is actuated to an ever-increasing extent (McFarland, 1971, pp. 16, 21).

To apply the idea of feedback to the problem of reinforcement, consider the possibility that drinking behaviour (with satiation for the moment eliminated) is represented by a closed-loop system as shown in Fig. 5.1. The "output" of this system is consumption of water, and the "input" is some initial activation from within the CNS of the command centre for drinking behaviour. We suppose that, in consequence of such an initial command, drinking has just begun; and, further, that the consumption of water provides positive feedback for drinking. Then one effect of water-consumption is that the signal carried back via the box labelled "feedback parameters" to the command centre for drinking further *increases* the strength of the command to continue drinking. (In the case of *negative* feed-back, which is involved in the *satiating* effect of water-consumption, the sign of this signal is reversed, and the effect it has on the command centre for drinking is to *reduce* the strength of the command to continue drinking: Fig. 5.1.)

In one sense, this description of positive reinforcement as a positive feedback mechanism is quite without explanatory power: it merely uses a different terminology from the one familiar in learning theory to describe the same facts as before. From another point of view however, the control-theory approach to positive reinforcement is potentially of great significance. Above all, it allows a powerful and wide-ranging mathematics to be used in the description of the effects of positive reinforcers (McFarland, 1971). Moreover, the mere fact that description of reinforcement as a positive feedback

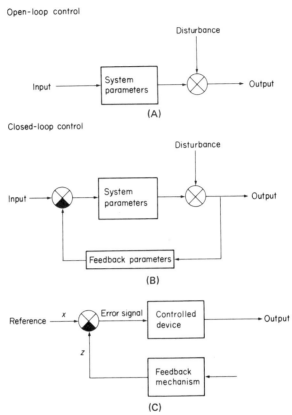

FIG. 5.1. Open-loop and Closed-loop (Feedback) Control Systems. A. Open-loop control, in which the output does not influence the input. B. Closed-loop control, in which it does. If the influence of the output is to increase still further the input, this is "positive feedback". C. A "negative feedback" system, in which the input to the "controlled device" (the "error signal") is proportional to the difference between the "reference" or "derived" level, X, and the feedback from output, Z. (From McFarland, 1971.)

mechanism aligns this behavioural phenomenon with a number of artefacts unmysteriously made by Man at once robs it too of some of its mystery. In addition, this new look at reinforcement suggests new ways of investigating it.

McFarland and McFarland (1968), for example, did a very simple experiment with the dove (in which, as we have seen, oral receptors stimulated by water communicate positive reinforcement uncontaminated by satiation) to show that there is indeed a positive feedback of drinking on drinking. Their argument was as follows. Suppose we first measure the temporal course of drinking up to the point of satiation in an uninterrupted session. Now we repeat the experiment, but with an interruption of drinking at some point during the session followed by a resumption some minutes later. If drinking is providing *positive* feedback for the continuation and strengthening of this same act of drinking, then after the interruption, during which time any feedback signals from drinking will have decayed, drinking should be resumed at a *lower* intensity than that observed in the uninterrupted drinking session. Fig. 5.2 shows that this is exactly the result McFarland and McFarland (1968) obtained.

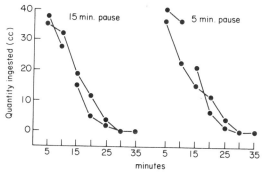

FIG. 5.2. Effect of Interruption of Drinking on Rate of Drinking. Continuous curve: rate of drinking under normal conditions. Broken curve: rate of drinking with 5- or 15-min. interruption. (From McFarland and McFarland, 1968.)

This is all right as far as it goes: and, indeed, the suggestion that reinforcement is a process of positive feedback is by no means new (Mowrer, 1954). But it leaves untouched the central problem posed by positive reinforcement: the *learning* of *new* responses which are followed by an S^{R+}. If an S^{R+} facilitates the behaviour which gives rise to it, in the manner of a positive feedback mechanism, it can only do so from that point in time at which the animal makes contact with it. But any new response on which the S^{R+} is made contingent must, of course, precede the moment of occurrence of the S^{R+}. It is this retrograde effect of an S^{R+} which is at the heart of the matter when we come to the *learning* aspect of reinforcement. In the last chapter we drew a distinction between this and the performance aspect of reinforcement (i.e. the maintenance of an existing response which is already being followed by an S^{R+}). It is only the latter to which the notion of positive feedback has a simple and obvious application. But it is the former—the learning aspect—which is more important.

Classical Conditioning of Reinforcement

There is, however, one other simple, but powerful, process which, allied to the notion of positive feedback, may be able to generate just such a retrograde effect as is required to account for the effects of reinforcement on learning: that of classical conditioning. This idea has been developed in particular by Mowrer in a series of papers beginning in 1953 (see Mowrer, 1960, p. 223). It grows in the first instance out of the well-established phenomenon of "secondary positive reinforcement"—the fact that an initially neutral stimulus which has been paired with an unconditioned S^{R+} itself takes on positively reinforcing properties.

An early study demonstrating this phenomenon is that of Saltzman (1949). Rats were first trained to run in a straight alley to obtain food in a distinctive goalbox. Following this training, they were placed in a U-shaped maze in which they could run to one of two goalboxes, neither of which was visible from the startbox. One of these goalboxes was the same as that in which reward had been delivered in the straight alley, the other was a different one. No reward was given in the U-maze in either goalbox. Nonetheless, the rats ran to that box in which they had been rewarded in the straight alley significantly more than to the other goalbox.

In this type of experiment, the animal shows that the initially neutral stimulus has become a secondary reinforcer by learning a new response which leads to its attainment. In other experiments, the secondary reinforcing effect of a stimulus paired with primary positive reinforcement is shown by the ability of the secondary reinforcer to delay extinction of the response already learnt for the primary reinforcer. Bugelski (1938), for example, trained rats to press a bar for a food reward. Operation of the bar was accompanied by a distinct click. After the animals had received thirty reinforcements they were divided into two groups and extinguished to a criterion of five minutes without a response. Half of the animals were extinguished with the click still accompanying depression of the bar; for the other half, the click was absent. The former group made significantly more responses during extinction.

This kind of experiment then (and there are many others which could have been cited) shows that a stimulus paired with an S^{R+} itself acquires reinforcing properties. It does not, however, implicate classical conditioning in any very direct manner. It is true that the secondary reinforcer could stand as CS to the UCS of the primary reinforcer, but since there is also an instrumental response at the same time (as in both Saltzman's and Bugelski's experiments) we have no guarantee that the classical conditioning contingency plays any functional role in the outcome. However, there are other experiments in which only classical conditioning contingencies are (explicitly) programmed during the establishment of the secondary reinforcer. A particularly interesting example is an experiment reported by Butter and Thomas (1958).

In this experiment one of two different concentrations of sucrose, 8% and 24%, was presented to rats after the audible click of the mechanism which delivered it. Following this classical conditioning phase of the experiment a bar was made available to the animals, depression of which produced the same click, but no other reinforcement. The rats pressed the bar more than controls for whom the click had never been associated with reward. This result demonstrates that classical conditioning with an S^{R+} serving as the UCS is able to confer secondary reinforcing properties on the CS paired with the UCS.

Butter and Thomas's (1958) experiment also demonstrates a second important point: that so-called "incentive motivation" may be a consequence of such classically conditioned secondary reinforcement. "Incentive" is defined by Logan (1968, p. 3), in the particular context of runway experiments, as follows: "If a rat's performance in an alley is differentially affected by the reward he has previously received in the goal box, then some internal consequent of the reward must be present while he is in the alley before the reward is received. 'Incentive' is our word for this consequent." Now there are a host of observations which show that the speed of learning and vigour of performance of an instrumental response (running an alley, pressing a bar etc.) are positive functions of the quantity, quality or frequency of reward by which the response is followed (Kimble, 1961; Logan, 1968), though there are occasional conflicting reports (Black, 1969). These then, are the major variables which determine "incentive motivation". (It is assumed, of course, that learning rate and performance vigour both increase with increasing incentive motivation.)

If we now return to Butter and Thomas's experiment we may note one further feature of their results. It is known that a more concentrated sucrose solution maintains a higher level of instrumental performance and learning than does a solution of lower concentration, if both are used as rewards in the normal way (e.g. Ison, 1964; Rosen, 1966). As we have already seen, Butter and Thomas exposed two different groups to classical conditioning with the click CS: one with 8% sucrose solution as the UCS, the other with 24% sucrose. In the test phase of the experiment the 24% group had a significantly higher rate of response on the lever producing the click than the 8% group. Thus a result was obtained with purely classical conditioning techniques which parallels the instrumental learning phenomena normally subsumed under the concept of incentive motivation.

Taken altogether, therefore, Butter and Thomas's results suggest the following possibilities: (a) that secondary reinforcement is normally based on classical conditioning; (b) that the degree of secondary reinforcing effect conditioned in this way is greater, the greater the effectiveness of the S^{R+} as a primary reinforcer; and (c) that incentive motivation is a consequence of the secondary reinforcement so conditioned.

These suggestions, however, take us beyond the notion of simple positive feedback as we have so far encountered it. In the example we used earlier, drinking behaviour, we saw positive feedback at work as a strengthening of the act of drinking in consequence of feedback signals derived from this very same act of drinking (McFarland and McFarland, 1968). If we assumed that this kind of system was general for all motivated behaviour, we would need only to suppose a set of pre-wired (i.e. independent of learning or experience) positive feedback mechanisms, one for each kind of behaviour (eating, copulation, sleeping etc.). Clearly, however, something more is involved in experiments such as Butter and Thomas's: the facilitation produced by the click associated with sucrose accrued, not to the innate activity of ingesting sucrose, but to the learned activity of pressing a bar. Is it possible to extend the notions we have encountered in this chapter to encompass this kind of learning?

Deutsch's Theory

A system which appears in principle to achieve this end has been proposed by J. A. Deutsch (1964b). Although the empirical evidence for Deutsch's theory is weak, it is worth describing in some detail, since it is the most thoroughly worked-out model available for a learning mechanism based on principles of positive feedback. The theory involves two basic kinds of elements, "links" and "analyzers", hypothetical entities deemed to be located somewhere in the CNS.

There is, to begin with, a "primary link" for each specific drive, e.g. hunger, thirst, sexual behaviour. This primary link is "set into activity by, or sensitive to, a specific change or state of the fluid surrounding it" (Deutsch, 1964b; p. 24). (For example, in the case of hunger, some correlate of blood-sugar level might, after a certain

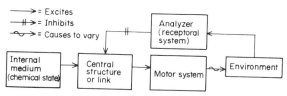

FIG. 5.3. Deutsch's Drive Model. See text for explanation. (From Deutsch, 1964b.)

period of time without food, cause activity to commence in special cells located in the lateral hypothalamus: Le Magnen, 1971.) This primary link causes activity in the motor system (which, in the case of purely innate behaviour, might consist, e.g. of eating) and this activity in turn produces stimuli which are received by an analyser which is joined to the link (e.g. an analyser sensitive to changes in blood-sugar level). The analyser, when activated in this way, turns off activity in the primary link. This part of Deutsch's theory (which is a simple *negative* feedback loop of the kind presented in Fig. 5.1) is shown in Fig. 5.3. (In the case of hunger, the primary link might be instanced by the cells in the lateral hypothalamus which appear to initiate eating behaviour, and the corresponding analyser by the cells in the medial hypothalamus which appear to terminate it: Grossman, 1967; Le Magnen, 1971.)

Deutsch goes on to postulate "secondary" links, each with a corresponding "analyser" attached to it. The function of all analysers is to receive a certain kind of stimulation. The function of all links is to produce a certain kind of motor output. The difference between a secondary link-plus-analyser and a primary link-plus-analyser is two-fold. (1) A secondary link receives its excitation, not from the change in the internal medium which excites a primary link, but in consequence of attachment to a chain of links, of which the first member is a primary link. (2) A secondary analyser does not turn off activity in a secondary link. On the contrary:

> When such a link is receiving excitation from a primary link and stimulation from the analyser, it will persist in exciting the same part of the motor system, and so maintain the same movement pattern, while the stimulation of it by the analyser increases. When there is a decrease, its motor output will vary, and will alter its movement pattern. *A link will thus tend to maximize its own stimulation* (Deutsch, 1964b, p. 36).

In other words, a secondary link-plus-analyser is a *positive* feedback loop.

According to Deutsch's theory, behaviour is controlled by chains of such links-plus-analysers, the first member of each chain being a primary link-plus-analyser. Excitation is transmitted down such a chain from the primary link, so that, in the absence of an appropriate input to the primary link (i.e. in the absence of the relevant specific drive), the whole chain is quiescent. If the primary link is being excited, excitation is transmitted to the last link in the chain. This link then gains control of the motor system, and varies the behavioural output of the organism until its attached analyser fires. The active link then maximizes its own stimulation as outlined in the previous paragraph.

A link whose analyser is firing ceases to transmit excitation further along the chain of links. It is this feature of Deutsch's model, together with the rules for the initial formation of a chain of links, which allows the organism to perform a goal-directed behavioural sequence, the end result of which is to attain a goal-object relevant to the drive state which triggers activity in the primary link of the chain. Let us look at each of these aspects of Deutsch's model, commencing with the formation of a chain of links-plus-analysers during learning.

Deutsch supposes, in fact, that the chain of links-plus-analysers which underlies a learned behaviour sequence is no different (except for how it comes into being) from a chain underlying an innate behaviour sequence (e.g. one involved in copulatory behaviour in, say, the rat): "for innate behaviour such a structure is present at birth; for learned behaviour it must be built up" (*op cit.*, p. 43). Deutsch goes on:

> It is supposed that prior to learning there are in the nervous system many units consisting of an analyser connected to a link. This link is in its turn connected to the motor system. During the course of learning, the links become attached to each other, according to the following principle.
>
> *When there is a link whose analyser is stimulated, another link, whose analyser has just ceased to be stimulated, will be attached to the first link, so that this first link will transmit excitation to it.*
>
> Thus temporal succession of the stimulation of analysers by cues will lead to an ordinal proximity of attachment when the row of links is formed . . . Therefore, when an animal is put in a maze and it sees cue *a*, which is then followed by cue *b*, then the link whose analyser is set off by cue *a* will be attached to the link whose analyser is set off by cue *b*. If cue *b* is then followed by the stimuli of food, then a similar connection will take place. As this food will be connected to a primary link, excited by a food deficit, the next time a food deficit occurs the primary link will be excited. This primary link will pass its excitation on to the food link, which will pass it on to the cue *b* link, which will pass it on to the cue *a* link. Thus the whole row which has been formed will be excited.

In this way, then, Deutsch sets up an ordered row of links-plus-analysers, corresponding to the sequence of spatial locations which an animal would encounter on its way through a maze to a food-baited goal. The navigation of the animal, placed at the beginning of such a sequence, along it to the goal is ensured by the rule that a link whose analyser is firing ceases to transmit excitation further along the chain of links. Deutsch supposes, reasonably, that, when the animal acts so as to maximize its stimulation by cue *a* (whose analyser is currently firing), it is highly likely to encounter stimulation from cue *b*, the next cue along in the direction of the goal (e.g. a rat placed in the startbox of a runway will almost certainly catch sight of the rest of the runway). When cue *b* fires its appropriate analyser, two things happen: (1) the attached link ceases to transmit excitation to the cue *a* link, which thus loses control of the motor system; and (2) the cue *b* link itself takes control of the motor system and the animal therefore acts so as to maximize stimulation from cue *b*, i.e. it approaches it. This action will, in turn, expose the animal to the next cue in the series, and so on until the goal object is reached.

This part of Deutsch's model is presented schematically in Fig. 5.4. Some such principle as this will need to be a feature of almost any model for learning which involves positive feedback, since, without it, the animal will remain permanently locked in to whatever secondarily reinforcing cue it first chances upon.

Earlier in this chapter I expressed the hope that an alliance between the principles of positive feedback and classical conditioning might be able to offer a solution to the problem of how positive reinforcers work. In effect, though not couched in these terms, Deutsch's theory accomplishes just this. The rule he enunciates for the chaining-together of links during learning (see above) is roughly equivalent to an S → S classical conditioning process. Together with

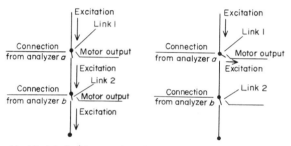

Fig. 5.4. Deutsch's Model for Approach Behaviour. The effect, in Deutsch's model, of stimulating an analyser on the flow of excitation. A link will transmit excitation to another link until the analyser attached to it is stimulated. The excitation will then be switched to control the motor system. For further explanation see text. (From Deutsch, 1964.)

the other rules of his model, it makes it possible to extend the principle of positive feedback beyond the limited function of maintaining behaviour directly focused on an S^{R+} (as in McFarland and McFarland's experiment on drinking in the dove) to the elicitation of goal-directed behaviour in the absence of the goal itself.

Incentive Motivation

These various lines of argument, then, appear gradually to be converging on a fairly powerful theory. In this theory, the process of secondary reinforcement seems destined to play an important part. (One way to view Deutsch's model is as a theory of the formation and functioning of secondary positive reinforcement.) As we have seen, the process of secondary reinforcement is not only likely to be involved in the retrograde effect of primary reinforcement which lies at the heart of goal-directed instrumental learning, but also to underlie the phenomenon of incentive motivation, i.e., the fact that the performance of an instrumental response chain has higher probability and/or vigour, the greater the degree of primary positive reinforcement (varied by quantity, duration, frequency or quality) which follows it. There is even a suggestion, from an ingenious experiment by Powell and Perkins (1957), that incentive motivation is *entirely* dependent on secondary reinforcement.

These workers first showed that different strengths of secondary reinforcement could be established by allowing rats to eat for 10 or

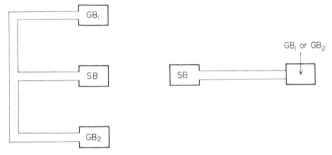

FIG. 5.5. Powell and Perkins' Experiment on Secondary Reinforcement. The E-maze (left) and straight alley (right) used by Powell and Perkins (1957). SB: startbox. GB$_1$ and GB$_2$: two goalboxes, each associated with different durations of access to food reward in the two apparatuses, as described in the text. (From Powell and Perkins, 1957.)

150 sec, respectively, in two distinctive goalboxes at the end of a straight alley along which they were first required to run. This demonstration of differential degrees of secondary reinforcement was accomplished by allowing the animals to choose in an E-shaped maze (Fig. 5.2) between two routes leading to the two different goal-boxes: the goalbox in which 150 sec feeding had previously been allowed was now chosen, even though 20 sec feeding was allowed in both goalboxes in this phase of the experiment. In a second experiment, trials in the straight alley and in the E-maze were interspersed with each other. In the E-maze (in which, of course, the animal could not see the goalboxes when it left the startbox) 10 sec eating was allowed in one goalbox and 150 sec in the second one. In the interspersed trials in the straight alley, the values of eating times associated with the two goalboxes was reversed, 10 sec being allowed in

the goalbox which, in the E-maze, was allocated 150 sec and 150 sec in the goalbox which, in the E-maze, was allocated 10 sec. Under these conditions, the rats *failed* to learn to choose the route to the 150 sec goalbox in the E-maze.

One interpretation of these results is as follows. The preference which would normally be shown for the goalbox associated with a longer reward is due to the differential degree to which secondary reinforcing value is conferred on the stimuli (i.e. in this particular experiment, the distinctive goalboxes and the routes leading to them) associated with the two durations of reward. However, in Powell and Perkins' second experiment, the interspersed trials in the straight alley, with the reversed association between goalbox and reward duration, equalized the degree of secondary reinforcement which accrued to the two goalboxes. There was therefore no basis on which the rats could learn the route to the goalbox associated in the E-maze with the longer reward. If this interpretation is correct, it implies that *different magnitudes of primary reinforcement have no additional effect on learning besides that of acting as UCSs for the conditioning of different magnitudes of secondary reinforcement to the stimuli immediatedly associated with them.*

A further implication of the Powell and Perkins experiment concerns the operation of what Hull (1932) called the "goal gradient". The most obvious experimental observation underlying the notion of a goal gradient is the fact that, in a straight alley, rats run faster, the closer they approach the goal (Hull, 1934). Since this kind of finding could be contaminated by purely physical factors determining initial inertia and the rate of gain of momentum, etc., it is comforting to have a similar report in a different situation in which such factors cannot apply: Becker and Bruning (1966) trained rats to turn five wheels successively in order to obtain a food reward and duly found that the rate of turning each wheel increased with closeness of the wheel-turn to the terminal point in time of food-delivery. Thus it seems in general to be the case that, the closer a response is in time and space to the terminal S^{R+}, the more vigorous is the response: this is the goal gradient. Now this could be attributed to the effects of delay of reinforcement: both in classical conditioning and in instrumental learning it is known that the strength of learning falls off rapidly as the interval between CS and UCS or R and S^{R+}, respectively, is increased. Obviously, if there is a five-part response chain of the kind used by Becker and Bruning, the first response in the chain suffers greater delay of reinforcement than does the fifth. However, the results of the Powell and Perkins experiment suggest that the principle of delay of reinforcement is insufficient, without further complication, to account for all the ways in which a terminal reinforcer transmits its effectiveness back along the chain of responses upon which it is contingent.

Consider rats in the Powell and Perkins E-maze which are simply trained to go to the one of two goalboxes containing the longer of two durations of reward. We may analyse this situation into two competing response-chains, each of the kind pictured in Fig. 5.6. We may suppose that S_2, S_3 and S_4, consequent upon R_1, R_2 and R_3,

$$S_1 \rightarrow R_1 \rightarrow S_2 \rightarrow R_2 \rightarrow S_3 \rightarrow R_3 \rightarrow S_4 \rightarrow R_4 \rightarrow S_5 \rightarrow R_G \rightarrow S^{R+}$$

$$S_1' \rightarrow R_1' \rightarrow S_2' \rightarrow R_2' \rightarrow S_3' \rightarrow R_3' \rightarrow S_4' \rightarrow R_4' \rightarrow S_5' \rightarrow R_G' \rightarrow S'^{R+}$$

FIG. 5.6. Stimuli and Responses Involved in Serial Response Chains. Stimulus-response chains involved in learning a task such as that posed by Powell and Perkins' E-maze (Fig. 5.5) may be analysed as shown: the upper chain may be taken as leading to the goalbox in which the longer duration of reward (S^{R+}) was available, the lower chain as leading to the goalbox in which the shorter duration of reward (S'^{R+}) was available. For further explanation, see text.

in each of these two chains have all acquired some secondary reinforcing properties and, further, that (in virtue of the goal-gradient) this property is stronger for S_4 than for S_3 and for S_3 than for S_2. Furthermore, it is natural to suppose that the secondary reinforcing effect of each stimulus in the chain leading to the shorter duration of reward is less than the secondary reinforcing effect of the corresponding stimulus in the chain leading to the longer duration of reward. Thus, at any point at which the two chains could be simultaneously evoked, the animal will make that response which leads him further along the chain terminating in the longer duration of reward. In this way, the principles of secondary reinforcement and the goal-gradient appear to be able to predict the known outcome: that animals will learn to go to the longer duration of reward under such conditions.

However, Powell and Perkins' results force us to examine more closely the way in which a secondary reinforcer (other than the one closest in point of time and/or space to the primary S^{R+}) obtains its secondary reinforcing property. As we have seen, Powell and Perkins were able to block learning of the route to the longer reward by interspersing trials in a straight alley in which the long-reward goalbox in the E-maze became a short-reward goalbox in the alley, and *vice versa*. We interpreted this blockage as being due to an equalizing of secondary rewarding effects as between the two goalboxes (which are the stimuli closest in time and space to the terminal reinforcers in the E-maze). In other words, if we have two response-chains of the kind pictured in Fig. 5.6, the secondary reinforcing effects of S_5 in the two chains have become equal. But reference to Fig. 5.6, and the response-chains which were required of the rats in Powell and Perkins' E-maze, will show that this will prevent the animals from developing a greater tendency to initiate the chain leading to the longer duration of reward only if the equalization of secondary reinforcement at S_5 is carried back along the chain to S_4, S_3 and S_2. That is to say, learning would be blocked only if the secondary reinforcing powers of stimuli early in the response-chain depended, not on their distance in time and space from the terminal reinforcer, but on the secondarily reinforcing powers of the stimulus which immediately follows them in the chain, S_4 depending on S_5, S_3 on S_4 and so on. It seems possible, therefore, that a response such as that of running down an alley or choosing the right path in a maze is based on a series of secondary reinforcers, the one standing closest to the goal having the goal object itself as the required UCS/S^{R+}, the next one in the chain then using this first secondary reinforcer as *its* UCS, and so on to the start of the response chain; each new secondary reinforcer being some-what weaker than the one which has served as its UCS for the conditioning of the secondary reinforcing effect.

If this analysis (which is essentially the same as Powell and Perkins' own) is correct, it implies that elimination of secondary reinforcement over an interval of time elapsing between a response and a primary S^{R+} would render learning and goal-directed behaviour with respect to this S^{R+} extremely difficult, if not impossible. The evidence on the effects of delay of reinforcement (now considered as a phenomenon in its own right *requiring* explanation rather than, as just previously, an explanatory principle which might account for the goal-gradient) is very much in agreement with this deduction. In conventional reinforcement situations it is no simple task to eliminate secondary reinforcement attaching (as it presumably does) not only to the environment in which, say, food or water is delivered, but also to the proprioceptive, postural, exteroceptive and other direct consequences of the actual making of the response upon which the S^{R+} is contingent, as well as those resulting from the consummatory response elicited by the S^{R+}. (Such response-produced stimuli are included among those pictured in Fig. 5.6, and we shall soon have occasion to talk to them again.) Even so, ingenious attempts have been made to achieve this end, and the results of such

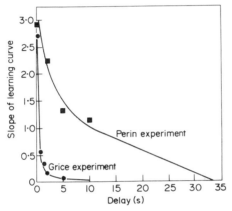

FIG. 5.7. Effects of Delay of Conventional Reinforcement on Learning. Results obtained by Perin (1943) in the Skinner box and Grice (1948) in a discrimination learning experiment. Grice's procedure was much more effective in eliminating secondary reinforcement. (From Kimble, 1961.)

experiments are clear in showing that, the more effective the elimination of secondary reinforcers, the poorer is the ability of the animal to learn to make the goal-response with an imposed delay of reward. Since these studies are reviewed in a number of accessible sources (e.g., Kimble, 1961, p. 150), we shall content ourselves here with showing the effects of delay of reward obtained in two experiments (Perin, 1943; Grice, 1948) which succeeded in eliminating secondary reinforcement to different degrees (Fig. 5.7).

More recently, the effects of delay of reinforcement have become dramatically evident in a situation in which it is possible to eliminate secondary reinforcement to a much greater degree than hitherto, while at the same time varying very precisely the interval between response and reinforcement. This situation is that of electrical self-stimulation of the brain. The lack of any consummatory response directed to the S^{R+} in this response effectively disposes of a major source of secondary reinforcement necessarily present when more conventional rewards are used. Perhaps for this reason there have been over the last decade a number of experimental indications that self-stimulation is extremely sensitive to delay of reinforcement. This problem has now been directly investigated by Hurwitz and James (1970). Their rats were implanted with electrodes in the medial forebrain bundle, the main focus for

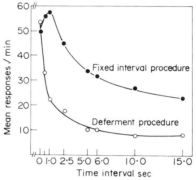

FIG. 5.8. Effects of Delay of Reinforcement on Learning in a Self-Stimulation Experiment. Mean barpressing rates when electrical stimulation of the medial forebrain bundle (the S^{R+}) was delayed by the time shown on the abscissa ("deferment procedure") or with fixed interval reinforcement at the intervals shown on the abscissa ("fixed interval procedure"). (From Hurwitz and James, 1970.)

the self-stimulation phenomenon. Rates of response were compared when the response (pressing a bar) was followed immediately by reinforcement and when delays ranging from 0.5 to 15.0 s were interposed between response and reinforcement, each rat being tested in each session at every delay value, including zero. (It should be noted that with this procedure "zero delay" truly is zero delay, since stimulation is delivered to the brain with a speed determined only by electrical delay in the circuitry.) As a control procedure to allow for the reduced rate at which stimulation is received by the rats as delay of reinforcement is increased, response rates were also recorded under a "fixed interval" procedure with the same intervals. (In a fixed interval schedule, a fixed time must elapse between successive reinforcements. The first response after this time has passed is reinforced with zero delay, but responses occurring earlier go unreinforced.) The results of the experiment are shown in Fig. 5.8. The steep decline in rate of response when reinforcement was delayed even by as little as 0.5 sec is evident (the curve labelled "deferment procedure"). Furthermore, this result was obtained *after* the animals had been fully trained with zero delay and with periods of zero delay of reward still occurring in every test session. Thus all the animal was required to do was to maintain a simple response which was already well learnt. It seems quite possible that, if the animal was trained from the start with delay of reward or was required to learn something more complex than barpressing, learning for electrical stimulation of the brain would be impossible even at very short delays. This possibility deserves further investigation.

The Mechanism of Positive Reinforcement

These various lines of argument, then, lead us to the following hypotheses concerning the mechanism of positive reinforcement. An S^{R+} is a stimulus which has two essential properties (though it may also have other, inessential ones, especially that of causing satiation):

(1) It activates a positive feedback mechanism to maintain behaviour directed towards itself, as in the McFarland and McFarland (1968) experiment on drinking in the dove.

(2) It acts as the UCS for the conferral, by classical conditioning, on stimuli which stand in relation to it as CSs of (a) the same kind of positive feedback properties as it possesses itself, and (b) the ability to act as a UCS in a further repetition of the same conditioning process.

Postulate (2), it should be noted, called on one process for which we have so far given only indirect empirical justification: that of "higher-order" classical conditioning. This refers to a classical conditioning pairing of the usual form, $S_1 \rightarrow S_2$, but in which the S_2 has itself previously been established as a CS by being paired with a primary UCS. Suppose, for example, the UCS is food, eliciting salivation as an innate UCR. First-order conditioning is carried out by pairing, say, a tone with food, until the tone produces a salivary CR. Pairing of a light with the tone (without direct pairing of light and food) may now result in the light acquiring the capacity to elicit a salivary CR (Pavlov, 1927). This is "second-order" conditioning. Pavlov, in his work with dogs, found evidence for "third-order" conditioning (in which some third CS would now be paired with the light) but only with an aversive primary UCS. In the rat, a clear demonstration of second-order conditioning has recently been reported by Rizley and Rescorla (1972), using conditioned suppression of barpressing behaviour with shock as the primary UCS. The theoretical importance of this phenomenon, however, calls for far more empirical investigation than it has so far received.

With two additional postulates, these hypotheses are able to provide a general mechanism whereby the animal is guided to the points in its spatio-temporal environment at which primary reinforcers are to be found. These additional postulates are:

(3) The degree to which a CS acquires secondary reinforcing property (1) listed above is proportional to, but always less than, the degree to which this property is possessed by the stimulus which has acted for it as UCS.

(4) Responding is directed towards that one of several simultaneously present stimuli which has the higher degree of reinforcing property (1). (This postulate is the equivalent of that part of Deutsch's model which was pictured in Fig. 5.4.)

Finally, with one further addition this mechanism is able to provide the animal with the ability to learn a response or response-chain which is followed by presentation of the terminal S^{R+}, viz.,

(5) Response-produced stimuli are able to serve as CSs and acquire secondarily reinforcing properties in the same way as any other stimuli.

This hypothesis is essentially the same as that proposed by Mowrer in 1960. In its general form, i.e. when applied to negative as well as positive reinforcers, it is known as "two-process theory": that is, a theory which supposes that observed instrumental learning and behaviour is the outcome of an interaction between two underlying processes, one (a classical conditioning component) responsible for the acquisition by initially neutral stimuli of reinforcing and motivational properties, the other (the instrumental component proper) responsible for the guidance of behaviour in such a way as to maximize positive reinforcement and minimize negative reinforcement. These two components correspond respectively to properties (2) and (1) given above to an S^{R+}. As we have seen, a very similar model, but couched in quite different terms, was also proposed by Deutsch, in 1960. Readers who wish to go further into the way in which such a learning mechanism might work are referred to these two sources. (We shall ourselves meet two-process theory frequently in later chapters.)

In the statement of two-process theory just given, there are two points which call for comment and amplification.

The first of these arises out of Postulate (2). By treating classical conditioning as a process whereby certain properties possessed by the UCS are transferred to the CS, this runs the risk of contradicting the modified stimulus substitution rule of classical conditioning which we adopted in Chapter 2. As we originally met this rule, it was stated thus: any component which exists in the vector of response changes elicited by the CS after conditioning also exists in the UCS vector and with the same direction of change. Stated in this way, the emphasis is on the actual *responses* elicited by the CS and the UCS. But Postulate (2) is couched in terms of *properties of stimuli*. And, while it is true that the only way to detect the properties of stimuli is by showing that they elicit or alter the animal's responses, the two kinds of terminology are not equivalent to each other. In particular, talk about properties of stimuli is *dispositional*. To say that a UCS possesses the property of activating a positive feedback mechanism is to suggest a whole range of responses which one might expect to observe under appropriate experimental conditions. Similarly, to say that the CS acquires this same property as a result of conditioning is to suggest that one might expect to observe the same range of responses under the same experimental conditions. But it does not imply that only those responses which were actually elicited by the UCS will actually be produced by the CS, as does the stimulus substitution rule expressed in terms of responses.

It is not difficult to see that data on secondary reinforcement, of a kind we have already considered in this chapter, render a response version of the modified rule of stimulus substitution untenable. Take for example, Butter and Thomas's (1958) experiment. In this, as we have seen, rats were exposed to the S → S pairing, click → sucrose. Following this, a bar was made available to them, depression of which produced the same click, but no other reinforcement. The rats pressed the bar at a significantly higher rate than controls for which the click-sucrose pairing had not been performed. Now it is clear from all that we know about barpressing and sucrose that, given the opportunity, most rats would learn to press a bar for a sucrose reward. So the fact that they press a bar to obtain a click previously paired with sucrose is fully in accord with a stimulus-property version of the stimulus substitution rule: the CS acquires a property possessed by the UCS. But it is equally clear that, in the actual conditions of Butter and Thomas's experiment, sucrose (the UCS) neither elicited nor reinforced barpressing—it could not, since the bar was not in the experimental chamber at the time. Thus, on a response version of the stimulus substitution rule, the fact that the CS came to act as a reinforcer for barpressing is inexplicable. Other similar examples will occur later in this chapter, when we look at the motivational properties of CSs paired with an S^{R+}/UCS (see for example the description below of Estes' 1948 experiment).

The modified stimulus substitution rule for classical conditioning must, therefore, be further modified to take a stimulus-property form: any property which the CS comes to possess in consequence of being paired with a UCS according to an $S \rightarrow S$ classical conditioning contingency is a property also possessed by the UCS (this excludes of course, properties already possessed by the CS prior to conditioning); though the UCS may possess other properties which do not pass to the CS in consequence of conditioning. It is in this form that we shall understand the modified stimulus substitution rule henceforth. (Of course, the response version of the stimulus substitution rule is subsumed under this new formulation.)

Given this reformulation of the stimulus substitution rule, it is worth re-examining a phenomenon we originally encountered in Chapter 2, namely, autoshaping. As will be recalled, this phenomenon was first observed in pigeons: a hungry bird comes to peck at a key which is regularly illuminated before the delivery of grain, even though no response contingency holds between pecking and grain-delivery (Brown and Jenkins, 1968). We considered several arguments in Chapter 2 which give rise to the view that the keypecking "auto-shaped" in this way is a classically conditioned response which mimics an operant response. This view has been questioned, however. In particular it has been pointed out that a rule to the effect that classical conditioning results in the elicitation by the CS of a response initially elicited by the UCS (i.e. the response version of the stimulus substitution rule) tells you nothing about the *direction* of the response so elicited. Thus, it is argued (Brown and Jenkins, 1968; Williams and Williams, 1969), to treat autoshaping as a case of classical conditioning may allow you to predict that the lighted key will elicit keypecking, but not that the keypecking will be directed at the key. Clearly, a prediction of pecking without any prediction of the target which is pecked is rather inadequate. So, it is maintained, to treat autoshaping as a case of classical conditioning is equally inadequate.

This general kind of point had in fact been made much earlier by Zener (1937). He commented on the fact that the conditioned salivary response, so extensively used by Pavlov, has no directional properties: the animal does not salivate in the direction of the CS, nor in some other direction, he just salivates. Furthermore, the traditional Pavlovian situation has the traditional dog tied down in a harness, so that, if the animal does acquire any directional response tendencies, he cannot display them. Zener therefore, carried out a Pavlovian salivary conditioning experiment with free-moving dogs, and he observed pronounced tendencies for animals to orient towards, approach and investigate CSs which were followed by a food UCS.

It is clear, then, both from the autoshaping studies and from Zener's earlier experiments, that a CS paired with a UCS/S^{R+} acquires the property of eliciting approach and investigatory behaviour (and sometimes consummatory behaviour: Moore, 1973; see chapter 2) *directed towards itself*. This, of course, merely repeats points already made in this chapter, especially in the form of Postulates (1) and (2) above. For these state that a CS which has been paired with a UCS/S^{R+} acquires a conditioned property of acting on a positive feedback mechanism so as to maintain behaviour directed towards itself. Thus the directional aspects of the auto-shaped keypeck are entirely in agreement with the theory proposed in this chapter, and also with the stimulus-property version of the stimulus substitution rule for classical conditioning.

The second point calling for amplification in the statement of two-process theory encapsulated in Postulates (1)–(5) concerns motivation. The theory treats classical conditioning as conferring on initially neutral stimuli paired with reinforcers both reinforcing and motivational properties. So far, however, we have been concerned with the acquisition of secondarily reinforcing properties and have said nothing about motivation. Operationally, the distinction between reinforcing properties and motivational properties is simply this: reinforcement is the term used in a case in which presentation of a stimulus following a response alters the probability or vigour of emission of the response on subsequent occasions; motivation is the term used in a case in which presentation of a stimulus prior to or simultaneously with the emission of a response alters the probability or vigour of emission of the response at that time.

Let us turn, then, to the evidence that pairing an initially neutral stimulus with an S^{R+} is able to confer on it motivational properties. An example is provided by an experiment of Estes (1948). Rats were

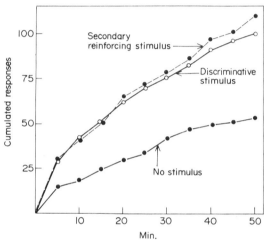

FIG. 5.9. Comparison between Secondary Reinforcing and Motivational Properties of a Discriminative Stimulus. Results from Dinsmoor (1950). For further explanation see text, in which the condition labelled "discriminative stimulus" is referred to as "motivational". (Figure from Kimble, 1961.)

first given pairings, according to a classical conditioning procedure, of tone as CS and food as UCS. The animals were then trained to press a bar for a food reward in the absence of any tone. In the final phase of the experiment the barpressing response was extinguished and at times during the extinction session the tone initially paired with food was sounded. Response rate on the bar was significantly higher when the tone was presented in this way. Note that the barpress did not alter in any way the presentation of the tone: this remained on whether the rats pressed the bar or not. Thus the effect described by Estes cannot be considered one of secondary reinforcement; though it is likely that a suitable test would have shown that the tone was *also* a secondary reinforcer.

An important aspect of Estes' procedure in this experiment is that the classical conditioning pairings were given under conditions in which the animal was not performing the instrumental response, changes in which were subsequently used to evaluate the effects of the CS. This procedure is sometimes referred to as classical conditioning "off the baseline", as distinguished from the case in which the CS → UCS pairings are presented to the animal "on the baseline", i.e. while it is actually engaged in performing the operant response. A number of recent experiments (e.g. Azrin and Hake, 1969; Henton and Brady, 1970; LoLordo, 1971; Miczek and Grossman, 1971), using the latter procedure, have obtained more complex, and conflicting, results when investigating the effects of CSs paired with the UCS of food on operant response rates for food. However, conditioning on the baseline is inherently more complex than conditioning off the baseline, and much more difficult to analyse theoretically. We shall, therefore, for the most part ignore such experiments, not only in dealing with the effects of CSs paired with rewards on rewarded operant behaviour, but also when we come to deal with other reinforcing events*.

A direct comparison between the secondarily reinforcing and motivational properties of a stimulus paired with an S^{R+} has been made by Dinsmoor (1950). He first trained rats on a discrimination in which barpressing in the light was reinforced by food, while barpressing in the dark was not. During this discrimination procedure, the light was turned on after the animal had remained in the dark for 30 sec without responding. The next response, which of course occurred in the light, was reinforced with food and the lights were then turned off again. After 200 reinforcements had been obtained, extinction was carried out under one of three conditions with three separate groups of rats: (1) in the dark; (2) in the dark, but with each response turning on the light for 3 sec in a test of secondary reinforcement; (3) in the light, each response turning off the light for 3 sec to see whether the light would increase responding by a motivational, as distinct from reinforcing, influence. The results of the experiment appear in Fig. 5.9. It can be seen that responding was higher under both conditions in which the light was present

---

* An exception to this rule is the treatment in Chapter 8 of the effects of CSs paired with an S^{R-} as UCS on rewarded operant baselines. In this instance the results of studies using classical conditioning on and off the baseline are in substantial agreement with each other.

during extinction, and to very much the same degree whether the light was acting in a reinforcing or in a motivating capacity. (That these results were not due to an effect of light *per se* is clear from the fact that half of Dinsmoor's subjects in fact had light and dark reversed both during acquisition and extinction. Essentially the same results were obtained when dark acted as the S^D for barpressing as when light played this role.)

Dinsmoor himself viewed his results in a slightly different way: namely, as showing that (as proposed by Skinner, 1938) a stimulus is a secondary reinforcer only to the extent that it is a discriminative stimulus. As we have seen before, an S^D is a stimulus in the presence of which an instrumental response is reinforced, while it is not reinforced in its absence. Clearly, the light in the training phase of Dinsmoor's experiment was just such a stimulus. Furthermore, the results he obtained in condition (3) of the extinction phase showed that the probability of emission of the barpressing response in the presence of light had been increased by this kind of training; and this is the evidence which is usually required as showing that a putative discriminative stimulus has indeed obtained discriminative control over the response.

A discriminative stimulus necessarily gives the animal information about the primary reinforcer: it says, in effect, "if you respond now, you will be reinforced, while responses at other times will not be reinforced". Egger and Miller (1962, 1963) have stressed the informational aspect of secondary reinforcers in a hypothesis which is closely related to the Skinner–Dinsmoor discriminative stimulus hypothesis. According to Egger and Miller, a stimulus paired with an S^{R+} takes on secondary reinforcing power only to the extent that it predicts the occurrence of the S^{R+}—mere temporal contiguity is not enough.

In a test of this hypothesis, Egger and Miller (1963) first trained rats to barpress for food, and then exposed different groups to one of the classical conditioning procedures pictured in Fig. 5.10. In the "redundant" condition, the CS whose secondarily reinforcing power was subsequently to be tested preceded the delivery of three food pellets, but was itself regularly preceded by one pellet. Thus, the initial pellet already conveyed to the rat with perfect certainty the information that three more pellets would be forthcoming, and the CS conveyed no additional information. In the "simple conditioning" procedure, the CS preceded the three pellets in the usual way and was predictive of their occurrence; additional deliveries of single pellets at other times in the session controlled for any non-informational aspects of the single pellets in the redundant procedure. In the "informative" procedure, the one pellet-CS-three pellets sequence was presented, as in the redundant procedure, but additional presentations of single pellets on their own had the consequence that the CS informed the

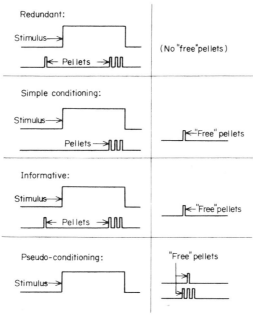

FIG. 5.10. Design of Egger and Miller's Experiment. For explanation see text. (From Egger and Miller, 1963.)

animal of those occasions on which the three pellets were also forthcoming. Finally, in the pseudoconditioning control procedure, the stimulus was presented without association with pellets at all. The effects of the stimuli set up in these four ways were evaluated by presenting them during a subsequent barpressing session under extinction conditions are far as the primary reinforcer (food) was concerned, but with the CS made contingent upon responding.

The results are shown in Fig. 5.11. It can be seen that the rate of barpressing was much higher after the simple conditioning and informative procedures than after the redundant procedure. The redundant procedure in fact (unlike the other two procedures) did not produce a significantly higher response rate than that observed in the pseudoconditioning control group; though it appears from Fig. 5.11 that some degree of secondary reinforcement was maintained by the CS in the redundant group. Egger and Miller suggest that this

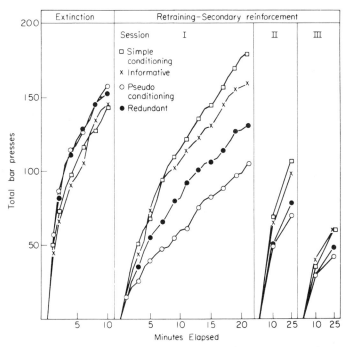

FIG. 5.11. Results of Egger and Miller's Experiment. The average cumulative response curves for the four groups (which had previously received the treatments diagrammed in Fig. 5.10) during extinction and in three subsequent "retraining" sessions in which only the CS was contingent upon barpressing. (From Egger and Miller, 1963.)

residual degree of secondary reinforcement can be explained in terms of the informational hypothesis by the temporal information which the CS offered to the rats in the redundant group: "three more pellets coming 1.5 sec after the stimulus begins". Be that as it may, it seems clear that the secondary reinforcing power of the CS under the conditions of their experiment was determined more by its informational content than by mere temporal contiguity, as their hypothesis holds.

Notice that this result does not contradict the view that secondary reinforcement is based on classical conditioning. On the contrary, it extends the conclusions we have already reached concerning classical conditioning to the case of secondary positive reinforcement. It will be recalled that, when we discussed in Chapter 2 the view that temporal contiguity between CS and UCS is both a necessary and a sufficient condition for classical conditioning to take place, we cited in opposition to this view the experiments of Kamin on blocking of the CER. Our conclusion there was that "in addition to temporal contiguity and a CS $\rightarrow$ UCS sequence with normally effective CS and UCS it is necessary, if classical conditioning is to take place, for the CS to convey some new information to the subject—i.e. the UCS should not be already fully predictable from the other CSs to which the animal is simultaneously exposed". This conclusion can stand without modification in application to Egger and Miller's experiment.

The conferral of motivational properties on a CS paired with an S^{R+}/UCS is also in harmony with the modified stimulus substitution rule for classical conditioning as it was formulated in Chapter 2: i.e. no response produced by the CS unless it is also produced by the UCS. This rule would lead us to expect (in parallel with effects of a CS, previously paired with a food UCS, on an operant baseline reinforced by food: see above) that food itself, delivered independently of the ongoing operant response, would increase the rate of this response. Just this result has been obtained in recent studies (Neuringer, 1969; Rescorla and Skucy, 1969) in which food has been delivered independently of responding during the extinction of an operant response previously reinforced with food.

Classical conditioning of an initially neutral stimulus which is predictive of the occurrence of an S^{R+}, then, confers both reinforcing and motivational properties on the stimulus. These properties, moreover, are quite general. Thus the secondary reinforcing property can be demonstrated when animals are tested under a different drive$_{DEP}$ (e.g. thirsty instead of hungry) from that operating when the secondary reinforcer was initially established (e.g. Wike and Casey, 1954; Estes, 1949), as can the acquired motivational property (Bacon and Bindra, 1967). The acquired motivational property has even been shown to cross the gap between appetitive and avoidance behaviour, changing sign as it does so: that is to say, whereas a secondary positive reinforcer presented to an animal responding for an S^{R+} increases the rate of response (as in the experiments by Estes and by Dinsmoor described above), presented to an animal responding to avoid an S^{R-} it *decreases* response rate (Grossen, Kostansek and Bolles, 1969; Overmier, Bull and Pack, 1971). But this effect (which one might call "demotivational") is a topic whose full consideration must await our treatment of active avoidance in Chapter 10.

It is particularly instructive to compare what classical conditioning with an S^{R+}/UCS can achieve with what, apparently, it cannot. Attempts to condition either drive$_{DEP}$ itself, in the shape of hunger and thirst either peripherally or centrally elicited (Miller, 1971; Myers and Miller, 1954; Novin and Miller, 1962; Cravens and Renner, 1970), or the drive-reducing effects of food (Miles and Wickens, 1953; Calvin *et al.* 1953) to initially neutral stimuli have been failures*. This is an interesting example of the point we made in Chapter 2 concerning the stimulus substitution theory of classical conditioning. We argued there that, if we list the response components which go to make up the total reaction to the UCS as a vector of changes with the directions of change noted, and if we do the same for the total reaction, after conditioning, to the CS, then it is in general the case that any component which exists in the CS vector also exists in the UCS vector and with the same direction of change; but the converse is not usually the case, that is, there will be components in the UCS vector which do not figure in the CS vector. In the case where the UCS is an S^{R+} with satiating effects (e.g. food for a hungry rat), it appears that classical conditioning can transfer

---

* There have been recent reports of both conditioned increases in drinking (Seligman *et al.*, 1971) and conditioned satiation of eating (Booth, 1972) which may mark the end of this series of failures. However, doubts remain (from the present point of view) in connection with both reports.

The Seligman *et al.* experiment used direct injection of angiotensin into the hypothalamus (thought to be a natural and direct precursor of thirst: Epstein *et al.*, 1970) as the UCS; the CS was the experimental chamber in which the rat was then allowed to drink. As expected, angiotensin injections produced a large unconditioned rise in water consumption. In a subsequent series of test sessions, the rat was placed in the experimental chamber without angiotensin injections. The experimental group (only four in number) showed a small and rapidly extinguished increase in water consumption in the first two of these test sessions as compared with a control group only ever given sham injections. In Booth's experiment it was shown that rats fed diets of two caloric densities, each associated with a particular odour and/or taste, came to eat less of the diet of high caloric density and continued to do so in response to the flavour associated with the high calorie diet even when the diets were equated in caloric density. In short, they learned to eat less of that diet of which less was needed for satiation to be reached (or more of the one of which more was needed: Booth's design does not allow a choice between these alternatives); and this learning was controlled by the associated flavour.

The difficulty with both experiments, for our purposes, is that they do not allow a discrimination between classical conditioning and instrumental learning effects. For a

from the UCS to the CS reinforcing and motivating properties, but not satiating properties*. Such a situation is unlikely to be a trivial consequence of the physical make-up of the world, as one might be tempted to assume for the case in which the animal does not make chewing movements when presented with a tone or a flash of light which has been followed by food (it is, after all, difficult to chew these stimuli). It seems, rather, that there has been adaptive evolution of conditionability for some of the properties of an S^{R+} to the exclusion of others. It is interesting to note that, on the hypothesis of reinforcement we have presented above, just those properties are conditionable which enable the animal to learn and perform goal-directed behaviour.

The Effects of Drive on Reinforcement

The demise of the drive-reduction theory of reinforcement left us, as we saw at the start of this chapter, with a number of unanswered questions. One of these—the question of how reinforcers work, if they do not work by reducing drives—we have examined in some detail in the preceding pages; and another—the question of what properties we might use to recognize an S^{R+} in advance of demonstrating its reinforcing effect—we shall return to in the next chapter. This leaves us with the question of how $drive_{TV}$ and $drive_{DEP}$ affect reinforcement (as we know they usually do), if it is not in virtue of the drive-reduction they allow the instrumental response to secure. To this question we now turn.

The answer we shall offer is a simple one: $drive_{TV}$ and $drive_{DEP}$ affect reinforcement by altering the magnitude or nature of the UCR which is elicited by the S^{R+}/UCS. This would have two consequences, corresponding respectively to the performance and learning aspects of positive reinforcement. (1) With regard to

---

demonstration of a classically conditioned increment in $drive_{DEP}$, it would be necessary to pair a neutral stimulus with increased hunger or thirst without the opportunity to drink. (Seligman *et al.* did in fact do this with one of the four animals in their experimental group; but this is, of course, insufficient.) Similarly, satiation would need to be paired, in the absence of eating or drinking, with a neutral stimulus for a demonstration of classically conditioned reduction in food- or water-drive. It is more reasonable to suppose, in the case of Booth's experiment, that the rats learned to eat less than that they came to feel less hungry when they were exposed to cues previously associated with the high-caloric diet.

* A similar view of the effect of classical conditioning with a UCS/S^{R+} has been proposed by Bindra (1972).

performance, there would be a change in the degree to which the S^{R+} activates its appropriate positive feedback mechanism. (2) With regard to learning, there would be a change in the degree of secondary reinforcing power conferred on the stimulus-response chain which is followed by presentation of the S^{R+}. The first part of this claim, concerning the effects of drive on the performance of goal-directed behaviour, is uncontroversial, and would probably be agreed to (though no doubt with changes in terminology) by theorists who otherwise hold quite diverse views as to the nature of reinforcement. The second part of the claim, concerning the effects of drive on the *learning* of goal-directed behaviour, is more idiosyncratic. For its empirical support it leans heavily on some ingenious experiments by Mendelson (1966).

In these experiments rats were used with electrodes implanted in the lateral hypothalamus at points where experimenter-applied stimulation elicited eating even though the animal was previously satiated with food; such stimulation also produces the other signs of hunger drive$_{GD}$, such as performance of a previously learnt response or the learning of a new response for the reward of food, in a manner we have become accustomed to earlier in this and the previous chapter. Thus it seems reasonable to think of this stimulation as turning on a hunger drive in the same way that results from a period of food-deprivation. The apparatus (Fig. 5.12) used by Mendelson was a maze shaped like a T, in which a food reward could be placed in one or other of the goalboxes situated at each end of the horizontal arm of the T. The animal, satiated for food, was placed in the startbox at the foot of the vertical stem of the T. Two conditions were compared. In one the current was switched on via the hypothalamic electrodes in the startbox and switched off when the animal turned into either of the horizontal arms of the T, irrespective of whether it was the arm leading to the goalbox containing the food or the unbaited arm. In the other condition the current was switched on only when the animal entered either arm of the T and was left on until it was removed from the apparatus. The results of the experiment showed that the rats in the first condition chose randomly between the two goalboxes, of which one contained food (which they did not consume); whereas, in the second condition, they learnt consistently to choose the goalbox containing food (which they duly ate).

The implications of this experiment can be considered from two points of view. The first is that provided by the group which did not learn to go to the arm containing food. The animals in this group regularly found themselves in the startbox hungry, and we may presume that it was well within their powers to learn that food was in, say, the left-hand goalbox. But the combination *hunger and knowledge of the whereabouts of food* was insufficient to motivate them to take the turning towards the food. The second point of view is that of the group which did learn to go to the arm containing food. The animals in this group regularly found themselves in the startbox

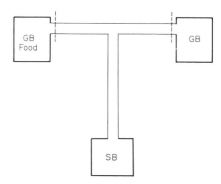

FIG. 5.12. Design of Mendelson's (1966) Experiment. T-maze used by Mendelson (1966). In one condition hypothalamic stimulation was turned on when the animal was placed in the startbox (SB) and turned off (dashed lines) when it entered either goalbox (GB), of which only one contained food. In the other condition the stimulation was off when the animal was placed in the startbox and turned on (dashed line) when it entered either goalbox. (From Mendelson, 1966.)

unhungry. They went to end of the T-maze, thus making themselves hungry, and then chose that arm of the maze in which they could satisfy their hunger. But, had they wished, they could have stayed put in the startbox and not made themselves hungry at all. Thus, in order to make a response which is eventually reinforced by food, it is not necessary to be hungry at the time of making it; but, for food to act as a reinforcer, it is necessary that the animal be hungry when the food is encountered.

These results go counter to the view, common to Hull and Deutsch, that drive impels an animal to action. They would follow, however, from the assumption that the role of hunger drive$_{DEP}$ or hunger drive$_{TV}$ (which, in these experiments, is presumably mimicked by hypothalamic stimulation) is to allow food to act as an

S^{R+}/UCS for the conditioning of secondary reinforcement to earlier members of that response-chain which takes the rat towards the goal containing food. Provided this secondary reinforcement is established, it is unimportant that the animal be hungry or not when it initiates the response-chain.

There are two objections which might be raised against this interpretation of Mendelson's (1966) experiment. The first is comparatively easily dealt with: it is the fact that animals do not usually initiate food-directed behaviour when they are not hungry; it requires the very special circumstances of hypothalamically induced hunger to demonstrate such a phenomenon. In answer to this objection we may echo Mendelson (1970), who suggests that under normal conditions "hunger and thirst may serve as cues signifying that instrumental responses for food and water will be followed by the rewarding activities of feeding and drinking". This suggestion is a reasonable one, since there is good evidence that specific instrumental responses may come under the discriminative control of internal stimuli characteristic of hunger or thirst (Bolles, 1967, p. 254).

A particularly interesting study of the cue properties of drive was reported by Yamaguchi in 1952. He trained different groups of rats to press a bar for a food reward at different levels of hunger drive$_{DEP}$, ranging from 3–72 h of food deprivation. Each group was then subdivided and one subgroup was tested at each level of drive used in training. In this way, Yamaguchi was able to determine whether drive$_{DEP}$ behaves like a normal stimulus dimension in displaying the phenomena of "stimulus generalization" and "generalization decrement" (see Fig. 3.9). Typical stimulus generalization results were in fact obtained, response vigour (measured by reaction time) falling off as the difference between training and testing drive levels increased. In groups tested at a higher level of drive than they were trained on, this generalization decrement was to some extent counteracted by the known tendency of animals on high drive to perform with greater vigour than animals on low drive*. Even so, in three out of six possible comparisons in Yamaguchi's data, the effect of shifting the rats from a lower training

---

* On the reasonable assumption that drive$_{DEP}$ is a dimension of stimulus *intensity* (analogous to brightness of light or loudness of noise), this tendency may possibly itself be explained as an instance of stimulus intensity dynamism (see Chapter 3 and Gray, 1965a). In fact Yamaguchi's results fit quite nicely with other data on the distortions in stimulus generalization curves produced by stimulus intensity dynamism (Gray, 1965a).

to a higher testing drive was to *decrease* the speed of response—a result which is predicted by the hypothesis that drive$_{DEP}$ possesses cue properties, but which is otherwise totally unexpected.

The second possible objection to Mendelson's (1966) experiment concerns the behaviour of the group which was stimulated when it entered the arm of the T-maze and learnt to go to the goalbox containing the food. It could be argued that the rats in this group learned two quite separate things. The first was to enter the horizontal arm, since they were there given hypothalamic stimulation (known to be powerfully reinforcing); the second was to go to that part of the horizontal arm in which food was contained, since the hypothalamic stimulation had also made them hungry. In other words, the effects of food on what they learnt were exerted only *after* they had made themselves hungry. However, this possibility can be excluded in the light of some later results reported by Mendelson (1970; and see Coons and Gruce, 1968; Mogenson and Morgan, 1967). In these experiments rats were used with electrodes at points in the lateral hypothalamus at which stimulation induced drinking, as well as being positively reinforcing. The threshold current was first obtained for self-stimulation in the absence of water. Water was then made available to the rat (previously satiated for water) in the self-stimulation situation. It was found that the presence of water caused the rat to respond at current intensities which had previously been too low to maintain self-stimulation. Furthermore, the animal, having induced in itself an artificial thirst in the presence of water, duly drank it. Thus the rat would not press the bar to turn on hypothalamic stimulation except when water was present; and it would not drink except when it had turned on its own hypothalamic stimulation; but given the chance it *would* do both. As Mendelson (1970) puts it: "rather than seeking out drive reduction, rats seek out drive induction in the presence of appropriate goal objects".

Mendelson presents a simple model to encompass the results of his experiments, a model which is entirely compatible with the arguments we have been developing in this chapter. This model is shown in Fig. 5.13. As explained by Mendelson himself:

Each box represents the neural circuit activated by the inscribed agent. Water deprivation, the sensory feedback from drinking and drinking-inducing intra-cranial stimulation (drink ICS) all send facilitation to reward circuits. No amount of water deprivation and no amount of drinking can in themselves ever deliver enough facilitation to the reward circuits to drive them over threshold. That is why neither water deprivation nor drinking by a satiated rat is reinforcing. Only the combined effects of both water deprivation and drinking can deliver supra-threshold facilitation to the reward circuits. On the other hand, the reinforcing effects of drink ICS depend on its intensity. At low intensities which may be sufficient to induce drinking, it too does not deliver enough facilitation to reward circuits. But, at slightly higher intensities (about 1 μA higher) or in combination with drinking, supra-threshold facilitation is delivered to the reward circuits (Mendelson, 1970, p. 928).

To bring this model into line with the hypotheses advanced in this chapter, it is only necessary to realize that Mendelson's "reward

FIG. 5.13. Mendelson's Model for Drinking and Self-Stimulation. Dashed lines represent subthreshold facilitation; solid lines, suprathreshold facilitation. The effects of satiation are not indicated; they are opposite to the effects of water deprivation. For further explanation, see text. (From Mendelson, 1970.)

circuits" are, in effect, a positive feedback mechanism concerned with the maximization of activity in themselves. The normal way in which such maximization is brought about is by the initiation of drinking behaviour. The self-stimulation experiment allows the animal to use the abnormal route of direct electrical input to the reward circuits. Furthermore, as Mendelson says, his model implies that drive is "subthreshold activation of reward circuits". Such subthreshold activation will produce consummatory behaviour (given a suitable S^{R+} to consume) whose intensity is proportional to the degree of activation. And, following the arguments we have been deploying in this chapter, the greater the UCR elicited by the S^{R+}, (1) the greater will be the vigour of performance of response-chains directed to the S^{R+} and (2) the greater will be the conditioning of secondary reinforcement, and so the greater the learning. Finally, the effects of satiation* can be regarded (again in agreement with Mendelson) as opposite to the effects of deprivation on the reward circuits, lowering both the intensity of food-directed behaviour and the possibility of using the S^{R+} as an efficient UCS for the conditioning of secondary reinforcement.

* See Morgan (1974) for an excellent review of the effects of satiation on behaviour. Morgan's conclusions are entirely compatible with the approach adopted here.

An interesting feature of Mendelson's model is that it makes sense of the way in which drive$_{DEP}$ and incentive motivation (the latter varied by size, frequency or quality of reward) combine to determine learning rate and response vigour. This problem has been approached principally within the framework of Hullian theory, which uses the symbols "D" for drive (e.g. number of hours of food deprivation) and "K" for incentive motivation (e.g. number of grams of food received). Hull's (1952) theory held that D and K combine multiplicatively. An alternative view (Spence, 1956) is that they are additive in their effects. The experimental data (Black, 1965) suggest that they combine multiplicatively when the value of either variable is close to zero, but additively if both have clearly non-zero values. A little consideration will show that this is exactly what Mendelson's model (Fig. 5.13) predicts; as he says, "no amount of water deprivation and no amount of drinking can in themselves ever deliver enough facilitation to the reward circuits to drive them over threshold"—so, with either D or K at zero, the combination of D and K is zero, i.e., multiplicative; but, if both water and drive are present, the inputs to Mendelson's reward circuits add to each other.

Mendelson's model completes our examination of the way in which positive reinforcement might work. It also completes the dethronement of drive. Once the central concept of Hullian theory, both impelling the animal to action and, by its reduction, allowing the animal to be reinforced, drive has now declined into a mere determinant of the magnitude of the UCR elicited by an S^{R+}/UCS. This is a role, in fact, which we have seen drive play once before—in our consideration of the effects of drive on classical conditioning (see the discussion of the experiment by De Bold *et al.*, in Chapter 4). In its place, we have put increasing emphasis on the classical conditioning of secondary reinforcement. As we have seen, the magnitude of the UCR is an important determinant of this process, so that drive in the original Hullian sense still has an important part to play in learning and motivation, albeit indirectly.

In the next chapter we consider the final question which the demise of the drive reduction theory of reinforcement poses: what independent properties do positive reinforcers possess, if any, which might allow us to identify them before we knew their reinforcing effects? Premack's answer to this question, as we shall see, takes still further the emphasis on the nature of the animal's responses to reinforcing stimuli which began to emerge in the present chapter.

6. Premack's Theory of Reinforcement

Physics has given the world the laws of conservation of energy and matter. One day psychology may be seen to be the mother of an equally important conservation law: the law of conservation of tautology. Loosely expressed, this law states that, once tautology has entered a system of thought, it is awfully difficult to get rid of it. In our discussion in the previous two chapters of the relations between drive and instrumental positive reinforcement we have more or less come round to a view which could be stated thus: reinforcement consists in drive-*induction*—in contrast to the defunct drive-reduction hypothesis. And this view (which appears to have originated in a paper by Sheffield *et al.*, 1954) is becoming increasingly common in contemporary texts on learning theory (e.g. Bolles, 1967, p. 254). Now, a statement such as this implies that the drive-induction hypothesis is an empirical claim which might conceivably be wrong. But a little thought shows that the drive-induction hypothesis of reinforcement is no more empirical than is the claim (whose purely tautological status we examined in Chapter 4) that drive$_{G D}$ is necessary for reinforcement. Indeed, it is the same claim: for the occurrence of drive-induction is detected precisely by goal-directed behaviour whose object is the (reinforcing) stimulus which is said to have induced the drive. (Consideration of the cases of electrical self-stimulation of the brain or the seeking-out of novelty—see Chapter 4—should sufficiently indicate to the reader that this is so.)

Our treatment in the last chapter of the performance aspect of positive reinforcement as activating a positive feedback mechanism (Fig. 5.1) is barely, if at all, less tautological than the drive-induction hypothesis of which it is, in effect, an illustration. As an attempt to describe the mechanism by which positive reinforcers produce their positively reinforcing effects, it goes very slightly beyond a verbal (and tautological) definition of positive reinforcement as a stimulus which induces a drive$_{GD}$. Of course, a really detailed description of such a positive feedback mechanisms, along with the many other kinds of feedback mechanism undoubtedly involved in the control of any particular example of goal-directed behaviour, would be of great practical value. (See, for example, Oatley's 1967 paper integrating much of the available experimental data on the control of water-intake into "a control model for the physiological basis of thirst".) But even if the machinery whereby positive reinforcing stimuli exert their positively reinforcing effects were known to us in exhaustive detail, we would probably be no better off when it came to answering the question: "by what properties can we recognize a positive reinforcer before we have actually tested it for its positively reinforcing effect"?

The drive-reduction hypothesis was an attempt to answer this question by saying, in effect: a stimulus, S_1, which reduces the intensity of already existing goal-directed behaviour, R_1 (directed to S_1), as an increasing function of the degree to which S_1 is in fact obtained, will serve as a positively reinforcing stimulus for the acquistion of new goal-directed behaviour, R_2, also directed to S_1. The demise of the drive-reduction hypothesis means that we have to seek an alternative answer. It is, of course, entirely possible that there is *no* general answer; that the only thing positive reinforcers have in common is that they *are* positively reinforcing. They do represent, after all, an extremely diverse set of stimuli. But we can presumably decide that positive reinforcers have no common property other than that of positive reinforcement only after trying as best we can to find some property and failing. And the time is surely premature to admit defeat.

The Drive Increment Hypothesis of Reinforcement

The drive-*induction* hypothesis of reinforcement, if it postulates that a positive reinforcer is a stimulus which *activates* a drive$_{GD}$, is, as we have just seen, an empty tautology. But there is a closely related hypothesis which is not: it states that a positive reinforcer is a stimulus which *increments* a drive$_{GD}$. This "drive-increment" hypothesis of reinforcement is the exact opposite of the drive-reduction hypothesis and it is equally empirical. Like the drive-reduction hypothesis (or, indeed, any other such hypothesis), it can come in two forms: a weak one, according to which any stimulus which acts as a reinforcer *also* increments a drive_{GD}; and a strong one, according to which reinforcement *consists in* drive increment, so that it is necessarily the case both that any stimulus which increments a drive_{GD} is a reinforcer, and also that any reinforcer is a stimulus which increments a drive_{GD}. The strong form of the drive-increment hypothesis, of course, entails the weak form, although the converse is not true. Thus it would be possible to infirm both hypotheses by finding a reinforcer which does not increment a drive. In a similar way, we argued in Chapter 4 that the drive-reduction hypothesis could be infirmed by evidence that there are stimuli which act as positive reinforcers but do not reduce drive_{GD} (e.g. electrical self-stimulation of the brain, air-drinking, breathing). In the case of the drive-increment hypothesis, however, it is rather premature to start looking for counter-instances to the generalization that all reinforcers increment drive_{GD}, since we do not yet have a sufficient number of positive instances even to make the generalization.

Indeed, it is rather odd even to be embarking on the making of such a generalization. Surely, all the mass of positive instances which made the drive-reduction hypothesis initially plausible (the fact that fed animals give up eating, watered animals drinking, mated animals copulating, etc) are clear negative instances for a drive-increment hypothesis, so why should we begin on such a hopeless task at all?

This reaction, however, is not justified. Consider, for example, two experiments we have encountered in earlier chapters. McFarland (1969) showed that in the dove the reinforcing and satiating effects of water pass along separate pathways: reinforcement depends on oral factors, satiation (i.e. drive reduction) on the amount of water reaching the stomach (see Chapter 4). McFarland and McFarland (1968) showed that there is positive feedback from drinking onto this same act of drinking, i.e. that the ingestion of water has a short-lived but definite drive-incremental effect on water-directed behaviour. In short, it is possible for there to be simultaneously drive reducing and drive-increasing effects of one stimulus on the behaviour directed towards that stimulus. Such effects have been shown in the feeding behaviour of doves, mice and rats, as well as in the example just described (McFarland, 1971, 1973). Thus it is entirely possible (a) that behind a visible satiation effect there lies a hidden drive-incremental effect and (b) that it is this drive-incremental effect which is critical for the occurrence of reinforcement.

However, it is a long way from saying that something is possible to showing that it happens. For the moment, we are only at the stage of simply collecting positive instances of reinforcement accompanied by drive increment. A few such examples exist. One is the McFarland and McFarland (1968) experiment on drinking in the dove already referred to, and the similar reports for feeding in mice (Wiepkema, 1971), rats (Le Magnen, 1968) and doves (McFarland, 1973a). Another is the "prefeeding" effect in runway experiments with hungry rats. It has been reported in several studies (e.g. Bruce, 1937; Morgan and Fields, 1938) that, if a rat is fed a small portion of food or water in the startbox of the runway, then it runs faster to a goalbox containing a rather larger amount of food or water-reward than controls not so "pre-fed". A third example comes from the sexual behaviour of the male rat. As shown by Beach and Jordan (1956), the time from first intromission to ejaculation (which is *prima facie* a measure of the intensity of the animal's sex drive$_{G D}$) gets smaller (i.e. drive is increased) over the first few consecutive bouts of copulation when the male is exposed to a female in estrus. A final example—and one which, with regard to the sheer bulk of the experimental data, is much weightier than the others—is the self-stimulation phenomenon. As we have already commented in Chapter 4, these data show very generally that an electrode from which self-stimulation can be obtained is also an electrode from which, when the experimenter applies stimulation, an increment is some drive$_{G D}$ or other is usually produced (Glickman and Schiff, 1967).

Recently, McFarland (1974) has provided a new method for demonstrating an increment in drive which may prove to have important application in tests of the drive-increment hypothesis of reinforcement. His method is an indirect one, which we cannot describe in detail here. It is based on the notion that, if an animal is simultaneously placed in two drive$_{D E P}$ states (e.g. hunger and thirst) and provided with the means of satisfying them both, then it has to use some strategy or other to allocate its time between the two appropriate drives$_{G D}$ (e.g. food-seeking and water-seeking). McFarland adduces evidence to show that, under such conditions, one drive$_{G D}$ activity is "dominant" over the other, in this sense: the subdominant activity is only able to occur when the dominant activity is, for some reason or other, temporarily switched off; conversely, when the dominant activity is switched on, the subdominant activity is automatically inhibited. The method which is relevant to our present concern is one whereby McFarland is able to determine which of two competing drives$_{G\,D}$ is dominant over the other and by how much.

Working with the Barbary dove, McFarland has shown that, if all other factors are held constant, the degree to which either feeding is dominant over drinking or drinking over feeding can be minipulated simply by altering the rate at which either food or water rewards are made available for pecking at a key. Take the case in which feeding is dominant over drinking. Then the degree of this dominance can be increased either by increasing the rate of delivery of food rewards or by decreasing the rate of delivery of water rewards. McFarland argues convincingly that these effects arise because the degree of positive feedback of food on eating (and of water on drinking) is greater, the greater the rate at which rewards are received. This conclusion is consistent with McFarland and McFarland's (1968) earlier observation that the positive feedback of water ingestion on drinking behaviour is subject to rapid temporal decay (see Chapter 5, Fig. 5.2). Thus, on this view (a) there is an increment in the drive$_{G\,D}$ for food which arises from the ingestion of food and which is greater, the greater the rate of food-ingestion, and (b) this drive-increment can be detected as an increase in the degree to which feeding is dominant over drinking. And similarly, *mutatis mutandis*, for the drive$_{G\,D}$ for water. Furthermore, McFarland (personal communication) has obtained data which indicate that these positive-feedback effects are mediated by oral, and not by gastric, factors, just as the reinforcing effects of drinking had previously been shown to be mediated by these factors (McFarland, 1969: see Chapter 4). Thus, there is some reason to suppose that the reinforcing and the drive-incremental effects of water ingestion in the Barbary dove are both initiated by the same peripheral signals, though whether the same neural pathways are then activated is, of course, another matter.

This kind of observation is encouraging for a drive-increment hypothesis of positive reinforcement. But the joint occurrence of two effects falls well short of indicating that the one is causally necessary for the production of the other, as would have to be the case on a strong interpretation of this hypothesis. To show such causal necessity, one would need to block the drive increment which normally occurs in consequence of drinking and show that the reinforcing effects of water were simultaneously eliminated. And such an experiment has yet even to be attempted. For the moment, therefore, we are justified only in concluding that there is a tendency for S^{R+}s to increase the intensity of the drive directed towards them; but there might be many other reasons for the existence of such a tendency, besides the fact that reinforcement *consists in* drive increment; and in any case, the universality of this tendency is still very much in doubt (a likely negative instance which springs to mind is that of the reinforcing effects of novelty).

An interesting view as to the functional value of having reinforcers produce an increment in drive has been suggested by McFarland (1973). He starts from a

> consideration of the fact that animals are always motivated to carry out a number of incompatible behavioural activities. Once an animal has started on one activity, feedback from that activity tending to reduce the level of motivation and fluctuations in the level of motivation for other activities will tend to disrupt the ongoing behaviour because of motivational competition. Although this problem can be partly overcome by means of time-sharing (McFarland, 1974), there remains a strong possibility that the animal will be continually dithering, unable to complete any task. To prevent dithering, it is necessary that the ongoing behaviour gain some momentum so that, once an animal has started on a particular course of action, it will continue. The momentum could be provided by positive feedback from the consequences of behaviour.

This view accounts nicely for the concomitance of positive-feedback or drive-incremental effects with the performance aspect of positive reinforcement; but it gives one little reason to suppose that drive increment should be essential for the *learning* aspect of positive reinforcement. Thus the most one can say at present about the role played by drive in positive reinforcement is that the drive-reduction hypothesis is almost certainly wrong; the drive-induction hypothesis is a tautology, and the drive-increment hypothesis only a gleam on the horizon.

Premack's Relational View of Reinforcement

A very different proposal concerning the nature of reinforcing stimuli (both positive and negative) has been made by David Premack (1965, 1971), as part of a general analysis of instrumental reinforcement. Since Premack's analysis has implications for a number of the problems we have considered in earlier chapters, we shall use the present one to examine his overall theory in some detail.

Premack begins his analysis by pointing out that previous theories of reinforcement have assumed—mistakenly, as he goes on to show—that stimuli either are or are not members of the class of reinforcers in virtue of their own inherent properties. In place of this "absolute" view of reinforcement, Premack proposes that reinforcement depends on a *relationship* between the reinforced activity and the activity evoked by the reinforcing stimulus. This relationship is, furthermore, *reversible*: with a change in the experimental situation it is possible for the reinforced and reinforcing activities to change roles. What is it, then, that determines which of two activities can positively reinforce the other? To this Premack's answer is, the relative probability of occurrence of the two activities: the one with the higher probability of occurring spontaneously (i.e. before any attempt has been made to make one activity contingent upon the prior occurrence of the other) can reinforce, but not be reinforced by, the one with the lower probability of occurrence. Thus, as a predictor of reinforcing capacity, Premack proposes "relative response probability". Finally, as a measure of relative response probability which can be applied to any kind of behaviour (and such a measure is otherwise not easy to find), Premack suggests the proportion of time allocated by the subject to each activity under unrestricted conditions which are identical (apart from such changes as are necessarily involved in the establishment of the $R \rightarrow S$ instrumental contingency) to those under which the experimenter assesses the instrumental reinforcing properties of the stimuli to which each activity is directed.

Notice that, in this approach, Premack lays great stress on the properties of the *response* as determining reinforcement rather than on the properties of the *stimulus* (the S^{R+}) which elicits this response or to which the response is directed. In this respect, Premack's approach is similar to that advocated by such ethologists as Tinbergen (1951) and by some earlier psychologists (e.g. Sheffield *et al.* 1954) who have held that it is the performance of a "consummatory" response, rather than the attainment of a particular stimulus, which reinforces goal-directed behaviour. A "consummatory" response is not easy to define. Roughly speaking, it is the final action in an innate species-specific behaviour chain, for example, copulatory thrusting and ejaculation at the end of a chain of male courtship and sexual behaviour. Premack's theory is broader than such consummatory-response theories insofar as it applies to *any* pair of responses: the one with the higher probability of occurrence should reinforce the one with the lower, irrespective of the nature of the response. Note also how well this approach fits with the evidence (especially Mendelson's experiments), considered in the previous chapter, that drive$_{DEP}$ affects the reinforcing capacity of an appropriate S^{R+} by altering the response elicited by this stimulus, rather than by affecting the initiation of a goal-directed behaviour chain. It is exactly in this way that Premack treats drive$_{DEP}$, i.e. as one of the determinants of response probability (with presentation of the S^{R+}, in his view, constituting merely another such determinant).

An example will help to make Premack's analysis clearer. Suppose that, under a given set of conditions, playing pinball (R_1) on a pinball machine (S_1) takes up a greater proportion of a child's time than does eating (R_2) candy (S_2) (and these are reinforcing activities actually used in some of Premack's experiments); then his theory predicts that eating candy can be reinforced by allowing access to the pinball machine contingent on candy-eating, but that playing pinball can not be reinforced by allowing access to candy contingent upon pinball-playing. If the conditions in which the child is maintained are changed, however, so that eating candy comes to take up proportionately more time than playing pinball, the latter will cease to be an effective reinforcer for candy-eating and candy-eating will become an effective reinforcer for pinball-playing.

It is clear that this theory genuinely does offer an empirical hypothesis as to the nature of positive reinforcers. Relative response probability measured in this way before any test of positive reinforcement is applied is in no way logically linked to the subsequent outcome of this test. It is logically possible for the reverse of Premack's theory to turn out to be the case; i.e. for the activity with the relatively lower response probability to reinforce the activity with the higher probability. As a matter of fact, however, Premack marshals an impressive array of evidence to show that it is indeed the higher-probability activity which reinforces the lower-probability one. We shall describe only a few of his experiments.

In one of these the two activities involved were drinking and running in a running wheel. In one condition, the subjects (rats) had free access to both food and an activity wheel, but access to water for only 1 h a day. During this hour, mean total drinking time was about 240 sec and mean total running time about 60 sec. Conversely, with free access to both food and water, but access to the wheel for only 1 h a day, mean total drinking time during this hour was only about 28 sec while mean total running time climbed to 329 sec in the same period. Premack's prediction was that, in the former case, drinking could reinforce running, but running could not reinforce drinking; and, in the second case, that running could reinforce drinking, but drinking could not reinforce running. This prediction was tested by either making insertion of the drinking tube contingent upon a certain number of turns of the running wheel or making unlocking of the running wheel contingent upon a certain number of licks at the drinking tube. The results confirmed the prediction in all respects. When drinking was the more probable activity than running (as in the usual experiment using water reward), the rats increased their rate of running in order to drink, but did not increase their rate of drinking in order to run. More interestingly (since it is the reverse of the usual experiment), when *running* was the more probable activity, the rats increased their rate of *drinking* in order to run, but did not increase their rate of running in order to drink.

In a second experiment Premack (1965) used electrical self-stimulation of the brain as one of the two activities. As he says, "the position which eating or drinking once held has now been pretty much usurped by intra-cranial self-stimulation (ICS); it is the new king of reinforcers." A particularly striking test of Premack's hypothesis can thus be made by showing that, king or not, this too is subject to the law of reversibility of reinforcement. "Do response probabilities produced by ICS act like other response probabilities as regards reinforcement? If so, and a response can be found more probable than the ICS-contingent response, then ICS should be subject to reinforcement." Holstein and Hundt (cited by Premack, 1965) were able to demonstrate precisely this phenomenon. They implanted three rats with electrodes in the midbrain tegmentum, the preoptic region and the median forebrain bundle, respectively. A current was found for each rat which produced "a moderate, stable response rate during daily sessions of 15 min length." The activity pitted against self-stimulation was the drinking of 25% sucrose solution; and, for all three animals, total duration of drinking in a 15 min session was greater than total duration of ICS barpressing during the same period. It could therefore be predicted on Premack's hypothesis that, when drinking sucrose was made contingent upon ICS barpressing, the rate at which the latter occurred would increase, i.e. be reinforced; but that the rate of drinking would not increase when ICS-barpressing was made contingent upon this. And this is what was found.

Premack describes many other experiments consistent with his view of the role of response-probability in determining reinforcing power. Among other things, these experiments establish the "indifference principle": it does not appear to matter what manipulations are undertaken to vary response probability (measured as before as the relative proportion of time spent on the activity in question), the instantaneous value of this probability, along with the corresponding probability for the other activity which enters into the contingency relationship, is all that is needed to predict which activity will reinforce and which be reinforced. This is so whether the manipulations undertaken to vary response probability involve capitalizing on a curve of temporal variation, the imposition of deprivation, or alterations in the quantity or quality of reward (Chapters 4 and 5).

In other experiments, concerned principally with the reversibility of reinforcement, Premack is able to show, even without varying response probability in these ways, that the traditional view that reinforcers are trans-situational (Meehl, 1950)—i.e. that a reinforcer which is effective with one particular instrumental response will be effective with all such responses—is wrong. To do this, he first measures the instantaneous response probabilities (by the same means as before) for a set of responses under given conditions. These can then be ranked from highest to lowest probability. The postulate of trans-situationality applies under these conditions to the member of the set with the highest instantaneous probability (H), for this is able to reinforce all other members of the set, according to the principles we have already seen at work. Similarly, the member of the set with the lowest instantaneous probability (L) offers no threat to trans-situationality, for it is able to reinforce no members of the set. It is members of the set lying between H and L which do offer such a threat. Premack's approach predicts, and his experimental results confirm, that a member of the set which is neither H nor L will reinforce the other members of the set which have lower response probabilities and be reinforced by members of the set with higher response probabilities. *Thus, the notion "S^{R+}" is both relational and reversible; and it appears to depend on the probabilities of spontaneous occurrence of the reinforced and reinforcing activities.*

So far, we have considered Premack's theory only as it applies to positive reinforcement. Recently, however, Premack (1971) has extended the theory to cover negative reinforcement as well. The extension is made via a simple reversal of perspective: "since a transition from a less to a more probable event facilitates responding, a transition from a more to a less probable event may suppress it" (Premack, 1971, p. 137).

As a test of this hypothesis Premack proposes the following experiment.

Consider that one established in rats a probability of running intermediate between two probabilities of drinking. For example, a thirsty rat will be more likely to drink than run, whereas a rat with an unrestricted water

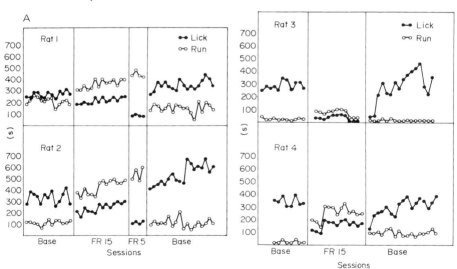

FIG. 6.1. Reinforcement and Punishment of Drinking by Running. A (see above). Duration of drinking and running, showing the base level of each behaviour, the suppression of drinking by running, and the subsequent return to base. B (see opposite). As A, showing the reinforcement of drinking by running and the subsequent return to base. (From Premack, 1971.)

supply will be more likely to run than drink. D_1 is a probability of drinking less than R_1 which is a probability of running less than D_2, i.e., $P_{D_2} > P_{R_1} > P_{D_1}$. The contingency if D_1 then R_1 should result in reinforcement, in increase in drinking, since running is more probable than drinking. But the contingency if D_2 then R_1 should result in punishment, a decrement in drinking, since running is less probable than drinking . . . One and the same event is predicted to produce both reinforcement and punishment, depending only upon the probability of the base event relative to that of the contingent event (Premack, 1971, p. 137).

This is essentially the experiment run by Weisman and Premack, using a running wheel which could be rotated by a motor, forcing the animal inside it to run. The wheel was also equipped with a drinking tube. Rats were run either with no deprivation or after 23 h water-deprivation. Operant levels (i.e. spontaneous frequencies before reinforcement operations were carried out) were recorded for drinking and running under both conditions, and then the effect of making running contingent on drinking in the two cases was determined. The results are shown in Fig. 6.1. It can be seen that Premack's predictions are fully supported: the consequence of

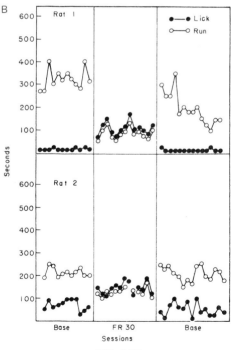

FIG. 6.1B.

making forced running contingent on drinking was to increase drinking above its operant level in the water-satiated condition but to decrease it below its operant level in the water-deprived condition.

Contiguity and Contingency in Instrumental Conditioning

Premack's analysis has not stopped short at the problem of what *stimuli* (or *activities*) can act as reinforcers. He has also made an important contribution to our understanding of what exactly constitutes an effective reinforcing *operation*. His exposition is, as usual, so lucid that we shall let him speak for himself.

Consider that we have two events, one of them incontrovertibly reinforcing (H) and the other incontrovertibly reinforcible (L). What is the minimal relation that can obtain between H and L that will produce reinforcement? How slightly can they contact each other and the contact still be effective? This is the question we want to examine now, as opposed to the matter of what are reinforcing and reinforcible events. We have already urged that the latter consists of any two responses that differ sufficiently in their probabilities of occurrence. Let us suspend debate on that topic in order to ask: What is the weakest relation that more and less probable responses can have that will eventuate in reinforcement?

We all know one sure-fire procedure for producing reinforcement: the contingency, the if L, then H operation which is used to produce virtually all reinforcement. But is the contingency a minimal or even a weak operation? Does it provide only temporal contiguity between H and L—the incontrovertibly reinforcing and reinforcible events—and nothing else?

Consider an ordered set of operations, all of which may conceivably produce reinforcement. The weakest will be pure temporal contiguity between H and L, while the strongest we need consider here will be the contingency. There are more than a few ways to produce temporal contiguity between L and H and these vary in strength according to the number and perhaps kind of additional conditions they superimpose upon temporal contiguity. Pure temporal contiguity, we will show in a moment, is rare or unknown.

In order to locate the weakest possible effective operation, we will start with the strongest operation in the set—which will give us the assurance that reinforcement is possible with the materials in question—and progressively denude the strongest operation of its surplus conditions until a point is reached where reinforcement is no longer produced. This point may be on either side of temporal contiguity.

What are the major surplus conditions of the contingency? Embodied in the contingency are at least three first-order conditions over and above simple temporal contiguity, not to mention some second-order conditions that are less evident though possibly important. Consider the first-order properties more or less in the order of their visibility. First, the heart of a contingency, which is a response requirement: the reinforcing event can occur only if L occurs first; this is a special constraint, for if a contingency did not obtain, the animal might enter H from any of a number of antecedents. But a typical contingency prescribes that H can be reached only through a preselected L. Second, the distribution of the organism's responding to H is circumscribed. The animal has a characteristic way of responding to H, both in terms of burst durations and intervals between bursts, but a contingency limits both maximum burst duration and minimum interburst interval; it sets these limits dramatically when the schedule is intermittent, though to some extent even when the schedule is continuous. That is, by its very nature a contingency involves intruding an experimenter-selected event, L, between the organism's successive responses to H, thereby disturbing to one degree or another the organism's response distribution on H. Third, a typical contingency leads to a reduction in the total amount or duration of responding to H, relative to what would occur were H free. The amount of food the animal eats, for example, in a typical contingency is substantially less than the amount it would eat were food freely available for a period of time equal to that of the contingency session. This reduction is not a necessary consequence of a contingency; as we shall see, a contingency can be arranged that leads to no such reduction, but historically the reduction appears to be an invariant concomitant of the contingency procedure, and thus it remains to be seen whether the reduction plays a role in reinforcement. To be sure, any of the constraints described above may be as inconsequential as they appear to be accidental; the mere fact that we find them in the test tube does nor prove that they are active ingredients; they may be inert accompaniments and temporal contiguity the only active factor . . .

A procedure which is weaker than the contingency and which is said to demonstrate that temporal contiguity is sufficient, is Skinner's (1948) noncontingency or superstition case. This procedure differs from a contingency principally in that it drops the response requirement. As you will likely recall, grain was available to pigeons in Skinner's classical demonstration according to a temporal schedule that was independent of the bird's responding. Since this procedure does not prescribe the path through which H is reached, the animal could enter H by any of a number of antecedents, different from bird to bird. Skinner reported pigeons to be reinforced by this procedure, to increase in the frequency of turning about or pecking the ceiling—any of a number of idiosyncratic responses which, though not required, occurred prior to H. Skinner concluded that temporal contiguity is a sufficient condition for reinforcement.

But we may note that although Skinner's procedure is weaker than the contingency, it is not yet a pure case of temporal contiguity. On the contrary, it retains from the surplus conditions of the contingency both a circumscription on the distribution of responding to H and a reduction in the total amount of responding to H. That is, the grain was not free but was available to the birds according to some program, and the amount they ate was almost certainly markedly less than they would have eaten in an equal period of time had grain been freely available.

Can temporal contiguity be achieved without either a response require-ment or any restriction on H? The free pairing of stimuli to which the subject has different probabilities of responding would appear to be one way. For example, suppose a rat is given unrestricted access to both an activity wheel and a source of water. Previous tests have established that with suitable water deprivation, the total duration for which the rat drinks when only water is available is greater than the total duration for which it runs when only the wheel is available. Accordingly, in this case, drinking will instance H, running will instance L.

Now when the rat is given both the tube and wheel at the same time, it will occasionally run and then drink—in the case of some of our rats, repeating this run-drink sequence perhaps 20 or more times in a 15-minute session. There will thus occur a temporal contiguity between incontro-vertibly reinforcible and reinforcing events. That is, if, with identical parameters, drinking were made contingent upon running, running would increase without question. The temporal contiguity that interests us now, however, is one that occurs without the encumbrances of the contingency. If there is no response requirement, no circumscription upon the dis-tribution of H responding, and no reduction in the amount of H responding, is temporal contiguity between H and L still a sufficient condition?

All the evidence we now have on this question is negative. Pure temporal contiguity has never proved to be a suffficient condition. By now a fair number of rats, upwards of 40, have been placed in a wheel containing a drinkometer and their running and drinking recorded on Esterline Angus tape. Despite the relatively large number of times these records show an instance of drink to follow (within 2 seconds or less) an instance of run, there are no cases in which the amount of running has increased over the base amount—the amount run when only the wheel is available; in fact, the rat typically runs more before the tube is inserted. Table 6.1 affords some idea of the number of times the would be effective temporal contiguities occur in this situation. This number of contiguities in a contingency situation would be more than sufficient to produce an increase in the frequency of running. Further, the number shown is an average per session, and many sessions are run before a negative outcome is accepted.

It might be considered that when the rat can both drink and run and drinking is more probable, running fails to increase simply because drink suppresses run. That is, although run is reinforced by drink, the increased disposition to run is not manifested because of response competition. This would make more sense if the total duration of run plus drink approxi-mated total session time, which it does not; even so, since a direct test can be made so simply, the point is worth considering. The possible suppres-

TABLE 6.1.   Number of noncontingent run-drink contiguities/15 min.
(From Premack, 1965)

Subject	1.	25	7.	19
	2.	24	8.	17
	3.	22	9.	13
	4.	11	10.	23
	5.	13	11.	21
	6.	8	12.	23

sive effect of drinking can be removed altogether simply by removing the tube. When this is done, the animal being placed in the wheel with the drinkometer removed, the amount it runs is not different from the base amount. Thus, no increase in running is seen either during a potential learning situation or subsequently during a potential extinction situation.

Thus far we have described three temporal contiguity-producing operations; ranging from the strong contingency to the weak pairing of two stimuli (wheel and tube); intermediate is Skinner's superstition paradigm, which appears to differ from the contingency only in dropping the response requirement. Since the latter produces reinforcement and the free-pairing procedure does not, this leaves in doubt the effect of the other two principal encumbrances of the contingency—circumscription of the H distribution and reduction of H total. Both are retained in the superstition paradigm, which is effective, and both are dropped in the free-pairing design, which is not effective. Accordingly, at least one and perhaps both of these conditions are necessary, i.e., must accompany temporal contiguity in order for reinforcement to occur.

One way to proceed now is to attempt to pervert the purpose of the contingency. Normally, a contingency is used to produce reinforcement, but is it possible to establish a contingency relationship and yet not produce reinforcement? The instructive consequence of attempting to divert the contingency from its usual end is that it leads to the abandonment of one of the normal surplus conditions of the contingency—specifically, the reduction in H. Although a circumscription on the distribution of H is all but inevitable, a result of the instrumental requirement, contingencies can be formed that do not reduce the animal's normal amount of responding to H. Indeed, the characteristic reduction in H is a coincidental by-product of another accidental feature of the standard contingency. The typical instrumental response, e.g., bar press, has a low operant level, and when access to H is made contingent upon such an instrumental event, a reduction in H, particularly when the contingency is first instated, is nearly inevitable. For example, when the rat can obtain a pellet only following a bar press, the low operant level of the bar press will almost certainly reduce the number of pellets the rat eats in the beginning . . .

The reduction in H can be avoided from the outset, however, by using an atypical instrumental response, one that has a substantial operant level.

For example, consider drinking to be made contingent upon running at a time when running has a high pre-reinforcement level, a thing which is easily established in the rat. By requiring only a "little" run for each relatively "large" drink, the arrangement can be made whereby the rat can provide itself the opportunity to drink the normal amount by running no more than the normal (base) amount. Now the striking thing about this kind of contingency is that it produces no reinforcement, no increase in the frequency of running. But, indeed, why should it? Without running more than it would otherwise, the animal can (and does) drink essentially the normal amount. We are thus led to see that a contingency *per se* is not a sufficient condition for reinforcement. Moreover, this completes the devaluation of the response requirement: Skinner's superstition paradigm showed that it is not a necessary condition for reinforcement*, and the present design shows that it is not a sufficient condition.

More instructive is the suggestion that, specifically, a reduction in H is needed in addition to temporal contiguity if reinforcement is to occur. Circumscribing the distribution of H is clearly not a sufficient condition (though it may be necessary), for the contingency will have this effect; yet if, despite the partitioning of H, H occurs in normal amount, there is no increase in instrumental responding.

But a main point may be considered to remain: if the rat drinks its normal amount, there is no reason for it to run more than its normal amount, but what if the tube is removed? Here too, there is no increase. After numerous sessions in which instances of run led repeatedly to instances of drink, but with no decrease in drink and no increase in run, the drinkometer was removed, as in extinction, and the animal given only the opportunity to run. No increase in running was observed in three such studies involving 19 rats . . .

In summary, a set of operations were shown that lead to temporal contiguity between events that are incontrovertibly reinforcing and reinforcible. If all such operations produced reinforcement, temporal contiguity could be accepted as a sufficient condition. As it turns out, however, only some of the operations produce reinforcement; we are thus led to search among the operations to discern the further conditions they embody. The present search indicates that a reduction in the total amount of H is a necessary condition (Premack, 1965, pp. 164–172).

The experiments described in this passage were all concerned with positive reinforcement. Although Premack has not reported a similar programme of research aimed at describing the necessary and sufficient conditions for a stimulus to act as a punishment, he has pointed to certain similarities between the effects of positive and negative reinforcers which suggest that something akin to "a

* More recent experimental work; not available to Premack at the time this passage was written, throws considerable doubt on this interpretation of Skinner's experiments on "superstition" (Staddon and Simmelhag, 1971).

reduction in the total amount of H" is also at work in the punishment situation.

He makes this point with reference to the experiment whose results are depicted in Fig. 6.1. In this experiment, as we have seen, running was able to act as a positive reinforcement for drinking; and also to act as a punishment for drinking when the pre-reinforcement operant level of drinking was higher than that of running. Now, if the reader will look at Fig. 6.1, he will be able to verify that Premack is correct in the assertion that (positive) "reinforcement involves not one change but two: an increase in the instrumental event (the defining outcome), but also a *decrement* in the *contingent response* which has gone unobserved or in any case does not enter standard discussions of reinforcement" (Premack, 1971, p. 149). This decrement in the contingent response is an indication that there has been a "reduction in the total amount of H" (i.e. running). According to Premack, there is a parallel to this in the case in which running is used as a punishment. Again, there is not one change but two: "a decrease in the instrumental event (the defining outcome), but also an *increase* in the *contingent response*. That is, when running contingent upon drinking suppressed drinking, the duration of running in the contingency was notably *greater* than in the base condition" (Premack, *loc. cit.*). The reader can verify that this is indeed so by looking once more at Fig. 6.1. Premack (*loc cit.*) finally sums up the parallel he has drawn thus:

> Operationally, reinforcement is produced by denying the subject the opportunity to occupy a state as long as it would choose to, whereas punishment is produced by forcing the subject to occupy a state longer than it would choose to. Neither outcome depends upon the intrinsic character of the state; we have seen the same state (running) produce both outcomes.

We shall need some shorthand to refer to these concepts. We shall call what Premack believes to be going on in the case of positive reinforcement ("reduction in the total amount of H") "restricted access" (to the reinforcer). The converse, over-exposure to the punishment, we shall refer to as "surplus access".

These are ingenious experiments, and the theory they support is a satisfyingly simple one. If correct, it offers us not only an independent way of identifying which events will positively reinforce what behaviour, but also an independent indication of which events will punish what behaviour. Furthermore, there is a powerful parsimony in the fact that essentially the same operations would provide both kinds of identification. The analysis of the contingency has, without question, thrown a bright light into previously murky corners; and it may have succeeded in replacing an essentially logical notion (iff R, then S—the contingency itself) with a glimpse of the machinery (temporal contiguity plus restricted or surplus access to the S) whereby the contingency is normally translated into behavioural outcomes. And yet, doubts remain: can it really be so simple?

Drive and Reinforcement Revisited

In an effort to bring these doubts out into the open, let us consider how Premack's treatment of positive reinforcement, radically new as it is in many respects, relates to the discussion of drive and reinforcement which has occupied us in previous chapters.

The answer to this question is clear, the moment we realize what techniques Premack uses to vary the probability of occurrence of the activities he investigates. This, as we have seen, is either by picking out the high or low points on a curve of spontaneous temporal variation, or by imposing deprivation schedules, or by the variation of incentive (the quantity and/or quality of the reinforcing stimulus). Thus, what Premack has in effect been claiming is that $drive_{TV}$ and $drive_{DEP}$, insofar as both are reflected in relative probability, are predictive of reinforcement (i.e. $drive_{GD}$). Furthermore, to the extent that his indifference principle is correct, he is claiming that $drive_{TV}$ and $drive_{DEP}$ are equivalent to each other (at least as far as reinforcement is concerned); and, indeed, that both are equivalent to variation in incentive for this purpose.

In Premack's own experiments, the data do indeed conform to this formulation. But it has always been the case that the various senses of drive and reinforcement which we distinguished in Chapter 4 hang together for the bulk of behaviour. That is why it has taken so long even to realize which parts of the tangle that unites the two kinds of concept are empirical and which logical. Thus we might find, when we look sufficiently far afield, that Premack's apparent "new look" at reinforcement leaves us with the same difficulties as before.

It turns out, however, that Premack's analysis is saved from most of the previous difficulties by the indifference principle. One consequence of this principle is that neither $drive_{TV}$ nor $drive_{DEP}$ need be regarded as *necessary* for reinforcement (and, empirically speaking, we concluded in Chapter 4 that neither in fact is); for each can substitute for the other. What is more, not even the disjunction, *either* drive$_{TV}$ *or* drive$_{DEP}$, need be regarded as necessary for reinforcement (as is again empirically the case, e.g. in responding for stimulus change); for incentive properties can substitute for either. Thus, for example, Premack's theory is consistent with Mendelson's model (Fig. 5.13), according to which "reward circuits" (which are responsible for the initiation of goal-directed behaviour) may be activated either by water-deprivation or feedback from the act of drinking. And this model, as we have seen, has much to recommend it.

What if we take the notion of relative response probability itself: are there counter-examples to Premack's view that, when this is high, the activity concerned can be a reinforcer and, when it is low, it cannot?

It is difficult to think of a case in which response probability could clearly be said to be low, while the activity concerned is nonetheless reinforcing. However, this difficulty is as likely to reflect Premack's definition of terms as some deep feature of the behaviour of organisms. The most obvious way to go about constructing such a counter-example is to find a rewarding activity which takes rather little time to perform; for, it will be recalled, Premack's definition of response probability is in terms of the proportion of time spent on the different activities concerned. Suppose, therefore, we measure the amounts of time a male rat spends, per 24 h, grooming and copulating (we thoughtfully provide him with an endless supply of receptive females). Undoubtedly, we shall find he spends more time grooming than copulating. It should follow, therefore, that we can reinforce copulatory behaviour with the opportunity to groom and not grooming with the opportunity to copulate. I have not done the experiment; but it seems implausible that this is the result one would obtain. But it would in any case be a waste of experimental time to test Premack's theory in this way: he has already protected himself against the outcome by decrying "the indiscriminate use of average response probabilities" on which my example is based.

Premack constructs his defence by reference to the diagram shown in Fig. 6.2.

Response A depicted in the curve on the right attains an extremely high probability at relatively long intervals, whereas response B shown on the left attains half that probability but at half the interval. The *average* probabilities of the two responses are thus equal; however, their momentary reinforcement values will not be equal. At T_x the reinforcement value of response A is $K \times 0$, that of response B, $K \times .5$; whereas at T_y, the reinforcement value of A is $K \times 1$, while that of response B is half that value. Response A is intended to afford at least a heuristic account of copulation, an explanation of the seeming incompatibility between the great appeal of this behaviour and its limited duration (Premack, 1971, p. 131).

The trouble with this defence is that it may well render Premack's theory incapable of *any* empirical disproof, at least, any of a kind purporting to be an instance of high reinforcement value coupled

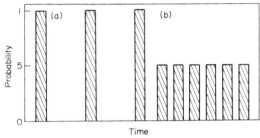

FIG. 6.2. On the Appeal of Copulation in Spite of its Limited Duration. See text for explanation. (From Premack, 1971.)

with low response probability; and a theory incapable even in principle of disproof is no longer an empirical theory at all. This danger looms still larger in another of Premack's statements from the same paper: "it is important that the parameter values used in the reinforcement session—contingent time and interstimulus interval, which can themselves affect response probability (e.g. Premack, 1965)—are also employed in the session used to measure the response probabilities" (Premack, 1971, p. 130). Thus, in the limit, Premack appears to be saying that the probability of the reinforcing activity must be high *at the instant when it is used as a reinforcer*. But, if it were not, it would not occur, and there could be (logically) no reinforcement from it. Thus the chief beneficiary from Premack's defence may turn out to be the law of conservation of tautology.

If the search for an instance of low response probability coupled with high reinforcement value appears to be blocked in this way, the other avenue—high response probability coupled with low reinforcement value—looks more promising. Indeed, we have already discussed such an instance in Chapter 4: the sexual behaviour of the estrous female rat. As we know, this animal, if provided with a constant supply of lovers, shows a high probability of engaging in copulatory behaviour with them on only one day in four. It should follow that access to a copulating male is reinforcing on these days and not on others. But in the Bolles *et al.* (1968) study, such access appeared not to be reinforcing either during estrus or out of it; and in Drewett's (1972) study it appeared to be equally reinforcing at both times. Thus the estrous female rat appears to be as great a stumbling block to Premack's theory of reinforcement as to every other one.

There is an interesting affinity between Premack's theory and the common belief that "all behaviour is motivated". As we have seen, Premack believes that response probability (i.e. proportionate time spent on the activity) can predict reinforcement value *for all activities*. That is to say, anything can reinforce anything else, just so long as the conditions of temporal contiguity and restricted access are met. Indeed, a great virtue of his experimental programme has been his willingness to try out new forms of behaviour with which to test this view of the ubiquity of reinforcement. His own words bear eloquent testimony to his efforts in this direction: "In a desperate attempt to produce revelatory illumination at a single stroke, I once successfully reinforced (horizontal) lever-pressing with (vertical) lever-pressing. But the scene lighted by the data showed few faces, and none with expressions of deep understanding" (Premack, 1971, p. 135).

Let us translate Premack's approach into the language of feed-back mechanisms which we introduced in the previous chapter (Fig. 5.1), bearing in mind the twin concepts of restricted access (for positive reinforcement) and surplus access (for punishment) as we do so. Let us suppose we are carrying out a Premackian experiment and have established an operant level for some form of behaviour or other. Premack believes that if we force the animal to engage in this behaviour less (presumably by some critical amount, but this is left unstated) than this operant level, we shall convert the opportunity to engage in it into a positive reinforcer; and, if we force the animal to engage in it more (presumably again by some critical amount) than the operant level, we shall convert the activity into a punishment. And, for selected forms of behaviour, he showed that this was indeed the case. But the view that this is true for *any* behaviour implies that any activity in which the animal engages is subject to control by negative feedback mechanisms sensitive to departure in *either* direction from the desired level of the activity which is manifest in the operant level. This, I take it, is Premack's version of the view that all behaviour is motivated.

But once again the behaviour of the estrous female rat appears to negate the principle, and for the reasons already stated: she allows herself to be pushed down below her operant level for copulation without demonstrating any greater desire to push this level up again by running to a male rat than when she is not in estrus (Drewett, 1972). It is clear that these important experiments on female sexual motivation in the rat (which, as we have seen, are none too conclusive) deserve replication and extension; much may turn on them. Of course, it is possible that all behaviour is motivated except for female sexual behaviour in one or two mammalian species. This unique case might arise because the motivation undoubtedly present in the male can be relied on to push a two-rat chain of sexual behaviour through to a happy conclusion. All estrus would need to do for the female, on this view, would be to sensitize her sexual reflexes to the stimuli provided by the male (Drewett, 1971)*. Clearly, we would be on stronger ground for attacking Premack if we could find a second example drawn from a different form of behaviour.

Premack's version of the "all behaviour is motivated" view is a particularly strong one in that it supposes that, for *all* behaviour, departure in *either* direction from the spontaneously exhibited level of a given activity is a motivating condition. As already pointed out, this is tantamount to equipping the control systems for all behaviour with negative feedback mechanisms sensitive to both shortfalls and excesses with respect to the desired level. (This point should be carefully distinguished from the view we adopted in the previous chapter that positive reinforcement is the activation of a *positive* feedback mechanism. The effect of the latter mechanism is to maintain ongoing behaviour directed to those features of the environment which allow reinforcement to be attained. That is to say, it is the *reinforced* activity which is maximized by positive feedback.

* Compare the Victorian view that nice girls don't like sex; though there is some reason to believe that the motivational structure of sexual behaviour in females of our own and other primate species is different from that present in the rat (Gray and Drewett, in press).

Premack's views, in contrast, are concerned with the conditions under which an activity becomes a *reinforcer*.) Premack holds then that, when the rate of emission of any activity falls below the desired level, this is sensed by a negative feedback mechanism which increases behaviour directed to correction of the deficit. Or, conversely, when the rate of emission of the activity exceeds the desired level, this too is sensed by a negative feedback mechanism which increases behaviour directed to elimination of the excess.

There is, of course, no reason in logic why behaviour of a particular kind should not be controlled by either or both kinds of negative feedback and by positive feedback as well; and, indeed, this appears to be the case for drinking (McFarland, 1971; Miller *et al.* 1968). Thus, when the rate of drinking is pushed down below its operant level, the consequent water-deficit is sensed and activates, by negative feedback, many mechanisms, including behavioural ones, aimed at the minimization and elimination of the deficit; but, when drinking is occurring, or when cues signalling the imminent arrival of water are received, positive feedback mechanisms are activated so as to maintain and strengthen the ongoing behaviour (McFarland, 1971; and see the previous chapter). (In cases such as this, where one activity—drinking—is simultaneously the source of positive and negative feedback, it is by no means clear whether this is a "reinforced" or "reinforcing" activity. Since the distinction consists in the way we choose to look at the complex systems involved, there is no reason why it should not, in fact, be both.)

However, *a priori*, it would seem a great luxury on the part of Nature to equip all forms of behaviour with negative feedback sensitive to both deficit and excess. Surely there are some forms of behaviour which might without danger or discomfort fall below (but not rise above) or rise above (but not fall below) a desired level, so that it would be sufficient to provide the animal with only a unidirectional sensor for negative feedback*. But, if that were so, there should be, in the light of Premack's analysis, some activities which were capable of becoming punishments (but not rewards) or rewards (but not punishments).

* In a related argument, McFarland (1973) has suggested that this must be so in the case of the "bait shyness" phenomenon (see Chapter 2), in which a taste stimulus is associated with a state of sickness which ensues many hours later. He points out the great difficulty there would be in designing a mechanism capable of forming *both* learned aversions *and* learned preferences over such long delays.

Unfortunately, *a priori* arguments of this kind are but a poor guide to reality. And support for Premack's approach comes from an unexpected quarter—the heart of traditional drive country. Miller *et al.* (1968) examined the motivating effect of an *excess* of water, as compared to the usual case of instigating motivated behaviour by water-deprivation. They preloaded rats with 20 ml of water delivered directly into the stomach and then entered them into a T-maze in which choice of one arm was followed by an injection of saline and choice of the other arm by an injection of anti-diuretic hormone (ADH). A control group of rats without water preloading were run in the same maze. Now the effect of ADH is to slow down the rate of excretion of water in the urine. Thus the preloaded rats would make their excess of water effectively more excessive by choosing the ADH arm. (All rats were forced to choose one arm or the other by the construction of the apparatus.) The control animals showed no preference between the two arms, thus demonstrating that, in the absence of preloading, ADH injections are neither rewarding nor aversive. However, the preloaded rats consistently chose the saline arm. Thus excess of water is a punishing condition, as Premack would expect.

Still, one swallow does not make a summer; the claim Premack's theory makes to universality means that many supporting instances will be needed to establish its foundations at all securely, whereas one or a few negative instances can shake them severely. The estrous female rat is a negative instance in that she does not respond as she should to a reduction in her operant level of sexual behaviour. Are there cases in which an animal does not respond as it should to an *increase* in operant level; does not respond, that is, as did Miller *et al.*'s rats to overloading with water? I do not know of any definite instances of this kind; but this may merely indicate that they have not been looked for.

What of the final claim which can be extracted from Premack's theory: that there is no punishment which does not consist in the elicitation of behaviour (or exposure to a stimulus) in excess of the operant level? The natural way to go about negating this would be to search for a punishing stimulus which has a high operant level of behaviour directed to it. The very odd sound of this suggestion makes one suspect tautology again. For how could a stimulus be a punishment if the animal showed a substantial operant level of self-exposure to the stimulus, given that a punishment precisely is a stimulus which suppresses behaviour on which it is contingent? Premack's answer might be that, in his experiments, running behaviour and the stimulation resulting from this behaviour fits exactly this description. But, unless it far exceeds the operant level, forced running is only a weak punishment. Behaviour directed towards stimuli generally used as punishers (electric shocks, slaps, very loud noises, etc.) has an operant level which is essentially zero. In consequence, even Premack's operational definition of a punisher loses much of its value, for activities which all have zero response probability (e.g. those elicited by electric shocks of 0.2, 0.5, 1.0 and 2.0 mA) differ considerably in their punishing power.

In an effort to use response probability to predict punishing power, Terhune and Premack (1970) introduced a new technique for its measurement which might overcome this kind of difficulty. Rats were first placed in a running wheel in which they were given an opportunity to drink (a drinking tube being inserted into the apparatus) for 10 sec every 40 sec on the average, and also forced to run for 10 sec in every 40 sec on the average. At this stage of the experiment there were no contingencies between running and drinking. The rat could stop the wheel turning, once it had started, by pressing a bar. In this way, the probability of the animal's stopping itself running could be measured as a function of the time after it had been forced to start running. This "probability of non-running" was then used as the independent variable in the second part of the experiment. For each of the three rats which took part in the experiment, forced running of durations corresponding to probabilities of non-running of 0.1, 0.5, 0.8 and 1.0 were made contingent upon drinking, and their punishing effects measured in the usual way as the size of the decrement brought about in the drinking behaviour. The results of the experiment are shown in Fig. 6.3. It will be seen that the degree of suppression of drinking was indeed greater, the greater the probability that the animal would have switched off the running wheel by the end of the duration of forced running used as the punishment.

This kind of experiment is impressive, so long as one keeps to the conceptual framework which Premack imposes on it. But, if one departs from that framework, one realizes that what he has demonstrated is: (a) the longer the duration of forced running, the more likely it is that a rat will emit an escape response to terminate its exposure to forced running; and (b) the longer the duration of forced running, the greater is the suppression of responding on which it is made contingent. But this, in effect, is a demonstration of co-variation between the two separate operational definitions of an S^{R-}: the punishment operation and the escape operation (Table 4.2). And, as pointed out in Chapter 4, though it is not a tautology to suppose that the results of these two operations will co-vary in this way, it is not at all clear which we would choose as *the* criterion for an S^{R-} if they did *not* agree. Thus the empirical content of the

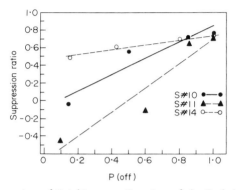

FIG. 6.3. The Suppression of Drinking as a Function of the Probability of Not-running. Each curve is for an individual rat. Abscissa: probability of the rat stopping forced running at a given duration of forced running. Ordinate: degree of suppression of drinking produced by running as punishment. 1.0 = total suppression, 0 = no suppression, negatives = acceleration. (From Premack, 1971.)

assertion that a punishment cannot be a stimulus which is the object of behaviour with a high spontaneous probability of occurrence is, to say the least, obscure.

Premack's work has the valuable quality that it causes us to look at old problems in a new light. We must be careful, however, to check whether the new perspectives he offers should cause us to alter any of the conclusions we have reached in previous chapters concerning issues to which his theory and experiments relate. One such issue is that of the relation between drive and reinforcement. In Chapter 4 we concluded that drive$_{DEP}$ is not necessary for positive reinforcement. But is not this conclusion contradicted by Premack's demonstration of the necessity of restricted access to the positive reinforcer if reinforcement is to occur?

The contradiction is, in fact, more apparent than real. There is an important difference in the kind of deprivation involved in Premack's restricted access and, say, the light-contingent barpressing or alley-running experiments on which we based the conclusion that reinforcement can occur without deprivation. In the former, the restricted access to the S^{R+} obtains at the time that its reinforcing effects are being *measured*; in the kind of experiment we discussed in Chapter 4, in contrast, the deprivation condition was imposed *before* the animal was introduced into the experimental situation in which reinforcement was investigated. And it is the latter kind of deprivation which we concluded was not necessary for reinforcement. From Premack's point of view, this kind of deprivation is one of the conditions which affect response probability, as we have seen earlier in this chapter. The distinction between the two kinds of deprivation is clear if we look again at the alley-running experiments of Fowler (1967) which we examined in Chapter 4 (Figs 4.3, 4.4 and 4.5). His "immediate" deprivation—i.e. the time the animal was detained in the black startbox before being allowed to run to the white goalbox—was the equivalent of a restricted-access condition; and his "maintenance" deprivation—i.e. the amount of exposure to white in the home cage before being put in the alley—was the equivalent of a drive$_{DEP}$ condition. And, as we saw, the former variable affected running speed for entry into the white goalbox, but only in complex interaction with goalbox detention time (Fig. 4.4), just as one would expect if this were a restricted-access variable at work; whereas the latter variable had little if any effect on running speeds (Fig. 4.5). Both in logic and given the evidence, therefore, it is possible to hold the view that restricted access, but not drive$_{DEP}$, is a necessary condition for positive reinforcement.

Premack's Theory Applied to Classical Conditioning

One last point we ought to examine is whether Premack's theory is applicable to classical conditioning (an issue he does not appear to have considered himself). In tackling this question, we shall take the opportunity to summarize the key features of Premack's work. These are the following:

(1) The hypothesis that the ability of a stimulus (or the activity elicited by that stimulus) to act as a positive or negative reinforcer

depends on the probability of occurrence of the elicited activity relative to the probability of occurrence of the reinforced activity. Relative probability of occurrence for the two activities in question is measured as the proportion of time devoted by the animal to each. Further: (a) the activity with the higher response probability can act as a reward for engaging in the activity with the lower response probability, but not the reverse; and (b) the activity with the lower response probability can act as a punishment for engaging in the activity with the higher response probability, but not the reverse.

(2) The analysis of the instrumental contingency for positive reinforcement as involving, as necessary and sufficient conditions: (a) temporal contiguity between the lower-probability response and the higher-probability response, the latter succeeding in time the former; and (b) restriction of access to the stimulus eliciting the higher-probability response to a level below the spontaneous self-exposure rate.

(3) A similar analysis of the instrumental contingency for punishment as involving, as necessary and sufficient conditions: (a) temporal continguity between the higher-probability response and the lower-probability response, the latter succeeding in time the former; and (b) exposure of the animal to the stimulus eliciting the lower-probability response to a degree in excess of the spontaneous self-exposure rate.

Is there anything analogous to these points in classical conditioning? With regard to points (2a) and (3a) we have already considered the relevance of the notions of temporal contiguity and contingency to classical conditioning in Chapter 2. There we concluded that this form of learning is, on the available evidence, more likely to reflect S → S contingencies than temporal contiguity. However, this conclusion is by no means so solid as to offer an impenetrable barrier to the application of Premack's theory to classical conditioning.

What about the notion of relative response probability (point 1)? A view of classical conditioning has been urged by Razran (1957, 1971) which bears some resemblance to Premack's emphasis on the relational character of the reinforcement operation. Razran has argued from the data gained in a large number of Soviet experiments on classical conditioning that, when S_1 and S_2 are temporally sequenced in that order in a classical conditioning paradigm, the possibility of using S_2 as a UCS and so of turning S_1 successfully into a CS depends, not on the absolute characteristics of S_1 and S_2 taken in isolation, but on the intensity of each relative to the other. There is, Razran argues, an optimal ratio of these intensities (which depends in part on straightforward physical stimulus intensity, stimulus modality and so on, but also on such things as biological significance, emotional meaning, etc) for conditioning to occur, the UCS being stronger than the CS, but not too much so. Now since the conditions which determine the intensity of a stimulus are complex, the only way in which this can be evaluated is, in effect, by the characteristics of the response it elicits. Thus Razran's view of the necessary conditions for classical conditioning to take place resembles Premack's view of instrumental reinforcement both in its relational nature and in its stress on the responses elicited by stimuli.

However, even if Razran's view is correct (and it cannot be entirely so, or experiments such as those by Varga and Pressman, discussed in Chapter 2, on "two-way conditioning" would be impossible), there is an essential difference between the classical and instrumental cases. Relative response probability determines not whether instrumental reinforcement can occur or not, but whether, assuming it does occur, it is of the positive (rewarding) or negative (punishing) variety. In contrast, on Razran's view, relative stimulus intensity as between potential CS and potential UCS determines whether or not classical conditioning can occur at all. If it does occur, it is always of the same variety—necessarily so, because (and this is, of course, a fundamental distinction between the two kinds of learning which we encountered in Chapter 4) classical conditioning does not come in two varieties, one appetitive and one aversive.

For the same reasons, the notions of restricted (2b) or surplus (3b) access cannot apply to the classical case in the way that Premack applies them to the instrumental case. For even if we assume that all successful UCSs in classical conditioning experiments are either restricted below or raised above the level of access the animal would like (an assumption which, if Premack's theory is correct, is tantamount to the view, examined and rejected at the end of Chapter 4, that only instrumental reinforcers, whether positive or negative, can serve as classical UCSs), it is still the case that the laws of classical conditioning apparently do not need to take account of which it is—restricted or surplus access, Food in the usual salivary classical conditioning experiment is restricted below the animal's desired level, while acid in an otherwise similar experiment is presented at a rate exceeding this level; but conditioning follows essentially the same course regardless. So the distinction between restricted and surplus access, fundamental as it may well be to instrumental reinforcement, is of no account for the classical case.

In sum, assuming Premack's views of reinforcement in the instrumental case prove to be substantially correct, they do not appear to offer any threat to the conclusion which we reached in Chapter 2, and derived further support for in Chapter 4, that classical and instrumental conditioning involve fundamentally different processes. As became apparent in Chapter 4, and again in the present chapter, one way in which this fundamental difference manifests itself is in the fact that instrumental learning involves two directions of change and two kinds of reinforcing event (positive and negative); whereas classical conditioning involves only one. How the two directions of instrumental change are handled by the CNS will be a major theme in the remainder of this book.

7. Emotion*

The term "emotion" has at times been dismissed with scorn by psychologists as being "no more than a chapter-heading". If so, it has usually headed the wrong chapter. For it is in the work of learning theorists that an understanding of the emotions has slowly emerged. Philosophers have been equally uncertain whether there is a real area of discourse hiding beneath the term "emotion" awaiting their tools of analysis; though some kind of consensus appears to be developing—and this is in complete agreement with the conclusion we shall reach in this chapter—that the emotion-words have to do with the appraisal as "good" or "bad" of the objects which give rise to the emotional states (e.g. Mischel, 1969). Given this doubt on the part of the experts, one would expect the layman to have great difficulty in understanding what emotions are all about. Yet is unlikely that anyone normally fluent in the use of the English language would have difficulty in deciding that "fear", "disappointment", "hope" and "anger", for example, are emotions, while "hunger", "thirst" and "drowsiness" are not. So somewhere there is a reasonably clear distinction being drawn between states which are or are not emotional.

Now it is clear that the term "emotion" is a theory-word: it refers to some kind of hypothetical internal state of the organism, not to something the experimenter does or directly observes. Equally clearly, "hunger", "thirst" and "drowsiness" are also hypothetical internal states of the organism: they are the ones which the learning theorist classifies as "drives" (Chapter 4). Such hypothetical internal states have to be invented in order to account for the fact that an organism's reactions to identical environmental inputs are not themselves invariant. We have to suppose that the variability inherent in the way organisms respond to their environments (assuming it is not totally random) reflects some systematic set of internal states

* This chapter is closely based on two earlier papers (Gray, 1972b, 1973).

which they may enter. The question, then, is: what differentiates those internal states we prefer to call "drives" from those we prefer to call "emotions"?

The answer, I think, is that "drives" are internal states which are principally caused by changes *internal* to the organism, while "emotions" are internal states which are principally caused by events external to the organism. Thus the states of hunger, thirst and drowsiness grow with the passage of time more or less independently of the environment in which the organism is placed; though it is true that they can be reversed or hindered in their development by environmental events (food, water or excessive stimulation, respectively). Fear, disappointment, hope and anger, on the other hand, are normally consequent upon the occurrence of particular kinds of environmental events. This analysis can be supported by a consideration of pathology. It is when drive states become dependent on specific environmental events, or alternatively cease to show the usual variation with time independently of environmental inputs, that we suspect illness; as in, say, the condition of anorexia nervosa (Dally, 1969), or the obese individuals described by Schachter (1967) as over-responding to the palatibility of their diet and other environmental conditions, but under-responding to the passage of time since their last meal, as compared with people of normal weight. Conversely, it is when emotional states arise with *no* precipitating environmental event that we smell pathology, as in "free-floating" anxiety or "endogenous" depression. Our vocabulary is particularly instructive in the case of erotic internal states. From the point of view of the distinction between internal and external control, sexual behaviour constitutes a border-line case: it is about equally dependent on the internal milieu (hormonal status, in particular) and on appropriate external stimuli (optimally, those associated with an attractive and willing member of the opposite sex). In line with the typically internal causation of drive and external elicitation of emotion, we do not, I think, regard "feeling sexy" (where the emphasis is on internal events) as an emotion, while we do so regard "being in love" (where the emphasis is on a particular environmental object).

Excursions into linguistic philosophy of this kind normally do no more than elucidate the use currently being made of the English language. The distinctions uncovered need not correspond to distinctions which exist in reality, and only the latter are of interest to the behavioural scientist. However, in this case, the distinctions apparently made in ordinary language turn out, I believe, to correspond rather well to distinctions which have arisen in the theory of learning (as well as to lines of demarcation within the neuro-endocrine system: Gray, 1973).

If the emotions are internal states elicited by external stimuli, what kinds of stimuli are these? An answer to this question is offered by two-process learning theory. We have already encountered this theory in one of its manifestations, in Chapter 5 when we considered secondary reinforcement and incentive. We shall consider it again in some detail in later chapters. Within this theory, it is possible to give a moderately simple definition of the emotions as *"those (hypothetical) internal states of the CNS which are produced by instrumentally reinforcing events or by stimuli which have in the subject's previous experience been followed by instrumentally reinforcing events"*. Thus the state we described in Chapter 5 as being produced by the presentation of initially neutral stimuli which have been paired (in a classical conditioning paradigm) with an unconditioned positive reinforcer could be called (as Mowrer, 1960, in fact calls it) "hope". This state, as we saw, is one in which the stimulus eliciting it possesses *(conditioned) reinforcing and (conditioned) motivational properties*. Similarly, "fear", as used by Miller (1951) and Mowrer (1947, 1960), is a state elicited by stimuli previously paired with unconditioned punishing events (Chapter 8); and "frustration", in Amsel's (1958) use, is a state produced by "frustrative nonreward", i.e. the omission of anticipated reward (Table 4.2 and Chapter 9).

If emotions are internal states elicited by reinforcing and secondary reinforcing stimuli, one is naturally led to ask how many distinguishable emotional states there are—a question which, given this approach to the problem, is closely related to a second one: "How many distinguishable classes of reinforcing events are there?".

The latter question is one we have already met, and to which we have already given a preliminary answer, as set out in Table 4.2. In general terms, one would naturally begin by dividing reinforcing events into the unconditioned and the conditioned variety. Unconditioned reinforcers are, of course, those which are effective for the species concerned without special training procedures. In the previous chapter, we examined Premack's attempt to identify the essential characteristics of such events; in the present context, however, we can ignore this question and take it for granted simply that we have at our disposal a stock of them (including, no doubt, food for a hungry animal, water for a thirsty one, electric shock etc.). Conditioned or secondary reinforcers, as we know, are those which do not have reinforcing properties *per se*, but acquire them only as a result of pairing with an unconditioned reinforcer. The

TABLE 7-1   Conditioned instrumental reinforcing events

Procedure used with primary reinforcement	Secondary positive reinforcement (Sec S^{R+})	Secondary negative reinforcement (Sec S^{R-})
Presentation	Rew—CS	Pun—CS
Termination	Pun!—CS	Rew!—CS
Omission	$\overline{\text{Pun}}$—CS	$\overline{\text{Rew}}$ CS

For significance of Rew, Pun!, etc., see Table 4.2. "Rew—CS" indicates a stimulus (CS) which has been paired with "Rew", and so on. !: termination. —: omission.

second major division of reinforcing events is that they can be positive (appetitive) or negative (aversive), another distinction with which we are already familiar. Finally, both unconditioned and conditioned reinforcers, whether positive or negative, can be presented, terminated or withheld, contingent upon some response or other. This leads to the set of classifications shown in Table 4.2 (reinforcing procedures with unconditioned reinforcing events) and Tables 7.1 and 7.2 (reinforcing procedures with conditioned reinforcing events).

In considering these three Tables and the symbols used in them, the reader should carefully distinguish between three kinds of classification.

(1) Classification of *stimuli*. A stimulus may classify as an S^{R+} in any one of three ways, by passing the presentation, termination or omission tests. Similarly, there are three ways in which a stimulus may classify as an S^{R-}. (See Table 4.2, Chapter 4.)

(2) Classification of *procedures*. A number of new symbols are introduced in these Tables which we have not yet used in the text.

TABLE 7-2   Reinforcing procedures with conditioned reinforcing events

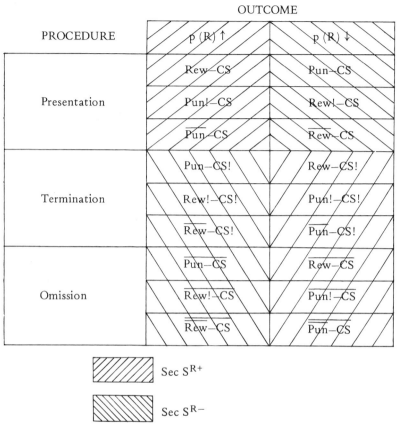

The abbreviations and symbols are as defined by the intersection of row (procedure) and column (outcome). p (R)↑: outcome is an increase in the probability of the response on which the reinforcing event is made contingent. p (R)↓: outcome is a decrease in the probability of this response. Crosshatching indicates those procedures-plus-outcomes which define a stimulus as a secondary (Sec) S^{R+} or S^{R-}, respectively. Rew—CS, etc., as defined in Table 7.1. !: termination. —: omission.

These symbols are defined by the intersection of the rows (representing the procedure by which the reinforcing effects of a stimulus are demonstrated) and the columns (representing the valence, positive or negative, of the reinforcing effect so demonstrated). Thus, "Rew" stands for the presentation of a positive reinforcer, "Rew!" and $\overline{\text{Rew}}$ for its termination and omission, respectively; and similarly for "Pun", "Pun!" and $\overline{\text{Pun}}$.

(3) Classification of *systems*. This is the point at which we go beyond operational definition to ask about the underlying systems in the CNS which mediate the observed changes of behaviour consequent upon the imposed experimental procedures. The question, "How many distinguishable classes of reinforcing events are there?" (which, in terms of two-process theory, is equivalent to asking how many distinguishable emotional states there are) is posed in this sense. The answer to it cannot be derived from purely logical considerations, but calls for experimental evidence. We shall consider some of the relevant data in the next few chapters.

An obvious hypothesis from which one might start on the search for underlying systems is that the operational distinction between positive and negative reinforcers corresponds to a real line of demarcation in the brain. This hypothesis is in direct opposition to Hull's theory of learning, which (as we saw in Chapter 4) treated all reinforcement as consisting in drive-reduction, it being unimportant whether the drive which was reduced was set up by, e.g. deprivation of food or the application of an electric shock. However, a major blow against this aspect of the Hullian monolith has been struck by the experiments on the reinforcing properties of direct electrical stimulation of the brain pioneered by James Olds (Olds and Olds, 1965). These experiments rather strongly suggest that rewards and punishments act on quite different systems in the brain.

We have come across this kind of experiment earlier. A rat is implanted with an electrode in one or other part of the brain and then one or both of two procedures may be followed. In tests for positive self-stimulation, the rat can press a lever or make some other response to cause the passage of a small electric current through the electrode into the tissue surrounding the tip. By the usual definition of an S^{R+}, if lever-pressing increases in probability under these conditions, it must be concluded that the electrical stimulation is rewarding. In tests for negative reinforcement, the current is applied by the experimenter and the rat is given the opportunity of terminating it by its response. If it does so, it is concluded that the electrical stimulation is an S^{R-}.

Olds and Olds (1965) have reviewed a large number of such experiments and have concluded that there are two anatomically distinct areas in the brain. Stimulation of one of them has purely rewarding effects, which begin at low current intensities and get greater as current intensity is increased. Stimulation of the other has punishing effects, and these too appear at the lowest stimulus intensity at which any reinforcing effects of any kind are observed and then get greater as current intensity is increased. According to Olds and Olds' analysis, mixed effects, such as reward at low current intensities and punishment at high intensities, or reward at brief current durations and punishment at long durations, are seen at points of anatomical overlap between the two main systems or in structures which have neural connections with both. (A Hullian view, especially if one follows Miller's, 1959, treatment of drive as a strong stimulus, would lead one to expect that stimulation of the brain would rather generally be innocuous at low intensities, but aversive at high intensities.) Thus it seems likely that, corresponding to the operational distinction between positive and negative instrumental reinforcers, there are two distinct brain systems, one for reward and one for punishment.

These, then, are the inter-twined themes we shall explore in the remaining chapters: two-process theory, the emotions, and the different kinds of reinforcing event. We start in the next chapter with the behavioural effects of punishment.

8. Punishment

The starting point for our consideration of the behavioural effects of punishment is Miller's (1951, 1959) research on "approach-avoidance conflict". It is an oddity of Miller's work that, though he explicitly regarded himself as a Hullian theorist, his analysis of approach-avoidance conflicts is one of the most important sources for the distinction between reward and punishment which has been stressed in this book, but which Hull ignored.

Miller's basic experimental situation is one in which a rat is first trained to run down an alley for a reward and is then given a punishment (usually an electric shock) each time it reaches the goal. In the terms set out in Table 4.2, it is clear that this situation involves the operation Pun (presentation of a negative reinforcer). Animals trained in this way show obvious signs of conflict. Under appropriate conditions they will start off towards the goalbox, stop, and then oscillate around this stopping point, slow approach behaviour being interrupted by sudden withdrawals. In analysing this behaviour, Miller supposed, naturally enough, that it results from an underlying conflict between separate approach and avoidance tendencies. We have already considered how the approach tendency might be set up, invoking the concepts of incentive and secondary positive reinforcement in our account (Chapter 5). In the present chapter we focus our attention on the avoidance tendency.

This we should call, more accurately, a *passive* avoidance tendency. The distinction between active and passive avoidance had, in fact, not been made fully explicit at the time Miller constructed his model. As we saw in Table 4.2 it consists, at the operational level, in this: passive avoidance is the fall in the probability of a response which is followed by an S^{R-} (Pun); active avoidance is the rise in the probability of a response which is followed by omission of an S^{R-} ($\overline{\text{Pun}}$). The behaviour of a rat in Miller's approach-avoidance conflict situation clearly fits the former, not the latter, definition.

On the face of it it is unlikely that a distinction between active and passive avoidance established in this way on operational grounds should correspond to anything real in the CNS. Consider the rat as having at its disposal an array of possible responses, R_1, R_2 ... R_j. In a passive avoidance situation, the experimenter designates one of these responses (R_p) as being followed by punishment and programmes nonpunishment to follow any other response; in an active avoidance situation, he designates one response (Ra) as being followed by nonpunishment and programmes punishment to follow

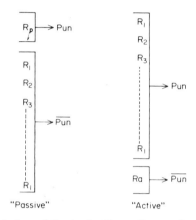

FIG. 8.1. Active and Passive Avoidance. See text for explanation.

any other response (Fig. 8.1). The apparently arbitrary nature of this distinction becomes apparent if we suppose that the experimenter now gradually expands the class of punished responses (to include 2, 3, 4 etc. different responses) in the passive avoidance situation, or that he gradually expands the class of nonpunished responses in the active avoidance situation. At what point during these expansions does the one form of avoidance change into the other? No doubt it is this kind of reasoning, whether explicit or implicit, which has caused learning theorists for the most part to consider active and passive avoidance as essentially the same species of behaviour. Mowrer (1960), for example, reduces the difference between them to the stimuli which become cues for each: in passive avoidance "these stimuli are produced by (correlated with) the behaviour, or response, which we wish to block"; whereas, in active avoidance learning, they are "not response-produced—they are, so to say, extrinsic rather than intrinsic, independent rather than response-dependent" (p. 32).

However, in spite of the pleasing parsimony of treating the two kinds of avoidance as alike, except insofar as the one is a learnt response to exteroceptive cues and the other to proprioceptive ones (Mowrer's proposal), the facts suggest otherwise. These facts derive from a number of different lines of research; some belonging to physiological psychology and some to research on individual differences. They concur in demonstrating the existence of a diversity of factors which affect an animal's ability to learn or perform an active avoidance response quite differently from the way they affect his prowess at passive avoidance. Among these factors are lesions to the septal area (McCleary, 1966; Gray, 1970b), the hippocampus (Douglas, 1967; Gray, 1970b), the cingulate gyrus (McCleary, 1966) and the frontal neocortex (Albert and Bignami, 1967; Grossman, 1967); the administration of the drugs sodium amylobarbitone and alcohol (Miller, 1959, 1964; Gray, 1970b); sex (Gray, 1971a, b; Denti and Epstein, 1972); selective breeding (Gray, 1971a); and stimulation in early infancy (Gray, 1971a). In the light of this remarkable convergence of information from quite diverse sources, it is obviously difficult to hold that active and passive avoidance are only trivially different from each other. We shall therefore assume that they are based on rather different processes, leaving active avoidance for later consideration in Chapter 10.

Miller's Equilibrium Model for Approach–Avoidance Conflicts

If we suppose, then, that the behaviour observed in Miller's experimental situation results from conflict between separate approach and passive–avoidance tendencies, the first step is to specify the conditions which affect the strength of each. Figure 8.2 shows some of these conditions in the form of a block diagram. Not surprisingly, we expect the approach tendency to be stronger if, for example, the animal is hungrier, the food reward is greater, and the number of previous rewards is greater; similarly, the avoidance tendency will be stronger, the more intense the electric shock and the more often it has been experienced.

But Miller's critical postulate concerns distance from the goal. We would obviously expect both the approach and avoidance tendencies

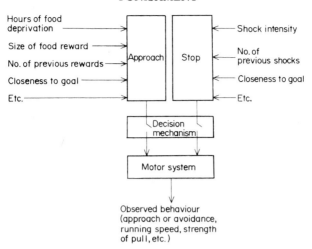

FIG. 8.2. Factors Affecting the Strengths of Approach and Avoidance. Miller's analysis of the factors which affect the strength of the approach and passive avoidance tendencies in a conflict situation drawn as a block diagram. The "decision mechanism" closes *either* the switch which allows the "motor system" to be controlled by the "approach" mechanism *or* the switch which allows it to be controlled by the "stop" or "passive avoidance" mechanism, but not both. Which switch is closed depends on the strength of the inputs to the decision mechanism from the approach and stop mechanisms, and these in turn depend on the factors listed to the left and right of the figures. (From Gray, 1971a.)

to get stronger, the closer the animal gets to the goal. But the strength of the two opposing tendencies cannot be affected in identical ways by distance from the goal. If they were, whichever was stronger at the furthest point from the goal would also be stronger at the nearest point to the goal and, in that case, the animal would either stop as far away as possible from it or approach it completely: the *part*-approach to the goal which is such a conspicuous feature of conflict behaviour simply could not occur. The only way in which the behaviour of part-approach, followed by hesitations and oscillations, can occur is if the strength of avoidance increases more rapidly with nearness to the goal than does that of approach; and this is the postulate which lies at the heart of Miller's conflict model.

The resulting approach and avoidance functions are shown in Fig. 8.3. It can be seen that the model now predicts that if the animal is placed further away from the goal than the point at which the two theoretical functions cross, he should move towards the goal until he reaches that point; if, on the other hand, he is placed nearer the goal than the equilibrium point, he should retreat towards it. Given both

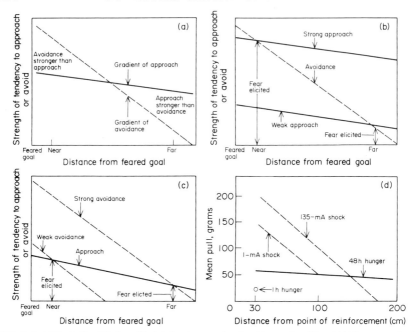

FIG. 8.3. Miller's Equilibrium Model for Approach–Avoidance Conflict. (A) The strength of
both the approach and the avoidance tendencies falls off with distance from the goal, but
the strength of the avoidance tendency falls off more rapidly. (B) Factors which increase or
decrease the strength of the approach tendency other than distance from the goal are
thought to raise or lower the height of the approach gradient without affecting its slope.
(C) Similarly, factors which increase or decrease the strength of the avoidance tendency raise
or lower the height of avoidance gradient. In every case, the animal should approach the
goal until the two gradients cross and then oscillate about this point. The fear finally elicited
depends on the height of the avoidance gradient at this equilibrium point. Empirical data
(D), obtained from rats wearing a special harness which made it possible to measure the
strength of the approach and avoidance tendencies separately when they were trained to run
in a runway with only food or only shock, support Miller's model. (From Miller 1959.)

physical and psychological inertia in this system, we should observe
the oscillation around the equilibrium point which is in fact typically
observed. The effects of those conditions which affect either the
approach or avoidance tendency, but not both, are conceived as
raising or lowering the entire function to which they relate without
affecting its slope. Thus, increasing hunger or decreasing shock
intensity should have the result that the animal will approach more
closely to the goal, perhaps even reaching it; and the reverse
operations should have the reverse effect.

These deductions have been confirmed in a series of experiments
from Miller's laboratory, especially those conducted by J. S. Brown,

who introduced a neat technique by which it is possible to measure, quite literally, the "strength" of the approach and avoidance tendencies. The rat is trained to run wearing a special harness which can be used to stop him at any chosen point in the runway. Since it is attached to a spring, it is possible to measure the strength with which the animal pulls against the harness at that point. Using this device (with animals trained only on the one habit, approach or avoidance), Brown was able to verify directly the crucial postulate that the strength of the avoidance tendency falls off more steeply with distance from the goal than does the strength of the approach tendency (Fig. 8.3, D).

Solomon (1964), however, has questioned the validity of these conclusions. He writes:

> Typically, the subject in an approach–avoidance experiment is trained to perform a specific sequence of responses under reward incentive and appetitive drive conditions. He runs to food when hungry. In contrast when the shock is introduced into the runway, it is usually placed near the goal, and no specific, long sequence of instrumental responses is required of the subject before the shock is terminated. Thus, the initial strengths of the approach and avoidance instrumental responses (which are in conflict) are not equated by analogous or symmetrical procedures. Miller has thoroughly and carefully discussed this, and has suggested that the avoidance gradient would not have as steep a slope if the shock were encountered by the rat early in the runway in the case where the whole runway is electrified. While this comment is probably correct, it does not go far enough, and I would like to elaborate on it. I would argue that if one wants to study the relative steepness of approach and avoidance in an unbiased way, the competing instrumental responses should be established in a *symmetrical* fashion. After learning to run down an alley to food the subject should be shocked near the goalbox or in it, and the shock should not be terminated until the subject has escaped all the way into the startbox. Then one can argue that two conflicting instrumental responses have been established. First, the subject runs one way for food; now he runs the same distance in the opposite direction in order to escape shock. When he stays in the startbox, he avoids shock entirely. Then the generalization or displacement of the approach and avoidance responses can be fairly studied (Solomon, 1964, p. 247).

At first sight Solomon's argument has considerable force. However, on closer scrutiny it becomes apparent that he has substituted for Miller's original approach–passive avoidance conflict one between approach and *escape* learning. Given the known differences between active and passive avoidance (involving Pun and Pun, respectively, contingent upon a designated response), one cannot assume that a hypothesis concerning the relationship between distance from the goal and the strength of passive avoidance can be translated into an equivalent hypothesis concerning escape behaviour. In fact, the underlying mechanisms controlling escape learning (i.e. increased probability of responses followed by Pun!) are more likely to resemble those controlling active avoidance (considered in Chapter 10) than those controlling passive avoidance. Nonetheless, Solomon's point is sufficiently powerful for one to seek confirmation that, at the very least, the principles Miller and Brown have demonstrated in the runway can be shown to operate in other situations as well.

Approach–avoidance conflicts have been much less studied in apparatuses other than the runway. However, there are two interesting experiments in the Skinner box which indicate that the same basic phenomena can be observed in this situation (although neither is directed to Solomon's point). In one of these, due to Millenson and McMillan (in press), we see the behaviour of part-approach to the goal which Miller observed in the runway. Rats are first trained to hold a bar down for ten seconds for a food reward. Shock is then also delivered at the end of the 10 sec period of bar-holding. The result (as shown in Fig. 8.4) is that the rat repeatedly initiates bar-holding behaviour, but only rarely completes the full 10 sec which will bring it both reward and punishment. In the second experiment (Hearst, 1967) rats are given "free" food (i.e. not contingent upon any specific response) on a variable interval schedule if they press a lever to make this schedule available. They are then exposed simultaneously to various schedules of "free" shock concurrently with the free food schedule, both the food and shock schedules being turned on simultaneously by pressing the same lever. A second press of the lever turns both schedules off. Hearst showed that, under conditions in which the total amount of time for which the animal exposed itself to these paired schedules was intermediate (i.e. food-seeking behaviour was neither completely suppressed by the associated shocks, not completely dominant over them), there was a maximum of "oscillatory" behaviour, defined as the number of times the animal both switched the paired schedules on and then rapidly switched them off again. This apparently corresponds to the oscillatory behaviour observed by Miller in the runway.

A further part of Miller's original series of runway experiments showed that stimulus similarity affects the approach and avoidance functions in the same way as distance from the goal. According to the principle of "stimulus generalization" (Fig. 3.9) the magnitude of the learnt response (whether classically or instrumentally conditioned) falls off as the similarity of a test stimulus to the original

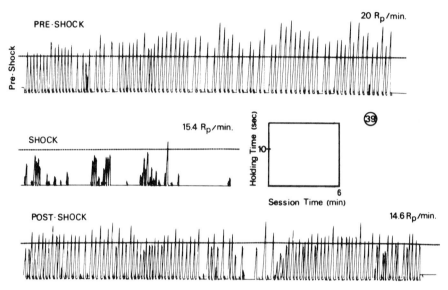

FIG. 8.4. Approach Avoidance Conflict in the Millenson–MacMillan Barholding Experiment. Representative record from a rat trained to hold down a bar for 10 sec to obtain a food reward ("preshock") and then also shocked for barholding ("shock"). The "post-shock" record shows recovery after punishment was discontinued. Vertical extents of pen-excursions show durations of bar-holds. Notice repeated initiation of bar holds, without completion of ten seconds necessary for reward and punishment, in shock phase. (From Millenson and MacMillan, in press.)

training stimulus (CS or S^D) becomes less. Again, then, we would expect both the approach and avoidance tendencies to be decreased if the original training situation is changed. Using runways of varying degrees of similarity, Miller has shown that this is indeed so, and that the decrease in the strength of the avoidance tendency is greater than the decrease in approach, for equal changes in stimulus stimilarity.

Given the critical nature of the assumption, in Miller's model, of a steeper fall-off in avoidance than in approach with change or distance from the goal it would obviously be desirable to be able to deduce this assumption from more fundamental principles. Miller and Brown have attempted to do this by considering the degree to which the cues providing motivational impulsion and direction for the two kinds of behaviour originate, on the one hand, from the environment or, on the other, from sources internal to the animal. It is only the former which should be affected by environmental change or spatial location. Now, when a rat runs down an alley for a food or water reward, there are two sources of motivational excitement. Internal to the animal there are cues emanating from the state of hunger or thirst, which depend on the number of hours of deprivation of food or water. (Even if, following the arguments we advanced in Chapter 5, we cease to regard the hunger and thirst drives as providing direct motivational excitement, we can still treat them, following Mendelson, 1970, as providing cues "signifying that instrumental responses for food and water will be followed by the rewarding activities of feeding and drinking".) External to the animal there are various stimuli along the runway which, in the way we traced in Chapter 5, have become conditioned stimuli signalling the imminence of food and thus providing "incentive" motivation. The strength of this incentive motivation will depend on such factors as the size of the reward, the number of conditioning experiences, distance from the goal, and so on.

Consider now an animal running down a runway towards a goalbox in which it has previously received shock on a number of occasions. Analogously to the acquisition by the stimuli in the runway of secondarily rewarding (or incentive) properties, we may suppose that they also acquire secondarily aversive properties. This process is often described by saying that they become conditioned "fear" stimuli. Later in this chapter we shall consider the nature of the properties possessed by such stimuli and the way in which they come to possess them. For the moment, let us simply regard them as the source of Miller's avoidance tendency (or "conditioned fear"). The strength of the conditioned fear will depend on the intensity of the punishment, the number of times it has been experienced, distance from the goal, and so on. But there is no internal source of motivation to do for the avoidance tendency what hunger does for the approach tendency. Now, since the strength of conditioning of both incentive and fear of external cues depends in the same way on distance from the goal, the approach and avoidance tendencies, to the extent that they result from exteroceptive stimuli, should be affected similarly by change in distance from the goal. But the cues which emanate from hunger and thirst are independent of distance from the goal (or of any other change in the external environment). Thus the avoidance tendency should be more purely determined by stimulus similarity and distance from the goal than the approach tendency.

In this way, then, it is possible, in general terms, to deduce the greater steepness of the avoidance than the approach function found in the typical Miller runway approach–avoidance conflict experiment. A more formal treatment shows that this deduction depends, however, on the hidden assumption that the rate of fall-off with stimulus change or distance from the goal in either the approach or the avoidance tendency is directly proportional to the magnitude of the external sources of motivation (and independent of the magnitude of the internal sources of motivation). Let us suppose that the approach and avoidance tendencies, in a typical Miller runway experiment, are in exact equilibrium in the goalbox itself, i.e. the animal risks taking the punishment in order to get the food reward on 50% of the possible occasions. Let the value of the avoidance tendency (or "fear") in the goalbox be x. Let the value of the approach tendency in the goalbox be $z = y + a$, where y represents the contribution from incentive motivation and a the contribution from hunger drive. Ex hypothesi, $x = z = y + a$ and therefore $x > y$. Suppose we now take some point earlier along the runway, or alternatively the same point in the goalbox but in a runway of changed appearance. Let the generalized values of the avoidance and approach tendencies under these new conditions be x' and $z' = a + y'$ respectively. Ex hypothesi $x' < z'$. Since a is constant, it follows that $x - x' > y - y'$. Assuming, as in the search for generality we must, that the difference between the decrement $x - x'$ and the decrement $y - y'$ is not due to the fact that the former relates to the avoidance function and the latter to the approach function, it follows that the magnitude of the decrement must be proportional to the value of x or y. The simplest assumption would be that, for equal steps of stimulus change (or equal increments of distance from the goal),the values of x or y are decreased by a constant divisor.

If this analysis is correct, it should be possible to alter the gradients of the approach and avoidance functions relative to each other by manipulating the degree to which each is controlled by internal and external sources of motivation. Hearst (1969) has conducted a number of experiments which offer indirect support for this inference.

In studies of both rewarded operant behaviour and active avoidance behaviour he has shown that gradients of stimulus generalization along exteroceptive stimulus dimensions are indeed shallower, the greater the degree to which the behaviour in question is simultaneously under the control of cues internal to the subject. For example, in one experiment pigeons were rewarded for keypecking on a schedule of "differential reinforcement for low rates" ("DRL"), on which only responses separated from one another by more than t seconds obtain reward. This schedule produced shallower gradients of stimulus generalization along an exteroceptive stimulus dimension (angle of orientation of a line projected on the key) than did reinforcement on a variable interval schedule. This would be predicted on the "internal cues" hypothesis, since DRL responding is controlled in part by the passage of time, and this must be assessed in some way by a mechanism which is internal to the animal. Similarly, Sidman avoidance behaviour, in which each response postpones the next programmed shock by t seconds, shows very little decrease when exteroceptive stimuli are varied from the training conditions (Hearst, 1965). However, Sidman avoidance is, of course, a form of *active* avoidance and, for reasons already discussed, we cannot automatically generalize from active avoidance to passive avoidance experiments, such as Miller's original experiments on conflict in the runway. Direct studies of the role of internal cues in the latter situation do not appear to have yet been carried out.

Passive Avoidance: Classical or Instrumental Conditioning

We have so far discussed Miller's passive avoidance tendency without saying very much about what sort of a tendency it is. In the first instance, as we already know (Table 4.2), passive avoidance may be operationally defined as the decrease in the probability of a response which is followed by presentation of punishment. This is evidently a form of instrumental learning, in that the contingency ostensibly programmed by the experimenter is an R → S one. But we have also linked what goes on in a passive avoidance experiment to the acquisition of incentive motivation by initially neutral stimuli in an approach learning experiment; a process which, in Chapter 5, we attributed to *classical* conditioning. That we are once again faced with the ambiguities surrounding the two kinds of conditioning is no accident; for the facts appear to indicate that passive avoidance learning partakes a little of both.

If one tries to consider passive avoidance as a pure case of instrumental learning, as it purports to be (operationally speaking), one immediately comes up against certain difficulties concerning the contingency and/or temporal contiguity which ought to hold between the R which gets suppressed and the S^{R-} which leads to its suppression. Now, as we saw in Chapter 6, Premack's work suggests that the full contingency is not necessary in the case of positive instrumental reinforcement, the weaker conditions of temporal contiguity and restricted access to the reinforcement being sufficient. The full contingency is equally unnecessary for the acquisition of passive avoidance. It is sufficient for pairings of the form, CS → UCS/ S^{R-} (e.g. electric shock), to be presented to an animal while it is engaging in positively reinforced behaviour for it to desist from this behaviour during the CS, even though the shock is not contingent upon performance of the positively reinforced response. But even temporal *contiguity* between R and S appears not to be necessary where passive avoidance is concerned; for the same outcome is obtained if the animal is presented, while engaged in positively reinforced behaviour, with a stimulus which has previously been paired, in a *different* environment, with electric shock as UCS according to a classical conditioning paradigm. Since these are the same outcomes as that seen when the positively reinforced response is explicitly followed by shock according to an R → S contingency, the question arises whether this contingency contributes anything in its own right to the observed behaviour.

This question has been examined by comparing the results obtained in the Skinner box when barpressing for food is punished by shock contingent upon the barpress (a full punishment paradigm, in principle identical to Miller's approach–avoidance design) with those obtained when shock or CSs previously paired with shock are presented to the animal while it is barpressing, but not contingent upon this response. (The suppression of operant behaviour observed in the latter case is often called a "conditioned emotional response" or CER: Estes and Skinner, 1941.) A recent paper by Church *et al.* (1970) reviews previous experiments in this field and contributes some important new findings. It is clear that (a) response-contingent punishment produces more suppression of the punished response than does shock delivered irrespective of the subject's responses, but also that (b) the latter kind of treatment produces considerable response-suppression on its own. Church *et al.*'s own experiments suggest, moreover, that the response-suppressive effects of non-contingent shock do not arise out of an adventitious temporal pairing between the response and the shock. Two of their experiments are relevant to this conclusion.

In the first of these experiments the animal could perform one of two responses to obtain positive reinforcement—barpressing or chain-pulling. Suppression of these responses was set up according to a punishment paradigm or to a CER one. In both cases the warning signal was a 3 min period of white noise. In the CER paradigm, shock occurred at random intervals during this warning signal; in the punishment paradigm, shocks were programmed at the same intervals, but actually delivered only when the animal made its first response (barpress or chain-pull) after this programming. The key measures were taken during extinction, i.e. with no further shocks delivered. Two separate conditions were investigated. In the first, the positively reinforced response was the same (barpressing or chain-pulling) during extinction of response-suppression as during acquisition. In the second, it was changed from acquisition to extinction; for example, if the animal had been barpressing during acquisition of conditioned suppression, the effects of the white noise were evaluated during extinction with the chain-pulling response. The results of this experiment are presented in Fig. 8.5. The important points to notice are that, first, the change of response had a much bigger effect on the degree of response suppression in the punishment than in the CER condition (indeed, there was no significant effect of change of response in the latter condition); and, second, that the degree of suppression of the *changed* response in the punishment condition was the same as the suppression of either changed or unchanged response in the CER condition.

Another of the experiments reported by Church *et al.* (1970) was similar, but this time comparison of the response-suppressive effects of the CER and punishment paradigms was carried out while the

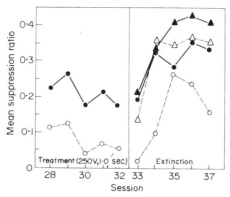

FIG. 8.5. Comparison of Suppression Produced by Response-Contingent and by Response-Noncontingent Shock. Mean suppression ratio (0 = total suppression, 0.5 = no suppression) as a function of response-contingent shock ("Pun") or response-noncontingent shock ("CER") during training (left-hand panel) and extinction (right-hand panel). During extinction the response studied was either the same as that during training or was changed to the alternative (barpressing or chain-pulling). (From Church, Wooten and Matthews, 1970.)

subject worked on both manipulanda (lever and chain) on a con-current schedule of positive reinforcement (i.e., both response were reinforced on variable-interval schedules independently of each other). In the punishment condition, during the warning signal the shocks programmed at random intervals were delivered after only one of the responses; in the CER condition the delivery of the shock was independent of both responses. The results of this experiment are shown in Fig. 8.6. It is clear that the degree of suppression of the unpunished response in the punishment condition is the same as the degree of suppression of both responses in the CER condition, and also clear that the animals in the punishment condition were able to make a clear discrimination between the response which was punished and the one which was not.

These results rather strongly suggest, in agreement with the conclusions reached by the experimenters, that the response suppression produced in the CER paradigm is a direct result of the pairing of the warning signal with the shock (i.e. of an S → S classical conditioning paradigm) and not of an adventitious pairing of the response itself with shock. This, at any rate, is the natural interpretation of the fact that the CER paradigm produced about the same degree of response suppression in both experiments as the punishment paradigm robbed of its specific response information (by change of response or by discrimination of the unpunished response in the concurrent schedule). The authors suggest—and we may well agree—that punishment may then be considered a CER *plus*: i.e. a degree of response suppression produced by pairing a signal with shock, as in the CER paradigm, plus a further degree of response suppression produced by pairing the specific response with shock.

These experiments, then, lead naturally to the conclusion that the bulk of the response suppression produced in either a passive avoidance or a CER experiment is due to the *classical* conditioning

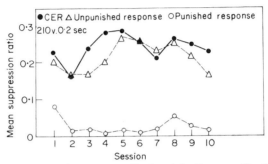

FIG. 8.6. Further Comparison of Suppression Produced by Response-Contingent and by Response-Noncontingent Shock. Mean suppression ratio (0 = total suppression, 0.5 = no suppression) when one of two responses (bar-pressing or chain-pulling), but not the other, was punished during the warning signal, or when shock was not contingent on either response ("CER"). (From Church, Wooten and Matthews, 1970).

which is a necessary feature of such an experiment. This conclusion has much in common with the view we took of autoshaping in Chapter 2: namely, that this is a case of apparent instrumental learning which is in fact disguised classical conditioning. Furthermore, given the finding by Williams and Williams (1969) that pigeons in an autoshaping procedure cannot learn to refrain from pecking under a negative response contingency (i.e. lighted key → grain *unless* the pigeon pecks, in which case grain is cancelled), it is likely that the pigeon's autoshaped keypecking is *entirely* a matter of classical conditioning. Might this also be the case for response suppression in the rat?

This question is tantamount to asking another one: if the punishment paradigm is a CER paradigm *plus*, then what is it that is added? Is it a genuine R → S component, i.e. instrumental learning? Or is it the result of a further S → S pairing, namely, that between response-produced stimuli (as CSs) and shock (as UCS)? If it were the latter, then the response suppression produced in both the CER and the punishment paradigms would be due entirely to classical conditioning.

In an attempt to answer this question, let us apply the Williams and Williams (1969) procedure—"autoshaping with a negative response contingency"—to response suppression. That is to say, we set up the contingency, CS → shock, unless the animal makes a designated response, in which case the shock is cancelled, and we compare the outcome of this experiment with that resulting from CS → shock pairings alone. In fact, we have no need to perform the experiment, since it has been done many times before: it is a standard active avoidance procedure of the kind we shall examine in detail in Chapter 10. And—in the rat—there is no doubt about the outcome. Although active avoidance learning of this kind is sometimes difficult in this species, it undoubtedly occurs. Thus the plus which is present in punishment but absent in the CER is probably genuine instrumental learning.

This same point can be made by reference to the susceptibility of instrumental, but not classical conditioning to "bidirectional conditioning" (Chapter 2). And, indeed, Williams and Williams' procedure is merely a special case of the bidirectional conditioning assay for instrumental reinforcement. As we saw in Chapter 2, this assay consists in showing that presentation of a putative instrumental reinforcer can either increase or decrease a designated response, depending only on whether the experimenter chooses to follow increases or decreases by the S^R. Classical conditioning, on the other hand, can lead to one or other outcome, but never both.

Suppose then, that we pair a tone CS with a shock UCS while a rat presses a bar. The outcome, as we know, is that the CS elicits response suppression; and this is invariably the outcome so long as we stick to a classical conditioning procedure with shock as the UCS. But let us now change to the instrumental mode. We can then do one of two things: we can follow barpressing by shock (punishment) or we can follow not-barpressing by shock (active avoidance with barpressing as the avoidance response). In the former case, we again obtain response suppression, but in the latter we obtain an increase in the rate of barpressing. The latter—the increase in barpressing as an active avoidance response—can only be a case of instrumental learning. And, whereas the former—the response suppression produced by punishment—could be entirely due to classical conditioning, it is more plausible to suppose that it too contains an element of instrumental learning*.

Response suppression in the CER then, is due only to classical conditioning (the CS → S^{R-}/UCS pairing); and in the case of punishment it is due in part to the same process, but in part also to an instrumental component (the R → S^{R-} pairing). Clearly, then, in both cases classical conditioning is very important. But what is it, in that case, that is getting conditioned? This question brings us to a rather odd feature of the experiments reported in this field.

The Behavioural Inhibition System

This oddity is that classical conditioning experiments in which the UCS is an S^{R-} constitute a clear-cut exception to the restricted version of the stimulus substitution view of classical conditioning which we endorsed in Chapter 2. According to this theory (see Fig. 2.2), there are no components (other than responses evoked by the CS before conditioning ever took place) in the vector of response changes evoked by the CS which do not also figure (with the same sign but not necessarily the same magnitude) in the vector of response changes elicited by the UCS. To the best of my knowledge, the only observations which are at variance with this rule have been made in experiments in which the UCS is a punishment. Thus, an electric shock elicits, as UCS, a great deal of activity (running, jumping, etc) and of noise (squealing) in the rat; but a CS which has been followed by such a UCS elicits exactly the reverse: immobility and silence (Myer, 1971). Heart-rate and respiratory responses have sometimes been seen to follow a similar pattern of inverse sign of change. In human subjects, for example, the heart-rate response to unconditioned electric shock is acceleration, but to a CS signalling shock it is deceleration (Notterman et al., 1952; Obrist et al., 1965).

But if these conclusions are correct, we are faced with the following situation. On the one hand, pairing according to a classical

---

* Interestingly, whereas pigeons show response suppression in punishment and CER situations of a kind which is very comparable to that shown by rats, it has proved much harder to teach them an instrumental avoidance response (Moore, 1973: see Chapter 10). Thus response suppression in *birds* may often be entirely a matter of classical conditioning. However, a recent report by Ferrari et al. (1973) shows clearly that pigeons, can, under the right conditions, be taught an avoidance response.

conditioning S → S paradigm of CS and punishment is responsible for much of the suppression of response in a passive avoidance experiment. On the other hand, such pairing of neutral stimuli with punishing ones fails to conform to the usual classical conditioning rule of modified stimulus substitution. So what at first looks like instrumental R → S learning turns out to be, at least in part, S → S conditioning in disguise, and this S → S conditioning, in turn, has a distinctly fishy smell.

I have considered this peculiar feature of passive avoidance behaviour (or "the conditioning of fear", depending on whether one prefers the instrumental or the classical vocabulary) before (Gray, 1971a). I suggested then that one might suppose that the rat (and no doubt many other species) comes equipped with an *innate* response to stimuli which have been followed by unconditioned punishing stimuli and only needs to learn (by classical conditioning) *which* originally neutral stimuli he should respond to. This kind of admixture of learning and innate behaviour would not be without parallel; and it makes good adaptive sense to respond to, say, pain inflicted by a predator by running and struggling but to stimuli which *warn* of impending danger by remaining still and perhaps escaping the predator's attention.

Razran (1971) has expressed views about what he calls "aversive inhibitory conditioning" (i.e. passive avoidance) which are in good agreement with this view, but which place this form of learning in a much broader context. He regards this kind of behaviour as *sui generis*, distinct from both classical and instrumental conditioning, and an earlier evolutionary development than either. In support of this view, he quotes, along with much other data, experiments which show that the coelenterates (the phylum which includes Hydra and its rather more complex relatives, the sea anemones) are capable of passive avoidance learning, but not of classical or instrumental conditioning (e.g. Ross, 1965), these latter forms of learning only developing at a more advanced stage of evolution. It cannot, of course, be taken for granted that, even supposing Razran is right in his evolutionary scheme, passive avoidance behaviour has remained an independent mode of learning in mammals. However, Razran's comparative and evolutionary approach certainly adds to, and gains weight from, the oddities of passive avoidance learning on which I have commented here.

In summary, then, it seems that there is quite good reason to conclude to the existence of a special "behavioural inhibition" system (as I shall henceforth call it), which is charged with the task of *inhibiting all ongoing positively reinforced behaviour* upon receipt of signals which, as a result of prior $S \to S$ pairing with unconditioned punishing stimuli (S^{R-}), have acquired the capacity to act on this system. In conformity with established practice, I shall call such stimuli indifferently "conditioned fear stimuli", "secondary aversive stimuli" or "warning signals"; for these three terms are about equally common.

It should be noted that the conditions under which behavioural inhibition, as I have introduced this term, occurs are quite different from those which give rise to "internal inhibition" in classical conditioning (see Chapter 3). The latter is caused by the omission of a UCS under conditions where a UCS might be expected to occur; and the effect of internal inhibition appears to be to activate a process which is opposite in sign to whatever process is activated by an excitatory CS. The distinction between internal inhibition and behavioural inhibition is clearest where an aversive UCS/S^{R-} is involved. Take the case in which S_1 is followed by shock and S_2 by non-shock. Then S_2 becomes an internal inhibitor (of fear and the behavioural symptoms of fear), as shown by the Rescorla and LoLordo (1965) experiment discussed in Chapter 3. But it is S_1 which activates the behavioural inhibition system to suppress positively reinforced behaviour, according to the present hypothesis and the data on which it is based.

Fight/Flight Behaviour

The same arguments which have led us to postulate a special behavioural inhibition system, activity in which is initiated by CSs previously paired with punishment, must lead us to ask, what is the nature of the behaviour elicited by punishment itself? Evidently, if the stimulus substitution theory of classical conditioning does not strictly apply to the case of aversive UCSs, we cannot regard the behaviour elicited by CSs and UCSs as essentially the same.

Descriptively, it is clear that unconditioned punishments, as eliciting stimuli, give rise to a great deal of activity directed either towards escape from the environment in which the punishment is received (wild jumping or running, for example) or towards attacking suitable objects in this environment (the most suitable object being another animal). Before pursuing the matter further, the kind of aggressive behaviour involved in the unconditioned responses to punishment has to be distinguished from a second kind of aggressive behaviour: predatory aggression.

The distinction seems intuitively plausible, and some species adopt characteristically different modes of attack in the two cases. For example, when a cat fights another cat or defends itself against a dog, it typically arches its back, raises its hair, hisses and growls. When, in contrast, it attacks a rat, this attack is preceded by a silent, stalking approach, with back low and hair smooth. Experiments in which behaviour has been elicited by electrical stimulation of the brain have strongly supported this distinction by showing, in both rats and cats, that the two kinds of aggression depend on different structures, the former ("intra-specific" or "defensive") kind of aggression being mediated by a system including the amygdala, the medial hypo-thalamus and the central grey of the midbrain (De Molina and Hunsperger, 1962; Gray, 1971a, 1972b), the latter ("predatory") kind being mediated by a system including the lateral hypothalamus and the medial forebrain bundle (structures which are also concerned with eating and food-seeking behaviour) (Roberts and Kiess, 1964; Hutchinson and Renfrew, 1966). Furthermore, whereas stimulation of the former set of structures is punishing (i.e. the animal will work to turn the stimulation off), stimulation of the latter set is rewarding by the self-stimulation test (Olds and Olds, 1965; Adams and Flynn, 1966). A final point which may be urged in support of the distinction is that, in rodents, there is a sex difference in the degree to which intra-specific aggression is displayed (males being more aggressive), but not in the display of predatory aggression (Gray, 1971b).

One kind of response to unconditioned punishments, then, is a pattern of species-specific defensive-aggressive behaviour. In addition the animal displays unconditioned escape behaviour. Can these types of response be separated from each other? To date, the answer to this question appears to be "No". Whether it is escape or aggression which is displayed in response to an unconditional punishment or to electrical stimulation of the brain appears to depend on compara-tively minor aspects of the environmental situation, not on the type

of punishment delivered nor on the precise brain structures stimulated: roughly speaking, if escape is possible, the subject will try
flight, if not, it will try fight (Ulrich, 1967; De Molina and
Hunsperger, 1962; Gray, 1971a). Thus no advantage would appear to
accrue, at least at this stage, from distinguishing, at the systematic
level, between unconditioned intra-specific aggression and unconditioned escape behaviour. We shall speak, therefore, of a single
"fight/flight" system, responsible for organizing behaviour elicited
by aversive UCSs and distinct from the behavioural inhibition system
for response to aversive CSs.

The intra-specific aggressive response to punishment appears not
to occur as a classical conditioned response to stimuli followed by
punishment; though this statement (like all such universal negatives)
may simply indicate that insufficient or the wrong research has been
carried out. In fact, one exception to this generalization is known to
exist: the aggressive response of the Siamese fighting fish to an
electric shock may be conditioned to an intially neutral CS paired
with the shock (Thompson and Sturm, 1965). However this may be a
rather special adaptation in a particular species, named after this
peculiar aggressive behaviour. And, in this book, we are above all
concerned to uncover regularities in the organization of mammalian
learning and behaviour. With regard to the conditionability of
escape behaviour, this is a topic we shall take up again in Chapter 10.
(It should be noted that the question whether aggressive or escape
UCRs can be turned into CRs is distinct from the point, already
made above, that the CR of behavioural inhibition is not a UCR to
aversive stimuli.)

Secondary Punishment

Let us return to the properties acquired by aversive CSs in
consequence of the classical conditioning which goes on in a passive
avoidance situation. It is implicit in the account we have given of
passive avoidance that such CSs themselves acquire the essential
reinforcing property which defines the primary S^{R-}/UCS with
which they are paired—that of suppressing responses which they
follow. If this were not so, given that the animal in a typical passive
avoidance situation is faced with a sequence of stimuli of which only
the very last ones in the chain are immediately followed by primary

punishment, Miller's avoidance function, with its gradual decline as distance from the goal increases, could not be set up. Instead, the animal would presumably go rapidly to a point quite close to the conflicted goalbox, and then suddenly halt. Thus, in a way which is analogous to the consideration we gave to the conditioning of secondary positive reinforcement in Chapter 5, we are led to the conclusion that a response which is followed by a CS which has previously been paired with an S^{R-}/UCS should show a decline in probability of recurrence of essentially the same kind as would be observed if it were followed by primary punishment.

An early demonstration of this phenomenon is due to Mowrer and Aiken (1954). As expected, they found that barpressing for a food reward was considerably reduced in rate if this response was also followed by a tone which had previously acted as the CS for the UCS of shock onset, even though the barpressing response itself had never been followed by primary punishment (see Fig. 10.4).

When we considered secondary positive reinforcers in Chapter 5 we distinguished between the reinforcing and the motivational properties which they seem to acquire in consequence of pairing with primary reinforcement. As pointed out there, reinforcing properties are those which are observed when the stimulus is presented contingently on a response, while motivational ones are observed by presenting the stimulus prior to or simultaneously with a response. A similar distinction can be drawn in the case of secondary negative reinforcers. We have just seen, in Mowrer and Aiken's experiment, an instance of the reinforcing property of such stimuli. We now consider their motivational properties.

In the parallel case of secondary positive reinforcement, we took as an instance of a motivational effect an experiment by Estes (1948) in which an initially neutral stimulus, paired as the CS with the UCS of food and subsequently presented to rats while they pressed a bar for a food reward, increased the rate of this response. If we are to preserve this parallel, then, we should look for a case in which a CS previously paired with a UCS of shock affects the rate of a response for which shock is a relevant reinforcing event. Such an experiment has been reported by Rescorla and LoLordo (1965). They first trained dogs in a shuttlebox on a Sidman avoidance schedule and then exposed them, in a separate environment, to classical conditioning trials in which the CS was paired with shock. Finally, this

CS was presented to the dog while it was performing the Sidman avoidance task. The rate of response rose significantly in the presence of the CS (see Fig. 2.3). (We shall return to these experiments in Chapter 10; and, in particular, to the problem raised by the fact that the relevant reinforcing event in a Sidman avoidance schedule is not, strictly speaking, shock, but shock-omission.) Similar effects can be produced when shock, rather than a stimulus previously paired with shock, is presented noncontingently to an animal performing a Sidman avoidance response (Sidman *et al.*, 1957).

However, there is another kind of motivational property, according to the definition we have just given of such properties, which attaches to secondary negative reinforcers. We are, in fact, already familiar with this second kind of motivational property: it is the one demonstrated in the CER paradigm. In this, it will be recalled, a stimulus previously paired with shock is able, when presented to an animal engaging in an instrumental response for positive reinforcement (such as food or water), to *depress* the rate of response. Thus, a description of the motivational properties of secondary aversive stimuli needs to take account of the kind of reinforcement which is used to maintain the baseline response, change in which is used as an index of a motivational effect. If this baseline response is maintained by Rew, the outcome of presenting the Pun–CS is a reduction in response rate (which could be termed a "demotivating" effect); if it is maintained by $\overline{\text{Pun}}$, presentation of the Pun–CS increases response rate (a motivating effect in the proper sense). A similar bifurcation can be observed in the motivational effects of a Rew –CS; we already know that it increases the rate of a response maintained by Rew, and we shall see in Chapter 10 that it reduces the rate of a response maintained by $\overline{\text{Pun}}$.

This pleasingly symmetrical picture, however, has to undergo considerable distortion to take account of one further set of findings: under some conditions, the effect of an aversive stimulus (whether primary or secondary) is, not to depress performance of a positively reinforced response, but rather to enhance it. To these conditions we now turn.

Summation of "Drive"

The invigorating properties of punishment have usually been studied as a way of testing the "drive summation" hypothesis advanced by Hull; and we, too, shall take this opportunity of completing the survey of uses of "drive"–like terms which we began in Chapter 4. Hull supposed that behaviour at any moment occurs because of the multiplication of a habit $(_SH_R)$ by the *sum* of existing drives (D). All drives, (hunger, thirst, sex drive, etc.) summate to produce D, and the application of a punishment or of a conditioned fear stimulus is conceived as setting up one such drive, namely, the fear drive. The habit which is energized by D on a particular occasion is the one which has the highest momentary rank in the "habit family hierarchy", and this rank depends above all on prior learning and the particular stimuli (the "S" in the symbol "$_SH_R$") to which the organism is exposed in its current environment.

The literature testing this notion by searching for summation between two appetitive drives (e.g. hunger and thirst) is confused, and it is certainly not possible to conclude that Hull's view has received very much support in this direction (McFarland, 1966). The notion that appetitive drives and aversive drives are in essence the same kind of thing has also failed to receive support from the kinds of consideration we looked at in Chapter 4. However, experiments in which the drive summation hypothesis has been examined by searching for summation between appetitive and aversive drives have, on the whole, supported Hull.

The Hullian prediction, however, is by no means a simple one. A typical experiment in this field would involve the application of a punishment or of a conditioned fear stimulus to an organism engaged in some form of appetitive behaviour (e.g. food-seeking or eating). From Hull's analysis we would expect the application of such a stimulus:

(1) To change the stimuli to which the organism is exposed. This may change the habit which is highest in the habit family hierarchy, and so *reduce the proportion of time spent by the subject on the original appetitive behaviour.*

(2) To increase D, by summation of drives, and so lead to an *increase in the vigour of whatever behaviour occurs, including the original appetitive behaviour*; provided that, as a result of effect (1), the proportion of time spent by the subject on this behaviour is not reduced to zero.

Unfortunately, experimenters have not usually distinguished between measures of the *probability*–p(R)–of occurrence of the appetitive behaviour (which should show a fall) and measures of the *vigour* or intensity—I_R —of the appetitive behaviour (which should show a rise). And, of course, in the absence of such a distinction, it is impossible to make precise predictions as to the behaviour of measures which partly reflect both probability and vigour (such as, for example, running speed or rate of barpressing); for the decrease in p(R) may be under- or over-compensated by the increase in I_R. A mathematical model (included as an Appendix to this book) which P. T. Smith and I (1969) have developed for the analysis of this kind of situation suggests that, if only measures of the overall amount of appetitive behaviour (probability multiplied by vigour) are available, then we are likely to observe an overall increase in the appetitive behaviour when the added aversive stimulation is low, but an overall decrease when the added aversive stimulation is high (Fig. 8.7).

The experimental findings on the effects of an added aversive stimulus on appetitive behaviour by and large fit this analysis well.

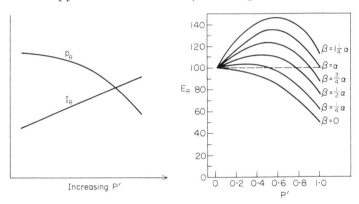

FIG. 8.7. Outline of Gray and Smith's Mathematical Model for Conflict and Drive Summation. The abscissa, P′, represents increasing degrees of the aversive drive, with appetitive drive held constant. That is, it represents increasing levels of input to the "stop" or "passive avoidance" mechanism in Fig. 8.2. When P′ = 1, the inputs to the approach and avoidance mechanisms are equal, and the animal is at the equilibrium point in Miller's equilibrium model (Fig. 8.3). The figure on the left shows how, in the Gray and Smith model, probability (P_R) of the approach behaviour is expected to decrease, and intensity or vigour (I_R) of the approach behaviour, when it occurs, is expected to increase, respectively, as the level of aversive drive approaches that of the appetitive drive. The figure on the right shows the resulting functions for E_R = P_R × I_R, i.e. the overall amount of appetitive behaviour when separate measures for probability and vigour are not available. The parameter, β, of the curves in the figure on the right reflects the degree to which increases in I_R over- or under-compensate (for high or low values of β, respectively) for decreases in P_R as P′ increases. This parameter is expressed as a proportion of the weighting, α, which is attached to inputs to the "approach" mechanism in Fig. 8.2. For further explanation see Appendix. (From Gray and Smith, 1969).

They may be summarized by saying that, with a relatively *low* intensity punishment or conditioned fear stimuli, and in an environment which is strongly associated with the appetitive drive, the addition of punishment or fear increases the overall consummatory behaviour observed (Amsel and Maltzman, 1950; Siegel and Siegel, 1949; Siegel and Brantley, 1951). If the shock used is of *high* intensity, or if the environment is not so strongly associated with appetitive behaviour, there is usually an overall reduction in the amount of appetitive behaviour (Amsel, 1950; Lawler, 1965). Finally, it is possible, when appropriate measures are taken, to observe the simultaneous decrease in the probability of the appetitive behaviour and increase in its vigour which the Hullian analysis suggests must always occur (Tugendhat, 1960a, 1960b; Beach and Fowler, 1959). The invigorating effect of aversive stimuli is common to both unconditioned and conditioned stimuli; so this appears to be a property which accrues to secondary aversive stimuli in consequence of classical conditioning, in accordance with the modified stimulus substitution rule examined in Chapter 2.

In Tugendhat's (1960a, 1960b) experiments, which offer empirical support for these conclusions, three-spined sticklebacks were kept in an experimental environment which was divided into a "home" area and a "food" area, separated from each other by a partition through which the fish were sometimes allowed to swim. Measurements were first taken of the fish's feeding behaviour at different levels of food deprivation. Shock was then introduced into the food area (though never in the home area). The effects of the shock were to reduce the amount of time the fish spent feeding (reduction in probability of response); but, while they were feeding, their behaviour was appropriate to a higher level of food deprivation than that on which they were in fact maintained (increase in response intensity). Beach and Fowler's experiments, though using quite different techniques, revealed a similar picture. The appetitive behaviour studied was the act of copulation in the male rat. It is known that, the higher the level of sexual arousal, the fewer the number of intromissions the male rat requires to reach the point of ejaculation (Beach and Jordan, 1956). Beach and Fowler first shocked rats for five successive days in a particular cage. The rats were then allowed to copulate with receptive females, either in the same cage or in a neutral one. In the cage associated with shock, fewer intromissions were required for ejaculation—i.e. there was an increase in I_R. Similar results were obtained by Beach in an earlier experiment in which the rats were actually shocked during the act of copulation: this led to a reduced total time spent copulating, i.e. a decrease in $p(R)$, together with the same reduction in the number of intromissions per ejaculation just described.

Comparison Between Positive and Negative Reinforcers

Both primary and secondary aversive stimuli, then, appear to possess the following properties, all of which accrue to the secondary aversive stimulus in consequence of classical conditioning with a primary aversive stimulus as UCS in accordance with the modified stimulus substitution rule:

(1) A reinforcing property: that of reducing the probability of a response on which they are contingent.

(2) A motivating property: that of increasing the rate of a response reinforced by $\overline{\text{Pun}}$ when presented to the animal while it is performing this response.

(3) A demotivating property: that of decreasing the rate of a response reinforced by Rew when presented to the animal while it is performing this response.

(4) An arousing or invigorating property: that of increasing the vigour of appetitive behaviour (whether instrumental or consummatory) when presented to the animal while it is engaged in this behaviour.

If we compare this list of properties with those we found to be attributes of primary and secondary *positive* reinforcers in Chapter 5, a number of similarities can be noted. They too were seen to possess a reinforcing property (with changed sign of the effect on response probability); a motivating property (but exercised on responses maintained by Rew); and a demotivating property (but exercised on responses maintained by $\overline{\text{Pun}}$, a topic not considered in detail until Chapter 10).

A further point of similarity concerns the process of "second-order conditioning". We concluded in Chapter 5 that a secondary reinforcer (Rew–CS) acquires the same ability to act as a UCS in a classical conditioning paradigm as the primary positive reinforcer with which it is paired. In this way, it is possible to account for the phenomenon of the goal-gradient and the outcome of the Powell and Perkins (1957) experiment on secondary reinforcement (Fig. 5.5). It would be desirable to come to the same conclusion with respect to secondary negative reinforcers (Pun–CS). In this way, Miller's approach and avoidance functions would involve the same basic conditoning mechanisms, the only difference being this: that, in the case of approach, what gets conditioned as a function of position in the spatio-temporal chain of stimuli leading to the goal is the capacity to activate a positive feedback mechanism; while, in the case of passive avoidance, it is the capacity to activate a behavioural inhibition mechanism.

Some such assumption as this can almost be justified on purely theoretical grounds. Consider, for example, the experiment by Mowrer and Aiken (1954), described earlier in this chapter, in which rats reduced their rate of barpressing for food if this response was also followed by a tone which had previously acted as the CS for the UCS of shock, even though the barpressing response itself had never been followed by primary punishment. In an experiment such as this, how can the Pun–CS act retrogressively in time so as to suppress the response on which it is contingent? It seems necessary to suppose that stimuli deriving from the to-be-suppressed response (i.e. barpressing in the Mowrer and Aiken experiment) themselves acquire the capacity to activate the behavioural inhibition system. But this is tantamount to concluding that the first-conditioned Pun–CS has the capacity to act as UCS for second-order conditioning of the CSs accompanying the act of barpressing.

In spite of the cogency of these arguments, there are rather few empirical demonstrations of second-order classical conditioning of fear. There are, however, two relevant experimental reports, which show the effect we seek.

McAllister and McAllister (1964) paired a tone with the UCS of shock and, interspersed with these tone-shock pairings, they also paired light as CS with the tone now as UCS. A first control group received the light tone pairings in a backward conditioning order (i.e. tone → light), and with a 15 sec delay between tone and light. All animals now received training in a double-compartment apparatus, one part of which was the same as that in which the tone-shock and tone-light (or light-tone) pairings had been conducted. When a door was opened they were able to cross over a barrier into the other compartment. The opening of the door was accompanied by the turning on of the same light as that used in the classical conditioning phase of the experiment, and this light was switched off when the animal crossed to the other side of the apparatus. A second control group had been exposed to the light-tone pairings in the first part of the experiment, but was not exposed to the light in the second part. The results showed that the group which (a) had had light-tone pairings, and (b) could turn this light off by crossing to the second compartment, learnt to perform the crossing response with a significantly shorter latency when the door was opened than either of the control groups.

This experiment demonstrates second-order conditioning of aversive properties, as we require; but of course, it cannot be taken for granted that the escape test, used by McAllister and McAllister (1964) to demonstrate these properties, is the equivalent of a punishment test. And it is the latter which is needed in the present context, if we are to assert with confidence that a CS paired with an S^{R-} as UCS acquires the capacity itself to act as UCS for the transfer to a higher-order CS of the *response-suppressive* effects of primary punishment. A direct demonstration of this phenomenon has, however, been reported recently by Rescorla (1972).

In this experiment rats were trained to press a bar for food and then received fear conditioning (assessed by the degree of conditioned suppression) "on the baseline". On the first two days of conditioning they received four ten-second flashing lights, after each of which a shock was delivered. Thereafter, on each day they received one trial of this kind and three trials in which a second-order stimulus (a tone) was presented for 40 sec, the last 10 sec of which was accompanied by the flashing light. On these tone-light trials, no shock was delivered. The results of the experiment are presented in Fig. 8.8. It can be seen that initially the tone produced considerable suppression of barpressing, but that this suppression became gradually less as the experiment continued. Indeed, by the end of the experiment, the tone had become a conditioned inhibitor of fear, as shown by the results pictured in the right hand panel of Fig. 8.8. This shows the degree of suppression produced in a test session conducted after Day 15 of conditioning by the light alone and by the light presented together with the tone. It can be seen that the conditioned suppression produced by the light was much reduced by

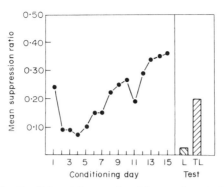

FIG. 8.8. Second-Order Conditioned Suppression. The panel to the left shows conditioned suppression to the tone over the course of a procedure in which the animal received either light → shock pairings or tone → light pairings. Development of suppression to the tone under these circumstances is an instance of second-order conditioning of fear, or more specifically, of the response-suppressive property of an S^{R-}/UCS. The right-hand panel shows suppression to the light (L) when presented alone and when preceded by the tone (TL) on a test session administered after Day 15. The reduction produced by the tone in the degree of suppression elicited by the light shows that, by this point in the experiment, the tone had become a conditioned inhibitor of fear. (From Rescorla, 1972).

simultaneous presentation of the tone—a result which indicates the presence of inhibitory effects (see Chapter 3).

That such conditioned inhibition should develop in the course of Rescorla's experiment is not surprising, for the paradigm used—CS_1 → UCS, $CS_2 + CS_1$ → no UCS—is precisely the same as the one used in experiments on conditioned inhibition. However, Rescorla used this paradigm, not because it was theoretically necessary to do so, but in order not to contaminate the measurement of the second-order conditioning of fear with that of the primary conditioning of fear, as would have occurred if the tone-light combination was itself followed by shock. Thus these experiments give no reason to doubt the stability of second-order conditioning of response suppression under conditions which do not involve the pairing of the second-order CS with absence of the UCS. Indeed, further experiments by Rescorla (personal communication) have demonstrated a quite remarkable stability of second-order conditioned suppression. For example, it has been shown to survive both complete extinction of the response-suppressive capacity of the first-order CS and a considerable degree of adaptation to the UCS itself (Rescorla, 1973).

One possible point of difference between the properties of positive and negative reinforcers lies in the arousing effects which we have attributed to primary and secondary aversive stimuli in the present chapter. No comparable property appears to exist in the case of primary and secondary positive reinforcers. This conclusion is based on "drive summation" experiments of a rather different kind from those we have so far considered in this chapter. In these experiments, the effects are investigated of adding an appetitive drive to behaviour maintained by aversive reinforcement.

This strategy, of course, is the reverse of the drive summation experiments which we have looked at till now, in which an aversive drive is added to behaviour maintained by appetitive reinforcement. There are, however, certain asymmetries between negative and positive reinforcers which should be borne in mind in considering such experiments (of which there are, in fact, very few). First, the added aversive "drive" in experiments of the kind we have so far considered is necessarily of external origin, i.e. it depends on presentation of punishment or the signal for a punishment. An added appetitive "drive", to be symmetrical with this operation, therefore, should depend on presentation of reward or the signal for a reward, In fact, however, it has usually been a drive of internal origin, i.e. a drive$_{DEP}$ (Chapter 4). Second, the positively reinforced baseline against which the effects of an added primary or secondary punishment have been evaluated in the experiments described earlier in this chapter has been maintained by Rew. To be symmetrical, therefore, a drive summation experiment of the reverse kind ought to examine the effects of a reward or a signal of reward on behaviour maintained by Pun, i.e. passive avoidance. In fact, however, the baselines used have been those of escape or avoidance behaviour, maintained, of course, by Pun! and $\overline{Pun}$.

Ideally, then, one would like to see an experimental investigation of the effects of a primary or secondary positive reinforcer presented during passive avoidance behaviour on the vigour of that behaviour. This would allow a true comparison, for positively reinforcing stimuli, with the arousing property we have been able to attribute to primary and secondary negative reinforcers. To my knowledge, no such experiments have been conducted. In order to conduct them, one would need to devise some method for measuring the *vigour* of a *passive* avoidance response; and while this is not an inconceivable thing to do, it is likely to be extremely difficult. One possible line of approach is suggested by a remark of Solomon's (1964, p. 241): "if a subject has been punished for touching some manipulandum which yields food, he may stay nearer to the manipulandum under low hunger drive and move farther away from it under high hunger drive, even though the probability of finally touching the manipulandum increases as hunger drive increases." Solomon goes on to say that he has observed this phenomenon in approach–avoidance conflicts in his laboratory, but these observations do not appear to have been published. It might be reasonable to treat distance from the conflicted goal in such an experiment as a measure of the vigour of passive avoidance behaviour; for, even though $drive_{DEP}$ must affect the approach tendency as well as the passive avoidance tendency, any such effect would presumably take the opposite direction from that observed by Solomon. If so, and if Solomon's informal observations can be verified, they may indicate that $drive_{DEP}$ increases the vigour of passive avoidance behaviour.

   More certain is the conclusion that $drive_{DEP}$ can increase the vigour of other forms of aversively motivated behaviour. Thus Amsel (1950b) showed that an escape response from stimuli previously associated with electric shock was performed faster by hungry than sated rats, without presentation of food-related incentives. In another experiment, departing from learning situations altogether, Meryman (cited by Brown, 1961) measured the amplitude of a startle response elicited by a pistol shot. Rats were either hungry or sated for food and either made fearful (by being given an electric shock in the test situation once a day) or not. The startle response was increased in magnitude by both hunger and fear, and the two effects summated with each other.

   In the same basic experimental situation, however, two experiments (Trapold, 1962; Armus et al., 1964) have failed to find any effect of a stimulus previously paired with food reward on the magnitude of the startle response to a pistol shot. Thus there is at present no reason to suppose that a Rew–CS shares with a Pun–CS arousing properties, though these do appear to be possessed by $drive_{DEP}$.

The Gray and Smith Model

   Let us close this chapter by summarizing, in the form of a block diagram, the conclusions we have reached in our discussion of the interactions between approach behaviour and passive avoidance. It is clear that in this diagram (Fig. 8.9), which is based on Gray and Smith's model (see Appendix), we must first carefully distinguish between the probability of occurrence of a rewarded response, $p(R)$, and the vigour with which it occurs, I_R. With regard to the motivation for the two kinds of tendency, approach and avoidance, we have distinguished between drive and incentive, in the case of approach, but we have only fear (or "negative incentive", as it is

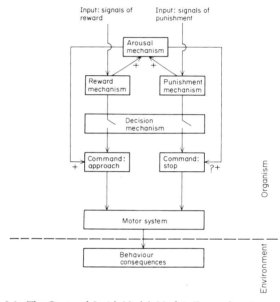

FIG. 8.9. The Gray and Smith Model, Mark I. For explanation see text.

sometimes called) in the case of avoidance. However, in keeping with the conclusion reached in Chapter 5 that drive effects approach behaviour by altering the magnitude of the UCR on which incentive is based, we can ignore this complication and base each tendency on only incentive-type motivation (remembering only that for some forms of behaviour this falls to zero if drive$_{D E P}$ is totally absent—see Chapter 5). The next point on which our block diagram must be based is the realization that, so far as probability of response is concerned, simultaneously elicited appetitive and aversive states will normally be in competition with each other. (Exceptions to this rule, which arise for example in consequence of the phenomenon of counter-conditioning, as discussed by Gray, 1971a, are ignored.) Finally, the evidence is strong, as we have seen, that aversively and appetitively based motivational excitement summate to affect the vigour of an *appetitive* response, though they may not do so in the case of aversive behaviour.

The box which in the block diagram of Fig. 8.9 mediates such drive-summation effects on vigour has been labelled "arousal". The reason for this is simple: the concept of "arousal", which we discussed in Chapter 3, was introduced precisely to handle variations in the intensity of behaviour irrespective of its direction, and it is just this phenomenon that the drive-summation experiments demonstrate. "Drive" is one of the determinants of "arousal level" as listed in Fig. 3.6; and, in general, the Hullian concept of "general drive", to the extent that it is viable, does not differ in any important respects from that of "arousal". I shall therefore treat them as the same. Thus the symbol, I_R, used by Gray and Smith (1969) for "intensity of response", is the equivalent of "arousal level" as used in Chapter 3.

This completes our survey of the behavioural effects of punishment. In the next chapter we examine the effects of frustrative nonreward, i.e. the omission of anticipated reward ($\overline{\text{Rew}}$). As we shall see, there are a number of striking similarities between the effects of this operation and those which we have seen in the present chapter to be produced by punishment.

9. Frustrative Nonreward

We have taken as our starting point for approaching many topics in this book the huge edifice of Hullian learning theory. Sometimes this theory has been found to conform to the facts, as far as experiment has been able to determine them; more often than not, it has been found to be wanting in both empirical accuracy and internal consistency. In the case of the next topic we turn to, however (the extinction of previously rewarded responses), Hullian theory is unable to offer even a useful starting point, for it is itself quite extinct.

Hull's theory of extinction involved a construct termed "reactive inhibition". Briefly, reactive inhibition was said to be a fatigue-like process which arises from the performance of a response, builds up with repetition of the response, and counteracts further repetition of the response. Moreover, this process occurs *irrespective of whether the response is followed by positive reinforcement or not.*

The logical tangles which ensue when this concept is used to account for phenomena whose very essence appears to be determined by the delivery or otherwise of reinforcement have been exposed in a well-known paper by Gleitman *et al.* (1954). Roughly speaking, these authors show that, in an experiment in which a repeated response is followed for a number of trials by reward and then by nonreward, Hull's theory must predict either that the response will rise to some maximum strength during the initial rewarded trials and then remain at that strength even when reward is discontinued, extinction never occurring; or that the strength of the response will first rise and then fall again to zero, even if reward continues to be given. Needless to say, even though both extreme resistance to extinction without reinforcement and extinction with reinforcement (e.g. Kendrick, 1958) are sometimes observed, neither is the norm; and the most critical event determining the extinction of a previously rewarded response is undoubtedly, under most circumstances, omission of reward.

For Hull, however, the omission of reward simply failed to constitute an event in the experience of the animal to which it occurred. Only reward had behavioural consequences—those of reducing drive and so increasing the strength of the response ("habit strength") which had been followed by such drive reduction. The distinctive feature of nonreward was seen as purely negative—it did *not* reduce drive and so could *not* increase habit strength. Whether extreme resistance to extinction without reinforcement or extinction with reinforcement was to be the outcome of a learning experiment involving reward and nonreward was thought to be determined only by the relative intensities attained by habit strength (a function of responses followed by rewards) and reactive inhibition (a function of responses alone).

The Omission of Expected Reward

In contrast to Hull's theory, an alternative approach, advocated by Abraham Amsel since the early 1950s, treats the omission of expected reward ($\overline{\text{Rew}}$ or "frustrative nonreward") as an event with very tangible behavioural consequences. Amsel's theory, and a number of related approaches (e.g. Spence, 1956; Capaldi, 1967), have been much more successful than Hull in dealing with the experimental data on extinction. It is to work in this tradition, therefore, that the present chapter is largely devoted.

Frustrative nonreward is defined as the omission of a reward following a response which has previously in the animal's history been rewarded. It will be evident that this definition presupposes the subject's ability to detect the non-occurrence of an expected event, for which we took pains to seek evidence in Chapter 1. There we concluded that, in the case of habituation of the OR, the evidence for expectancies and the ability to detect their fulfilment or disappointment is very good. But we also concluded that it cannot be taken for granted, from the fact that expectancies are employed in the control of habituation of the OR, that they will also be used in the control of other forms of behaviour. Thus, we must re-establish our right to talk of expectancies in each new context. Are we, then, justified in speaking of the non-occurrence of expected reward as a behaviourally effective event?

A series of experiments (Amsel and Roussel, 1952; Wagner, 1959; Gray and Dudderidge, 1971) which appear to establish our right to do this have been performed in the double runway situation pictured in Fig. 9.1. Reward is available in the second goalbox of two consecutive runways on a continuous reinforcement schedule (CRF)—i.e. on every trial. In the first goalbox, however, reward is available, in one version of the experiment, on a random 50% partial reinforcement (PRF) schedule—i.e. on one trial in two, chosen at random; and, in a second version, on CRF for an initial block of trials, followed either by PRF for a subsequent block of trials or by no further reward in goalbox 1. In both versions of the experiment it

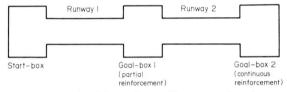

FIG. 9.1. Amsel and Roussel's Double-Runway Experiment.

is found that running speed in the second runway is greater after nonreward in goalbox 1 than after reward in goalbox 1.

Now, this result could be due to a slowing-up effect of reward (e.g. a consequence of reduced hunger) or to a speeding-up effect of nonreward. If it were the former, the experiment would have failed to demonstrate that nonreward is a behaviourally effective event in its own right. The appropriate controls, needed to demonstrate a true effect of nonreward, consist of groups which are run in the same situation, but with reward either given on every trial in goalbox 1 or on no trials in goalbox 1. The results of such experiments (Wagner, 1959; Gray and Dudderidge, 1971) show that rats always rewarded and rats never rewarded in goalbox 1 both run in the second runway at speeds which are like those of PRF rats after reward in goalbox 1. Thus, the difference in runway 2 speeds after goalbox 1 reward and nonreward, respectively, must, at least in part, be attributed to a specific speeding-up effect of *the omission of reward under conditions where reward sometimes occurs.* Frustrative nonreward is thus shown to be a behaviourally effective event.

Frustrative Nonreward Compared to Punishment

If this conclusion is correct, we may go on to ask what, in fact, the effects of frustrative nonreward are. In examining these effects, it will be as well to keep in mind the list of properties established in the previous chapter as attributes of primary and secondary punishment; for there are very great similarities between the effects of Pun and $\overline{\text{Rew}}$ and between those of Pun–CS and $\overline{\text{Rew}}$–Cs (i.e. stimuli previously associated with primary frustrative nonreward, or "conditioned frustrative stimuli"). So great are these similarities, in fact, that they have given rise to the hypothesis that the events of $\overline{\text{Rew}}$ and Pun, and the processes to which they give rise, are functionally (Wagner, 1966) or even physiologically (Gray, 1967, 1970b) equivalent.

If this hypothesis is to be taken at all seriously, the first thing to establish is that $\overline{\text{Rew}}$ possesses the chief defining property of an S^{R-}, namely, that of being aversive. This would involve showing that the probability of a response followed by $\overline{\text{Rew}}$ decreases—as, of course, it does, for this is simply a description of what happens when a previously rewarded response is extinguished. However, it is more natural to attribute this to the fact that reward no longer occurs than to any actively punishing effects of *non*reward. This logical difficulty, in many experimental situations, of distinguishing between the active effects of $\overline{\text{Rew}}$ and the removal of the effects of Rew will force us to rely in the main on data concerning the effects, not of $\overline{\text{Rew}}$ itself, but rather of $\overline{\text{Rew}}$–CS, stimuli associated with $\overline{\text{Rew}}$.

In the case in point, we wish to demonstrate that $\overline{\text{Rew}}$ is an aversive event. If we wished to do this for some conceptually simpler kind of event (e.g. exposure to loud noise), we could show that the event in question was aversive by demonstrating either that it decreased the probability of response on which it was contingent (the punishment test) or that it increased the probability of responses followed by its termination or omission (the escape and avoidance tests). However, it is clear that one can only terminate or omit nonreward by the provision of reward; thus, just as extinction of a response followed by nonreward cannot be attributed to a punishing effect of nonreward (as distinct from removal of the effects of reward), so a rise in the probability of a response followed by "termination of nonreward" or "omission of nonreward" is naturally attributed to the simple presentation of reward. Instead, therefore, we must seek evidence that presentation of a $\overline{Rew}$–CS decreases the probability of a response on which it is contingent, or that termination or omission of such a stimulus increases the probability of a response on which it is contingent. Such a demonstration need not be contaminated in any way by changes in reward. If it is successful, we shall be able to argue that it is unlikely that initially neutral stimuli paired with $\overline{Rew}$ could acquire such aversive properties unless the primary event of $\overline{Rew}$ itself also possessed them.

Such demonstrations have, in fact, been made, using the escape test of aversiveness. The avoidance test has not been used successfully in a way which eliminates the effects of changes in the frequency of primary reward; and the punishment test has only been used with the pairing of $\overline{Rew}$ and the CS conducted "on the baseline" (see Chapter 5), a technique which produces confusing results (Leitenberg, Bertsch and Coughlin, 1968). Results in which escape from a $\overline{Rew}$–CS has been investigated, however, have been consistently positive, even though quite diverse procedures have been used. Since the aversive nature of a $\overline{Rew}$–CS is a point of considerable theoretical importance, I shall describe three rather different experiments of this kind.

In the first of these, Adelman and Maatsch (1956) trained rats to run down a straight runway for a food reward and then placed them on extinction. Now, the usual way to measure resistance to extinction is to count the number of trials run to zero reward before the animal stops in the runway without reaching the goalbox. This fails to show that $\overline{Rew}$ is actively aversive for the reasons already discussed: it is more reasonable to regard the animal as simply not bothering to go to the now empty goalbox. In order to show actively aversive effects of $\overline{Rew}$, Adelman and Maatsch modified the usual extinction technique in the following way. Their apparatus had a ledge around the goalbox to which the rat could jump up. During extinction, the experimental rats were allowed to exit from the goalbox by this route. A control group of hungry rats was rewarded with food on the ledge for jumping up to it. A second control group was never given food, either in the goalbox or on the ledge, but merely placed in the goalbox the same number of times as the experimental group entered the goalbox during rewarded acquisition of the running response. The key finding was that the experimental rats, which were jumping out of an environment in which they were exposed to frustrative nonreward, learned to jump out more quickly even than the food-rewarded controls, while both did much better than the control group which was neither rewarded nor frustrated. The essential findings of this experiment have been replicated by Gray (1969).

A second demonstration of the aversive properties of $\overline{\text{Rew}}$–CS is due to Daly (1969), using essentially the same design as one previously tried out with encouraging results by Wagner (1963a). Daly trained four groups of rats in the straight alley, all with 15 pellets of food as reward during initial acquisition. After the running response was fully established, the size of the reward was shifted to 1 pellet for two of the groups and to zero (i.e. extinction) for the other two. For one of each of these pairs of groups the changed reward condition was accompanied by a new stimulus (a light) in the goalbox. Subsequently, the animals in all groups were tested to see whether they would acquire a new hurdle-jumping response to take them out of the goalbox into a discriminably different compartment. On these hurdle-jumping trials, the rat was placed in the goalbox with the same reward and stimulus conditions (i.e. light or no light) which they had experienced in the reward-shift phase of the runway part of the experiment. Four control groups were also used, two with 1 pellet at all stages of the runway training and two with no pellets at any stage of the runway training. Each of these pairs of control groups were divided into one which received exposure to light in the goalbox and one which did not, in the same way as the equivalent experimental groups.

The results of the hurdle-jumping phase of the experiment are presented in Fig. 9.2. In this figure, the four control groups have been collapsed into one, since they did not differ from each other. It is apparent that, in comparison with the controls, all four experimental groups showed a higher level of hurdle-jumping. Furthermore, there was a higher rate of hurdle-jumping if the downward shift in reward magnitude was to zero pellets than if it was to one pellet, and a higher rate of hurdle-jumping when the light stimulus was added to the goalbox as the environment from which the hurdle-jumping response permitted escape. Finally, it is to be noted that 1 pellet compared to a previously experienced reward of 15 pellets was able to maintain a higher rate of escape behaviour than 1 pellet when 1 pellet was what the animal had experienced all along (the latter condition being represented among the controls).

Thus, Daly's experiment appears to permit the following important conclusions:

(1) A goalbox in which the rat is exposed to extinction after previous reward becomes aversive (supporting Adelman and Maatsch's findings).

(2) The addition of an explicit CS (the light) paired with this omission of reward increases the level of aversiveness of the total

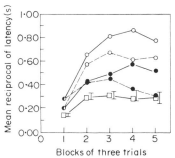

FIG. 9.2. Aversive Properties of Conditioned Frustration. Speed of hurdle jumping based on conditioned frustration as a function of trial blocks. Magnitude of reward (0 or 1 pellet) and presence (CS) or absence (NCS) of a discrete CS during frustration conditioning and hurdle jumping: 0 CS (open circle, solid line): 0 NCS (open circle, dashed line); 1 CS (solid circle, solid line); 1 NCS (solid circle, dashed line); controls (open square). Data from Daly (1969); (Figure from McAllister and McAllister, 1972.)

situation. Thus we may speak of this light as a $\overline{\text{Rew}}$–CS and as aversive.

(3) A reduction in reward from an experienced level of 15 pellets to a non-zero, but lower level (in this case 1 pellet) is also able to confer aversive properties on stimuli associated with this reduction, and thus appears to be functionally equivalent to (though evidently less intense than) total removal of reward.

A final experiment in which escape from a $\overline{\text{Rew}}$–CS has been demonstrated is reported by Terrace (1971). He trained pigeons to peck a key for a food reward, delivered on a variable-interval schedule, when a vertical line was projected onto the key. When a horizontal line was projected on the key, responses were not reinforced. (In the terminology used to describe operant conditioning procedures, these stimuli are described as S^D and S^Δ, respectively. For our purposes, they are presumed instances of a

Rew–CS and a $\overline{\text{Rew}}$–CS, respectively.) The two stimuli, and the accompanying reward (or extinction) schedules, alternated throughout a session in a "successive discrimination" procedure. The pigeon also had available a second key, lit up but with no other stimulus projected on it. For one group of pigeons, pecking this second key turned off S^Δ on the first key for a period of 5 sec, during which time the first key was blank. Neither the availability of reward nor the time of onset of the next period of S^D was in any way affected by these responses on the second key. At the end of the five-second blank period, the stimulus on the first key came on again. Terrace's results showed clearly that this "escape-from-S^Δ" contingency was able to maintain a high rate of responding on the second key, even when the response requirement was increased to "fixed ratio 5 (FR 5)", i.e. the pigeon had to make five successive responses for S^Δ to be turned off. Control groups, in which responses on the second key either had no effect or turned off the light behind the second key, showed no such high levels of response.

In this experiment, Terrace also used a further control group. This was a group of pigeons which learnt the discrimination "without errors". Terrace (1963a, b, 1966) had previously pioneered a technique of so-called "errorless discrimination training". In this, the S^Δ is introduced initially for very brief periods of time and at very low intensity; both stimulus duration and stimulus intensity are then gradually increased as the experiment proceeds. As a result (though for reasons which are obscure) the pigeon makes hardly any responses at all when the S^Δ is displayed on the key, even in the later stages of the experiment when it is fully intense and present for much of the time. In a series of experiments, Terrace has shown that discriminations learnt in this way are different from those learnt in the usual way (when the animal makes a very considerable number of unrewarded responses in the presence of S^Δ) in quite a number of important respects. Without going into detail (see Terrace, 1966, 1972b), these differences are consistent with the view that, in the usual procedure, the learning of a discrimination results in the S^Δ acquiring the capacity to elicit highly emotional behaviour, whereas in the errorless procedure these emotional effects are absent. In agreement with this general picture, Terrace found that the errorless discrimination group in the experiment just described did *not* press the second key in order to turn off S^Δ –that is to say, they showed no evidence that this stimulus was aversive to them, unlike the pigeons which had undergone the normal discrimination training procedure.

Terrace's results suggest the conclusion that a $\overline{\text{Rew}}$–CS becomes aversive if and only if the subject responds in its presence and has its response go unrewarded. This formulation, however, is probably incomplete as it stands.

Let us make the reasonable supposition that the same events which are critical in making nonreward aversive are also critical in producing the double-runway frustration effect, another consequence of nonreward considered earlier in this chapter. Let us compare, then, the results which Terrace obtained in the errorless training experiment with the performance of one of the groups in the double-runway experiment. The group in question is the one which is never rewarded in the first goalbox and which then runs in the second runway at a speed which is essentially the same as that shown by a group always rewarded in the first goalbox (Wagner, 1959). From the behaviour of this group we concluded earlier that it is only nonreward in the context of reward which has a frustrative effect. Viewed slightly differently, however, this group is also an instance in which the animal makes plenty of responses in the presence of a stimulus (the first goalbox), has these responses go unrewarded, and yet fails to show an effect of nonreward.

Thus if we wish to integrate the findings from the double runway experiments and those from the Skinner box discrimination experiments into one formulation, this formulation will have to read as follows: a stimulus becomes aversive and frustrative if and only if it is present when (a) the animal expects reward, (b) it makes the appropriate response, and (c) it fails to have its response rewarded*. There is no difficulty in applying this formulation to Terrace's results. For the animals which, after the usual training procedure, *do* respond in the presence of the S^Δ presumably do so in the expectation of

---

* Compare this formulation with that for the development of internal inhibition as given at the end of Chapter 3. The critical difference appears to be that frustration arises when the aminal *makes an instrumental response* in the light of its expectation and has its expectation disappointed. If no instrumental response is involved, but merely the disappointment of an expectation established in a purely S → S paradigm, internal inhibition develops. If this view is correct, it might perhaps be possible to use the occurrence of frustration effects (of the kind described in this Chapter) as diagnostic of instrumental behaviour. (See in this connection the discussion of Razran's evolutionary approach to the distinction between classical and instrumental conditioning at the close of Chapter 2.)

reward. The puzzling feature of Terrace's experiment is why the errorless training procedure prevents the pigeon from acquiring such an expectation, or results in its acquiring it but nonetheless not responding. As for the double runway experiments, even though the group never rewarded in the first goalbox keeps repeating the unrewarded response of running down the first runway, we must suppose that it does not expect a reward for doing so.

Between them, then, these three experiments (Adelman and Maatsch, 1965; Daly, 1969; and Terrace, 1971) offer convincing evidence that the termination of a $\overline{Rew}$–CS is aversive; from which it seems likely that the primary event of $\overline{Rew}$ is aversive, and would prove to be so by any of the appropriate tests, presentation, termination or omission, could we but apply them.

A closer look at Daly's (1969) experiment suggests in fact a possible way to circumvent the difficulties attached to applying these tests to frustrative nonreward *per se*. The clue lies in the fact that *reduction* in reward to a *non*-zero amount had the same effect (that of conditioning aversive properties to a $\overline{Rew}$–CS) as did reduction completely to zero. Further, the design Daly used, in which a control group was given only a low value of reward without ever experiencing the higher one, allows one to disentangle the effects of absolute level of reward from those of reward-reduction. Thus, if we may treat reward reduction as the equivalent of complete removal of reward, the way is open to investigate the aversive effects of the primary event of frustrative nonreward, as distinct from those of $\overline{Rew}$–CS.

Viewed in this light, a very well-established phenomenon, known since the 1940s, can be seen to be evidence of the punishing effects of frustrative nonreward. This is the "Crespi depression effect" (Crespi, 1942). In this, animals are first trained to run down a runway for a reward of a relatively large size, e.g. 15 pellets as in Daly's experiment described above. They are then shifted to a low reward, e.g. 1 pellet. A control group is kept on 1 pellet throughout. In such an experiment, as is well known, the animals running to 15 pellets will normally run faster than those rewarded with 1 pellet. We now shift the high-reward group to the low reward, leaving conditions for the low-reward group unchanged. The key observation, replicated many times since Crespi's original report (e.g. Spence, 1956), is that the shifted group runs for a number of trials after the shift more slowly than the unshifted low-reward group. Thus low reward for a response which has previously been followed by high reward appears to be aversive by a punishment test (suppression of the response of running to the goalbox). If this is so for reduced but non-zero reward, it would be surprising if it were not also so for the case where reward reduction is to zero.

Direct evidence that frustrative nonreward of zero value is aversive by a punishment test comes from an experiment by Amsel and Surridge (1964). This experiment also provides a further instance of the way in which an experienced event depends on what other events the animal experiences in the same context; i.e. of the way in which an animal compares what is happening now with what might reasonably be expected to happen, given what has happened before. In the Crespi depression effect, the operation of such expectations is shown in the fact that a low reward has aversive consequences if and only if the animal has previously experienced high reward for the same response. In the Amsel and Surridge experiment, nonreward of zero value was shown to have more powerfully aversive consequences if the previously experienced reward was high than if it was low.

The design of this experiment was as follows. Four groups of rats were trained in a runway with either 50% random partial reinforcement or continuous reinforcement, and with either large reward (a 500-mg food pellet) or small reward (a 94-mg pellet). On half the trials, for all four groups, a light came on over the goalbox, too late to affect running speed. This was always on the nonrewarded trials for the two PRF groups. After the running response was fully established, the conditions were changed in such a way that the light came on just before the rat entered the last section of the runway, still on the nonrewarded trials in the case of the PRF groups. Only in the case of the PRF groups was running speed affected, being slowed down after the light came on. This finding by itself might simply indicate that, since the light signalled that no reward was going to be found in the goalbox on these trials, the rat, informed of this circumstance, did not bother to keep running. However, if that were so, there should be no difference between the effects of the light in the PRF group given high reward and in the PRF group given low reward. In fact, there was a very marked difference, the slowing down effect of the light being much greater in the high-reward group. The most reasonable interpretation of this result, given the other evidence that nonreward is aversive, is that zero reward for rats used to a large pellet was more aversive (i.e. punishing) than zero reward for rats used to a small one.

Properties of Frustrative Nonreward

Both $\overline{\text{Rew}}$ and $\overline{\text{Rew}}$—CS, then, are aversive. What other properties can be attributed to these events? The best established one is probably the equivalent of what, in the case of Pun and Pun—CS, we termed an "arousing" property (Chapter 8): that of increasing the vigour of ongoing behaviour, irrespective of its motivation. As in the case of the invigorating effects of punishment, experiments in this area have been largely conducted within the framework of Hull's hypothesis of drive summation. For Amsel treats the state ("frustration") produced by $\overline{\text{Rew}}$ and $\overline{\text{Rew}}$—CS as a Hullian drive, in the same way that other theorist have treated the state ("fear") produced by Pun and Pun—CS as one.

The increased vigour which results from frustrative nonreward has been shown in a simple and direct manner by investigations of the changes which occur in a barpressing response which is subjected to extinction after previously having been rewarded. In such experiments extinction has been found to induce transient increases in the force, duration and rate of response (Notterman, 1959; Margulies, 1961; Thompson and Bloom, 1966). Similar increments in the vigour of ongoing behaviour can be produced by $\overline{\text{Rew}}$—CS, as well as by $\overline{\text{Rew}}$ itself. Wagner (1963), for example, showed that a stimulus encountered by rats just before they entered the goalbox on the nonrewarded trials of a PRF schedule was subsequently able to potentiate the startle reflex when presented together with the stimulus for the latter response. Another example of the invigorating effects of $\overline{\text{Rew}}$—CS is probably to be found in the partial reinforcement acquisition effect (PRAE). This consists in the fact that, if two groups of rats are run to rewards in the runway, one on a CRF schedule and the other on a PRF schedule, the PRF group usually runs faster than the CRF group by the end of training, especially in the sections of the runway which are furthest from the goal (Goodrich, 1959; Haggard, 1959). This phenomenon has been theoretically analysed by Amsel (1958, 1962) as being due to the invigorating effects of the frustration conditioned in the PRF group to cues in the runway. (See also the paper by Gray and Smith reproduced in the Appendix.)

As well as reinforcing and arousing properties, we concluded in the previous chapter that Pun and Pun–CS possess two kinds of motivational properties: a "motivating one", that of increasing the rate of performance of a response reinforced by $\overline{\text{Pun}}$; and a "demotivating one", that of decreasing the rate of performance of a response reinforced by Rew. Can anything analogous be found in the case of $\overline{\text{Rew}}$ and $\overline{\text{Rew}}$–CS?

As we saw in Chapter 8, the motivational properties of Pun and Pun–CS have been demonstrated by exposing animals to these events while they are performing an avoidance response on a Sidman schedule (Fig. 2.3) and observing an increased rate of avoidance behaviour. In an exactly similar experiment using $\overline{\text{Rew}}$–CS, Grossen, Kostansek and Bolles (1969) paired, in a classical conditioning paradigm, a tone either with food or with "no food" as UCS. The groups of rats assigned to these two conditions were treated as follows. The tone-food group had a 5 sec tone presented on a variable-interval (VI) 1 min. schedule, and each tone was followed by presentation of one food pellet. The tone-no food group also received tones on a VI 1 min. schedule, but food pellets were programmed on a VI 30 sec schedule, of which only those deliveries scheduled for 30 sec or more *after* tone onset were actually made. In addition, a "random control" group received the same series of tones, but food pellets were independently programmed on another VI 1 min. schedule, so that the temporal relationship between tone and food was random. For all three groups, the tone was then presented to the rats while they were performing an avoidance response on a Sidman schedule in a different apparatus (a shuttle box).

The results (see Fig. 10.10) showed that the tone *reduced* the rate of shuttling in the tone-food group; *increased** the rate of shuttling in the tone-no food group; and had no effect in the random control group. We shall consider the significance of the first of these findings in Chapter 10. For the moment, it is the effect of the tone in the tone-no food group which concerns us. For this group, the tone is a

---

* Note that this appears to be an instance of the "reaction of the reverse sign" which we met in Chapter 3. Since the reaction which is reversed is itself inhibitory (reduction of Sidman shuttling by a tone paired with food), we must presumably treat it as a "*disinhibitory*" reaction of the reverse sign.

$\overline{\text{Rew}}$–CS. And Grossen, Kostansek and Bolles', results therefore, demonstrate that such a stimulus has the same "motivating" effect on a response reinforced by $\overline{\text{Pun}}$ as is produced by Pun–CS: one more strand in the net of similarities which binds punishment and nonreward. A similar experiment involving the primary event of $\overline{\text{Rew}}$, rather than $\overline{\text{Rew}}$–CS, has yet to be performed.

   Intuitively, one might expect to find the demotivating effect of $\overline{\text{Rew}}$ and $\overline{\text{Rew}}$–CS more readily than the motivating one. For this expectation does not require bolstering from the hypothesis that the effects of $\overline{\text{Rew}}$ are similar to those of Pun: it is rather natural to expect that nonreward, or stimuli associated with nonreward, will reduce the performance of a rewarded response. Unfortunately, using the primary event of $\overline{\text{Rew}}$, the appropriate experiment may well be impossible to perform, for the same kind of reason we have already encountered in other connections. However, using $\overline{\text{Rew}}$–CS, the experiment had been done, and with success.

   Trapold and Winokur (1967) placed rats in a Skinner box and, with the lever removed, paired the delivery of food pellets with the sounding of a tone (making the tone a Rew–CS) according to a classical conditioning procedure. The rats were also presented with a clicking noise and with a light. For one group of rats, the clicker was followed by food and the light by no food and for a second group the opposite procedure was used, light being followed by food and clicker by no food. In the case of two control groups, either all three stimuli were followed by food or none of them. The animals were then trained to press a bar for the delivery of a food pellet upon presentation of the tone, and the latency of the response to the onset of the tone was measured. When this behaviour was fully established, the clicker and the light were occasionally presented in place of the tone (and were also followed by food reward if the bar was pressed). The critical data were the latencies to press the bar in response to these two stimuli in the different groups.

   The main finding was that the response to the clicker in the group which had had classical conditioning of this stimulus to no food (and of light and tone to food) was significantly slower than that of any other group, including the group which had had no food after any of the three stimuli during the classical conditioning phase of the experiment. Thus, provided the pairing clicker → no food had been experienced in the same context in which other stimuli were paired with food, the clicker stimulus slowed down the food-rewarded response. The results with the light stimulus were less clear-cut, but the authors attribute this with some plausibility to the generally low level of response commanded by this stimulus.

In a further part of the same experiment, some of the rats were given a "pre-extinction" classical conditioning session in which, with the lever once more removed from the Skinner box, the tone was repeatedly presented without food following it, while the clicker and light were presented with food. Controls were given all three stimuli followed by food. The lever was then re-inserted and the three stimuli each presented to the animal in an irregular sequence; bar-presses in response to tone-onset were never reinforced by food, those given in response to the other two stimuli were. The latency of response to the tone fell off much more rapidly in the "pre-extinguished" group than in the control animals, and this difference was clearly apparent in the first four trials. Further results of a similar kind have been reported by Trapold *et al.* (1968) and by Brown and Jenkins (1967).

These experiments are important in three ways. First, they offer evidence that a $\overline{Rew}$–CS does indeed possess the capacity to retard performance of a rewarded response. The relevant research appears so far to have been performed only under conditions in which the S^{R+}/UCS used in the classical conditioning phase of the experiment is the same as the S^{R+} used in the instrumental conditioning phase. Thus one cannot be sure that $\overline{Rew}$–CS *in general* are able to retard the performance of *any* rewarded instrumental response, irrespective of the nature of the reward. However, given the evidence that $\overline{Rew}$–CS can influence behaviour maintained by $\overline{Pun}$, as in the Grossen *et al.* experiment described above, it is unlikely that their demotivating effects are limited to the same kind of reward as that used in their initial establishment.

Second, experiments such as Grossen *et al.*'s and Trapold's are important in that they show that classical conditioning, in the absence of explicit instrumental contingencies, is sufficient to confer motivating and demotivating properties on a stimulus paired with nonreward. Thus they offer support for the general form of two-process theory outlined in Chapter 5, according to which classical conditioning is responsible for the acquisition by initially neutral stimuli of reinforcing and motivational properties and these then serve as the basis for instrumental behaviour. Unfortunately, the experiments considered earlier in this chapter as demonstrating the aversive and arousing properties of $\overline{\text{Rew}}$–CS did not explicitly separate the classical conditioning component of this hypothetical dual process of learning from the instrumental component. It would clearly be desirable to apply the kind of design used by Trapold and by Grossen to these properties also.

The third way in which Trapold's and Grossen's experiments are important is that they show the operation of expectancies and their disappointment in a classical conditioning situation. In Trapold's experiment, a rat for which a stimulus was paired with no food alongside another stimulus paired with food subsequently showed a quite different response to this stimulus from that elicited in a rat exposed to *both* stimuli without a food UCS following. And, in Grossen's experiment, a difference emerged between the response of a rat to a stimulus paired with periods of food-free time (food being at other times delivered to the animal) and the response of a rat to the same stimulus presented in random association with the delivery of food. The most plausible interpretation of this kind of result is that the animal develops an expectation of food in the experimental environment; and that the nondelivery of food after a $\overline{\text{Rew}}$–CS represents a mismatch for this expectation. Thus experiments of this kind establish our right to talk of a "non-UCS" (specifically a "non-UCS/S^{R+}") as an active event in classical conditioning, paralleling the similar right we derived from the double-runway experiment in the case of instrumental nonreward. We shall come across a further example of this kind of phenomenon in Chapter 10, when we deal with the active effects of a "non-UCS/S^{R-}", or "nonpunishment".

There is evidence, then, for reinforcing, arousing, motivating and demotivating properties attaching to frustrative nonreward and to signals of frustrative nonreward. This leaves two other properties which, in the previous chapter, we attributed to punishment: an eliciting property, that of giving rise to unconditioned fight/flight behaviour; and a conditioning property, that of acting as UCS for the conditioning of secondary punishing effects. With regard to Pun–CS, we concluded that these do not possess the same eliciting property as primary punishment: instead of eliciting fight/flight behaviour, they give rise to activity in the special "behavioural inhibition" system which we postulated in the previous chapter as underlying the response-suppression caused by punishment. With regard to the conditioning property of Pun, we concluded (but on the basis of a single experiment) that this is conferred on a Pun–CS, which can thus itself act as UCS for the higher-order conditioning of fear. Let us again seek parallels in the case of $\overline{Rew}$ and $\overline{Rew}$–CS.

As far as the UCS property of the primary event of frustrative nonreward is concerned, we have already seen good instances of this in the experiments by Trapold and by Grossen and their collaborators described above. Unfortunately, experiments to determine whether or not this UCS property can be passed on to $\overline{Rew}$–CS (that is to say, experiments on the higher-order conditioning of frustration) do not appear to have been performed.

Turning to the eliciting properties of frustrative nonreward, the evidence is now very good that this event can elicit aggressive behaviour directed towards conspecifics who happen to be present in the environment in which frustrative nonreward occurs, thus supporting a hypothesis proposed in 1950 by Dollard and Miller according to which "frustration produces aggression". Two experiments which illustrate this point are due to Azrin (1967) and the Gallup (1965). Azrin trained pigeons to obtain food by pecking at a key. Another pigeon was kept in the experimental chamber, restrained and inactive. When the working pigeon was placed on an extinction schedule, it turned and attacked the restrained pigeon viciously. Gallup's experiment shows that this kind of behaviour is not restricted to pigeons. He trained a pair of rats to run simultaneously down two adjacent and parallel runways for food on a partial reinforcement schedule. After thirty seconds in the goalbox a door separating the two boxes was opened and the two animals were allowed one minute together. The amount of aggression displayed by the two animals was measured by means of a rating scale running from 1 to 7. After nonrewarding trials the mean aggression score was 6.8, significantly greater than the score of 1.7 observed after rewarded trials.

With regard finally to escape behaviour elicited by frustrative nonreward, there is no clearcut instance of this phenomenon. The experiment by Adelman and Maatsch (1956), described earlier in illustration of the aversive properties of nonreward, seems to deal with learnt or skilled escape behaviour, rather than with an unconditioned locomotor response to nonreward. (The distinction between unconditioned and learnt escape is one which will occupy us in Chapter 10.) At any rate, the animals displayed a definite learning curve in the acquisition of the relevant response (jumping up onto a ledge around the now empty goalbox in which reward had previously been obtained). The double-runway experiment of Amsel and Roussel (1952), which was historically the first to establish the reality of the state of frustration, is a better candidate; and indeed, I believe that the speeding up in the second runway after nonreward in the first goalbox (which constitutes the frustration effect in this apparatus) probably does represent an unconditioned escape response to frustrative nonreward. In support of this view is the fact that it is a very rapidly developing response. In one of my own experiments (Gray, 1969), for example, it was present at a statistically high level of confidence during the first eight trials of a 50% random mixture of reward and nonreward in the first goalbox. However, Amsel and Roussel initially treated the frustration effect as an instance of drive summation, or of what we have termed the "arousing" property of nonreward. According to this argument, the drive or arousal produced by frustrative nonreward summates with the hunger and incentive motivation which underlies performance of the running response in the second runway so as to produce the observed increase in running speed. There appear to be no data available which would allow one to choose between these two interpretations of the FE in the double runway.

I know of no experiments which have been directly concerned with the conditionability of unconditioned escape behaviour to Rew–CS (as distinct from experiments showing that subjects will learn a *new* response to terminate a Rew–CS, discussed earlier); nor of any experiments on the conditionability of aggressive behaviour elicited by frustrative nonreward.

This then, brings to a close our general survey of the properties of Rew and Rew–CS, and the similarities between these and the corresponding properties of Pun and Pun–CS. (There are many other similarities between Pun and Rew of a more detailed nature, which could also have been mentioned: see, for example, the experiments by Brown and Wagner, 1964, and Grusec, 1968.) In making this survey we have considered a number of diverse phenomena which appear to be attributable to the effects of frustrative nonreward or to stimuli conditioned to this event, including, for example, the frustration effect in the double runway, the partial reinforcement acquisition effect, the Crespi depression effect, and frustration-produced aggression. This by no means exhausts the list of phenomena which appear to be explicable in terms of frustration theory; one could add the partial reinforcement extinction effect (Amsel, 1962), behavioural contrast and peak shift (Terrace, 1966; and see Appendix), the depression effect in the Skinner box (Baltzer and Weiskrantz, 1970; Ridgers and Gray, 1973), and transposition (Hebert and Krantz, 1965; and see Appendix). However, this is not the place to go into detail concerning these various phenomena.

The Behavioural Inhibition and Fight/Flight Systems: A Second Look

Given the number of parallels drawn in this chapter between the effects of, on the one hand, Pun and Pun—CS and, on the other, $\overline{\text{Rew}}$ and $\overline{\text{Rew}}$—CS, it is reasonable to entertain the hypothesis that both kinds of reinforcing event and their associated conditioned stimuli act on essentially the same systems in the CNS. In the case of Pun—CS we concluded in the previous chapter that the system involved is the one I have termed the "behavioural inhibition" system. Thus we may now extend that conclusion to cover the effects of $\overline{\text{Rew}}$—CS. In other words, the behavioural inhibition system, which (a) inhibits any on-going positively reinforced behaviour and (b) increments level of arousal (Fig. 8.9), is set into operation either by stimuli which have in the animal's experience been followed by punishment or by stimuli which have been followed by frustrative nonreward.

Similarly, we may extend the black box diagram shown in Fig. 8.9 into the one shown in Fig. 9.3. The new component contained in this figure is a "comparator for reward". This is essentially the same sort of mechanism as Sokolov's "neuronal model" for habituation of the OR (see Chapter 1). It stores the expected level of reward given the Rew—CS (Chapter 5) to which the animal is currently exposed, and compares it with the level of reward actually received in consequence of the animal's instrumental response. If the received level of reward is less than the expected level, there is (1) an input to that part of the system which is responsible for evaluating aversive UCSs (whether punishing or nonrewarding) and (2) in consequence an increment to the conditioned frustrating properties of stimuli in the animal's environment (including those emanating from its own instrumental behaviour) which have occurred in sufficient spatiotemporal proximity to the UCS ($\overline{\text{Rew}}$) to act as CSs in relation to it. When these stimuli (which, as in a random partial reinforcement schedule,

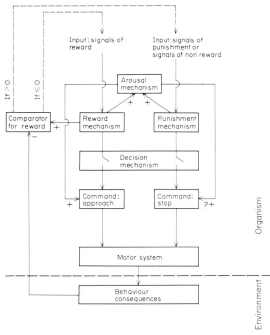

FIG. 9.3. The Gray and Smith Model, Mark 2. Expanded version of Fig. 8.9. For explanation see text. Dashed lines indicate inputs which occur on trial $n + 1$ as a result of classical conditioning of exteroceptive, interoceptive or proprioceptive CSs to the consequences of behaviour on trial n.

may be the same as those which act as Rew—CS) recur, they set up activity in the behavioural inhibition system exactly in the same way that Pun—CS do. (This model is taken further in the Gray and Smith paper reprinted in the Appendix.)

We have used the term "behavioural inhibition" to describe the system set out in Fig. 9.3 without as yet justifying it as we did for Sokolov's use of "inhibition" in his two-stage model for habituation of the orienting reflex (Chapter 1). There we agreed to confine our use of the term "inhibition" to the case where there was a definite response-suppressive mechanism at work. As we saw in that context, the best evidence for the existence of such a mechanism is the recurrence of the previously inhibited response if the mechanism is in some way removed from the scene. Evidence of this kind does in fact exist in the case of the behavioural inhibition system. Furthermore, the same experimental treatments which lead to the recurrence of responses which would otherwise be suppressed in the presence of Pun-CS also lead to the recurrence of responses suppressed in the presence of $\overline{Rew}$—CS, thus adding strongly to the evidence that these two kinds of stimuli act on one and the same system.

The evidence on which this claim is based comes from experiments in which changes in behaviour are observed after the injection of various drugs or after lesions to various parts of the brain. These experiments have shown that damage to a number of structures in the so-called "limbic system" of the brain causes an impairment both in passive avoidance and in the extinction of previously rewarded behaviour, as well as other related behaviour changes. These structures include most notably the hippocampus (Douglas, 1967) and the septal area (McCleary, 1966). Since the electrical activity of the hippocampus is strongly controlled by neurons in the septal area, it seems likely that these two areas form part of a single integrated system (Stumpf, 1965; Gray, 1970b). Furthermore, the drugs sodium amylobarbitone and alcohol produce a very similar pattern of behavioural impairment to that resulting from lesions to these two areas of the brain (Miller, 1959, 1964; Gray, 1970b); and there is evidence to connect this similarity of behavioural action with an influence of both drugs on septal control of hippocampal electrical activity (Gray, 1970b, 1972b; Gray and Ball, 1970).

This is not the place to go into further detail concerning what are essentially physiological experiments. In lieu of such detail, we offer Fig. 9.4, which summarizes the author's conclusions (Gray, 1972c) regarding the neurological basis of behavioural inhibition; and Table 9.1, which summarizes the pattern of behavioural change produced in a large number of experiments by injections of sodium amylobarbitone.

The behavioural selectivity of this drug is truly remarkable. This is brought out very clearly if we consider its action on behaviour produced by $\overline{Rew}$—CS (Miller, 1964; Wagner, 1966; Gray, 1967, 1969, 1972b; Ison and Rosen, 1967; Ison and Pennes, 1969; Rosen *et al.*, 1967). Across an extraordinarily wide diversity of forms of behaviour produced by such stimuli, the action of amylobarbitone can be described quite simply as follows: it causes the behaviour of animals exposed to Rew–CS to resemble the behaviour of animals not so exposed, but it does not alter the behaviour of animals exposed only to Rew and Rew–CS. This statement is true for simple extinction; for the partial reinforcement acquisition effect; for the effects of partial reinforcement on acquisition even when these take the reverse direction to the usual one (PRF animals running

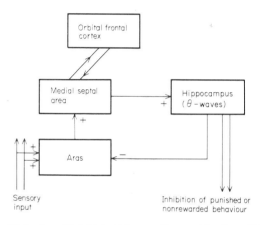

FIG. 9.4. "Behavioural Inhibition" System Proposed by Gray (1972c).

slower than CRF ones); for the partial reinforcement extinction effect (see below); for the Crespi depression effect and the depression effect in the Skinner box; and for suppression of the response to the negative stimulus during discrimination learning (see Table 9.1 for references); and this list is by no means exhaustive. Although the variety of phenomena studied is smaller, the available evidence (Table 9.1) is consistent in showing an equally strong impairment of response suppression produced by Pun–CS, as in passive avoidance.

In contrast to the impairment by amylobarbitone of response suppression to Pun–CS and Rew–CS, unconditioned escape behaviour elicited by punishment appears not to be affected by the drug (Barry and Miller, 1965). A similar disparity between behaviour

TABLE 9.1.   Effects on behaviour of sodium amylobarbitone

Behaviour	Reinforcing Event*	Effect†	Selected References
Approach	Rew; Rew–CS	?	Barry and Miller, 1965; Gray, 1969.
Crespi elation effect	Rew; Rew–CS	0	Ison and Northman, 1968; Ridgers and Gray, 1973.
Escape	Pun!	—	Barry and Miller, 1965.
Passive Avoidance	Pun–CS	— —	Barry and Miller, 1962; Kumar, 1971.
Formation of CER	Pun–CS; Pun	— —	Singh and Eysenck, 1960.
"Potentiated Startle" response	Pun–CS	— —	Chi, 1965.
Active avoidance	$\overline{\text{Pun}}$; $\overline{\text{Pun}}$–CS	?	Lynch et al., 1960; Domino et al., 1965; King, 1970.
2-way active avoidance (shuttlebox)	$\overline{\text{Pun}}$ + $\overline{\text{Pun}}$–CS vs Pun + Pun–CS	+§	Kamano et al., 1966.
Extinction	$\overline{\text{Rew}}$; $\overline{\text{Rew}}$–CS	— —	Barry, Wagner and Miller, 1962: Gray, 1969.

PRAE	Rew; Rew–CS	– –	Wagner, 1963b; Gray, 1969.
PREE	Rew; Rew–CS	– –	Ison and Pennes, 1969; Gray, 1969; Gray and Dudderidge, 1971.
Crespi depression effect	Rew; Rew–CS	– –	Rosen, Glass and Ison, 1967; Ridgers and Gray, 1973.
Discrimination learning	Rew; Rew–CS	– –	Ison and Rosen, 1967.
Double-runway FE	Rew	0	Ison, Daly and Glass, 1967; Freedman and Rosen, 1969; Gray, 1969; Gray and Dudderidge, 1971.
Small-trial PREE	Rew	0	Ziff and Capaldi, 1971.
Response-contingent time-out	Rew!–CS	– –	Ferster et al., 1962.

* Abbreviations as defined in Tables 4.2, 7.1 and 7.2.
† Symbols have following significance:
+ facilitation
– slight impairment
— marked impairment
0 no effect
? inconsistent reports
§ Presumably due to reduced effectiveness of Pun + Pun–CS.

due to Pun–CS and behaviour elicited by Pun is found in the brain lesion data. Thus the same septal lesions which impair passive avoidance greatly increase intra-specific aggressiveness and lower the threshold of response to electric shock (Fried, 1973; Lints and Harvey, 1969). Furthermore, unconditioned escape and aggressive behaviour can easily be elicited by stimulation of the brain via

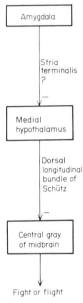

FIG. 9.5. Possible Neural Structures Subserving Unconditioned Escape and Intra-Specific Aggression. —: inhibits.

implanted electrodes; but, when this is done (e.g., de Molina and Hunsperger, 1962), the brain structures from which these effects are elicited are quite separate from those, damage to which impairs behavioural inhibition (Gray, 1972b; see Fig. 9.5). Thus these physiological experiments add to the purely behavioural evidence adduced in the previous chapter that quite separate systems mediate the behavioural effects of Pun and those of Pun–CS.

There is also evidence, albeit scanty and inconclusive, that different systems mediate the behavioural effects of $\overline{\text{Rew}}$–CS and those of $\overline{\text{Rew}}$, leaving open the possibility that the system (Fig. 9.5) mediating the behavioural effects of the primary event of Pun also mediates those of the primary event of $\overline{\text{Rew}}$. The evidence in question arises principally from studies of the FE in the double runway. Clear interpretation of these studies is made difficult by the fact that, as discussed above, the exact nature of the FE is still in doubt. However, on the assumption that it represents an unconditioned escape reaction to the primary event of frustrative nonreward, we might expect the FE to separate out from the effects of Rew–CS and perhaps to go together with those of Pun. In accord with the first part of this deduction, the FE is unaffected by any of the three physiological interventions—injections of amylobarbitone, septal or hippocampal lesions—which attenuate the effects of both Pun–CS and Rew–CS, but not those of Pun. It is, of course, always difficult to establish a negative conclusion of this kind, and in the case of the lesion effects the case rests on only two experiments, one dealing with septal (Mabry and Peeler, 1972) and one with hippocampal (Swanson and Isaacson, 1969) destruction. However, there are now several independent reports that amylobarbitone fails to affect the FE (Ison et al., 1967; Gray, 1969; Gray and Dudderidge, 1971; Freedman and Rosen, 1969).

One particularly convincing experiment of this kind has come from my own laboratory (Gray and Dudderidge, 1971). In this experiment we showed, in the same animals at the same time, that amylobarbitone *did* affect the partial reinforcement extinction effect (PREE) and yet left the FE quite untouched. Now the PREE is perhaps the most robust phenomenon yet discovered by students of learning. It consists in the fact that, if two groups of animals are trained on a rewarded response for an equal number of trials, one on random partial reinforcement and the other on continuous reinforcement, the PRF group is subsequently much more resistant to extinction than the CRF group. This phenomenon has been the subject of intensive experimental investigation and theoretical speculation (Lewis, 1960; Robbins, 1971; Amsel, 1962; Capaldi, 1967; Sutherland and Mackintosh, 1971). Before considering the Gray and Dudderidge experiment, therefore, we shall need to delve a little into the literature which deals with the PREE itself.

The Partial Reinforcement Extinction Effect

The PREE appears, in fact, not to be one phenomenon, but two closely related ones. This has become clear from the separate, but parallel, lines of investigation pursued by Amsel and by Capaldi. These two workers hold theories of the PREE which are in many ways quite similar, but which differ in one important respect. According to Capaldi (1967), $\overline{Rew}$ sets up a distinctive after-effect (which Amsel, who agrees about this point, would call "frustration"). This after-effect is the source of distinctive stimuli to the animal. Consider now a rat on a PRF schedule in a runway, when it gets a rewarded trial following a nonrewarded one (an "N–R transition" in Capaldi's terminology). At the start of the trial the rat is experiencing the stimulus after-effects of $\overline{Rew}$, he runs down the runway and is rewarded for doing so. Thus running is rewarded in the presence of the stimulus after-effects of nonreward; and, according to familiar principles of instrumental learning, the presence of these stimuli (now discriminative stimuli, S^D) should increase the probability of running on future occasions. The rat on a CRF schedule, of course, has no after-effects of $\overline{Rew}$ to experience. Thus, when extinction commences $\overline{Rew}$ is a new event for the CRF rat, but for the PRF rat it provides a further instance of stimuli, the after-effects of $\overline{Rew}$, in whose presence the instrumental response has been rewarded. Hence PRF rats will have a greater probability of running, producing the observed difference in resistance to extinction.

Amsel's theory includes one process which is absent from Capaldi's, but it presupposes (either explicitly or implicitly) everything postulated by Capaldi. The new process is one of classical conditioning. Amsel proposes that stimuli (e.g. those emanating from the startbox and stern of the runway) which regularly precede the occurrence of $\overline{Rew}$ become, by classical conditioning, $\overline{Rew}$–CS. These "conditioned frustrating" stimuli recur every time the animal is placed in the apparatus and each time they elicit a state of "conditioned frustration" (symbolized by Amsel as "r_f"), with the properties we have already described in this chapter. The next step is to suppose that this internal state of conditioned frustration is itself the source of distinctive stimuli ("s_f") which, because they are present on trials when running is rewarded, come to stand as S^D in relation to this response exactly as do Capaldi's after effects of nonreward. Again, no such process can occur in the case of CRF animals. Thus, when extinction commences, the CRF rat experiences for the first time primary frustration and, after some number of trials of extinction, conditioned frustration. Since the probability of running is higher for the PRF rats in the presence of stimuli emanating from the states of both unconditioned and conditioned frustration, their observed superiority of performance during extinction, relative to CRF rats, is once more predicted.

The two theories, Amsel's and Capaldi's, are presented schematically in Fig. 9.6. It should be noted that Amsel's theory is an example of two-process theory, postulating as it does (a) two separate processes of learning, one classical conditioning and the other instrumental, and (b) an interaction between them.

It is clear from Fig. 9.6 that the major difference between Amsel's and Capaldi's theories can be summarized by calling the former an

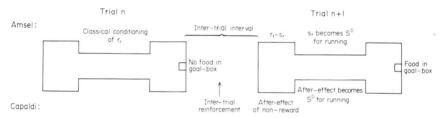

FIG. 9.6. Amsel's and Capaldi's Theories of the Partial Reinforcement Extinction Effect. For explanation, see text.

"intra-trial" theory and the latter an "inter-trial" one. The problem, as it were, is to get stimuli characteristic of nonreward into the startbox at the beginning of trial $N + 1$: Amsel does this by getting them conditioned to stimuli in the experimental environment, Capaldi by crossing the temporal gap which separates trial N from trial $N + 1$. There is, of course, no reason why both theories should not be correct. Indeed, it is clear that Amsel must suppose that Capaldi's after-effects occur (for this is the unconditioned frustration response which is to be conditioned). He could deny that the unconditioned frustration response is the source of any stimuli to the animal. But such a denial is unnecessary; and it would in any case be unusual to claim that an unconditioned response was imperceptible, and yet that the conditioned form of the response constituted an effective source of stimuli. Amsel could also deny that the unconditioned response to frustrative nonreward has any appreciable duration in time: but again such a denial is in no way called for by his own theory. Capaldi, on the other hand, does not presuppose Amsel. He could, if he wished, claim that his after-effects of non-reward are unconditionable; but, again, nothing about his own theory makes such a claim necessary. So a useful first approach might be to suppose that both theories are correct; or rather that a single theory involving both Capaldi's inter-trial effect and Amsel's intra-trial effect might be correct.

This approach, in fact, appears to cope with most of the available experimental data. This is not the place to summarize the considerable evidence that Capaldi and Amsel have been able to amass each for his own theory; and these workers have in any case done this job expertly themselves (Capaldi, 1967, 1971; Amsel, 1962, 1967; see also Sutherland and Mackintosh, 1971). What is striking, when one compares the two bodies of work, is that Capaldi has usually employed one set of conditions and Amsel another; and these conditions are just those one would expect to increase (in Capaldi's case) or decrease (in Amsel's) the relative importance of inter-trial processes. That is to say, Capaldi has, for the most part, used short inter-trial intervals (1–20 min), which are easier to cross with an after-effect; large rewards, so that the after-effect of their omission is likely to be large; and small numbers of trials, minimizing the degree of Amselian conditioning which can take place. Amsel, in contrast, has tended to use long inter-trial intervals (several minutes to 24 h), small rewards and many trials.

The likelihood that both Capaldi's after-effects and Amsel's conditioned frustration are operative in the PREE is supported by some experiments from K. W. Spence's laboratory (Black and Spence, 1965; Spence *et al.*, 1965). In these experiments use was made of Capaldi's technique of "inter-trial reinforcement". This consists in giving the rat an additional reward (after placing it in the goalbox by hand) between the trials on which the instrumental response is performed. This reward may be given between the nonrewarded and rewarded trials of an N–R transition (see Fig. 9.6) or after a rewarded trial. In the former case, according to Capaldi's theory, the inter-trial reinforcement would be expected to substitute for the after-effect of nonreward an after-effect of reward, and so block the behavioural effects of nonreward. Giving the inter-trial reinforcement after reward trials, in a different group of animals, is the control procedure. Using this technique, under his preferred conditions, Capaldi has been able to provide good experimental support for the inter-trial theory.

Spence and his collaborators argued, however, that the inter-trial reinforcement technique should only work if Amsel's conditioned frustration had not yet had an opportunity to become established; for, once there is an *intra*-trial mode of crossing the gap between nonrewarded and rewarded trials, the inter-trial route is no longer essential, and blocking it should have no effect. They therefore examined the effect of inter-trial reinforcement on the PREE under two conditions: with a relatively small number of trials (which should emphasize inter-trial processes), or with a relatively large number of trials (which should emphasize intra-trial processes). Their results showed that in the former *but not the latter* case, inter-trial reinforcement delivered during the N–R transition succeeded in blocking the PREE.

This result, then, suggests that the PREE may arise in two ways. The first (which is favoured by large rewards, few trials and short inter-trial intervals) is Capaldi's: the after-effect of nonreward becomes directly a discriminative stimulus for performing the instrumental response by crossing the N–R inter-trial interval. The second (which is favoured by small rewards, many trials and long inter-trial intervals) is Amsel's: a conditioned frustration response provides the appropriate discriminative stimuli, obviating the need for direct crossing of the temporal gap between nonrewarded and rewarded trials. This conclusion is questioned by Capaldi (1967, 1971), who has recently provided evidence that after-effects (which he now describes as "memory stimuli") can last much longer than one might anticipate, at least up to 24 h. However, independent evidence for the distinction between the two kinds of PREE comes from experiments which have employed amylobarbitone.

It has now been reported a number of times that injections of amylobarbitone during training on a partial reinforcement schedule, with extinction subsequently carried out in the absence of the drug, is able to considerably attenuate or even block completely the PREE (Ison and Pennes, 1969; Gray, 1969, 1972b; Gray and Dudderidge, 1971; Capaldi and Sparling, 1971), and we have further replicated the phenomenon in a number of unpublished studies in our own laboratory. An example of this effect of the drug is shown in Fig. 9.7. It can be seen that it is entirely attributable to a reduction in resistance to extinction on the part of the drugged PRF animals, the drugged CRF animals being indistinguishable from placebo-injected controls. Thus the effect of amylobarbitone on the PREE is entirely in accordance with the conclusion reached earlier in this chapter: the drug reverses the effects of nonreward and does not alter those of reward.

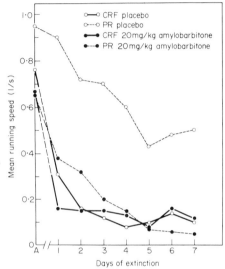

FIG. 9.7. Abolition of the Partial Reinforcement Extinction Effect by Injections of 20 mg/kg Sodium Amylobarbitone During Acquisition. The four groups represented by the curves in the figure received either continuous reinforcement (CRF) or partial reinforcement (PR) combined with injections of either amylobarbitone or a saline placebo during training. The point marked "A" on the abscissa is the last day of acquisition. During extinction all groups were given placebo injections and no further reward. The PR placebo group is much more resistant to extinction than the CRF placebo group but the two amylobarbitone groups both extinguish rapidly. (From Gray, 1969.)

Now all the experiments in which amylobarbitone has been reported to block the PREE in this way have employed conditions which favour *Amselian* processes. In particular, they have used fairly large numbers of trials; and the greater the number of trials employed, the greater appears to have been the effect on the PREE of amylobarbitone (Gray, 1969, 1972b). There is, moreover, one published experiment in which the PREE is quite unaffected by injections of amylobarbitone. And this (Ziff and Capaldi, 1971) employed conditions which favour Capaldi's inter-trial process: very few trials, short inter-trial interval and large reward. In contrast to the absence of any effect of the drug on the small-trial PREE in the Ziff and Capaldi experiment, we have recently obtained the largest effect of amylobarbitone on the PREE yet observed in an experiment using a 24 h inter-trial interval, likely to favour the Amselian process to a considerable degree. The results of this experiment

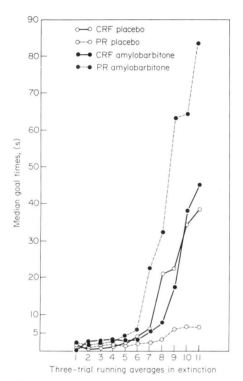

FIG. 9.8. Abolition of the Partial Reinforcement Extinction Effect by Amylobarbitone During Training with a 24 h Intertrial Interval. The design of this experiment was essentially the same as that of the experiment whose results are shown in Fig. 9.7, except that only one trial was run per day. Note that, in extinction on placebo, the previously drugged PR group shows considerably *less* resistance to extinction than the previously drugged CRF group.

(Dudderidge *et al.*, in preparation) are presented in Fig. 9.8. It can be seen that, after amylobarbitone injections during training, the CRF group is actually *more* resistant to extinction that the PRF group, an unusual result which probably reflects the smaller number of rewards received by the PRF animals (only 19 acquisition trials having been run in this experiment).

These results, then, offer support for the view that the PREE can arise in two ways (both of which, of course, are likely to be operative simultaneously under most conditions): one of these involves only the after-effects of nonreward and is insusceptible to the drug amylobarbitone; the other involves the conditioning of frustration and is highly susceptible to the effects of this drug. This conclusion in turn suggests that there is a physiological distinction between the effects of $\overline{Rew}$ and the effects of $\overline{Rew}$–CS, paralleling the distinction between two different systems which mediate the behavioural effects of Pun and Pun–CS. This view is further supported by the results of the Gray and Dudderidge (1971) experiment referred to earlier and to which we now return.

In this experiment we attempted to use amylobarbitone as a kind of pharmacological scalpel to separate the FE from the PREE (the latter under conditions favouring the Amselian process). We trained rats in the Amsel and Roussel double runway (Fig. 9.1). All rats received food on a CRF schedule in the second goalbox. Two of the four groups studied also received CRF in the first goalbox, the other two getting PRF on a random 50% schedule. One each of these pairs of groups was trained with amylobarbitone injections, the other with saline as a placebo. In this way, we were able to observe the effect of the drug on the FE: as in previous experiments there was none, a clearcut FE being observed in both placebo and drug conditions. All rats were now extinguished, without further drug injections, in the first half of the double runway. In the rats which had received placebo during training, a PREE was observed. The rats which had received the drug also showed a PREE, but significantly reduced; and, as in previous experiments, this reduction was entirely due to a lowered resistance to extinction in the drugged PRF group. Thus, though amylobarbitone had failed to affect the FE at the time it was actually present in the animal's blood-stream, it nonetheless attenuated the PREE tested later, when the animal was no longer directly under the influence of the drug. This experiment, then, adds to the evidence that the direct after-effect of nonreward (which, on whatever view one adopts of the FE, is presumably involved in this phenomenon) is immune to amylobarbitone, and that this drug affects only the behavioural consequences of *conditioned* frustration.

This view is not without its difficulties (Capaldi and Sparling, 1971; Gray, 1969, Experiment 3; Gray, 1972b). However, it is probably the most reasonable one to adopt in the light of existing data; and it offers the only available solution to the otherwise puzzling problem posed by the immunity of the double-runway FE (alone among frustration effects, apart from the small-trial PREE) to amylobarbitone, as well as to septal and hippocampal lesions. Tentatively, therefore, we conclude that $\overline{\text{Rew}}$ and $\overline{\text{Rew}}$–CS activate different systems in the CNS, and that the system activated by $\overline{\text{Rew}}$–CS is identical to the one activated by Pun–CS–i.e. it is the amylobarbitone-sensitive behavioural inhibition system. Whether or not the system activated by the primary event of $\overline{\text{Rew}}$ is the same as that activated by Pun is still an open question, and there are at present very few data to bring to bear on it. The desire for parsimony and simplicity bids us hope that it is so; but only further experiment can resolve the issue.

10. Active Avoidance and Relieving Nonpunishment

As we saw in Chapter 8 the distinction between active and passive avoidance is that, in the former, a response followed by omission of punishment increases in probability while, in the latter, a response followed by presentation of punishment decreases in probability. Two questions of possible identity arise from this distinction:

(1) Are the classes of *stimuli* which may be used to produce the two kinds of avoidance behaviour identical?

(2) Are the *processes* involved in the two kinds of avoidance behaviour identical?

Since there is a third way of using a negative reinforcer, i.e. so that its termination leads to *escape* behaviour, each of these questions, for completeness, should be expanded to cover three terms. Escape behaviour, however, has received much less theoretical or empirical attention than the two forms of avoidance behaviour. We too shall mention it only briefly.

The tendency has been, until comparatively recently, to answer both the above questions in the affirmative. Certainly, casual observation suggests that it is correct to answer Question 1 in this way, though there has been, in fact, little systematic investigation of the problem. We have already discussed one such investigation in Chapter 6: Terhune and Premack (1970) showed that the degree to which a stimulus would act as a punishment in a passive avoidance paradigm could be predicted by the probability with which the animal would escape from it. I know of only one negative instance to the rule of identity with respect to Question 1: this has arisen in experiments involving aversive electrical stimulation of the brain. With electrodes implanted in certain areas of the brain, rats readily learn an escape response to terminate the stimulation, but only with difficulty, if at all, an anticipatory avoidance response (Roberts,

1958; Olds and Olds, 1962; Stein, 1965). With this exception (the significance of which is obscure) we may proceed on the familiar assumption that stimuli which pass one of the three tests of negative reinforcement (passive avoidance, escape or active avoidance) will normally also pass the other two tests. The affirmative answer to Question 2, however, is almost certainly wrong, as we have already seen in Chapter 8.

Since we cannot generalize the explanation of passive avoidance developed in Chapter 8 to active avoidance, we must ask what processes underlie the establishment of an active avoidance response. This question has proved to be one of the most difficult ones with which learning theorists are faced, and they have often got themselves into some formidable tangles in their attempts to answer it. In this chapter we follow them though some of these tangles.

The difficulty that active avoidance learning has posed for the dominant tradition of learning theory during the last forty years or so has arisen from the joint operation of two preconceptions: (1) for learning to occur there has to be a source of reinforcement; (2) the non-occurrence of punishment is a non-event from the subject's point of view. It follows that, since the omission of punishment cannot provide the necessary source of reinforcement, some other source must be found. It is the search for such an alternative source of reinforcment which has produced most of the tangles; but, it has also been a most fruitful spur to the development of two-process learning theory.

The reader trained in the sophistries of Chapter 1, in which we argued the case for the existence of expectancies and the detection of departures from expectancies during habituation of the orienting reflex, will want to ask why the omission of anticipated punishment cannot provide the reinforcement for active avoidance learning. After all, the omission of anticipated reward ($\overline{\text{Rew}}$) has been shown to be a potent event in its own right (Chapter 9), so why not the omission of anticipated punishment ($\overline{\text{Pun}}$)? And, indeed, as we shall see when we come to the experiments of Herrnstein and Hineline (Herrnstein, 1969) and Rescorla and LoLordo (1965), there is good evidence that $\overline{\text{Pun}}$ is a distinctive event for animal subjects. However, before coming to these experiments, let us follow the debate which began with Mowrer's (1947) and Miller's (1951) independent attempts to salvage a reinforcement theory of active avoidance learning while leaving $\overline{\text{Pun}}$ in the mentalistic limbo where it was thought to belong: for out of these attempts the main lines of two-process theory have emerged.

The Miller–Mowrer Theory

The essential claim made by both Mowrer and Miller (although they differed in other important respects, as we shall see) was that, in an active avoidance situation, animals do not learn to avoid the punishment at all. Instead they learn to *terminate* stimuli regularly followed by punishment (i.e. Pun–CS, or "secondarily aversive stimuli", "conditioned fear stimuli" or "warning signals"), and, by so doing, in most situations prevent (but as an unintended consequence of their acts) the occurrence of the punishment. Active avoidance behaviour, then, on this view: (1) is not reinforced by $\overline{\text{Pun}}$; (2) *is* reinforced by the termination of warning signals (Pun–CS!, as defined in Tables 7.1 and 7.2). These claims have stimulated a great deal of experimental work from which a number of conclusions may be drawn.

It is clear that, by regularly pairing an initially neutral stimulus with punishment, it is indeed possible to create a secondarily aversive stimulus, and that the termination of this stimulus may then increase the probability of behaviour on which it is made contingent. This was shown in a number of classic studies in the 1940s. In one of Miller's experiments (1948), for example, a rat was first shocked in a white compartment and allowed to escape from the shock by running into a black compartment. It was soon found that the rat would run from the white to the black compartment even in the absence of the shock. A stronger demonstration of the aversive properties acquired by the white compartment was provided by making the animal learn a totally new response to get out of it, even though it was never shocked again. This was done by interposing a barrier between the two compartments which could be removed if the rat turned a wheel. The rat duly learned to turn the wheel. A bar was then substituted for the wheel, whereupon the rat abandoned wheel-turning and took up the now effective barpressing instead. Evidently, the rat's initial experience with shock in the white compartment had left some fairly permanent residue which was sufficiently strong to motivate the learning of several new forms of behaviour.

There are many other reports of similar phenomena, allowing us to conclude that Pun–CS are aversive, not only by a punishment test (Chapter 8), but also by an escape test. However, behaviour upon which termination of a warning signal is made contingent does not always increase in probability. On the contrary, there are a number of experiments in which the animal treats *presentation* of a warning signal as a *positive* reinforcer. The experimental design which produces this apparently paradoxical result is one in which the subject is given a choice (e.g. by occupation of one side or other of a two-compartment apparatus) between unsignalled shock and shock preceded by a warning signal. The results of such experiments (Lockard, 1963; Perkins *et al.*, 1966) are unequivocal: rats prefer shock-with-warning to unsignalled shock. On an uncomplicated Miller–Mowrer view, this is unexpected, since the total aversiveness of the situation should be increased by adding the aversive CS to the already aversive UCS. We shall return to this point later.

A further conclusion which can be drawn from work on the Miller–Mowrer theory is that $\overline{Pun}$ *under certain conditions* may indeed be ineffective as a reinforcement, as both these theorists claimed. The necessary conditions appear to be (1) that $\overline{Pun}$ be pitted against Pun–CS! and (2) that the task required of the animal be a rather complex one.

The experiments demonstrating the ineffectiveness of $\overline{Pun}$ under these conditions are due to Kamin (1956, 1957). He used four groups of rats in the shuttle-box. One was given the usual escape-avoidance procedure, in which a response (of jumping to the other side of the apparatus) terminated the shock if it was already one, avoided the shock if it was not yet on, and terminated the Pun–CS (a buzzer) in either case. A classical conditioning control group was given the same buzzer-shock sequences but could not affect either by their responses. As was to be expected, the former of these two groups learned to shuttle, while the latter did not. Of the other two groups, one had shuttling reinforced by CS-termination without shock-avoidance, the other by shock-avoidance without CS-termination. (All groups could terminate the shock once it was on by shuttling.) The results of the experiment are shown in Fig. 10.1. It is clear that termination of the Pun-CS, without avoidance of punishment, was able to sustain a respectable level of shuttling, confirming the conclusions we have already drawn, that this is indeed a reinforcing event. Our present interest, however, is in the performance of the group given shock-avoidance but not CS-termination for shuttling. Clearly, the level of responding attained by this group was below that of the escape-avoidance rats, indicating that the reinforcing effect of $\overline{\text{Pun}}$ may be reduced by pitting it against Pun-CS!

At first sight however, the outcome of Kamin's (1956) experiment was less than satisfactory for the Miller–Mowrer theory, since that

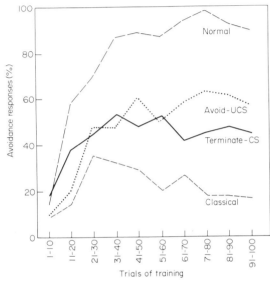

FIG. 10.1. Results of Kamin's Experiment on CS-Termination and Shock-Avoidance in the Shuttlebox. The four curves are for groups of rats which could both terminate the CS and avoid the shock ("normal"), terminate the CS only, avoid the shock only, or do neither ("classical"). (From Kamin, 1956.)

theory predicts that the CS-termination-only group should have learned as well as the escape-avoidance group, and the shock-avoidance-only group should not have learned to shuttle at all. The former of these difficulties is, however, only apparent: since rats in this group were in fact *punished* for shuttling (shock occurring when they reached the other side of the apparatus), it is not surprising that their level of shuttling was lower than that in the escape-avoidance group. Indeed, given the punishment received by this group for shuttling, Kamin's experiment is a striking demonstration of the effectiveness of Pun–CS! as a reinforcer. As for the second difficulty, a further experiment of Kamin's (1957) showed that it is possible to render P̄u̅n̅ totally ineffective as a reinforcer, as the Miller–Mowrer theory predicts.

Kamin argued that, since the duration of the Pun–CS in his first experiment was fixed at five seconds, and since the rats tended to respond about three seconds after the onset of the CS, the group which nominally had shock-avoidance-only for shuttling was in fact also receiving CS-termination, but with a delay of the order of two seconds. He therefore repeated the experiment, but arranged for the duration of the CS to be timed from the moment of the animal's response. Under these conditions, a group which had shuttling reinforced by shock-avoidance and by CS-termination at a delay of 5 sec from the moment of response did not learn to shuttle at all. Thus, though immediate CS-termination may sustain a moderate level of shuttling in spite of the occurrence of punishment for shuttling, the avoidance of punishment is unable to sustain shuttling if CS-termination is delayed by only 5 sec from the time of the response.

This problem has been further examined by Bolles, Stokes and Younger (1966). They repeated Kamin's (1956) experiment in the shuttlebox, but in addition investigated the effects of a contingency which Kamin had held constant in all conditions: termination by the response of the shock if it was already on when the animal responded. For half their groups they eliminated this contingency by using a duration of shock which was so short (0.3 sec that it terminated before the rat had had time to escape. Their results are shown in Table 10.1. It will be seen that they replicated Kamin's results in the groups which escaped shock, but that the escape contingency was itself partly responsible for maintaining shuttling both when it was combined with shock-avoidance and when it was combined with CS-termination. Shock-avoidance entirely on its own, i.e. combined with neither CS-termination nor shock-escape, resulted in only 15 avoidances out of 100, compared to 14 when shuttling had no effect at all. Thus, in the shuttlebox, Bolles *et al.* confirm Kamin's finding that shock-avoidance *per se* is extraordinarily weak in maintaining avoidance behaviour. But it is also to be noted from Table 10.1 that CS-termination entirely on its own fares no better: 10 responses out of 100.

However, when Bolles *et al.* repeated essentially the same experiment in a running wheel, rather than a shuttlebox, they obtained

TABLE 10.1. Median CRs in 100 training trials as a function of whether the CR terminates the CS (T), avoids the US (A), or escapes the US (E). (From Bolles, Stokes and Younger 1966.)

Experimental condition			Median CRs
T	A	E	70
		—	37
	—	E	31
		—	10
—	A	E	40
		—	15
	—	E	9
		—	14

very different results. They defined the avoidance response as a quarter-turn of the running wheel in either direction. This offered the rat a much less complex problem than the response of shuttling, which requires the subject continually to return to the side of the apparatus from which it has just fled, thus introducing an element of conflict into the situation. It may be this element of conflict that accounts for the different results obtained in the two kinds of apparatus. Whatever the reason, it is clear from Fig. 10.2 that they are different: avoidance alone (without either shock-escape or CS-

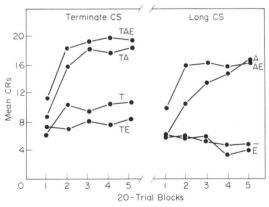

FIG. 10.2. Effects of CS-Termination, Shock-Escape and Shock-Avoidance on Performance in the Running Wheel. The acquisition of a running response in a running wheel as a function of whether the CS could be terminated (T) and of whether the shock could be avoided (A) or not and escaped (E) or not. The group marked — affected neither CS nor shock by running. (From Bolles, Stokes and Younger, 1966.)

termination) was sufficient in the running wheel to maintain a respectably high level of responding. This result, furthermore, was not due to delayed termination of the CS, as Bolles et al. showed in a further experiment using a trace conditioning procedure. In this procedure the CS is presented for a period of time which is too brief (0.5 sec in the present case) to allow completion of the avoidance response, and the shock then follows (on non-avoidance trials) after a relatively long interval (10 sec in the present case). There can therefore be no question of apparent termination of the CS by the avoidance response. Nevertheless, avoidance alone was once more able to maintain responding at the same level as before.

At least under some conditions, therefore, Pun is able to act as a reinforcement without help either from Pun–CS! or from Pun! We shall meet even more convincing demonstrations of this point later in the chapter. Before pursuing the matter further at this point, however, let us follow the fate of two-process theory in another part of the experimental forest: that dealing with the *extinction* of avoidance behaviour.

The term "two-process theory" is, in fact, only properly applicable to Mowrer's version of the Miller–Mowrer theory. Miller postulated only *one* process, a Hullian one for which reinforcement was essential and took the form of drive reduction (specifically, reduction in fear). Mowrer, in contrast, explicitly distinguished between a classical conditioning process (for which temporal contiguity was sufficient) responsible for the conditioning of fear to a Pun–CS, and an instrumental learning process (requiring drive reduction) responsible for the conditioning of the instrumental learning response by means of reduction in fear. (The famous paper in which Mowrer, in 1947, made this proposal was seminal for the construction of two-process theory.) This difference between the two theories is critical when we come to examine how they deal with the extinction of avoidance behaviour.

Let us approach the difference between the two theories by considering the problem that they each set out to solve. From the point of view of Hull's theory of learning, which both Miller and Mowrer took as their starting point, it was necessary to find a source of drive-reduction (Chapter 4) to provide the reinforcement for a successful avoidance response. Let us suppose the experimental animal is in a conventional escape-avoidance situation in which his response terminates shock once it is on and prevents its occurrence if it is made between the onset of the warning signal and the programmed onset of the shock. It is easy for a Hullian to find a source of drive-reduction to reinforce the escape response: he regards the onset of shock as the equivalent of a rise in drive and he regards the termination of the shock which is contingent on the response as a reduction in drive: QED. (We saw, however, in Chapter 4 that, used in this way, the drive-reduction hypothesis of reinforcement is an empirically empty tautology.) Now let us suppose that, after making a series of escape responses, the animal makes his first avoidance response. This too can be accounted for within the Hullian framework simply enough. It can be argued that the escape response occurs in the presence of stimuli which are also present during the period when the warning signal is on (including most notably the warning signal itself, given the usual procedure in which this and the shock overlap in time). These stimuli will acquire the power to act as discriminative stimuli for the escape response even in the absence of the shock, thus enabling the escape response to occur as an anticipatory avoidance response. We finally suppose that the avoidance response now occurs in this way on several successive trials. Here is where the difficulty arises for Hullian theory. Since the avoidance response gets no reinforcement (i.e. no shock-termination, so no drive-reduction), it should rapidly extinguish. Once it has extinguished, the animal should revert to escape responding, and the cycle should recommence. In this way, the simplest Hullian prediction is that the experimental animal should endlessly alternate between bouts of escape responding and bouts of avoidance responding.

Now there has been the occasional report (see Turner and Solomon, 1962) that this is precisely what a rat does in an escape-avoidance task. However, this is certainly not what usually happens*: indeed, one of the most remarkable features of active avoidance behaviour is its extreme resistance to extinction after only a few initial punishments and over a long series of successful avoidance responses which no longer encounter any punishment. There are, in any case, other reasons to discount this simplest Hullian account of avoidance behaviour, e.g. the fact that animals can learn

* As pointed out by Turner and Solomon (1962), it occurs when the response designated by the experimenter as the active avoidance response is a highly reflective one (i.e. is elicited with high probability and short latency by the to-be-avoided S^{R-}: see Chapter 2).

one response to terminate shock and a different one to avoid it, in the same situation at the same time (Mowrer and Lamoreaux, 1946). For both Miller and Mowrer, then, the problem was to find a continuing source of reinforcement to prevent the extinction of successful avoidance responses, once these had begun to occur. Now, if one examines the theories they each constructed to do this job, it turns out that Miller's theory is logically water-tight, but empirically wrong; and Mowrer's is theoretically incapable of doing what it set out to do, but is supported by a considerable amount of experimental evidence.

Both postulate a hypothetical drive state called "fear", elicited by stimuli which are regularly associated with punishment (i.e. Pun—CS). "Fear" is a theoretical hybrid: it is simultaneously a *response* (it is the result of conditioning and resembles the set of responses evoked by the unconditioned punishing stimulus); a *drive* (it invigorates ongoing behaviour and its reduction is reinforcing); and a source of internal *stimuli* (stimuli which, in a manner familiar from the notion of conditioned frustration—Chapter 9—can become the eliciting cues for an overt instrumental response). So far the two theories are in agreement. They differ in the way in which fear is conceived to become conditioned to stimuli associated with punishment.

Mowrer's view was that the conditioning of fear takes place by *classical* conditioning, that classical conditioning requires temporal contiguity between CS and UCS but no drive-reduction, and that the learning of the instrumental avoidance response is based on a separate process which *does* require drive-reduction. This drive-reduction consists in reduction in the level of fear; and the animal provides this for itself by terminating the warning signals which, as the result of classical conditioning, are the eliciting stimuli for fear. Thus Mowrer made a radical departure from the Hullian uni-process framework, so creating the model for much theorizing since, including Amsel's frustration theory considered in the previous chapter.

Miller's theory, in contrast, kept much closer to the Hullian framework. It maintained Hull's uni-process view of learning and sought all reinforcement in drive-reduction. Thus, for the conditioning of fear to take place, there must be a reduction in drive to reinforce *this* conditioning too. But if fear is called in to provide the source of drive-reduction for the avoidance response, and a new source of drive-reduction then has to be called into account for the conditioning of fear, there is a danger of an infinite regress. To circumvent this danger, Miller found the drive-reduction for the learning of fear in *reduction in the fear itself*. His argument runs as follows.

In the presence of certain stimuli, a shock is delivered to the animal. This shock elicits an internal drive state which we may call "unconditioned fear". The shock is of limited duration, whether because the experimenter terminates it after a fixed time or because the animal terminates it by an escape response. At the termination of the shock, there is a reduction in the level of unconditioned fear. This provides reinforcement (i.e. drive-reduction) for the learning of those responses which occurred prior to the termination of shock. These responses included the *onset of the unconditioned fear*, and this response occurred in the presence of stimuli emanating from the experimental environment. Thus, by Hullian principles of reinforcement, these stimuli acquire the capacity to elicit as a *conditioned* response the fear that was initially elicited by the shock itself. We are now, then, in the situation that stimuli in the experimental environment are able to elicit conditioned fear before shock occurs. Let us suppose that chief among these stimuli is an explicit warning signal, say a buzzer. When the buzzer sounds, the animal experiences a rise in conditioned fear. If he now does something which terminates the buzzer, there is in consequence a fall in the level of conditioned fear. This fall in conditioned fear is a reduction in drive, and it provides Hullian reinforcement *simultaneously for the instrumental resonse which terminated the buzzer and for the onset of the fear itself*. Thus, if we suppose (as in the usual experimental procedure) that the response which terminates the warning signal also avoids the shock, this response, on Miller's theory, continues indefinitely to be followed by reinforcement (a fall in the level of conditioned fear) both for itself and for the further conditioning of fear.

We have spent many words in expounding Miller's theory of fear and avoidance learning because it is a difficult theory to grasp. It is highly counter-intuitive and it makes some very odd predictions, as we shall see in a moment. It had the great advantage over Mowrer's theory, however, that, had it worked, it provided a source of reinforcement for avoidance responses which need never, in principle, disappear. It thus explained the extreme resistance to extinction of avoidance responses which is actually observed. Mowrer's theory, in contrast, as a little thought shows, barely alters the essential dilemma posed by avoidance learning for Hullian theory.

This, as we have seen, predicts that the animal will go through an endless cycle of escape followed by avoidance and back to escape. The best Mowrer's theory can do to improve on this is somewhat to lengthen the duration of the avoidance bouts in this cycle. Conditioned fear, in his theory, is reinforced by the temporal contiguity between CS (e.g. an explicit warning signal) and UCS (shock) according to the principles of classical conditioning. But, once the animal starts successfully avoiding, the UCS by definition ceases to occur. The avoidance response itself is maintained for a while by the reduction in fear which follows it, according to the drive-reduction principle of Hullian instrumental learning. But the conditioned fear itself must start to extinguish as soon as the shocks stop coming, according to the usual laws of Pavlovian extinction. Eventually, then, there is no longer any conditioned fear elicited by the warning signal for the avoidance response (which terminates this signal) to reduce; i.e. there is no longer any drive-reduction, so the avoidance response itself should extinguish, until the animal re-enters a phase of escape responding and the whole cycle, lengthened from the original Hullian prediction but essentially unchanged, starts up again.

Given this situation, it would be natural to hope that, in spite of its baroque flavour, Miller's theory (which was at least logically capable of doing the job) would prove correct. Unfortunately, experiments designed to choose between the two theories have unequivocally favoured Mowrer's.

It will be sufficient to give here two examples of the kind of paradoxical prediction Miller's theory makes and of the experiments which have tested and infirmed these predictions. Mowrer and Aiken (1954) and Mowrer and Solomon (1954) argued that, if drive-reduction is what reinforces the fear that is conditioned to a secondarily aversive stimulus, then the closer the onset of this stimulus is to the *offset* of shock, the more easily will fear be so conditioned. Conversely, common sense and Mowrer's theory would both lead one to expect that fear would be most readily conditioned, the closer the onset of the initially neutral stimulus is to the *onset* of the shock. The experiments they conducted to test this deduction involving pairing a 3 sec flickering light with a 10 sec shock according to the various procedures shown in Fig. 10.3, and then testing for the fear-arousal properties of the would-be secondarily aversive stimuli formed in these ways. The assessment of fear was carried out by presenting the flickering light to the subjects (rats) either non-contingently while they pressed a bar for a food reward (in Mowrer and Aiken's experiment) or contingently upon the food-rewarded barpresses (in Mowrer and Solomon's experiment); as we know from Chapter 8, in both techniques secondarily aversive stimuli would be expected to depress the rate of barpressing, and the degree of depression may conveniently be used as a measure of the extent of aroused fear. As can be seen in Fig. 10.3, barpressing was reduced in Mowrer and Aiken's experiment most when the onset of the light was paired with the onset of shock and least when it was paired with shock-offset. Furthermore, the Mowrer and Solomon experiment showed that, given the association between the CS and shock-onset, it is of no consequence how long it is after the occurrence of the CS that shock-offset occurs, nor whether shock-offset occurs abruptly or gradually. Miller's theory in contrast, would predict that more fear would be conditioned (1) when shock-offset follows the CS at a short interval rather than a long one, and (2) when shock-offset is an abrupt, clearly noticeable event, rather than a gradual waning in intensity. However, stimuli paired by Mowrer and Solomon according to the four procedures shown in Fig. 10.3 all elicited equivalent amounts of fear.

It seems then, that Miller's theory, at the critical point where it differs from Mowrer's, is wrong, so that Mowrer's two-process theory is all we are left with. Moreover, in spite of its logical incompleteness, there is in fact a considerable body of evidence to show that the essential claims made by this theory are correct. These claims are:

(1) There are two distinct processes of learning, one, classical conditioning, depending only on temporal contiguity between stimuli, the other, instrumental learning, depending on reinforcement following a response.

(2) As a result of the first kind of conditioning, stimuli acquire emotional and motivational significance; in particular, they become secondarily aversive.

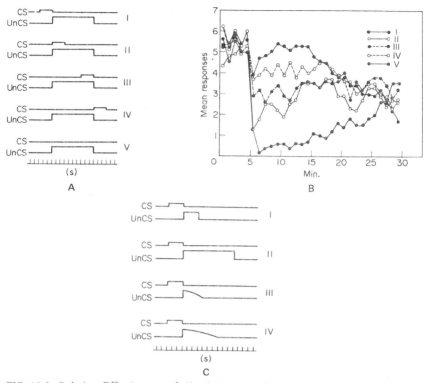

FIG. 10.3. Relative Effectiveness of Shock Onset and Shock Offset as Unconditioned Stimuli in Conditioning of Fear. A. Relationships between CS and shock UCS ("UnCS") for various groups in the Mowrer and Aiken (1954) experiment. B. Conditioned suppression produced in Mowrer and Aiken's experiment by CSs paired with shock under conditions shown in A. C. Various arrangements of CS and shock ("UnCS") employed in Mowrer and Solomon's (1954) experiment on the effect of shock duration and rate of cessation upon conditioned fear. See text for further explanation. (Figure taken from Kimble, 1961.)

(3) These stimuli then influence instrumental learning (a) by providing new sources of reinforcement for it, and (b) by altering the direction and level of motivation.

We have, in fact, already considered much of the evidence which supports these claims. With regard to point (1), we gave this exhaustive consideration in earlier chapters, especially Chapter 2. With regard to points (2) and (3a), the evidence that under most, though not all, conditions animals will work to terminate their exposure to stimuli previously paired with punishment has been reviewed earlier in this chapter. It remains to consider the evidence for point (3b). In this connection, the recent experiments of

Rescorla and Solomon (1967) and their associates show that stimuli paired with punishment do indeed acquire the capacity to affect motivation, as required by Mowrer's theory.

In these experiments (e.g. Rescorla and LoLordo, 1965) an explicit separation is made between the two phases of classical conditioning and instrumental learning which are usually only inferred in studies of avoidance learning in, say, the shuttlebox. The instrumental learning phase of the experiment is carried out using a Sidman avoidance schedule (see Fig. 2.3). The advantage of this schedule is that it does not involve a special warning signal. It can therefore provide a baseline against which the motivational significance of stimuli can easily be evaluated. The stimuli whose effect was evaluated in this way had been paired with shock (i.e. Pun) according to a classical conditioning procedure. The experimenters argued that, if such stimuli acquire the capacity to increase the level of fear (as they should), then they ought to increase the rate of Sidman avoidance responding. Since presentation of the test stimuli in this procedure is independent of the performance of the Sidman avoidance response, this is a motivational, rather than a reinforcement, method of assessing fear (see Chapters 5 and 8). The basic result obtained by Rescorla and LoLordo (1965)—that a stimulus paired with shock according to a classical conditioning paradigm acquires the power to raise the rate of Sidman avoidance responding—has now been repeated many times (e.g. Riess and Farrar, 1973)*.

Soltysik's Emendation of Mowrer's Theory

Give the relative success of Mowrer's two-process theory of active avoidance, and the failure of Miller's uni-process theory, it is tempting to seek for some way of repairing Mowrer's logical

---

* However, there are also a number of reports of the opposite effect, i.e. a stimulus paired with shock producing conditioned *suppression* of Sidman avoidance. It is not entirely clear under what conditions each of these two effects, conditioned acceleration as in the original Rescorla and LoLordo (1965) experiment or conditioned suppression, can be obtained. However, one variable which has definitely been shown to be operative is the intensity of the shock UCS relative to the intensity of the shock used in maintenance of the Sidman avoidance behaviour: if the shock UCS is equal to or less intense than the Sidman shock, acceleration is obtained; if the UCS is more intense than the Sidman shock, suppression (Scobie, 1972). Other studies relevant to this problem have been reported by Blackman (1970), Roberts and Hurwitz (1970) and Scobie (1973).

structure so that it no longer predicts rapid extinction of fear and hence of avoidance behaviour. Such a repair has been attempted by Soltysik (1964).

Soltysik's starting point lies in the phenomenon of Pavlovian conditioned inhibition, which we considered in Chapter 3. The basic experimental paradigm for conditioned inhibition is: CS → UCS, CI + CS → no UCS; the abbreviation "CI" standing for "conditioned inhibitor". As a result of such pairings, the combination CI + CS ceases to elicit the CR, although this continues to be elicited by the CS on its own. Now, in an avoidance situation, it is possible to regard the stimuli which arise from the making of the avoidance response (e.g. proprioceptive and kinaesthetic feedback or the changes in the external environment produced by the response) as conditioned inhibitors of the conditioned response of fear elicited by the warning signal. This is because the animal experiences pairings of the following kinds: warning signal → shock, warning signal + stimuli produced by the avoidance response → no shock. The key point in Soltysik's version of Mowrer's two-process theory is the assumption that a pairing of the form, CS + CI → no UCS, not only prevents the CR from occurring (conditioned inhibition, properly speaking), but also *protects the CR from extinction*, so that this continues to be elicited by the CS presented on its own. That a CI can protect a CR from extinction in this sense has been shown for ordinary salivary conditioning by Chorazyna (1962).

One difficulty in the way of this theory is that, in the usual Pavlovian paradigm, the CI precedes the CS, whereas, in an avoidance situation, the warning signal necessarily precedes the avoidance response, and so also the putative conditioned inhibitory stimuli emanating from this response. However, this difficulty was overcome by the demonstration (Soltysik, 1960) of conditioned inhibition in a straightforward Pavlovian salivary conditioning situation, but using the temporal pattern characteristic of the avoidance situation. Using a dog as subject, Soltysik set up a salivary CR with food as UCS and the whirring of a fan as CS. He then interspersed CS → UCS pairings with pairings in which the CS was presented simultaneously with a conditioned inhibitor (a buzzer), in the sequence CS + CI → no food. Once the conditioned inhibition was established (i.e. the CS + CI combination ceased to elicit salivation, whereas the CS on its own continued to do so), Soltysik changed the sequence to CS → CI, the onset of the CI occurring three seconds after CS onset, without disrupting the conditioned inhibitory effect. He now presented this sequence to the dog for 120 consecutive trials, with no interspersed CS-only trials. At the end of this part of the experiment, he presented the dog with the CS on its own again. This was the critical trial for testing his emendation of Mowrer's theory. According to this emendation, the CS → CI pairings, even though they had continued for so long without any interspersed positive conditioning trials, should have preserved intact the CR to the CS presented alone. This in fact turned out to be the case: when presented alone the CS produced a full-blown salivary response which became apparent when the three seconds usually intervening between CS and CI had elapsed, but the latter failed to occur.

Soltysik's theory of avoidance behaviour, then, suggests the following series of processes. On the early trials of avoidance conditioning the warning signals paired with punishment acquire secondarily aversive properties by the usual processes of classical conditioning. Performance of the instrumental avoidance response replaces these signals by others (response-produced feedback, new exteroceptive stimuli, or the termination of the warning signals) which, again as the result of classical conditioning, come to be conditioned inhibitors of fear, along the lines indicated in Soltysik's (1960) salivary conditioning "model" of avoidance behaviour. The resulting inhibition of fear constitutes reinforcement (i.e. fear-reduction) for the instrumental avoidance response. At the same time, the power of the warning signals to elicit fear is preserved from extinction, again along the lines indicated in Soltysik's salivary conditioning experiment.

It should be noted that the time course of fear postulated in this theory (briefly elicited by the warning signal and then inhibited by the avoidance response) can be matched by observations made of heart-rate changes during avoidance conditioning by Soltysik and Kowalska (1960). These workers monitored heart rate in dogs pressing a bar to avoid shock after presentation of the warning signal: heart rate rose upon presentation of the warning signal (a frequent observation, usually taken to indicate an increase in fear) and fell again, in some cases below the prewarning baseline, after performance of the avoidance response. Furthermore, the cardio-acceleration response to the onset of the warning signal continued unchanged for hundreds of trials during which the dogs consistently avoided the shock, thus supporting the view that fear does not extinguish during successful avoidance but is merely inhibited by the avoidance response.

Both theoretically and empirically, then, Soltysik's modification of Mowrer's two-process theory looks moderately sturdy. Unfortunately, a direct test of the theory in an avoidance situation, reported by LoLordo and Rescorla (1966), proved to be negative.

These workers first trained dogs in a Sidman avoidance shuttling response. They then carried out classical conditioning, using unavoidable shock as UCS, to two CSs. They also established a conditioned inhibitor by pairing it with each of the two CSs in the temporal sequence, CS → CI, and not following the combination by shock. They had previously shown (Rescorla and LoLordo, 1965) that these techniques are sufficient to produce conditioned fear-inducing and fear-reducing stimuli, as judged by increases or decreases in Sidman avoidance response rate when the CS or the CI, respectively, is presented to the animal in the shuttlebox. The phase of the experiment specifically directed to testing Soltysik's theory now followed. The dog was presented with both CSs, but no more shock, in a second Pavlovian conditioning situation. One of the CSs (CS_1) was repeatedly presented by itself, the other (CS_2) together with the previously established CI in the temporal sequence CS_2 → CI. If Soltysik's theory is correct, it would be expected that the pairings CS_1 → no UCS would lead to extinction of fear to CS_1, but the pairings CS_2 → CI would fail to extinguish fear to this CS. To see whether this had indeed occurred, both CSs were presented to the animal while it performed in the Sideman avoidance task. The results did not disclose any difference between the two CSs in their effects on Sidman avoidance rate, thus failing to support Soltysik's theory.

It is never wise to abandon a theory because of a single experimental result, especially one consisting in the *absence* of an expected effect: there are innumerable experimental parameters which one might just not have set right, thus obscuring the phenomenon one seeks. In particular, in the LoLordo and Rescorla (1966) experiment just described, there was no evidence that extinction of fear had been produced in the second, and critical, Pavlovian conditioning phase of the experiment; for, in the final test phase, *both* CSs, the one given extinction protected by the CI and the one given unprotected extinction, produced substantial increases in Sidman avoidance rate.

Nonetheless, for the moment we must conclude that Soltysik's valiant attempt to save Mowrer's theory lacks direct supportive evidence.

Safety Signals

Whether it is correct in detail or not, Soltysik's theory contains an important element which may serve as a signpost for future progress: it focuses our attention on the stimuli to which the avoidance response gives rise, as distinct from those which it terminates. Let us consider in more detail what the properties of such stimuli might be.

Let us take as our point of departure the properties possessed by an explicit conditioned inhibitor of fear of the kind used by Rescorla and LoLordo in their experiments. Rescorla and LoLordo (1965) demonstrated that a CI (set up by pairings of the form, CS → shock, contrasted with CS → CI) is able to reduce the rate of performance of a Sidman avoidance response. This, of course, is the opposite change to that produced by a stimulus paired with shock, which increases the Sidman avoidance rate. Earlier in this chapter we took the latter observation to indicate that one result of Pavlovian conditioning is to confer motivational properties on the CS which is paired with an unconditioned punishment. These motivational properties can be described, in the language of the emotions, as "fear-inducing". Rather naturally, therefore, one may take the opposite effect accruing to the CI in Rescorla and LoLordo's experiment as also indicating the acquisition by the CI of motivational properties; and one may describe these, as Rescorla and LoLordo themselves do, as "fear-reducing".

The same kind of motivational property can be conferred on an initially neutral stimulus by at least two other Pavlovian paradigms, as we have already seen in Chapter 3: differentiation (CS_1 → Pun, CS_2 → $\overline{Pun}$), and conditioned inhibition maintaining the usual Pavlovian temporal parameters (CS_1 → Pun, CI + CS_1 → $\overline{Pun}$) (Rescorla and LoLordo, 1965; see Fig. 2.3). Thus pairing a stimulus with $\overline{Pun}$ (so creating a $\overline{Pun}$–CS) according to any one of a number of Pavlovian paradigms confers on the stimulus motivational properties which are opposite in sign to those conferred by a pairing with Pun. (We have met this change in motivational sign before: it is the "reaction of the reverse sign" of Chapter 3.) And it seems reasonable to suppose that, among such $\overline{\text{Pun}}$–CS, are the stimuli which arise from or accompany a successful avoidance response.

Before continuing this examination of the properties of the stimuli which arise from a successful avoidance response, there is one more implication we should draw from Rescorla and LoLordo's (1965) experiments. They demonstrate once more the behavioural significance of the non-occurrence of an expected event. In this way they add to the series of demonstrations of the operation of expectancies which we have encountered throughout this book: the stimulus-omission experiment for habituation of the orienting reflex (Chapter 1); the double-runway frustration effect produced by nonreward in instrumental appetitive learning (Chapter 9); and the experiments by Trapold and Winokur (1967) and Grossen, Kostansek and Bolles (1969) which demonstrated the effects of a "non-UCS/$S^{R\,+}$" in a classical conditioning paradigm (Chapter 9). Later in this chapter, we shall come across Herrnstein and Hineline's experiments (Herrnstein, 1969) showing the effects of "nonpunishment" in instrumental avoidance behaviour. To this list, the Rescorla and LoLordo experiments add a demonstration of the effects in a classical conditioning paradigm of a "non-UCS/$S^{R\,-}$".

To see that this is so, consider the results of the Rescorla and LoLordo experiment employing the differentiation paradigm ($CS_1 \rightarrow$ UCS, $CS_2 \rightarrow$ no UCS; the UCS being a punishing electric shock). As we have seen (Chapter 3) the result of such pairings is that both CS_1 and CS_2 acquire altered properties as compared to a control procedure in which an initially neutral stimulus is paired neither with the UCS nor its absence. (In this control procedure–Rescorla and LoLordo's "truly random control"–the probability of occurrence of the UCS is the same whether the CS occurs or not.) Now, how can the differential stimulus acquire its altered properties? In the first place, the change only occurs if the pairing $CS_2 \rightarrow$ no UCS takes place under conditions in which the pairing $CS_1 \rightarrow$ UCS also takes place. Pairings of the form, $CS_2 \rightarrow$ no UCS on their own fail to alter the effects of the CS (except insofar as the externally inhibitory effects of novelty–Chapter 3–become habituated). Thus any theory is likely to begin by postulating some initial generalization of conditioning from CS_1 to CS_2. In the terms of two-process theory, one might say that it is conditioned fear which generalizes in this way.

Suppose the animal is now giving this response to CS_2. Eventually, a change must take place so that exactly the opposite response is given to this stimulus (a process which was complete within 90 trials in the Rescorla and LoLordo, 1965, experiment). It is difficult to see anything else at work in this simple experiment which could account for such a change other than the animal's detection of the *non-occurrence* of shock at the time when, after CS_1, it usually occurs (see Fig. 10.4).

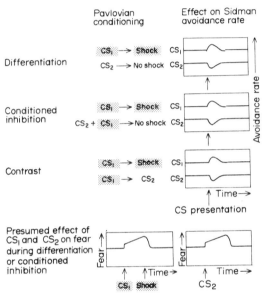

FIG. 10.4. Design and Results of Rescorla and LoLordo's Experiment. Three Pavlovian conditioning procedures used by Rescorla and LoLordo (1965) to establish CSs which either increased or decreased the rate of Sidman avoidance responding (Fig. 2.3) when presented to dogs in a shuttlebox. The two panels at the bottom of the figure depict the changes in the level of fear which can be presumed to occur after the presentation of the two kinds of CS during the Pavlovian conditioning phase of the experiment. For further explanation see text. (Figure from Gray, 1972a.)

It is this kind of argument which gives us licence to describe the pairings in the Rescorla and LoLordo experiments as "$CS_2 \rightarrow$ no UCS" or "$CS_2 \rightarrow \overline{Pun}$", rather than "$CS_2 \rightarrow$ nothing": the animal detects the non-occurrence of a specific expected event at a specific moment in time. It is ironic that this demonstration forms part of an extremely successful programme of research by proponents of two-process theory; for, along with the Herrnstein and Hineline experiments considered below, it shows that the problem which two-process theory was intended to solve—how to substitute some other reinforcement for the non-event of $\overline{Pun}$—was never a problem at all. It would have been perfectly reasonable at the outset to treat avoidance behaviour as being reinforced by avoidance of punishment.

Let us return to the properties of the stimuli which arise from a successful avoidance response, i.e. of $\overline{Pun}$–CS. So far, we have considered only a motivational property of such stimuli—their ability to reduce the rate of Sidman avoidance responding when presented to the subject independently of his performance of this response. We have previously described effects such as this as "demotivating". Thus, the capacity of a Pun—CS to reduce the rate of a rewarded operant response in the CER paradigm was described as a de- motivating effect in Chapter 8; and the capacity of a $\overline{Rew}$–CS to produce a similar reduction in rewarded response rate was so described in Chapter 9. It is natural, therefore, to describe the rate-reducing effects of a $\overline{Pun}$–CS on a Sidman avoidance baseline also as "demotivating"; especially since this conforms to the view that these effects arise from a reduction in fear caused by pre- sentation of the $\overline{Pun}$–CS.

In the case of the other three kinds of secondary reinforcing stimuli—Rew—CS, Pun—CS and $\overline{Rew}$–CS—we have seen that there exists a motivating property as well as a demotivating one: a Rew—CS increases the rate of a rewarded operant response (Chapter 5) and both Pun—CS and $\overline{Rew}$–CS increase the rate of a Sidman avoidance response (Chapters 8 and 9). These findings are sum- marized in Table 10.2. It can be seen from this table that symmetry would lead us perhaps to expect a motivating property in the case of $\overline{Pun}$–CS also; and that such a property might take the form of an increased rate of performance of a rewarded operant response. Such an effect has not been unequivocally demonstrated, though two experiments have come close to doing so.

Hammond (1966) investigated the effects of a $\overline{Pun}$–CS in a CER experiment. He showed that presentation of this stimulus did indeed increase the rate of performance of the rewarded response. But this rate-increasing effect disappeared when the baseline performance of the operant (i.e. performance in the absence either of the Pun—CS or the $\overline{Pun}$–CS) recovered to the level displayed before any shocks had ever been presented. Thus the simplest interpretation of Hammond's results is that the $\overline{Pun}$–CS inhibited the fear which had generalized from the explicit Pun–CS to the total experimental situation. There is no need, therefore, to postulate any effect of this stimulus on the performance of rewarded operants *per se.*

A more convincing demonstration of a similar effect is described by Hearst (1969). Rats pressed a lever for a food reward on a variable-interval schedule. An exteroceptive stimulus (auditory for some animals, visual for others) was occasionally presented for periods of one minute and, during this stimulus (S^Δ), lever pressing was never rewarded. After the subjects had learned the discrimination, as shown by a reduced response rate in S^Δ, a second

TABLE 10.2. Motivational effects of secondary positive and negative reinforcers on baselines maintained by Rew and $\overline{\text{Pun}}$

Direction of Effect	Type of Stimulus			
	Rew–CS	$\overline{\text{Pun}}$–CS	Pun–CS	$\overline{\text{Rew}}$–CS
Motivating	Rew ↑ (5)	? Rew ↑	$\overline{\text{Pun}}$ ↑ (9)	$\overline{\text{Pun}}$ ↑ (8)
Demotivating	$\overline{\text{Pun}}$ ↓ (5)	$\overline{\text{Pun}}$ ↓ (10)	Rew ↓ (9)	Rew ↓ (8)

Type of stimulus (Rew–CS, etc.) is as defined in Table 7.1. Arrows indicate response rate increase (↑) or decrease (↓) when baseline responding is maintained by reward (Rew) or Sidman avoidance ($\overline{\text{Pun}}$). Numbers in brackets indicate chapter in which the relevant effect is described. A motivating effect of $\overline{\text{Pun}}$–CS on a Rew baseline has not yet been described, but might be expected on grounds of symmetry. Note the opposite effects produced by each kind of stimulus on baselines maintained, respectively, by Rew and $\overline{\text{Pun}}$.

stimulus was introduced, also for occasional periods of one minute. This stimulus terminated in an unavoidable shock, i.e. it was a Pun–CS. Responding during the Pun–CS continued to be rewarded, but, of course, a considerable degree of conditioned suppression developed in its presence. At the same time, responding considerably increased in the presence of S^Δ. Now, since neither shock nor the Pun–CS were ever presented in combination with the S^Δ, this might be expected to become a safety signal, i.e., a $\overline{\text{Pun}}$–CS. Thus the rise in response rate in S^Δ may represent an instance of a $\overline{\text{Pun}}$–CS producing an increase in the rate of performance of a rewarded operant. However, the dual significance of this stimulus (as a $\overline{\text{Rew}}$–CS as well as a $\overline{\text{Pun}}$–CS) makes interpretation of Hearst's observations somewhat hazardous.

Besides motivational properties, it is clear that $\overline{\text{Pun}}$–CS (and also Pun!–CS) possess secondary reinforcing properties; specifically they act as positive reinforcers, i.e. the animal will work to attain them.

There are now several demonstrations of this type of effect (Lawler, 1965; Kinsman and Bixenstine, 1968; Rescorla, 1969; Weisman and Litner, 1969)*.

In Rescorla's (1969) experiment, for example, dogs were trained to press either one of two panels on a Sidman avoidance schedule. They then received Pavlovian fear conditioning in which CS_1 signalled a shock UCS, together with conditioned inhibition trials using Soltysik's temporal sequence of CS_1 → CI. Returning to the avoidance task, the CI was made contingent upon pressing one panel, a neutral control stimulus following presses on the other. The results showed that the dogs distributed their responses so as to produce the CI (which is, of course, a $\overline{\text{Pun}}$–CS) more often than the neutral stimulus, though the overall rate of panel-pressing was not changed. In a somewhat similar experiment using rats, Weisman and Litner (1969) demonstrated that a Pavlovian CS which signalled a period of shock-free time in an experiment in which shocks were being delivered on a random schedule acquired the capacity to modulate the rate of Sidman avoidance wheel-turning when subsequently presented contingently upon this response. When the $\overline{\text{Pun}}$–CS was made contingent upon an increase in the avoidance response rate, this rose; and when it was then made contingent upon a decrease in the avoidance response rate, it fell. Notice that, in both the Rescorla and the Weisman and Litner experiments, the demonstration of secondary positive reinforcing effects was made with a $\overline{\text{Pun}}$–CS which had been established in an explicit classical conditioning session carried out separately from the instrumental learning task.

$\overline{\text{Pun}}$-CS (or "safety signals"), then appear to be the mirror images of Pun–CS ("warning signals"). The latter are fear-inducing and secondarily aversive, the former fear-reducing and secondarily rewarding. But, in the light of this analysis, it becomes necessary to re-examine our conclusions concerning Pun–CS. In a typical avoidance situation, termination of Pun–CS and production of $\overline{\text{Pun}}$–CS are simultaneous or even identical events (for the termination of a stimulus is itself a stimulus). Thus we have to be careful if we wish to claim that *both* termination of a Pun–CS *and* production of a $\overline{\text{Pun}}$–CS are positively reinforcing.

Bolles and Grossen (1969; Bolles, 1970) have performed a number

* And see for a critical review LoLordo (1969); and for some recent positive results Morris (1973).

of experiments which demonstrate the positively reinforcing properties of P̄un–CS and at the same time cast doubt on the reinforcing properties of termination of Pun–CS. They ran rats in a running wheel or in a shuttle-box and compared the results obtained when the effective avoidance response (a) terminated the warning signal, (b) produced no exteroceptive stimulus change other than shock avoidance, and (c) produced a brief change in illumination which occurred only on successful avoidance trials and was thus a safety signal. Their results are shown in Fig. 10.5. It can be seen that the safety signal was as successful in maintaining avoidance behaviour

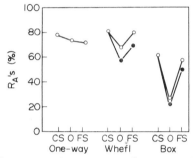

FIG. 10.5. Relative Effectiveness of Termination of Warning and Onset of Safety Signal in Maintaining Avoidance Responding. Graphs show percentage of avoidance responding in a one-way runway, a running wheel and shuttlebox when responding produced CS termination (CS), presentation of a safety signal (FS) or neither (0). (Data from Bolles and Grossen, 1969; figure from Bolles, 1970.)

as was termination of the warning signal. Since termination of the warning signal was itself a safety signal, whereas the explicit safety signal in condition (c) was not associated with shock, these results could be interpreted as showing that the production of a safety signal is the critical event and that termination of a warning signal is only effective insofar as it also provides this.

That this conclusion should not be over-generalized, however, is clear from the early experiments of Neal Miller with which this chapter began. As we saw, a rat shocked in a compartment was able to learn two new responses—wheel-turning and barpressing—to escape from it, even though it was no longer receiving shocks there. Thus, if it was learning to approach a safe place, this could only be by contrast with a dangerous place: i.e. for P̄un–CS to be effectively rewarding in this experiment, it was necessary that Pun–CS also be effectively aversive. Thus the most reasonable conclusion is that safety signals and warning signals both operate in their own right and in interaction with each other. In an initially neutral environment, some stimuli come to stand out as secondarily fear-inducing and aversive, others as secondarily fear-reducing and rewarding, and still others remain neutral; all presumably as the result of classical conditioning, operating along the lines we examined in Chapter 2.

The demonstrated properties of $\overline{\text{Pun}}$–CS may offer an alternative possibility, besides Soltysik's conditioned inhibition proposal, for the salvation of Mowrer's two-process theory. The problem with this theory, it will be recalled, is that it ought to predict the fairly rapid extinction of fear, and thus of avoidance behaviour. Suppose, however, that what an animal does, after an initial phase during which it terminates warning signals, is to learn to approach or produce safety signals. Then after the initial phase fear could indeed extinguish and yet leave avoidance behaviour intact. This proposal has much to recommend it.

In the first place, once an animal has thoroughly learnt a successful avoidance response and is no longer getting punished very often, it does not necessarily *look* frightened. When the warning signal is presented, it calmly completes the avoidance response, and in between warning signals it gets on with whatever portion of the ordinary business of living the experimental environment allows it. More formal demonstrations of the transience of fear in avoidance situations are available. For example, Kamin et al. (1963) measured the fear evoked by the warning signal in a standard escape-avoidance shuttle-box task by presenting the signal to the animal while it was barpressing for a food reward on a variable-interval schedule of reinforcement. The conditioned emotional response (suppression of barpressing) increased in magnitude during the early stages of training in the shuttlebox, but as performance reached successively higher criteria the suppression ratio fell again (Fig. 10.6). This finding is, of course, unexpected from the point of view of an unmodified Mowrer two-process theory, according to which, as fear of the warning signal goes down, so ought performance of the avoidance response. According to the present view, however, this result makes good sense: fear of the warning signal extinguishes as it is no longer followed by punishment (because the animal is successfully avoiding it), but the avoidance response is now maintained by the positive reinforcement of safety signals (those produced by shuttling to the currently safe side of the apparatus).

Another experimental report which is in good agreement with this view of avoidance learning is by Lawler (1965). He showed that, once safety signals have come to act as such, their effectiveness as positive reinforcers is relatively independent of the degree of fear aroused in the experimental situation. Rats were first trained to run

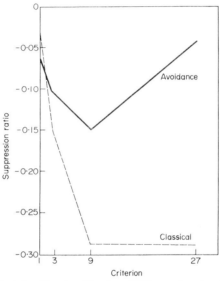

FIG. 10.6. Fear Elicited by Warning Signal at Different Levels of Avoidance Training. Conditioned suppression (0 = no suppression) produced by a warning signal paired with unavoidable shock 1, 3, 9 or 27 times in the "classical" group, or to which the animals have made 1, 3, 9 or 27 consecutive avoidance responses in the "avoidance" group. (From Kamin, Brimer and Black, 1963.)

into a distinctive box to escape shock. A buzzer was sounded at the same time as the animals were shocked. The animals were later tested to see whether the escape box had become a secondary reward. They were placed in a start box, as in the original training trials, and given the choice of two boxes to enter, one of which was the original escape box. For half the animals, the test trials used the same start box as in the training trials and the buzzer was sounded; for the other half, a different start box was used and there was no buzzer. Controls were treated identically, except that they were not shocked during training. No animals were shocked during the test for secondary reward. All the animals shocked during training chose the original escape box more often than the controls, thus demonstrating that this box had indeed become a secondary reward. Furthermore, this tendency was no less (indeed it was stronger) in the group given a changed startbox and no buzzer during test trials (i.e. the group which was presumably less fearful). Thus the secondary rewarding effects of safety stimuli (strictly, in this experiment, Pun!–CS) appear to be relatively independent of the degree of fear aroused in the situation.

The safety signal modification of Mowrer's two-process theory, then, has many advantages. It leaves the Mowrer theory logically capable of doing the job it set out to do, and most of its postulated processes have empirical support: the two fundamental processes of classical and instrumental conditioning and their interaction; the aversive and fear-inducing properties of Pun–CS; the rewarding and fear-reducing properties of $\overline{\text{Pun}}$–CS; the eventual independence of safety signals from the current level of fear; and the reduction of fear which occurs as avoidance learning becomes well established. Above all, this theory no longer suffers from the major defect of the original Mowrer theory: it no longer predicts that avoidance behaviour will extinguish very quickly.

Indeed the question arises, on a safety signal view of avoidance learning, how extinction of avoidance could ever take place at all. If safety signals are similar to other secondary rewarding stimuli, extinction of the instrumental behaviour which gives rise to such stimuli should only occur when the expectation of reward is disappointed, along the lines of the frustration theory discussed in Chapter 9. But how could such disappointment occur? The animal expects, upon receipt of safety signals, non-punishment, i.e. nothing. If therefore, the experimental conditions remain unchanged, successful avoidance should continue indefinitely to produce the expected outcome of non-punishment, and there is no reason for extinction to occur. (The fact that the experimenter may have taken the decision, uncommunicated to the animal, no longer to administer the punishment in the event that the avoidance response is not made—which is what "extinction" usually means in descriptions of experimental procedure—is neither here nor there.) It is in agreement with this deduction that, in simple one-way avoidance situations, such as running from a box in which shock has occurred into one in which it has never occurred, the experimental animal's persistence in performing the avoidance response usually lasts longer than the experimenter's in allowing him to do so. Spontaneous extinction does occur in more complicated environments, especially the shuttle-box; but this is theoretically very complex, involving as it does a conflict between active avoidance of the side of the apparatus where shock is next programmed to occur and passive avoidance of the now safe, but recently dangerous side. Such exceptions apart, unless special measures are taken to eradicate it (Gray, 1971a), active avoidance is often virtually inextinguishable.

The safety-signal modification of Mowrer's theory also enables us to take account of a difficulty for the uncomplicated Mowrer theory which we encountered earlier in this chapter: the fact that animals prefer shock preceded by a warning signal to unsignalled shock. Suppose the rat has a choice between an environment in which shocks occur randomly with a mean frequency m per minute and a second environment in which shocks occur randomly with the same mean frequency, but each shock is preceded by a warning signal t sec long. On the uncomplicated Mowrer theory, as we have seen, the warning signals in the second environment merely add to the overall level of aversiveness, so that the animal should prefer the former environment. However, a safety signal view is more complicated: the added aversiveness of the warning signal is more than outweighed by the *reduction* in the average level of fear which (by comparison with the unsignalled case) must occur during the intervals of time which are *not* filled by the warning signal; for, by arguments which are now familiar, the absence of the warning signal can serve as a safety signal. Evidence in favour of this interpretation of the difference between signalled and unsignalled shock has recently been reviewed by Seligman, Maier and Solomon (1971).

Bolles' Approach

A very similar view to the present one has been advanced by Bolles (1970). Its chief difference is that Bolles suggests that safety signals are only of importance for the learning and maintenance of responses which do not come easily to the experimental animal. He points out that there is a very great difference in how easily experimental animals can learn different responses by which to avoid shock. Whereas, for example, the rat can learn to run from a box where shock may occur into a safe box in one or two trials, it takes many tens or hundreds of trials to learn to press a bar or to run from one side to the other of a two-compartment shuttlebox. Bolles suggests that the critical difference between these two kinds of task—the easy and the hard ones—is that the former allows the animal to avoid shock by employing an innate species-specific defence reaction, in particular freezing, fleeing and fighting (though virtually all the relevant experimental work has been concerned with fleeing). Only when the experimenter requires the animal to learn something which is not in this innate repertoire of defensive reactions does it have to go through the hard grind of learned aversiveness and learned safety signals.

There may well be something in this distinction. Certainly, as Bolles remarks, any species which, in its natural environment, took the hundreds of trials often required in the laboratory to learn how to avoid danger would long ago be extinct. And there does seem to be a good case for describing some instances of avoidance behaviour observed in the laboratory as the elicitation of species-specific defence reactions (SSDRs) by a stimulus situation associated with punishment. Consider, for example, experiments of a kind in which an animal is first given a series of shocks in an environment from which, at that time, it cannot escape and is then given an opportunity to escape from this environment into a different one, with no further shocks delivered. Many such experiments have been reported (Bolles, 1971) and they concur in showing that an animal treated in this way will rapidly run or jump out of the environment in which it has experienced shock, the moment the experimenter makes it possible for him to do so. It is clear that, in such an experiment, the animal cannot have acquired a new, instrumental response to terminate or avoid the *shock*. Furthermore, since it escapes very rapidly as soon as it has the opportunity, it is also difficult to describe the animal as learning a new, instrumental response to terminate its exposure to the Pun—CS constituted by the environment associated with shock. Thus Bolles account, according to which the animal has an SSDR of flight which is elicited by Pun—CS in a rather automatic fashion, is a very plausible one. Indeed, in many ways, it is equivalent to the description of Pun—CS as aversive, a description we have adopted in this chapter, and also in Chapter 8.

There is an important parallel between, on the one hand, the kind of experiment I have just described and Bolles' account of it and, on the other, the autoshaping phenomenon and Moore's (1973) account of that (see Chapter 2). Indeed, the experiment in which a rat escapes from a CS previously paired with inescapable shock is, in effect, an exact equivalent, but using an aversive instead of an appetitive UCS, of the autoshaping experiment. In the latter, it will be recalled, the animal comes to direct food-appropriate consummatory behaviour to a CS paired with response-independent food. In the former, the animal comes to direct shock-appropriate "consummatory" behaviour (i.e. flight) away from a CS paired with response-independent shock. In both cases the learning principle which appears to be operative is the S–S contingency of classical conditioning. And Bolles' account of avoidance behaviour, like Moore's account of autoshaping, says that ostensibly instrumental behaviour (running or jumping out of the secondarily aversive environment) is in fact a classical conditioned response in disguise.

This is all right as far as it goes. But, just as Moore's account of autoshaping cannot be generalized to the whole of rewarded instrumental behaviour, so Bolles' account of avoidance behaviour cannot be generalized to deal with such obviously novel response patterns as barpressing in the rat or panel-pushing in the dog. Nor, indeed, does Bolles wish to treat all avoidance behaviour as a classically conditioned SSDR. He himself admits that "rats do sometimes learn such unnatural avoidance responses as pressing a bar, and in fact they occasionally become fairly proficient at it" (Bolles, 1972, p. 132) (though, to be sure, they take longer to learn this kind of response than to exhibit a conditioned SSDR).

It is worth pausing a moment to consider what evidence one would advance to defeat someone who might wish to propose that *all* avoidance behaviour in fact consists of classically conditioned SSDRs. The answer is clear: one would need to show that some avoidance behaviour had passed the bidirectional conditioning test for instrumental learning (Chapter 2). For it cannot plausibly be the case that some response, R_1, is an SSDR and *also* R_2, the exact opposite of R_1. The best such evidence is probably that obtained in Miller's (1969) experiments on instrumental conditioning of autonomic responses. For example, he and Di Cara managed to train rats to avoid shock by either increasing or decreasing heart rate, and by either increasing or decreasing blood pressure. In each of these pairs of avoidance responses, one may perhaps be regarded as an SSDR (though how could one decide which?), but hardly both.

If we accept Bolles' treatment of conditioned SSDRs, then, as being applicable to some kinds of avoidance behaviour but not others, the problem becomes that of distinguishing in an actual case between the two. This, in effect, boils down to the task of distinguishing between behaviour controlled by S → S and by R → S contingencies, i.e. that of distinguishing between classical and instrumental conditioning discussed at length in Chapter 2. In this connection, it is of some interest that it has so far been found very difficult to establish anything resembling truly instrumental avoidance behaviour in the pigeon, although much effort has been expended in that direction (Moore, 1973). Moore (1973) points out that, where the pigeon has come to respond so as to avoid shock, it tends to do so by flapping its wings or by making use of other parts of its natural defensive response pattern (i.e. by making an SSDR, according to Bolles' definition)*. Thus, in the case of instrumental avoidance behaviour as in the case of instrumental rewarded behaviour (Chapter 2), it is possible that the instrumental R → S principle only becomes fully operative at the phylogenetic level of mammals†.

If we leave aside the kind of avoidance which can be satisfactorily accounted for as a conditioned SSDR, Bolles' (1970, 1971, 1972) theory is essentially the same as the one proposed in the present chapter. It seems, then, that the leading contender for an account of "skilled" avoidance behaviour (e.g. a rat pressing a bar or a dog in a shuttlebox) remains Mowrer's version of two-process theory, buttressed with safety signals, whose importance has been suggested in one way or another by a number of workers, including Rescorla and Solomon (1967), Woodworth and Schlosberg (1954), Denny (1971), Olds and Olds (1965) and Mowrer (1960) himself.

The resilience of two-process theory is remarkable, considering that the major motive for its development—the presumed ineffective-

---

* However, Ferrari et al. (1973) have recently reported keypecking to avoid shock in the pigeon which appears to be truly instrumental, and not a conditioned SSDR.

† Given the view, considered below, that active avoidance behaviour is maintained by the same positive reinforcement system as is concerned with rewarded behaviour, the two kinds of instrumental behaviour would necessarily emerge at the same evolutionary level.

ness of P̄ūn as a reinforcer—is now known to have been spurious. However, some recent experiments by Herrnstein and Hineline (Herrnstein, 1969) and Taub and Berman (1968) have provided the biggest challenge that it has yet had to face.

The Herrnstein and Hineline Experiment

The Herrnstein and Hineline experiments are a refinement of the procedure introduced by Sidman (1953). As we know already, a Sidman avoidance schedule (see Fig. 2-3) is defined by two parameters, the response—shock (R—S) and the shock—shock (S—S) intervals. If the animal does not respond, shocks occur regularly at the S-S interval; if it does respond, each response postpones the next shock by the R-S interval. If the animal responds regularly with inter-response times which are less than the R-S interval, it need never be shocked. Note that no exteroceptive stimulus is correlated with the delivery of shock, i.e. there is no overt warning signal. Thus, it might be expected from the Miller-Mowrer theory that the animal would not learn Sidman avoidance. In fact, it does. The usual way out of this difficulty for the theory, and for other similar theories, is to point out that there must be internal stimuli which are correlated with the passage of time since the last response and with the passage of time since the last shock, providing, as it were, an internal clock to measure the R-S and the S-S intervals. As the time approximates the moment when shock is next due to be delivered, the postulated internal stimuli which act as the "hands" of the clock become more and more aversive (because of prior conditioning, according to a familiar pattern). By responding, the animal replaces these stimuli with the stimuli characteristic of a shorter time since responding (these being negatively correlated with shock), i.e. he replaces a secondarily aversive stimulus with a safety signal. QED, and the Miller-Mowrer theory is saved.

The Herrnstein and Hineline experiment takes the Sidman avoidance schedule one critical stage further. In effect, these workers offered rats a choice between two frequencies of being shocked. If they pressed a lever they were shocked at unpredictable intervals, with the mean frequency of shock equalling, say, m times a minute. If they did anything else at all, they were shocked at equally unpredictable intervals with a frequency, n times a minute, which was greater than the frequency associated with lever-pressing, i.e. $n > m$. A lever-press obtained for the rat a period of time on the schedule with the lower frequency of shocks. This period lasted until the next shock programmed on this schedule. After that shock had been delivered, control reverted to the schedule with the higher shock frequency until the rat's next lever-press.

It seems clear that the Miller–Mowrer theory must predict that it is impossible for the rat to learn to press the lever under these conditions. And again the rat proves to be able to learn to do so with remarkable efficiency (Herrnstein, 1969). That reduction in shock frequency is the effective variable in producing this learning, more over, is indicated by the fact that the rate of lever-pressing was proportional to the degree of reduction in shock-frequency brought about by the animal's response.

The implications of this important experiment are numerous. In the first place, it seems effectively to dispose of the notion that avoidance must be CS-termination in disguise. As Herrnstein (1969) points out in detail, the difference between the schedule associated with pressing and that associated with not pressing is a purely statistical one: the mean frequency of shocks. There is no external stimulus and no internal stimulus which can be said to vary with this mean frequency. We cannot appeal to internal stimuli which fluctuate with the passage of time (as in disposing of the Sidman avoidance results) because, since the actual moments of delivery of shock are randomly distributed around the mean frequency of shocks in both schedules, shock sometimes occurs in any interval of time both after responding and after not responding: only the *average* number of shocks in each interval of time is different after responding and not responding. It seems necessary to conclude, then, that the animal can:

(a) measure the average frequency of shocks it receives when not responding;

(b) store this frequency;

(c) measure the same quantity during periods of time after it responds;

(d) compare this with the stored frequency for shocks when not responding; and

(e) choose that behaviour which is associated with the lower shock frequency.

Much of this analysis will be unsurprising to a reader who has already accepted the implications of the stimulus omission experiment in Chapter 1, the active effects of nonreward described in Chapter 9, and the Rescorla and LoLordo experiments discussed earlier in this chapter. He has already become accustomed to talk of expectancies, comparators, match-mismatch decisions and so on. However, the behaviour of Herrnstein and Hineline's rats actually forces us to go a good deal further than this.

In nearly all the other kinds of experiment which demonstrate the operation of expectancies, the stimulus whose non-occurrence is shown to be effective in influencing behaviour could have been expected to occur *at a particular point in time*. Thus, the stored representation of past events could be activated at that time, in a manner made unmysterious by Sokolov's model for habituation of the OR and by the experimental evidence considered in Chapter 1; and comparison with current input could duly be made. The activation of the stored representation could, furthermore, be represented as fitting familiar patterns of classical conditioning. In all the experiments we have discussed previously the point in time at which the expected event might occur had been preceded by other events (even if these were only inferred internal correlates of the passage of time, as in the stimulus omission experiment) in a regular fashion; these preceding events, therefore, could be regarded as CSs and activation of the expectancy as the CR. In the Herrnstein and Hineline experiment, however, the expected frequencies of shock associated with responding or not responding on the lever *do not have a locus in time*: they are statistical properties of collections of events spread out over an extended period of time. The only events which do occur at points in time are the shock themselves: it is impossible to say at any particular moment "a shock which the animal might have expected has just failed to occur."

Thus the Herrnstein and Hineline experiments appear to offer an insuperable difficulty to two-process theory as we have considered it in this and previous chapters. Yet we should be careful not to throw the baby out with the bath water. Exactly where is the difficulty? What is it that we *should* throw out?

Earlier we listed the essential claims of two-process theory as applied to avoidance learning as follows:

(1) There are two distinct processes of learning: one, classical

conditioning, depending only on *temporal contiguity between stimuli*; the other, instrumental learning, depending on reinforcement following a response.

(2) As a result of the first kind of conditioning, stimuli acquire emotional and motivational significance as "secondarily aversive" (and, given the safety-signal modification of two-process theory, "secondarily rewarding").

(3) These stimuli then influence instrumental learning (a) by providing new sources of reinforcement for it, and (b) by altering the direction and level of motivation.

As we have seen in this chapter, there is substantial evidence in support of each of these claims. The force of the Herrnstein and Hineline experiments is directed principally against the phrase set in italics in (1) above: temporal contiguity between stimuli, even when some of these stimuli are allowed to be events such as $\overline{\text{Pun}}$—the *non*-occurrence of a stimulus at an expected point in time—cannot be all that is involved in what the animal learns in these experiments. But this inference must come as something less than a surprise if we recall our discussion of temporal contiguity in simple classical conditioning experiments in Chapter 2. We concluded there that the evidence from classical conditioning experiments suggests a process which

enables the organism to compute the probability of the UCS following the CS at a number of different intervals of time following CS onset, and to compare this with the probability of the UCS occurring without the CS preceding it by the interval in question. If the probability of the UCS occurring at the specified interval after CS onset is greater than it would be without the CS having occurred at that time, the CS acquires a positive conditioned significance. If the two probabilities are alike, the significance of the "CS" remains neutral. If the probability of the UCS occurring at the specified interval after CS onset is actually lower than if the CS had not occurred at that time, then the stimulus becomes a negative or inhibitory CS.

If for "UCS" we substitute "shock" in this statement, and for "CS" "the stimuli resulting from barpressing in the Herrnstein and Hineline experiment", we have all the apparatus we need (considerable though it is) to generate learned safety signals out of the latter.

It is not, then, two-process theory which is threatened by the Herrnstein and Hineline experiments, it is an over-simple conception of classical conditioning. If classical conditioning has in any case to be understood in the kind of terms we developed in Chapter 2, these experiments—important as they undoubtedly are—are quite neutral with respect to two-process theory. What they suggest, rather, is either that the classical conditioning involved in two-process avoidance learning is able to call upon the full complexity of the calculus of probabilities which we outlined in Chapter 2; or that single-process avoidance learning, based on reduction in the average density of punishment as the reinforcing agent, requires the same calculus.

Taub and Berman's Experiments on the Deafferated Monkey

Accepting, then, the still unsolved and central mystery of how classical conditioning itself works, the lines of an acceptable theory of active avoidance learning appear still to be intact. But this theory has to withstand a further onslaught: from Taub and Berman's experiments on avoidance learning in the deafferented rhesus monkey.

It is a key assumption of two-process theory that instrumental behaviour is guided by the consequences of actions in producing secondary reinforcers, both aversive and rewarding. The only difference between Mowrer's original theory and the modified version of this theory we have arrived at so far is that the latter includes, besides the termination of secondary aversive stimuli, the onset of secondary rewarding stimuli (i.e. safety signals) as potential sources of reinforcement for avoidance behaviour. Such secondary reinforcing stimuli may be in any modality, exteroceptive, interoceptive or proprioceptive. When there are no obvious sources of exteroceptive secondary reinforcement around, as in Sidman avoidance behaviour, it is the habit of the harassed two-process theorist to fall back on postulated, but generally unobserved, interoceptive or proprioceptive sources. However, a very thorough series of experiments by Taub and Berman (1968) and their collaborators shows that it is possible to maintain efficient avoidance behaviour in monkeys which have been deprived, by one means or another, of virtually all sensory feedback from the avoidance response, exteroceptive, proprioceptive and interoceptive.

These experiments employed rhesus monkeys which had the responding limb surgically deafferented by section of the appropriate dorsal roots in the spinal cord. In this way, the proprioceptive stimuli which normally indicate to the central nervous system that a limb has moved in a certain way were eliminated. The monkey was trained, in some cases before this operation and in some cases after, to avoid shock upon receipt of a warning signal (a buzzer) by flexing the deafferented limb. View of the limb was impeded, thus eliminating visual feedback. Whether the monkey was trained in this task pre- or post-deafferentation, it performed the task perfectly well. In the first experiments carried out by Taub, Berman and their collaborators, the warning signal was response-terminated, so that the Miller-Mowrer theory was unthreatened—termination of a secondary aversive auditory signal could provide all the reinforcement needed for the avoidance response. In a further refinement, however, the warning signal was changed to a click of fixed duration (which was too short for there to be any question of its being apparently terminated by the response), and a trace-conditioning procedure was used (i.e. an interval elapsed between the offset of the warning signal and the delivery of the shock on non-avoidance trials). Again, whether surgical deafferentation was carried out before or after avoidance training, the monkeys were able to learn and perform the required avoidance response. Taub and Berman (1968) describe several other experiments involving more extensive deafferentation procedures, both surgical and pharmacological and affecting inter-oception as well as proprioception, as well as a number of further refinements in the behavioural situation (most importantly, limitation of the amplitude of the motor pattern designated as the avoidance re-sponse, thus reducing the possibility of unsuspected sensory feedback via unlikely routes). It is difficult to quarrel with the conclusion they draw from these experiments: "avoidance responding proceeded in a situation in which secondary negative reinforcement could not be presented over either proprioceptive, interoceptive or exteroceptive pathways" (Taub and Berman, 1968, p. 185). To which one might add that secondary *positive* reinforcement was equally thoroughly eliminated.

It is extremely difficult to maintain, in the face of this evidence, that the two processes of two-process theory are *necessary* for avoidance learning to occur. The rhesus monkey, deprived of all information other than the issue from the CNS of one or other kind of command to the motor system and the occurrence or otherwise of shock, is able to correlate these two kinds of event and determine which motor commands are followed by shock and which by non-shock. Thus the only items which can develop secondary aversive or secondary rewarding properties are *the motor commands themselves*. But to push the language of classical conditioning and secondary reinforcement this far is obviously to take two-process theory beyond the point up to which it remains useful.

Taub and Berman have this to say themselves concerning the implications of their results:

> Another issue raised by the experiments described above relates to the question of how an animal could learn to make use of a deafferented limb in the absence of vision. Instrumental conditioning involves the ability to repeat consistently certain movements; but how can the animals with a deafferented limb that they cannot see learn to repeat movements, when by all classical considerations they should not know where the limb is, whether it has moved, and if moved, in what way? Since the required information concerning the topography of their movements could not have been conveyed over peripheral pathways, it must have been provided by some central mechanism that does not involve the participation of the peripheral nervous system. Such a mechanism could be one of two general types: either it would involve feedback, but of wholly central origin, or it would involve no feedback whatever.
>
> The former mechanism requires the existence of a purely central feedback system that could, in effect, return information concerning future movements to the CNS before the impulses that will produce these movements have reached the periphery. An animal could thus determine the general position of its limb in the absence of peripheral sensation. Indeed, just such a mechanism has been demonstrated electro-physiologically, first by Chang (1955) and Li (1958), subsequently by a large number of investigators (for a partial summary see Levitt, Carreras, Lui and Chamers, 1964), and anatomically by Kuypers (1960). It would seem to involve afferent collaterals from the medullary pyramidal tracts to the nuclei gracilis and cuneatus, thence back to the cerebral cortex through ventralis lateralis. In fact, in the last 15 years it has been found, in contrast to the classical view, that most of the thalamic nuclei are really two-way streets. Indeed, if central feedback is of significance for behaviour following deafferentation, it seems reasonable to assume that not one but several "loop" pathways would be involved. That is, if one were to set out *a priori* to construct a servo-mechanism that was maximally effective and sensitive to control, one would certainly establish a feedback loop at *each* level of the system from command centre to output.
>
> The second type of central mechanism referred to above involves the possibility that behaviour can be learned and performed in the absence of all topographic feedback from either movement or its associated neural events, either peripheral or central. This implies that "neural traces" or

"engrams" can be laid down (by whatever process) entirely on the basis of centrifugal impulses without requiring the return of centripetal impulses from the normally resulting motor and neural activity to, as it were, stamp them in. To reduce the proposal to its simplest terms we might say that the neurones of a motor centre do not have to be told that they have fired, they know.

Whatever the precise nature of the central mechanism responsible for the mediation of the phenomena observed in these experiments, we clearly have in them situations in which the CNS displays a considerable amount of automony and independence from the periphery in the acquisition and maintenance of behaviour. Indeed, we could even say that the most general conclusion that can be drawn from our research is that in mammals, once a motor program has been written into the CNS, the specified behaviour, having been initiated, can be performed without reference to or guidance from the periphery. Moreover, there does not appear to be any reason why the initiation, the trigger, cannot also be wholly central in nature.

Finally, it might be appropriate to return to a subject that was touched upon earlier. Learning theorists have frequently resorted to proprioception as an explanatory device in accounting for the behaviour that develops under such diverse conditions as trace avoidance conditioning, delay of reinforcement, delayed response, sensory preconditioning, temporal discrimination, bridging temporal gaps, chaining, and indeed any situation where an appeal to some sort of central or interior mechanism as a mediating process would otherwise be necessary. It would hardly be an exaggeration to say that proprioceptive hypotheses have been used as a sort of glue to hold a number of learning theories together on what appeared to be empirical grounds, in the face of apparently contradictory evidence. And, after all, there can be no doubt that proprioceptive feedback almost invariably accompanies all behaviour. It should be pointed out, however, that when proprioception is invoked as an explanatory device in situations where its relevance has not received specific demonstration, it begins to assume a mythological character, notwithstanding its undeniable existence.

We can go further. If proprioception or response-produced stimulation cannot account for counting or the discrimination of number, for bridging temporal gaps, or for the performance of long coherent chains of behaviour—what can? We have previously referred to the demonstration of the existence of wholly central processes by virtue of which an organism could monitor its own behaviour and, therefore, presumably edit, censor or delete it before it is emitted. This is clearly a type of thinking by any worthwhile definition (Taub and Berman, 1968).

Indeed, it is. And, for that matter, so is the calculus of probabilities which seems to be involved in Herrnstein and Hineline's experiment. But we may reasonably suppose that rhesus monkeys, dogs and rats, like the rest of us, only think when they have to. In other words, though the two processes of two-process theory may not be *necessary* for the rhesus monkey to perform an avoidance response, he may nonetheless make use of them when he can. Furthermore, we have no guarantee that, because monkeys can solve the difficult problem with which Taub and Berman faced them, the same would be true of animals lower down the phylogenetic scale. As Taub and Berman themselves point out, monkeys appear to be very different from amphibia with regard to the effects of spinal deafferentation: amphibia manifest complete inability to ambulate after such treatment (Gray and Lissman, 1940, 1946; Weiss, 1941), whereas Taub and Berman's monkeys displayed very extensive movement. However, current evidence (Jankowska, 1959; Gorska and Jankowska, 1961; Gorska *et al.*, 1961) does not suggest any great difference between monkeys, dogs, cats and rats in the extent to which deafferentation incommodes the use of a limb for instrumental behaviour.

As far as concerns mammals, then, given both the extensive evidence in favour of two-process theory and the difficulties posed for this theory by Taub and Berman's and, to a less extent, Herrnstein and Hineline's experiments, the safest conclusion is that the two processes of two-process theory are normally operative in the acquisition and maintenance of avoidance behaviour; but that, if necessary, the animal is able to make a direct correlation between its motor commands and the non-occurrence of expected punishment, or even (in the light of Herrnstein and Hineline's results) between its motor commands and a reduction in the average frequency of punishment from some expected level. On this view, two-process theory is unlikely to be totally abandoned because of results such as Taub and Berman's. Rather, it may turn out to be like Newtonian physics in relation to the theory of relativity, a special case of a more general theory. Such a theory would have to encompass both the data to which two-process theory is easily applicable and experimental results which indicate more abstract computational powers of the kind indicated above. With this hope in mind, let us return to two-process theory on its home ground.

Relieving Nonpunishment Compared to Reward

It has been implicit in much of what has been said about the modified version of two-process theory developed in this chapter that safety signals—$\overline{\text{Pun}}$—CS—are functionally equivalent to secondary rewards—Rew—CS. Such an equivalence, if real, would be the counterpart to the equivalence, postulated in the previous chapter, between $\overline{\text{Rew}}$—CS and Pun—CS. However, whereas the latter hypothesis has a fairly substantial body of experimental evidence in its favour, the former is as yet virtually innocent of contact, positve or negative, with the harsh world of experimental fact. Indeed, apart from the general point that both kinds of stimuli may serve as positive reinforcers (as considered in this chapter for safety signals and as demonstrated in a long line of experiments for Rew—CS: see Chapter 5 and Kimble, 1961, p. 167 *et seq*), I know of only a handful of experiments which bear on the hypothesis that there is a functional equivalence between $\overline{\text{Pun}}$—CS and Rew—CS (and also between the corresponding primary events, $\overline{\text{Pun}}$ and Rew).

One relevant kind of experiment stems from the work of Rescorla and LoLordo discussed earlier in this chapter. It will be recalled that the basic experimental design used by these workers consists in classically conditioning a stimulus so that it comes to have shock-predictive or non-shock-predictive significance (creating a Pun—CS or a $\overline{\text{Pun}}$—CS, respectively), and then investigating the effects of these stimuli when presented to the animal while it performs a Sidman avoidance response. In a comparable study, Grossen, Kostansek and Bolles (1969) established food-predictive and non-food-predictive stimuli (i.e. a Rew—CS and a $\overline{\text{Rew}}$—CS, respectively) in the classical conditioning phase of the experiment, and then evaluated the effects of these stimuli against the same type of Sidman avoidance baseline. (The detailed design of this experiment has already been discussed in Chapter 9 in connection with the observed effects of the $\overline{\text{Rew}}$—CS.) Now, if there is a functional equivalence between $\overline{\text{Pun}}$—CS and Rew—CS, we might expect the Rew—CS to produce the same kind of change in the rate of avoidance responding as does the $\overline{\text{Pun}}$—CS, that is, to decrease it, Fig. 10.7 shows that this is exactly what happened in the experiment by Grossen *et al.* (1969).

This effect of Rew—CS was described as "demotivating" in Chapter 7, where we first encountered it. However, such a description does nothing to explain the phenomenon, any more than does the hypothesis (motivated largely by considerations of parsimony and symmetry) that a Rew—CS is functionally equivalent to a $\overline{\text{Pun}}$—CS. How, then, can we account for it?

One possibility is that it is in some way an artefact arising from some specific motor pattern which is adventitiously conditioned to the Rew—CS during the phase of classical conditioning and which is incompatible with rapid performance of the Sidman avoidance response. In this way the rate of performance of the response would fall, but the observed phenomenon would have no systematic significance. This kind of explanation (or rather, explaining away) can, of course, be applied in principle to any of the interactions between classical and instrumental conditioning which we have

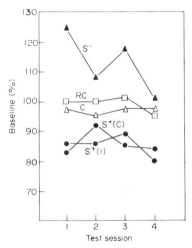

FIG. 10.7. Effects of Stimuli Paired with Reward or Nonreward on Sidman Avoidance Responding. Performance of a previously learned avoidance response over 40 test trials by groups of subjects for which the test tone had signalled no food, S^-; had been unrelated to food, RC; had not been previously presented, C; or had signalled the occurrence of food in either a classical conditioning, S^+ (C), or an instrumental S^+ (I), situation. (From Grossen, Kostansek and Bolles, 1969.)

considered in this book, and it is not always easy to exclude it (Trapols and Overmier, 1972). In the Grossen *et al.* experiment, however, an attempt was made to show experimentally that it could not account for the results obtained.

For this purpose, an additional control group was included, labelled "CS+(I)" in Fig. 10.7. In contrast to Group CS, which received classical conditioning of the form CS → food, this special control group was not exposed to a pure classical conditioning contingency. Instead, it was required to run down a runway to obtain food, the tone stimulus (used as the CS for all the groups in the experiment) being sounded just as the startbox door was opened.

In this way, this group too had a tone-food positive pairing. It can be seen from Fig. 10.7 that, in the final test phase of the experiment, it behaved exactly as did the CS+ group, the tone decreasing the rate of Sidman avoidance responding in the shuttlebox to exactly the same degree. This result makes it unlikely that the results obtained in the CS+ group are due to an incompatibility between the Sidman shuttling response and some kind of adventitious motor response learned by this group during the classical conditioning phase of the experiment. For the running response learned by the CS+(I) group was deliberately chosen so as to be compatible with shuttling; and, even if it were not, it is unlikely that the CS+ group was hampered by an unobserved motor response exactly to the same degree that the CS+(I) group was hampered by the running response in which it was given explicit training. It is more plausible to suppose that the decrease in Sidman avoidance responding was produced in both groups by the classical conditioning contingency which the the two groups had in common, and that this affected some central process, motivational or otherwise. A similar experiment has been reported by Overmier *et al.* (1971), who also found that a CS for food suppressed Sidman avoidance behaviour under conditions which made it unlikely that specific motor responses to the CS were involved.

It seems reasonable to suppose, then, that the effects of a Rew–CS on Sidman avoidance behaviour are due to some kind of central change, rather than to peripheral motor effects. What might this change be? We have described the comparable effects produced by Pun–CS as representing an inhibition of fear. Might a Rew–CS similarly act so as to reduce fear? In Chapter 3 we considered the methods which need to be applied if one wishes to demonstrate an inhibitory process at work. It will be recalled that, following Rescorla (1969), we distinguished there between "summation" and "retardation" tests of inhibitory effects. In a summation test the presumed inhibitory stimulus is presented simultaneously with an excitatory stimulus and is expected to subtract from the latter's effects. This, in effect, is what happened in the Grossen *et al.* experiment just described. In a retardation test, the attempt is made to turn the inhibitory stimulus into an excitatory stimulus for the same response in respect of which it is thought to possess inhibitory properties. It is expected to be more difficult to do this with the inhibitory stimulus than with a neutral control stimulus. Thus if Rew–CS depress Sidman avoidance behaviour in the summation test in consequence of an inhibition of fear, it should be relatively difficult to turn a Rew–CS into a warning signal for the performance of an avoidance response. This deduction was tested in an experiment with dogs by Overmier and Payne (1971). They found, however, that a CS paired with food in a classical conditioning session, when subsequently used as the warning signal for an avoidance response in the shuttlebox, led to *faster* acquisition of this response when compared with the performance of groups for which the same stimulus had either been paired with no-food or had been presented in random association with food. Similar results were reported by Bacon and Bindra (1967) in an experiment using rats, water in place of food in the classical conditioning session, and a runway avoidance response.

Although no investigator has yet carried out the summation and retardation tests with the same group of animals and the same avoidance response (as would be necessary for any definite conclusion to be reached), it would obviously be incautious in the face of these results to conclude that a Rew–CS reduces Sidman avoidance in consequence of an inhibitory effect on fear. On the contrary, the pattern of results so far reported (response-suppression by the summation test, facilitated acquisition by the retardation test) suggests an attentional effect (Sutherland and Mackintosh, 1971; Rescorla, 1969; and see Chapter 3). That is to say, the pairing of a stimulus with a reward may give it an attention-catching quality which distracts from performance in the summation test, but makes learning easier in the retardation test. But, if this interpretation is correct, it offers no support for the hypothesis of equivalence between Rew–CS and Pun–CS. This hypothesis relates to motivational and reinforcing effects; and attentional effects are in any case too general to be of significance in the present context.

A second series of experiments bearing on the possible functional equivalence of safety signals and secondary rewards involves physiological techniques. It is due to Olds and his collaborators (Olds and Olds, 1965). These workers trained rats both to press a lever for the reward of electrical stimulation delivered to electrodes implanted in rewarding sites in the brain, and to perform this response in order to terminate electrical stimulation delivered by the experimenter to punishing sites in the brain. The unconditioned reaction to the latter kind of stimulation—that is, the response elicited before the animal had learnt that the most rapid and effective way to terminate it was to press the lever—was the kind of wild running, leaping and aggressive behaviour which we described as "fight/flight" in Chapter 8. The important feature of Olds' experiment was the alterations induced in these three kinds of behaviour—self-stimulation, unconditioned fight/flight, and skilled escape from punishment—by two physiological treatments: injections of chlorpromazine and spreading cortical depression produced by applying potassium chloride to the neocortex. Both treatments abolished self-stimulation and skilled escape behaviour, but left unconditioned fight/flight behaviour intact. Thus these results support both (1) the distinction between unconditioned fight/flight behaviour and skilled escape responding, and (2) the functional equivalence of behaviour directed to reward and behaviour directed to the minimization of punishment.

In other experiments, Olds and his group have recorded single neuron activity in the brain areas involved and have shown that skilled escape behaviour is impaired with the same time course as the disruption caused by chlorpromazine and spreading cortical depression in the activity of neurons in the reward areas of the brain. These observations are consistent with Olds' view that it is activity in these areas which reinforces skilled escape and active avoidance behaviour; a view which is physiologically isomorphic to the behavioural hypothesis, suggested here, that active avoidance is reinforced by $\overline{Pun}$—CS and that $\overline{Pun}$—CS are functionally equivalent to Rew—CS. Further support for this view, from the same experimental tradition, comes from the reports by Stein (1965) and Margules and Stein (1968) that the learning of active avoidance, both in the shuttlebox and in a Sidman barpressing task, is improved if rats are simultaneously given noncontingent electrical stimulation of sites in the reward areas of the brain.

It is clear that the evidence in favour of the equivalence between Rew and $\overline{Pun}$ and their associated secondary reinforcers is much weaker than the evidence for the corresponding equivalence between Rew and Pun (Chapter 9). Furthermore, we have not yet mentioned the biggest difficulty in the way of accepting the former equivalence, though the alert reader may have noticed it. It lies in the data summarized in Table 10.2, earlier in this chapter. From that table it is clear that there is a systematic difference in the results obtained from presenting secondary reinforcers, positive and negative, to animals while they are performing operant responses which are reinforced respectively by Rew or by $\overline{Pun}$. Those stimuli (Rew—CS) which increase response rates on a rewarded baseline *decrease* response rates on a Sidman avoidance baseline; and those stimuli (Pun—CS and $\overline{Rew}$—CS) which decrease response rates on a rewarded baseline *increase* response rates on a Sidman avoidance baseline. On the hypothesis of a functional equivalence between Rew and $\overline{Pun}$ it is difficult to see how such a difference could arise.

Nonetheless, especially in view of the intriguing physiological experiments reported by Olds and by Stein, it may be of heuristic value to incorporate these ideas (of safety signals as being essentially equivalent to secondary positive reinforcers, and as providing the reinforcement for an established active avoidance response) into the black box diagram which we commenced in Chapters 8 and 9 (see Figs 8.9 and 9.3).

The Gray and Smith Model Completed

In this expansion (Fig. 10.8) we add a "comparator for punishment", which receives information from CSs previously followed by punishment and predicts from these the level of punishment likely to occur on the present occasion. At the same time, operation of the "punishment" mechanism leads to the inhibition of ongoing behaviour along the lines discussed in Chapters 8 and 9. At this point, we introduce a new notion concerning the behavioural inhibition system: that, by inhibiting behaviour patterns which are normally dominant in the particular environment, it allows new or improbable patterns of behaviour to occur. The outcome of such behaviour is fed back to the "comparator for punishment". If the punishment received matches the punishment expected (or is greater), the CSs arising from the behaviour pattern just tried out (proprioceptive, kinaesthetic, exteroceptive, etc.) are added to the list of learned aversive stimuli; their re-occurrence on some future occasion will now both act as an input to the punishment comparator and operate the behavioural inhibition system.

However, if any behaviour pattern is followed by tbe receipt of *less* punishment than expected, there is an input from the com-

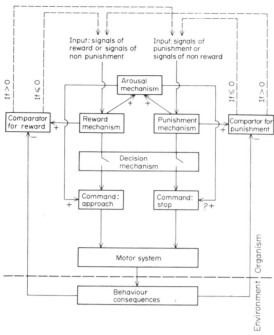

FIG. 10.8. The Gray and Smith Model, Mark 3. Expanded version of Fig. 9.3. Dashed lines indicate inputs which occur on trial *n + 1* as a result of classical conditioning of exteroceptive, interoceptive or proprioceptive CSs to the consequences of behaviour on trial *n*. For further explanation see text and Appendix.

parator for punishment to the reward mechanism. This input acts as a UCS for the conditioning of secondary rewarding (or "safety") significance to the CSs arising from the appropriate behaviour pattern. Thus, on future occasions, receipt of such stimuli (e.g. sight of a lever the pressing of which was followed by non-shock) activates the reward (or "approach") mechanism. This is the same positive feedback system which was described in Chapter 5 as underlying the learning and performance of rewarded instrumental behaviour.

This completes the model which we have been engaged in constructing in the last three chapters (together with Chapter 5). In effect, it is a model of the instrumental component of a general two-process learning system, able in principle to deal with reward, omission of reward, punishment, and omission of punishment as reinforcing events. Supplied with a simple mathematics, it is described in more detail in the paper by Gray and Smith which forms the Appendix to this book.

11. Conclusion

As pointed out in the Preface, one purpose of this book is to serve as a scaffolding for an eventual theory of the physiological basis of personality. The relation between such a theory and a theory of learning may be expressed in this way. Learning theory is the attempt to describe the general structure of the conceptual nervous system which is common to all the members of a given species (or even of a group of species). A theory of personality is an attempt to account for differences in behaviour between individual members of the species in terms of systematic variation in the properties of the subsystems or components which go to make up this general conceptual nervous system. If one can then go one step further and align these subsystems with neural and/or endocrine structure and function in the real neuro-endocrine system, one has constructed a theory of the physiological basis of personality (Gray, 1972a, 1973).

In order to carry out this program, one needs in the first instance some idea of the number and nature of the separate subsystems in the general CNS, variation in which might account for some portion of individual differences in behaviour. It is partly for this reason that throughout this book we have paid much attention to problems of difference and identity; questions such as, "does latent inhibition differ from internal inhibition?" (Chapter 3); or "is the state produced by nonreward identical to that produced by punishment?" (Chapter 9). In this final chapter I shall attempt to summarize the decisions we have reached on these and similar questions. In this way I hope both to remind the reader of the ground we have covered in the preceding chapters on the theory of learning and to construct a set of signposts to possible future developments in the theory of personality.

I have drawn up this summary in the form of Table 11.1. There are two very obvious omissions in this table. Clearly, any

TABLE 11.1.

System/Phenomenon	Features of Processes Involved		Chapter and References
1. Orienting Reflex (OR) subsuming: external inhibition; disinhibition.	Stimuli	Novel, irrespective of modality.	Chapter 1, 3 (external inhibition) Sokolov (1963a), Gray (1964b), Lynn (1966).
	Responses	Specific ORs; orienting behaviour; increase in capacity to process sensory information; inhibition of CRs; disinhibition.	
	CNS*	Sokolov's model (Fig. 1.7); Tribe–Webb model (Fig. 3.5). Includes increment in level of arousal.	
	RNS†	ARAS (Fig. 1.8).	
2. Increment in Arousal Level subsuming: trans-marginal inhibition; general drive.	Stimuli	See Fig. 3.6.	Chapter 3, 8 (general drive) Sokolov (1963a), Gray (1964b), Lynn (1966).
	Responses	See Fig. 3.6; includes at high levels, inhibition of both CRs and instrumental behaviour.	
	CNS	Sokolov's model (Fig. 1.7).	
	RNS	ARAS (Fig. 1.8).	
3. Habituation of OR subsuming: latent inhibition.	Stimuli	Familiar, not CS or S^D	Chapter 1, 3 (latent inhibition). Sokolov (1963a), Lynn (1966).
	Responses	Inhibition of OR.	
	CNS	Sokolov's model (Figs 1.7, 1.9).	
	RNS	Cerebral cortex; hippocampus.	

TABLE 11.1—continued

System/Phenomenon	Features of Processes Involved		Chapter and References
4. Excitatory Classical Conditioning	Stimuli	$S \rightarrow S$ contingency	Chapter 2, 5 Pavlov (1927, 1928), Rescorla and Wagner (1972), Wagner and Rescorla (1972).
	Responses	Formation of CR by modified stimulus substitution rule (Fig. 2.2).	
	CNS	Wagner–Rescorla theory.	
	RNS	Cerebral cortex unnecessary.	
5. Internal Inhibition	Stimuli	$S \rightarrow \bar{S}$‡ contingency	Chapter 2, 3 Pavlov (1927, 1928), Wagner and Rescorla (1972).
	Responses	Inhibition of CRs	
	CNS	Wagner–Rescorla theory.	
	RNS	?	
6. Set of UCRs to UCS/S^{R+}	Stimuli	Various and different for different species (food, water, etc)	Chapter 4 Glickman and Schiff (1967).
	Responses	Various and different for different UCS/S^{R+} (eating, drinking, etc).	
	CNS	Modulated by drive$_{DEP}$ and drive$_{TV}$	
	RNS	Lateral hypothalamus, midbrain	
7. Instrumental Approach Learning subsuming: drive$_{GD}$; active avoidance; skilled escape.	Stimuli	Rew—CS; $\overline{Pun}$—CS	Chapter 4, 5, 10 Deutsch (1964b), McFarland (1971), Olds and Olds (1965), Glickman and Schiff (1967).
	Responses	Approach behaviour.	
	CNS	Activation of positive feedback mechanism (Fig. 5.1); Deutsch's model (Figs 5.3, 5.4).	

			References
	RNS	Lateral hypothalamus and medial forebrain bundle; amygdala; cerebral cortex.	Chapter 8, 9 De Molina and Hunsperger (1962), Olds and Olds (1965), Gray (1971a).
8. Set of UCRs to UCS/S^R—	Stimuli	Various and different for different species, but especially painful stimuli, threats from conspecifics and $\overline{Rew}$.	
	Responses	Unconditioned fight or flight.	
	CNS	?	
	RNS	Amygdala, medial hypothalamus, central gray (Fig. 9.5).	
9. Behavioural Inhibition	Stimuli	Pun—CS, $\overline{Rew}$—CS	Chapter 8, 9 Gray (1971a, 1972c).
	Responses	Inhibition of instrumental approach behaviour.	
	CNS	See Fig. 9.3; includes increment in level of arousal.	
	RNS	Septo-hippocampal system (Fig. 9.4).	

* CNS: conceptual nervous system.
† RNS: real nervous system.
‡ $\overline{S}$: nondelivery of expected stimulus similarly for $\overline{Rew}$, $\overline{Pun}$ (nondelivery of expected reward or punishment, respectively).

conceptual nervous system must start with perceptual systems for the receipt of stimuli and finish with motor systems for the execution of responses. Neither of these, however, have figured in this book, and they therefore have no place in our summary of conclusions. Rather, Table 11.1 contains guesses as to what lies between stimulus reception and response execution: that is, guesses about motivation, about analysis and learning of the significance of stimuli, and about decisions as to gross modes of response (e.g. approach or avoidance).

It is hoped that the table is self-explanatory. If not, reference to the chapters listed in the right-hand column should serve to clarify and justify the conclusions it contains. One major point, however, deserves some final discussion. As Table 11.1 stands, nine separate systems or phenomena are listed. Three of these, however, have much in common, and can perhaps be reduced to one: the orienting reflex, increment in arousal level and behavioural inhibition.

Perusal of the appropriate rows in Table 11.1, and of the earlier parts of this book dealing with each of these phenomena, shows that the chief points of difference between them are as follows:

(1) *Stimuli.* The operations which increase arousal level (Fig. 3.6) are more varied than those (presentation of novel stimuli) which elicit the OR, but include the latter. The operations which produce behavioural inhibition (presentation of Pun–CS or $\overline{\text{Rew}}$–CS) do not figure in the list shown in Fig. 3.6 as affecting arousal level. However, we have discussed the evidence (Chapters 8 and 9) that these stimuli do in fact increase level of arousal (or "general drive", which is synonymous with arousal level). Thus the OR and behavioural inhibition are each produced by a subset of those stimuli which increment level of arousal.

(2) *Responses.* The OR includes a heterogeneous group of responses which, at least in some cases, appear to have the function of increasing the animal's capacity to process sensory information (Sokolov, 1963a). It also includes inhibition of classical conditioned reflexes (Pavlov's "external inhibition"). Behavioural inhibition is defined by the inhibition of instrumental behaviour which it involves. However, no-one who has watched an animal in an appropriate experiment can doubt that presentation of a Pun–CS or a $\overline{\text{Rew}}$–CS also elicits the whole gamut of visible orienting responses, i.e. those which are clearly directed towards analysing such stimuli as are present in the animal's environment (head-and-eyes-turning,

pricking-up of ears, etc). More formally, it has been demonstrated that frustrative nonreward in a partial reinforcement experiment increases the amount of information which the animal takes in concerning the experimental environment (Sutherland, 1966); and also that, like other effects of $\overline{\text{Rew}}$–CS (Table 9.1), sodium amylobarbitone blocks this increase (McGonigle et al., 1967). Thus the chief difference between the OR and behavioural inhibition appears to be that the former involves inhibition of CRs and the latter inhibition of instrumental responses.

There is even a parallel in the instrumental case to the curious phenomenon of disinhibition, described by Pavlov in classical conditioning experiments. It will be recalled (Chapter 3) that this consists in the fact that, if a novel stimulus is presented to an animal in conjunction with a recently established internal inhibitory stimulus (e.g. a recently extinguished CS), the inhibited CR is re-elicited. In a closely similar fashion, Wagner (1966) changed the colour of a runway half-way through the extinction of a previously rewarding running response and found that this caused the experimental animals to resume running towards the empty goalbox.

Turning to level of arousal, it is generally accepted (Gray, 1964b) that at high levels of arousal there is an overall loss of behavioural efficiency, including decrements in both classical and instrumental conditioned responses. Transmarginal inhibition, whether of intensity or repetition (Figs 3.3 and 3.4), can probably be regarded as the manifestation of this phenomenon in the classical conditioning case (see Gray, 1964b, for an extended treatment of this argument). With regard to the set of specific orienting responses (lowered skin resistance, heart-rate and respiratory changes, peripheral vasoconstriction, EEG desynchronization, etc: Sokolov, 1963a; Lynn, 1966), these have all been used by various workers as "indices" (Fig. 3.6) of arousal level. Furthermore, physiologically, they are known to depend on the same midbrain structures which are thought to be central to the control of level of arousal (Sokolov, 1960, 1963a). Thus, as in the case of the stimuli which elicit the OR, behavioural inhibition and increments in arousal, so we can conclude for the responses which constitute each of these that those relating to the OR and to behavioural inhibition are both subsets of those relating to increased arousal level.

(3) *Arousal level.* An increment in arousal level has been shown to be part of both the OR (Sokolov, 1960, 1963a: Chapters 1 and 3)

and (under the name of "general drive") behavioural inhibition (Amsel, 1958, 1962; Gray, 1971a: Chapters 8 and 9).

Given these great points of similarity it is parsimonious to suppose the existence of a single system, responsive to novel stimuli and to Pun–CS and Rew–CS, as well as to the treatments listed to the left of Fig. 3.6, and whose functions are: (a) to inhibit all ongoing behaviour, whether instrumental or classically conditioned (or, indeed, innate); and (b) to perform the maximum possible analysis of environmental stimuli, especially novel ones. The orienting responses would then be one consequence of activity in this system. The other major outputs of the system would be an initial inhibition of all previously operative behaviour patterns; coupled with an increment in arousal level, i.e. an increment in the intensity of whatever behaviour finally does occur. These two apparently contradictory elements—increased behavioural intensity and behavioural inhibition—are already built into the Gray and Smith (1969) conflict model (Figs 8.9, 9.3 and 10.8; and Appendix). As for the various CNS models and RNS substrates which have been proposed for arousal, the OR and behavioural inhibition (Figs 1.7, 1.8, 3.5, 3.6, 9.3, 9.4), these all have much in common, especially the central role played by the ascending reticular activating system of the brainstem (Magoun, 1963). In particular, the behavioural inhibition system proposed by Gray (1972c; Fig. 9.4) incorporates most of the features of the earlier models. Thus the only embarrassment which seems to stem from conjoining the orienting reflex, high arousal and behavioural inhibition into one system is a plethora of names. Perhaps one way out would be to coin yet another one: the "Stop, look and listen system".

By whatever name—and I shall continue to talk of "behavioural inhibition"—this system is likely to be of particular importance for the study of personality, and especially for the clinical application of personality theory to problems of neurotic behaviour (Gray, 1971a, 1973). For there is some reason to suppose that it is chronic overactivity in the behavioural inhibition system which underlies extreme degrees of neurotic introversion—to use Eysenck's (1967) terminology—or "manifest anxiety"—to use the Spences' (Spence and Spence, 1966). At least, that is the theory I have proposed (Gray, 1970a, 1971a, 1972c, 1973) and for which we have recently obtained some experimental evidence (Nicholson and Gray, 1972). But that is another story.

Appendix: An Arousal-Decision Model for Partial Reinforcement and Discrimination Learning

(This paper originally appeared in 1969 as Chapter 10 by J. A. Gray and P. T. Smith in "Animal Discrimination Learning" edited by R. M. Gilbert and N. S. Sutherland)

A Difficulty in Frustration Theory

Amsel's (1958, 1962) theory of frustration is able to predict with some degree of success a number of phenomena in learning experiments. However, it also encounters certain difficulties. It was in attempting to cope with these difficulties that the impetus for the model outlined in this paper arose. At the same time, the model is intended to have wider application than to the runway experiments with which Amsel's own theory has largely been concerned. In particular, it also applies to a number of phenomena which have been observed in operant conditioning experiments and which bear an obvious resemblance to frustration effects observed in runways— notably, "behavioural contrast" (Reynolds, 1961) and "peak shift" (Hanson, 1959; Friedman and Guttman, 1965). We shall follow the logic of the actual development of the model and start with partial reinforcement experiments in runways. We shall then deal with the application of the model to the operant conditioning experiments.

The need for a modification of Amsel's frustration theory springs in the first instance from the way in which the partial reinforcement acquisition effect in a straight alley depends on distance from the goal. Compared to continuously reinforced animals, animals on a random partial reinforcement schedule run slower early on in training, then catch up, and finally, late in training, run faster (Goodrich, 1959; Haggard, 1959). According to Amsel's theory both the initial decrement in speed and the final increment in speed shown by the partial reinforcement group relative to continuously re-inforced (CRF) controls are due to conditioned frustration (r_f). This occurs in the following manner.

After a number of rewards have been received the partially reinforced animal develops an expectation of reward (defined in Hullian terms as an "anticipatory goal response", r_g). If reward is now not received after the instrumental response is made, there is an unconditioned response* termed "frustration"; the operation which leads to frustration is termed "frustrative nonreward". Frustration is deemed to be subject to classical Pavlovian conditioning, so stimuli in the stem and startbox of the runway (which regularly precede the occurrence of the primary frustration response) are able to become conditioned stimuli eliciting conditioned frustration. Frustration (whether of the conditioned or unconditioned form) is said to be an aversive state, so that the animal's initial reaction will be to attempt to escape from the stimuli which elicit it. It is this aversive property of conditioned frustration which is said to lead to the initial decrement in speed shown by the partially reinforced animal. In effect, the animal is in an approach-avoidance conflict of the kind analysed by Miller (1959) in experiments in which the aversive state is set up by a noxious stimulus, such as an electric shock.

The final superiority in running speed displayed by the partially reinforced animals is accounted for in the following manner. The conditioned frustration response is said to set up stimulation (s_f) which is able to act for the animal like a cue. Since this cue is followed on a proportion of trials by the instrumental behaviour of running down the alley and the receipt of primary rewards, it becomes a discriminative stimulus (S^D) for running. In this way, the initially disruptive effects of anticipatory frustration are overcome and the animal continues to run to the goalbox in spite of the aversive aspects of the situation. However, more than this is needed if we are to account for the actual *superiority* in speed of running shown by the partially rewarded animals. This something else is provided by the joint assumptions that frustration has drive pro-perties (i.e. increases the vigour of ongoing behaviour) and that summation can take place between the frustration drive and the approach drive. Empirical support for these assumptions can be found in the double-runway "frustration effect" demonstrated by

* i.e. an unconditioned change in a state of the "conceptual nervous system".

Amsel and his co-workers (Amsel, 1958; Amsel and Roussel, 1952). Other evidence in favour of these assumptions is reviewed by Gray (1967); while McFarland's (1966) review of work relevant to drive-summation leads to the conclusion that, though the evidence for drive-summation in general may be weak, there is ample evidence that an *aversive* drive may add to the vigour with which an appetitive response is performed*. It follows, then, that, once the disruptive effects of conditioned frustration in a partial reinforcement experiment are overcome by the associative process described above, partially rewarded animals will actually run faster than their continuously reinforced controls.

This, then, is the account given by Amsel's frustration theory of the effects of partial reinforcement on performance during acquisition. Without considering the adequacy of this theory in more general terms, we wish to focus attention on one particular difficulty which it encounters. This difficulty arises from the fact that the initial slowing down shown by the partially reinforced animals is strongest the *closer* the animal is to the goal; whereas their final superiority in speed is greatest the further away the animal is from the goal (Wagner, 1961; Goodrich, 1959). The same thing is found when distance from the goal is measured, not in spatial terms, but by setting up an operant response chain (Becker and Bruning, 1966). Thus in terms of frustration theory, the early aversive effects of conditioned frustration are greatest nearer the goal, but its later drive-inducing effects are greater further away from the goal. There is nothing in the theory as it stands which would lead one to expect this difference. Since r_f is set up by the normal processes of classical conditioning, it should be strongest nearest the point of reinforcement, so the spatial gradient shown by the early aversive effects is as expected; the difficulty arises rather with the late drive-inducing effects. Why should these too not be strongest nearest to the goal?

The Model

In an attempt to answer this question, we have called upon the distinction between *intensity* and *direction* of behaviour which is

---

* It is clear that the addition of an aversive drive may also reduce the performance of an appetitive response, as in the case of conditioned suppression. The analysis proposed in this paper is an attempt to predict *when* these incremental and decremental effects will each be observed.

emphasized by the so-called "energetics" group (Freeman, 1948; Duffy, 1962). Briefly, it is supposed that animals on a partial reinforcement schedule in a runway are in an approach-avoidance conflict, in which the approach and avoidance functions* may be depicted in the type of diagram used by Miller (1959) and shown in Fig. A.1. (The significance of the symbols in this figure is explained later.) This diagram calls for two comments. We have not allowed the avoidance function to rise higher than the approach function, since we are only concerned (in partial reinforcement experiments) with the case in which the animal *does* reach the goal, and we have

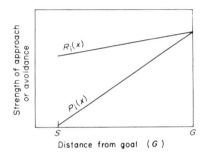

FIG. A.1. Approach $R_i(x)$ and avoidance $P_i(x)$ functions. The x-axis represents distance along an ideal runway stretching from the point S, where the avoidance level is zero, to the point G, where the two functions meet.

assumed that the greater steepness of the avoidance than the approach function which has been shown in the runway in experiments using electric shock to set up the avoidance drive (Miller, 1959) also holds for the partial reinforcement situation†.

The distinction between intensity and direction of behaviour is then made in the following way. It is supposed that, at any instant, the animal may be engaging in one of two kinds of behaviour: he

---

*To avoid the ambiguity of the word "gradient" (in learning theory it often refers to a generalization curve, in mathematics it would be taken to mean the *slope* of this curve) we use the terms *function* to denote a complete generalization curve and *level* to denote its value at any particular point.

† It is clear from Hearst's (1965) experiments that the avoidance function is not always steeper than the approach function. A comparison between Miller's results and Hearst's suggests that the steepness of the two functions depends on the extent to which each of them is controlled by exteroceptive or interoceptive stimuli: the greater the contribution of interceptive (including drive) stimuli, the flatter the function. In the case which we are considering, there is every reason to suppose that a "frustration" function would behave in the same way as a "fear" function, since both are largely controlled by exteroceptive stimuli in the type of runway experiment concerned.

may be moving toward the goal or avoiding it, by which we mean suppressing approach behaviour. It is then postulated that the proportion of time for which S engages in the one kind of behaviour or the other depends on the relative heights of the two functions at that point in the runway. In symbolic terms $p_R(x) = f[R_i(x), P_i(x)]$, where $p_R(x)$ is the probability of engaging in approach behaviour at the point x and $R_i(x)$ and $P_i(x)$ are the approach and avoidance levels at the point x. For fixed R_i, f decreases as P_i increases; for fixed P_i, f increases as R_i increases. The variable x could be a measure of the physical distance along a runway or (in the case of other experimental situations which we shall be considering later) of the position of a stimulus along a stimulus similarity continuum. So much for the direction of behaviour. The postulate concerning the intensity of behaviour is that, *whichever* direction the behaviour takes, its intensity is the result of a combination of the contributions of the approach and avoidance functions: $I_R(x) = g[R_i(x), P_i(x)]$, where $I_R(x)$ is the intensity of approach behaviour occurring at x, and g is a monotonic increasing function of both $R_i(x)$ and $P_i(x)$.

Before proceeding further, we wish to recast these basic ideas in a slightly different form, giving them at the same time a degree of physiological underpinning. Let us suppose that there are two basic drive-and-reinforcement mechanisms of the kind described by Olds and other workers (Olds and Olds, 1965; Stein, 1964) on the basis of self-stimulation studies with implanted electrodes: a reward mechanism and a punishment mechanism*. It is assumed that these mechanisms are set into operation by the positive and negative reinforcers and also that activity in them is subject to the laws of classical conditioning. It is further assumed that the operation of frustrative nonreward causes an increment in the activity of the punishment system. [Data supporting the view that frustrative nonreward and noxious stimuli act on the same physiological system are reviewed by Wagner (1966) and Gray (1967).] Level of activity in the reward and punishment systems, then, would, underlie the approach and avoidance functions, respectively. We now suppose that both these mechanisms feed into a general arousal mechanism such as the "ascending reticular activating system" (Samuels, 1959).

---

* I would not now (1974) identify the punishment mechanism of the model with points in the brain, stimulation of which is negatively reinforcing as in Olds, experiments. Rather I believe the relevant physiological system to be that depicted in Fig. 9.4.

This is to adopt Hebb's (1955) suggestion that this system is the basis of Hull's construct of general drive. Next, we suppose that the reward and punishment mechanisms are in competition for control of the motor apparatus, and that there is a decision mechanism whose job it is to choose between them. Whichever behaviour occurs, it is then facilitated by the output it receives from the arousal mechanism. These ideas, which are essentially identical with those developed in the preceding paragraph in less concrete terms, are depicted in Fig. A.2, in a block diagram of the kind described by McFarland (1966) in his model for frustration and attention. In terms of this diagram, the problem is to specify (1) how the inputs to the "behaviour command" for "approach" depends on the inputs to the reward and punishment mechanisms and (2) how the decision mechanism arrives at its decision.

Before leaving Fig. A.2, a few further comments are necessary. (1) The negative feedback loop linking the reward mechanism to the consequences of approach behaviour is to allow the animal to compare the *actual* reward or punishment received with the *expected* reward. It is the outcome of this comparison which determines whether there is now an input to the reward mechanism or to the punishment mechanism. For the sake of greater generality, it is supposed that there will be an input to the punishment mechanism not only if the consequence of approach behaviour is *zero* reward, but also if it is some non-zero reward which is *less* than the expected reward.*

If the consequence of approach behaviour is the receipt of a reward which is equal to or greater than the expected reward, there is an input to the reward mechanism. (2) It should be noted that the reward and punishment mechanisms have been given reciprocal inhibitory links with each other. This has been done partly because of the evidence from the central stimulation studies that such links do in fact exist (Olds and Olds, 1965; Stein, 1964) and partly

---

* A recent experiment by Peckham and Amsel (1967) has succeeded in showing that the magnitude of the double-runway frustration effect is positively correlated with the degree of reward reduction in spite of earlier failures (McHose and Ludvigson, 1965) to obtain this result. The design of this experiment, however, involved a reduction to zero reward from two different non-zero values. It still remains to be shown that a reduction of reward to a non-zero value has frustrating effects, and the available data (McHose and Ludvigson, 1965; McHose, 1966) do not support our assumption. However, it is a necessary assumption if the model is to deal with the phenomenon of behavioural contrast when the negative stimulus (S^Δ) is associated with a non-zero reward. (Addendum 1974: positive evidence in support of this assumption, gathered since 1969, is discussed in Chapter 9.)

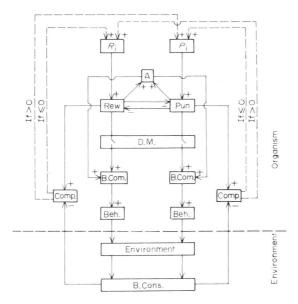

FIG. A.2. Block diagram of the arousal-decision model. R_i and P_i: inputs to the reward and punishment mechanisms, Rew and Pun. D.M.: the decision mechanism. A: the arousal mechanism. B.Com.: behaviour command to "approach" (on the reward side) or to "passively avoid" or "stop" (on the punishment side). Beh.: the observed motor behaviour. B.Cons.: the consequences (rewarding or punishing) of the behaviour that occurs. Comp.: comparator mechanisms which compare the actual consequences of behaviour with the expected consequences and make appropriate reward or punishment inputs. Dashed lines indicate inputs which occur on trial $n + 1$ as a result of classical conditioning of exteroceptive, introceptive or proprioceptive CSS to the consequences of behaviour on trial n. See text for further explanation.

because changing the values of the transmittances* along these links is one way (though not the only one) of providing for trial-by-trial changes in the output of the system (see below). (3) Finally, we should note that the system depicted in Fig. A.2 is symmetrical for approach and avoidance behaviour. We shall confine our analysis, however, to the approach behaviour predicted by the model.

Our analysis has taken us to the point where, if we symbolize the predicted approach behaviour by E_R, we have:

$$E_R = p_R(x) \times I_R(x) = f[R_i(x), P_i(x)] \times g[R_i(x), P_i(x)] \qquad (1)$$

The problem, then, is to specify the functions f and g. Let us deal with the intensity component, $I_R(x) = g[R_i(x), P_i(x)]$, first.

---

* The transmittance is the function that must be applied to the input (i.e. the upstream node in a flow graph) to obtain the value at the output (downstream node).

We may approach a specification of the function, g, by use of the method of flow-graph simplification described by McFarland (1965). Fig. A.3 shows a translation of the relevant parts of the block diagram of Fig. A.2 into an equivalent flow-graph. We are interested

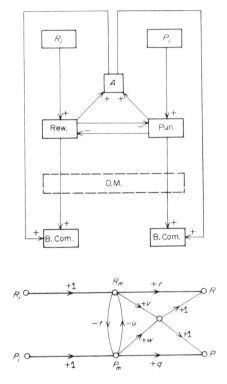

FIG. A.3. Block diagram and equivalent flow graph of parts of the arousal-decision model required to specify the function

$$I_R(x) = g[R_i(x), P_i(x)]$$

R_m is the same as Rew and P_m is the same as Pun. R is the Behaviour Command for approach. P is the Behaviour Command for avoidance. For general method, see McFarland (1965).

for the moment in analysing only for the output along the reward or approach path, R, so we can ignore the branches connecting P_M to P (the output of the punishment pathway) and A (the arousal mechanism) to P. The transmittances (small letters written along the branches) are assumed to be constants. As a result of flow-graph simplification (McFarland, 1965), the following result is obtained:

$$I_R = R = R_i \times \left(\frac{r + v - tw}{1 - tu}\right) + P_i w - P_i u \left(\frac{r + v - tw}{1 - tu}\right)$$

Putting $m = (r + v - tw)/(1 - tu)$ and $n = w - um$, we obtain:

$$I_R = R = mR_i + nP_i \qquad (2)$$

It may also be noted that, if we make use of a simpler model and omit the assumption of reciprocal inhibitory links between the reward and punishment systems, we obtain (by setting $t = u = 0$)

$$I_R = R = (r + v)R_i + wP_i \qquad (2a)$$

It is clear, then, that the value obtained for the intensity of the approach behaviour is a linear combination of the values for the inputs to the reward and punishment systems*. If we consider the behaviour of this function, as we move to the right along the abscissa of Fig. A.1 (from startbox to goalbox in a straightway), taking the ordinate in this figure to represent the values of the inputs to reward (approach function) and punishment (avoidance function) mechanisms, we see that it increases linearly with a slope that will depend on the values of the constants in Eqn (2).

We have so far dealt with the function $I_R(x) = g[R_i(x), P_i(x)]$; that is, in terms of Fig. A.2, we have supposed that the action of the decision mechanism has been to favour approach behaviour. We now turn to the problem of specifying $p_R(x) = f[R_i(x), P_i(x)]$. In other words, we must specify the decision rule followed by the decision mechanism. Let us suppose that R_d and P_d (the inputs along the reward and punishment pathways, respectively, to the decision mechanism) vary randomly and independently in time about some mean values, $R'(x)$ and $P'(x)$. The simplest initial assumptions are that they are normally distributed with the same standard deviation, σ. The simplest decision rule in such circumstances is that the animal responds with approach behaviour if $R_d > P_d$ and with avoidance behaviour if $R_d < P_d$. This gives us $p_R(x)$ as a simple function of $[R'(x) - P'(x)]/\sigma$, i.e. the number of standard deviations separating the means of R_d and P_d. Such a function can be calculated with

---

* The linearity is, of course, a simple consequence of the assumption of linear transmittances; the value of the derivation is that it specifies the contribution of the various components in the model to the coefficients in the equations.

the use of noraml probability tables. The variation of $p_R(x)$ with $[R'(x) - P'(x)]/\sigma$ is indicated by Table A.1.

TABLE A.1.   The variation of $p_R(x)$ with $R'(x) - P'(x)$

$\dfrac{R'(x) - P'(x)}{\sigma}$	0	1	2	3	4	5
$p_R(x)$	0.500	0.692	0.841	0.933	0.977	0.994

The relation of $R'(x)$ and $P'(x)$ to the other parameters in our model can be achieved if we return to our flow-graph analysis. Fig. A.4 shows the truncated part of Fig. A.3 which it is necessary to submit to analysis in order to obtain the inputs R_d and P_d into the decision mechanism. The results of this analysis are that

$$R_d = R_i \frac{r}{1 - tu} - P_i \frac{ur}{1 - tu} \tag{3}$$

$$P_d = P_i \frac{q}{1 - tu} - R_i \frac{tq}{1 - tu} \tag{4}$$

and if we consider mean values in this system we can replace R_d and P_d by R' and P', respectively, in (3) and (4), on the understanding

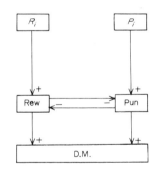

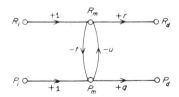

FIG. A.4. Block diagram and equivalent flow graph of parts of the arousal-decision model required to specify the inputs, R_d and P_d, from the reward and punishment mechanisms to the decision mechanism.

that R_i and P_i represent the means of the initial inputs to the system. We can eliminate R_i and P_i between Eqs (2), (3) and (4) to obtain:

$$I_R = \alpha R_d + \beta P_d \tag{5}$$

where $\alpha = (r + v)/r$ and $\beta = w/q$; that is, α and β are constants determined by the flow-graph analysis. Our assumptions about the variability of R_d and P_d and the constancy on any given trial of the transmittances in our flow-graph imply (because of Eqn (5)) that I_R is also subject to random variation, but since from the point of view of Eqn (1) we are only interested in the mean value of I_R, we can take means in Eqn (5), and adopting the convention that from now on $I_R(x)$ refers only to the *mean* intensity at the point x, we obtain:

$$I_R(x) = \alpha R'(x) + \beta P'(x) \tag{6}$$

This, together with our equation for the decision mechanism,

$$p_R(x) = f\left(\frac{R'(x) - P'(x)}{\sigma}\right)$$

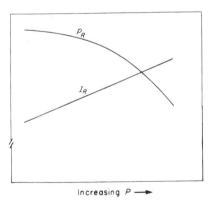

Increasing P ⟶

FIG. A.5. Probability of approach behaviour (p_R) and intensity of behaviour (I_R) as the mean punishment input (P') to the decision mechanism approaches the mean level of reward input.

forms the basis of our further analysis. Fig. A.5 shows the way in which probability of approach behaviour (p_R) and the intensity of approach behaviour (I_R) each varies as the input to the punishment mechanism approaches the level of the input to the reward mechanism. It is the multiplication of these two functions upon which Fig. A.6 is based.

The question also arises of how the values of α, β influence the behaviour of the function $E(x) = I_R(x) \cdot p_R(x)$. The relation between E and P', for α and R' fixed and for various values of β is shown in Fig. A.6. For $\beta = 0$, P' has no effect on I_R and reduces $f[(R' - P')/\sigma]$ as P' increases, thus E must decrease as P' increases. For $\beta \geqslant \alpha$, increases in I_R due to the presence of P' more than compensate for the decreases in $p_R(x)$, and thus E is never less than its level when P' was absent. For intermediate values of β, low P' produces an increase in E, high P' a decrease in E. For our analysis, the natural assumption is that β is intermediate between 0 and α. The assumption that there

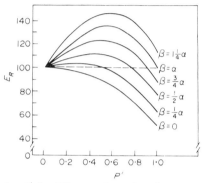

FIG. A.6. E_R plotted against P' for different values of β. R' is held constant. P' is expressed as a fraction of R'. E_R is expressed as a percentage of the value it would take if P' were absent.

is a general arousal mechanism means that we are taking β as significantly different from zero. We also note that if all the transmittances in Fig. A.3 are equal (remembering that, in analyzing for I_R, the pathways to P make no contribution), then $\beta = \frac{1}{2}\alpha$. This is the value we tentatively adopt in our analysis: a different value of β within the general restriction $0 < \beta < \alpha$ will give qualitatively the same results.

The Partial Reinforcement Acquisition Effect

We return now to the partial reinforcement acquisition effect. Because of the linear equations (3) and (4), $R'(x)$ and $P'(x)$ will have the same general form as $R_i(x)$ and $P_i(x)$ respectively, and the latter, according to Miller's (1959) data and theoretical analysis, take the form shown in Fig. A.1. The argument x is the distance along the runway. It is not critical to the model that $R'(x)$ and $P'(x)$ be *linear* functions of x: almost any continuous monotonic functions with the same end points will produce the same qualitative results. For convenience, measure $R'(x)$ and $P'(x)$ in standard deviation units (i.e. take $\sigma = 1$). The points S and G on the abscissa of the figure are to be taken, in any real situation, as lying beyond the real start and goal boxes, and they mark, respectively, the point at which the avoidance function falls to zero and the points at which the approach and

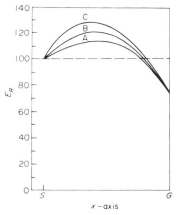

FIG. A.7. E_R plotted against distance along runway for various slopes of the approach and avoidance functions. All the curves are plotted with $R'(S) = 5$, $P'(S) = 0$, and $R'(G) = P'(G)$. They differ only in the value of $R'(G)$; $R'(G) = 6$ in Curve A, 10 in Curve B and 20 in Curve C. E_R is expressed as a percentage of the value it would take if P' were absent. For the significance of "S" and "G" on the x-axis see the text.

avoidance functions meet (i.e. the probability of approach behaviour = 0.5). $P'(S)$, then, = 0 and $R'(G) = P'(G)$. Now, in a runway situation, it is experimentally difficult to separate intensity from direction of behaviour, so what we are interested in is $E_R = p_R(x) \cdot I_R(x)$. We are now in a position to show how E_R depends on x and on the slope of the intensity function, $I_R(x)$. Fig. A.7 shows the general form of this dependence. The abscissa of this figure is distance along an ideal runway stretching from $x = S$ to $x = G$. The ordinate shows E_R as a percentage of the net approach behaviour in the absence of any input to the punishment system (i.e. for a CRF control group).

The curves differ only in the slope of the approach and avoidance functions from which they are derived. We see that choice of a suitable set of parameters (e.g. $R'(S)$ = 5, $R'(G)$ = 6) results in a curve which, over its middle range (which is where the real runway would lie) depicts what is in fact obtained for a partial reinforcement group relative to CRF controls early in training: a decrement in performance which is greater, the nearer the animal is to the goalbox.

The next thing to consider is what happens during continued training. In this connection, Amsel talks of the stimulus feedback from conditioned frustration $(r_f–s_f)$ becoming a cue for approach behaviour. Here we intend to part company with him. Instead, we shall make use of the inhibitory loops connecting the reward and punishment mechanisms. (This could be viewed as giving content to the expression "counter-conditioning", which is sometimes used to describe the tolerance for frustration which the animal appears to develop in a partial reinforcement situation.) We suppose that, whenever an animal is exposed to both rewards and punishments in the same situation over and over again, the transmittances along the reciprocal inhibitory links, t and u, are gradually adjusted so as to increase the more powerful input at the expense of the less powerful*. (The reader is referred in this connection to Eqns (3) and (4), from which it is clear that increasing t and decreasing u increases R_d and decreases P_d. Decreasing t and increasing u would have the reverse effects.) In the case of a partial reinforcement experiment, it is clear that reward is more powerful than punishment.

With continued training, then, the approach and avoidance functions (Fig. A.1) will rise and fall, respectively, thus increasing the separation between them. (It should be noted that essentially the same results are obtained if the approach function only rises, as it perhaps might on the hypothesis that s_f becomes a cue for running; or if the avoidance function only falls. Furthermore, very similar effects are obtained if the mean inputs to the decision mechanism, $R'(x)$ and $P'(x)$, are left unaltered, but their variability is reduced—see below, in connection with behavioural contrast.) It is clear that increasing the separation between $R'(x)$ and $P'(x)$ is going to have

* When a reward is *followed* regularly by a punishment, or vice versa, some adjustment appears to be made to enhance the event which comes later in this sequence at the expense of the earlier one (perhaps by classical conditioning); for an animal will accept a more intense punishment to get to a subsequent reward than he will accept when it is contingent upon taking a preceding reward (Solomon, 1964). On a random partial reinforcement schedule, this consideration does not apply, as reward and punishment follow each other equally often and, in any case, the intervals between them are ordinarily too large.

rather similar effects to moving the "real" runway along the abscissa of Fig. A.6 to the left. Fig. A.8 shows the curves that result from altering the heights of the approach and avoidance functions in this way. We see that continued training results in a reduction in the speed decrement shown by the partial reinforcement group near the goal, and an increase in their superiority early on in the runway. Thus our model appears to be able to accommodate the results obtained by such workers as Wagner (1961) and Goodrich (1959).

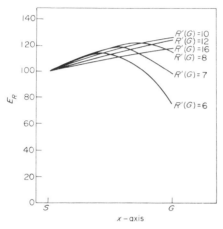

FIG. A.8. E_R plotted against distance along runway for different separations between the approach and avoidance functions. In this particular set of curves $P'(x)$ is kept constant $[P'(S) = 0, P'(G) = 6]$ and $R'(x)$ is varied so that its slope is constant $[R'(G) - R'(S) = 1]$. The same type of result is obtained if $R'(x)$ is held constant and $P'(x)$ reduced, or $R'(x)$ increased and $P'(x)$ reduced simultaneously. E_R is expressed as a percentage of the value it would take if P' were absent; i.e. for the partial reinforcement case, we plot the performance of partial reinforcement animals relative to constant reinforcement controls.

However, it is clear that it also predicts further changes with continued training. Thus, the maximum locus of superiority for the partial reinforcement group should move towards and eventually reach the goal; while with still further training the superiority of the partial reinforcement group should become smaller and eventually disappear.

The model, then, makes predictions about the effects of continued training which could be tested in the partial reinforcement situation for which it was initially developed. (Ordinarily, experiments on partial reinforcement effects in runways are not continued beyond about 100 trials, so there do not appear to be any data in the literature which we could use for this purpose at present.) It also makes predictions about the effects of increasing the lengths of the runway. Although it does not seem possible to extend a real runway to approach any closer to the ideal point "G" in Fig. A.1, increasing its length should take one closer to the point "S". Thus the model predicts (Fig. A.7) that, for a given number of training trials, the locus of maximum superiority of the partial reinforcement group should move forward from the startbox as the runway is lengthened. Finally, it is clear that the model predicts the greater variability of running times observed in the partial reinforcement group, relative to CRF controls, during the phase of acquisition at which the decremental effects of partial reinforcement are greatest (Amsel, 1958). For, according to the model, these decremental effects occur when $p_R(x)$ tends to 0.5; and the variability of a sampling distribution of two alternatives is greatest when they are equally likely.

Extensions of the Model to Induction, Transposition and Peak Shift

An adequate test of our model would obviously be much easier to carry out if it were possible to obtain separate measures of $p_R(x)$ and $I_R(x)$. It is impossible to do this using running speed in the typical runway experiments which we have so far considered. Operant conditioning techniques are more promising, since it should not be difficult to obtain measures of both proportion of time spent responding (p_R) and rate of response while responding (I_R). Fortunately, there are a number of phenomena observed in operant conditioning experiments which bear considerable similarities to runway frustration effects. The most important of these are "behavioural contrast" (Reynolds, 1961, 1963; Terrace, 1966a) and "peak shift" (Hanson, 1959; Friedman and Guttman, 1965).

Since the terminology in this area is a little confusing, it will help if we first define a number of terms used in the following discussion. It has been found in a number of experiments (see Terrace, 1966a, for review) that response rate in the presence of a stimulus correlated with a given frequency and magnitude of reward (which we shall call "reward value") can be altered by exposing the animal, in the same experimental environment, to a different stimulus correlated with a different reward value. We shall use the usual Skinnerian terminology and indicate the stimulus associated with the higher reward value by

S^D and the stimulus associated with the lower reward value by S^Δ. The alterations in response rate which have been observed take four forms: an *increase* in response rate in S^D as a result of exposure to S^Δ; a *decrease* in response rate in S^D as a result of exposure to S^Δ; an *increase* in rate in S^Δ as a result of exposure to S^D; and a *decrease* in rate in S^Δ as a result of exposure to S^D; in each case relative to the rate obtaining when S^D or S^Δ is the only stimulus to which the animal is exposed and its associated reward value is the same. Very similar phenomena were observed by Pavlov (1927, p. 188), using classical conditioning techniques. The four kinds of alterations in response are indicated in Table A.2, together with the terms used to describe them by Reynolds (1963) and by Pavlov (1927). The confusion of terminology evident in this Table requires no further comment.

Our own practice will be to use the term "induction" to refer to the general phenomenon whereby response vigour in the presence of one stimulus correlated with a certain reward value is altered by the presence of another stimulus correlated with a different reward value—i.e. to cover all four rows of Table A.2. We shall follow Pavlov in describing the case in which the inducing stimulus is S^Δ and the change is observed in S^D as "positive induction", though including by this term his "irradiation of inhibition" as well. Similarly, the case in which the inducing stimulus is S^D and the change is observed in S^Δ will be called "negative induction", which includes Pavlov's "irradiation of excitation". Where the change in S^D or in S^Δ is an increment in response vigour, we shall describe it simply as an "increment"; and similarly a fall in response vigour, whether in S^D or S^Δ, is a "decrement". Reynolds' "behavioural contrast" includes, therefore, incremental positive induction and decremental negative induction.

In showing how our model may be applied to induction, we shall for the present limit ourselves to the case of positive induction in which the S^Δ is correlated with zero reward. Later in the paper, we shall extend the analysis to cover both negative induction and non-zero reward values associated with S^Δ.

A limitation on our analysis in the present paper is that we shall consider only "sustained" induction effects, as distinct from "transient" ones (Bloomfield, 1966a; Nevin and Shettleworth, 1966). A transient effect is one whose duration is measured in terms of

TABLE A.2.   Four kinds of alteration in response

Inducing stimulus	Stimulus in which changed response observed	Direction of change in response vigour	Pavlovian term	Reynolds' term	Suggested term	
1 S△ or CS −	S^D or CS +	Increment	Positive induction	Behavioural contrast	Positive induction	Incremental
2 S△ or CS −	S^D or CS +	Decrement	Irradiation of inhibition	Induction		Decremental
3 S^D or CS +	S△ or CS −	Decrement	Negative induction	Behavioural contrast	Negative induction	Decremental
4 S^D or CS +	S△ or CS −	Increment	Irradiation of excitation	Induction		Incremental

minutes or seconds after temination of exposure to the inducing stimulus; a sustained effect is one whose duration is measured in hours or days after exposure to the inducing stimulus.

The other phenomena to which we intend to apply our model are the "peak shifts" (Hanson, 1959; Friedman and Guttman, 1965) and "transposition" and "transposition reversal" (Hebert and Krantz, 1965). Although the latter have not usually been studied in operant experiments, they are most easily discussed alongside the peak shifts. If we use "positive" and "negative" in the same way as above, we may distinguish both a "positive peak shift" and a "negative peak shift". Both kinds of shift are concerned with changes in generalization gradients (or, better, generalization functions) produced by discrimination training between two values along a stimulus continuum. In the positive peak shift (Hanson, 1959) maximum overall response rate is shifted along the stimulus continuum from S^D in the direction away from S^Δ; in the negative peak shift (Guttman, 1965), minimum overall response rate is shifted along the stimulus continuum from S^Δ in the direction away from S^D. In these definitions, we have used the words "*overall* response rate", in the same sense as $E_R = I_R \cdot p_R$, to distinguish the peak shifts from transposition. Transposition refers to the fact that an animal trained to discriminate S^D from S^Δ chooses a stimulus removed along the stimulus continuum from S^D in the direction away from S^Δ in preference to the S^D itself; here, then, we are concerned only with *probability* of approaching one or the other stimulus. If pairs of stimuli both removed from S^D in the direction away from S^Δ are offered to the animal, at some distance from S^D the animal will choose the stimulus *closer* to S^D; this is termed "transposition reversal" (Hebert and Krantz, 1965).

Induction

With these definitions in hand, we turn first to positive induction with the S^Δ reward value set at zero. Terrace (1966a) in his review of the relevant data, concludes that this phenomenon is probably a type of frustration effect, and we shall not repeat his arguments here. In terms of our model, the experimental situation may be pictured as in Fig. A.9. The animal is trained with a stimulus correlated with reward, S^D, whose position on a stimulus continuum is x^D and a stimulus correlated with zero reward, S^Δ (whose position is x^Δ). An approach function, $R'(x)$, has its peak at x^D and an avoidance function, $P'(x)$—set up by the frustrative nonreward experienced during exposure to S^Δ—has its peak at x^Δ. $R'(x)$ and $P'(x)$ are assumed to be smooth curves (their differential coefficients are continuous) and asymptotically zero for extreme values of x. For convenience, we define the stimulus scale such that $x^D > x^\Delta$.

In Fig. A.9, we sketch $E(x) = I_R(x) \cdot p_R(x)$. It can be seen that, according as $E(x)^D$ is greater than or less than the level of the

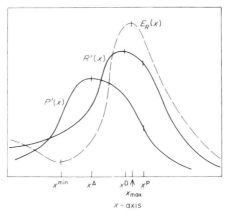

FIG. A.9. $E_R(x)$, $R'(x)$ and $P'(x)$ in a discrimination learning task. $R'(x)$ has a peak at x^D and $P'(x)$ one at x^Δ. $E_R(x)$ has a peak at x^{max} and a minimum at x^{min}. x^P is where $R'(x) - P'(x)$ is maximum.

approach function at x^D, so incremental or decremental positive induction will occur. To establish the conditions under which the one or the other type of induction will be observed we may refer to Fig. A.6. From this we see that the effect of introducing a small value of $P'(x)$ at x^D is to increase E, but a large value of $P'(x^D)$ will decrease $E(x^D)$. It follows that incremental induction (Reynolds' "behavioural contrast") will be observed if $P'(x^D)$ is small and decremental induction (Reynolds' "induction") if $P'(x^D)$ is large. The size of $P'(x^D)$ can be manipulated by changing the separation between the two stimuli or by altering the overall height of the avoidance function. (The latter effect may be obtained by, for example, increasing the reward value associated with S^Δ to some non-zero value which is still less than the S^D reward value.) Increasing stimulus separation for fixed overall level of $P'(x)$ will reduce $P'(x^D)$ and increasing the overall level of $P'(x)$ for fixed stimulus separation will raise $P'(x^D)$. Thus the relation between the size and direction of the positive induction effects, stimulus separation and overall frustration level will be that shown in Fig. A.10.

The predictions of the model are thus in general agreement with the experimental finding (Hanson, 1959; Bloomfield, 1966b) that, if S^D and S^Δ are separated by a small amount, decremental induction occurs, but if they are separated by a large amount, incremental induction (behavioural contrast) is observed. Note, however, that our

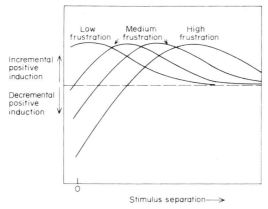

FIG. A.10. Positive induction as a function of overall frustration level and stimulus separation.

model predicts that only incremental induction, no matter what the stimulus separation, would occur in a situation in which the overall frustration is small.

Another way in which the predictions of the model agree with existing data concerns the effects of continued training on induction. It has been shown that positive incremental induction (behavioural contrast) disappears after lengthy periods of testing. (Terrace, 1966b). As we have discussed earlier in connection with runway partial reinforcement effects, there are several ways of representing the effects of continued training in our model, but they all lead to similar conclusions, as shown in Fig. A.8. The most natural assumption for continued discrimination training is that $R'(x) - P'(x)$ gets larger at x^D. Fig. A.8 shows that, on this assumption, continued training should lead to the disappearance of an incremental induction effect as observed.

Note further that the curves shown in Fig. A.10 plot $E(x) = I_R(x) \cdot p_R(x)$. That is, in terms of operant measures, they show relative change in overall number of responses in a unit testing period, which is in fact the way in which most of the data in this field are presented. However, the model makes quite detailed predictions concerning the separate changes in $I_R(x)$ and $p_R(x)$ which may easily be translated into observational terms for an operant experiment. If a distribution of inter-response times (IRT) for a single S^D is obtained, this may be used as a base-line for estimating changes in both I_R and p_R as a result of introducing S^Δ. Increases in I_R should appear as a shortening of IRTs *when the animal is responding*. Decreases in p_R should appear as unusually long pauses. Thus the model predicts that, when incremental induction occurs, the overall increase in number of responses should be accompanied by an increased variability of IRTs, both shorter and longer times being observed. When decremental induction occurs, the overall fall in number of responses should be accompanied by the same kind of change in the IRT distribution, though, of course, the lengthened IRTs should be longer or more in number, and the shortened IRTs shorter or fewer in number than for incremental induction.

Transposition

We turn now to consider transposition and transposition reversal. Our analysis here is essentially the same as Spence's (1937).* We assume that an animal faced with a choice between two stimuli S', S'' will more often choose the stimulus for which $p_R(x)$ is larger.

Now at x^D, $R'(x) - P'(x)$ is an increasing function of x (since $dR'/dx = 0$ and dP'/dx is negative), but $p_R(x)$ is continuous and tends to zero as x becomes large. Therefore $p_R(x)$ reaches a peak[†] at a point x^P (see Fig. A.9), $x^P > x^D$. Thus for any x', x'' such that $x^P \geqslant x' > x'' \geqslant x^D$, transposition will occur (since $p_R(x^P) \geqslant p_R(x') > p_R(x'') \geqslant p_R(x^D)$). Similarly, for $x' > x'' > x^P$, transposition reversal will occur. The conclusion is that if S', S'' are both sufficiently close to S^D transposition will always occur, and if S', S'' are both sufficiently far from S^D transposition reversal will always

---

* Spence's model can handle transposition with no difficulty, but, because he treats an S^Δ as setting up purely *inhibitory* tendencies, he cannot cope with incremental induction.

† This is assuming that $R'(x) - P'(x)$ is sufficiently well behaved to have only one peak: if $R'(x) - P'(x)$ has more than one peak, the argument is more complicated but leads to essentially the same results.

occur (this latter conclusion assumes $R'(x) > P'(x)$ for all large x, a not unreasonable assumption).

If we consider the relations between transposition and peak shift, we see that the model predicts that x^P (the critical point for transposition/transposition reversal) is greater than x^{max} (see Fig. A.9), the point where the overall number of responses is maximum. This can be seen as follows:

$$E = I_R(x) . p_R(x),$$
$$= [\alpha R'(x) + \beta P'(x)] f(R'(x) - P'(x)) \tag{7}$$

Taking logarithms and differentiating with respect to x gives:

$$\frac{1}{E}\frac{dE}{dx} = \frac{1}{\alpha R' + \beta P'}\left[\alpha\frac{dR'}{dx} + \beta\frac{dP'}{dx}\right] + \frac{1}{f(R' - P')}\frac{df}{dx} \tag{8}$$

At $x = x^P$, $df/dx = 0$ (x^P is at the peak of $p_R(x)$) and dR'/dx and dP'/dx are both negative (since $x^P > x^D$ and x^Δ),

$\therefore$ since all other terms in (8) are positive, dE/dx is negative;

i.e. E (the overall response measure) has already passed its peak, therefore $x^P > x^{max}$.

This result offers another test of our anlysis of E into p_R and I_R components: as far as we know, no published data looks at transposition* (based on $p_R(x)$) and response rate (based on E) at the same time.

A similar analysis around S^Δ will yield a similar set of predictions (which, however, are different in detail) for preferences between stimuli in this region. As far as we know "negative transposition" of this kind has not been observed.

Peak Shift

The requirement for positive peak shift is that $x^{max} > x^D$, i.e. when $dR'/dx = 0$, dE/dx is positive.

Developing Eqn (8):

$$\frac{1}{E}\frac{dE}{dx} = \frac{1}{\alpha R' + \beta R'}\left[\alpha\frac{dR'}{dx} + \beta\frac{dP'}{dx}\right]$$

$$+ \frac{1}{f(R' - P')}\left[\frac{df(y)}{dy}\right]_{y = R' - P'}\left[\frac{dR'}{dx} - \frac{dP'}{dx}\right]$$

---

* Honig's (1962) experiment measures what he calls "transposition" in terms, not of choice responses, but overall number of responses directed to each member of his pairs of stimuli.

when

$$\frac{dR'}{dx} = 0, \frac{dE}{dx} > 0 \text{ if}$$

$$\frac{1}{I_R} \beta \frac{dP'}{dx} - \frac{1}{P_R} \left[\frac{df(y)}{dy} \right]_{y = R' - P'} \times \frac{dP'}{dx} > 0$$

Dividing by $(dP'/dx)(< 0)$ and rearranging we obtain

$$\frac{1}{\beta} \left[\frac{df(y)}{dy} \right]_{y = R'(x^D) - P'(x^D)} > \frac{p_R (x^D)}{I_R (x^D)} \tag{9}$$

Now $df(y)/dy$ is a function entirely dependent on the properties of the normal distribution (it is the probability density function), and it is bounded: moreover,

$$\text{as } p_R (x) \to 1, \quad \left[\frac{df(y)}{dy} \right]_{y = R' - P'} \to 0,$$

∴ by suitable selection of large $p_R (x)$ or small $I_R (x)$ it would be possible to violate Eqn (9). Thus positive peak shift will *not* occur—and there may be a shift in the opposite direction—if $R'(x^D)$ − $P'(x^D)$ is too large (implying that the separation between S^D and S^Δ is too large) or if $I_R (x)$ is too small, i.e. there is a low level of arousal.

Hanson's (1959) paper affords some evidence relating to these last derivations from the model. If we consider the expectations for peak shift together with those for positive induction (see below), it is clear that there should be a greater positive peak shift, the greater the decremental positive induction at S^D, for both these phenomena should increase with decreasing separation between S^D and S^Δ. As positive induction at S^D changes from decremental to incremental (with increasing stimulus separation), peak shift should be reduced and eventually the peak might even move away from S^D in the direction of S^Δ. Hanson's data suggest that this is exactly what occurs: in his curve (Fig. A.11) for the smallest stimulus separation there appears, together with decremental induction, a swing of the peak still further away from S^D; and in the curve for the greatest stimulus separation, together with incremental induction, there is a swing of the peak back towards S^D.

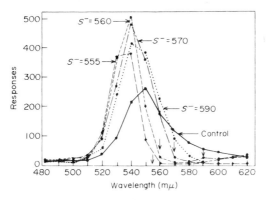

FIG. A.11. Stimulus generalization curves for different distances along the wavelength continuum between S^D ("CS" at 550 mμ) and S^Δ ("S—" at 555, 560, 570 and 590 mμ) compared to a control condition without S^Δ. (Data from Hanson (1959). *J. exp. Psychol.* 58, 321-324 copyright by the American Psychological Association, and reproduced by permission.)

The same type of condition applies to negative peak shift: the condition for negative peak shift will in fact be that

$$\frac{1}{\alpha} \left[\frac{df(y)}{dy} \right]_{y = R'(x^\Delta) - P'(x^\Delta)} > \frac{p_R(x^\Delta)}{I_R(x^\Delta)} \qquad (10)$$

Although it is possible to construct pathological cases when (9) is satisfied but (10) is not, and vice versa, generally speaking presence or absence of positive peak shift should be coupled with presence or absence of negative peak shift.

Non-zero Frustrative Reward

Now behavioural contrast (incremental positive induction) has been observed with nonzero reward correlated with S^Δ (Reynolds, 1961, 1963; Terrace, 1966a). Furthermore, the magnitude of the contrast which is observed is a function of the disparity between the reward values associated with S^D and S^Δ (Reynolds, 1963). It is clear, then, that if our theoretical framework is to be of any value it must also deal with this case. In considering the case in which S^Δ is correlated with zero reward we had to take into account only an approach function centred on S^D, and an avoidance function centred on S^Δ. When reward is also received during S^Δ it becomes necessary to take explicit account of the effects of this reward as well.

We do not propose to present a detailed solution to the problem of non-zero S^Δ reward, though detailed solutions involving a few additional assumptions and a little more mathematics could easily be developed; these solutions would take the form of specifying the amount of unconditioned frustration at S^Δ associated with the difference between expected and actual reward. All we need assume for our present purposes is that a steadily increasing reward value at S^Δ, with reward at S^D fixed, will produce a steadily decreasing frustration input to the punishment mechanism at S^Δ and thus a

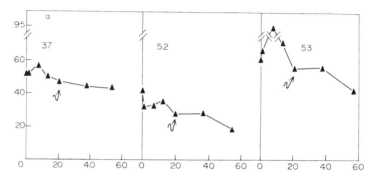

FIG. A.12. Responses per minute (ordinate) in the presence of a stimulus associated with 20 reinforcements per h as a function of number of reinforcement per h (abscissa) in the second component of a multiple schedule. (Data for three separate pigeons from Reynolds (1963). *J. exp. Anal. Behav.*, **6**, 131-139 copyright (1959) by the Society for the Experimental Analysis of Behavior, Inc., and reproduced by permission.)

steadily decreasing generalized frustration input at S^D. As far as the effects of S^Δ reward on the approach function at S^D are concerned, there are several sorts of assumptions one can make. For example, we could assume that the input to the reward mechanism at S^D is entirely dependent on the larger reward which is actually obtained during S^D. In that case, with reward at S^Δ steadily decreasing from a value the same as or close to the S^D reward value, one of the family of curves for E_R presented in Fig. A.6 is obtained. Similar curves would be obtained by the alternative assumption that the reward actually experienced at S^Δ adds by generalization to the approach function at S^D. The predicted joint effects of varying S^Δ reward value and stimulus separation, with S^D reward value fixed, have already been presented in Fig. A.10.

The available empirical data fit these predictions reasonably well. Reynolds' (1963) data (Fig. A.12) show that with fixed stimulus separation, the greatest degree of incremental positive induction (behavioural contrast) occurred at an intermediate value of S^Δ reward, though Bird 52 shows a particularly high S^D response rate with zero S^Δ reward. Furthermore, it is of some interest (since our analysis began with runway data) to note that Mackinnon (1967) has observed very similar phenomena in an experiment in which rats ran in two runways for different reward values. His data are shown in

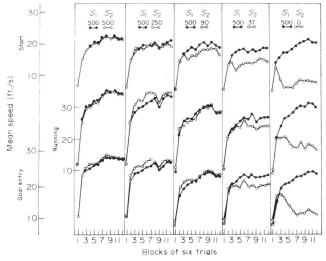

FIG. A.13. Start, run and goal speeds in an S^D alley with reward = 500 mg as a function of the magnitude of the reward given for running in a second, S^Δ, alley. $S_1 = S^D$, $S_2 = S^\Delta$ and the numbers indicate magnitude of reward in mg. (Data from Mackinnon (1967) *J. exp. Psychol.* **75**, 329-338. Copyright (1967) by the American Psychological Association, and reproduced by permission.)

Fig. A.13, from which it can be seen that, for fixed stimulus separation and fixed S^D reward value (500 mg), running speeds in the S^D alley varied systematically with the reward given for running in the S^Δ alley, For S^Δ reward = 250 mg, there is an increment in speed of running the S^D alley; for S^Δ reward value decreasing below 250 mg, there is a steadily greater decrement in S^D alley running speed. Moreover, it is clear from our earlier discussion that, in terms of the model, movement towards the goalbox in a runway experiment is the equivalent of reducing stimulus separation in an operant experiment. We would therefore predict, in line with Fig. A.10, that the incremental positive induction observed in

Mackinnon's experiment will be transformed into decremental positive induction by a joint decrease in S^Δ reward value and closer approach to the goal. It is clear from Fig. A.13 that these predictions are a reasonably accurate description of his results.

We turn finally to consider the predictions of the model for negative induction with nonzero S^Δ reward, inductive effects being measured against the response rate maintained when S^Δ and its correlated reward value are the only conditions to which the animal is exposed. It is clear that, as S^Δ reward value decreases, the frustration input at S^Δ increases. Thus we would again make the

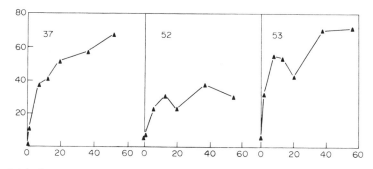

FIG. A.14. Responses per minute (ordinate) in the presence of a stimulus associated with the number of reinforcements per h shown on the abscissa. Reinforcement frequency in the second component of the multiple schedule was always 20 per h. (Data for three separate pigeons from Reynolds (1963), *J. exp. Anal. Behav.* **6**, 131-139. Copyright (1963) by the Society for the Experimental Analysis of Behavior, Inc., and reproduced by permission.)

predictions shown in Fig. A.6: for S^Δ reward value close to S^D reward value, there should be an increment in S^Δ responding; as S^Δ reward value approaches zero there should be a reduction in this increment which turns into a decrement for very low reward values. From Fig. A.14 it can be seen that Reynolds' (1963) data again fit these predictions well in the case of two of his three pigeons.

This completes our extension of the model to situations other than the runway partial reinforcement experiments with which we began. The model has still wider generality than we have been able to indicate here. It can obviously be applied to experiments involving interactions between rewards and punishments (e.g. food in one stimulus, shock in another), for it is a key assumption in the model that frustrative nonreward acts on a punishment system.

Summary

Arising from a critique of Amsel's theory of frustration a mathematical model is developed for application to situations involving conflict either between reward and punishment or between reward and frustrative non-reward. The model consists essentially of a translation of Amsel's theory into a "black box" with various interacting components. By specifying the mathematics of the interactions between the components, the model is able to achieve a higher degree of precision and to overcome certain difficulties and ambiguities contained in Amsel's theory. Behaviour is analyzed into separate "direction" and "intensity" components which multiply together to produce the final observed performance. The direction of behaviour (approach or avoidance) is determined by a "decision mechanism" whose activity is analyzed according to statistical decision theory. The intensity of behaviour is determined by a weighted function of the inputs to "reward" and "punishment" mechanisms. The model is couched in terms which should facilitate attempts to match its components with elements in the central nervous system. Its application to existing data on the effects of partial reinforcement in runway studies and on behavioural contrast, peak shift and other inductive phenomena in operant conditioning situations is illustrated and new predictions are deduced.

References

* See also additional references added in proof, p. 407.

Adams, D. and Flynn, J. P. (1966). Transfer of an escape response from tail shock to brain-stimulated attack behaviour. *J. Exp. Anal. Behav.* 9, 401-408.

Adelman, H. M and Maatsch, J. L. (1956). Learning and extinction based upon frustration, food reward, and exploratory tendency. *J. Exp. Psychol.* 52, 311-315.

Albert, M. and Bignami, G. (1967). Effects of frontal median cortical and caudate lesions on two-way avoidance learning by rats. *Physiol. Behav.* 3, 141-147.

Amsel, A. (1950a). The effect upon level of consummatory response of the addition of anxiety to a motivational complex. *J. Exp. Psychol.* 40, 709-715.

Amsel, A. (1950b). The combination of primary appetitional need with primary and secondary emotionally derived needs. *J. Exp. Psychol.* 40, 1-14.

Amsel, A. (1958). The role of frustrative nonreward in non-continuous reward situations. *Psychol. Bull.* 55, 102-119.

Amsel, A. (1962). Frustrative nonreward in partial reinforcement and discrimination learning; some recent history and a theoretical extension. *Psychol. Rev.* 69, 306-328.

Amsel, A. and Maltzman, I. (1950). The effect upon generalised drive strength of emotionality as inferred from the level of consummatory response. *J. Exp. Psychol.* 40, 563-569.

Amsel, A. and Roussel, J. (1952). Motivational properties of frustration: I. Effect on a running response of the addition of frustration to the motivational complex. *J. Exp. Psychol.* 43, 363-368.

Amsel, A. and Surridge, C. T. (1964). The influence of magnitude of reward on the aversive properties of anticipatory frustration. *Canad. J. Psychol.* 18, 321-327.

Armus, H. L., Carlson, K. R., Guinan, J. F., and Crowell, R. A. (1964). Effect of a secondary reinforcement stimulus on the auditory startle response. *Psychol. Rep.* 14, 535-540.

Asratian, E. A. (1965). "Compensatory Adaptations, Reflex Activity and the Brain", Pergamon Press, Oxford.

Azrin, N. H. (1967). Pain and aggression. *Psychology Today* 1 (1), 26-33.

Azrin, N. H. and Hake, D. F. (1969). Positive conditioned suppression: conditioned suppression using positive reinforcers as the unconditioned stimuli. *J. Exp. Anal. Behav.* 12, 167-173.

Bacon, W. E. and Bindra, D. (1967) The generality of the incentive-motivational effects of classically conditioned stimuli in instrumental learning. *Acta Biol. Exp.* **27**, 185-197.

Ball, G. G. (1970). Hypothalamic self stimulation and feeding: different time functions. *Physiol. Behav.* **5**, 1343-1346.

Ball, G. G. (1972). Self-stimulation in the ventromedial hypothalamus. *Science, N.Y.* **178**, 72-73.

Ball, G. G. and Adams, D. W. (1965). Intracranial stimulation as an avoidance or escape response. *Psychon. Sci.* **3**, 39-40.

Baltzer, V. and Weiskrantz, L. (1970). Negative and positive behavioural contrast in the same animals. *Nature (Lond.)* **228**, 581-582.

Barry, H. and Miller, N. E. (1962) Effects of drugs on approach-avoidance conflict tested repeatedly by means of a "telescope alley". *J. Comp. Physiol. Psychol.* **55**, 201-210.

Barry, H. and Miller, N. E. (1965). Comparison of drug effects on approach, avoidance and escape motivation. *J. Comp. Physiol. Psychol.* **59**, 18-24.

Barry, H., Wagner, A. R. and Miller, N. E. (1962). Effects of alcohol and amobarbital on performance inhibited by experimental extinction. *J. Comp. Physiol. Psychol.* **55**, 464-468.

Beach, F. A. and Fowler, H. (1959). Effects of "situational anxiety" on sexual behaviour in male rats. *J. Comp. Physiol. Psychol.* **52**, 245-248.

Beach, F. A. and Jordan, L. (1956). Sexual exhaustion and recovery in the male rat. *Quart. J. Exp. Psychol.* **8**, 121-133.

Becker, P. W. and Bruning, J. L. (1966). Goal gradient during acquisition, partial reinforcement, and extinction of a five part response chain. *Psychon. Sci.* **4**, 11-12.

Benedict, J. O. and Ayres, J. B. (1972). Factors affecting conditioning in the truly random control procedure in the rat. *J. Comp. Physiol. Psychol.* **78**, 323-330.

Berger, B. D., Yarczower, M. and Bitterman, M. D. (1965). Effect of partial reinforcement on the extinction of a classically conditioned response in the goldfish. *J. Comp. Physiol. Psychol.* **59**, 399-405.

Berlyne, D. E. (1950). Novelty and curiosity as determinants of exploratory behaviour. *Brit. J. Psychol.* **41**, 68-80.

Berlyne, D. E. (1960). "Conflict, Arousal and Curiosity", McGraw Hill, New York.

Bindra, D. (1972). A unified account of classical conditioning and operant training. *In* "Classical Conditioning II: Current Research and Theory" (A. H. Black and W. F. Prokasy, Eds), 453-481. Appleton-Century-Crofts, New York.

Black, A. H. (1965). Cardiac conditioning in curarized dogs: the relationship between heart rate and skeletal behaviour. *In*: "Classical Conditioning" (W. F. Prokasy, Ed.), Appleton, New York.

Black, A. H. (1971). Autonomic aversive conditioning in infrahuman subjects. *In*: "Aversive Conditioning and Learning" (F. R. Brush, Ed.), 3-104. Academic Press, New York, London.

Black, R. W. (1969). Incentive motivation and the parameters of reward in instrumental conditioning. *Nebraska Symposium on Motivation* **17**, 83-137.

Black, R. W. and Spence, K. W. (1965). Effects of intertrial reinforcement on resistance to extinction following extended training. *J. Exp. Psychol.* 70, 559-563.

Blackman, D. E. (1970). Conditioned suppression of avoidance behaviour in rats. *Quart. J. Exp. Psychol.* 22, 547-553.

Bloomfield, T. M. (1966a). Two types of behavioral contrast in discrimination learning. *J. Exp. Anal. Behav.* 9, 155-161.

Bloomfield, T. M. (1966b). Behavioural induction in multiple reinforcement schedules. Unpublished Ph.D. thesis, University of Exeter, England.

Blurton-Jones, N. G. (1968). Observations and experiments on causation of threat displays of the Great Tit (*Paris major*). *Animal Behav. Monogr.* 1 (2), 75-158.

Bolles, R. C. (1967). "Theory of Motivation" Harper and Row, New York.

Bolles, R. C. (1970). Species-specific defence reactions and avoidance learning. *Psychol. Rev.* 77, 32-48.

Bolles, R. C. (1971). Species-specific defence reactions. *In*: "Aversive Conditioning and Learning" (F. R. Brush, Ed.), 183-233. Academic Press, New York, London.

Bolles, R. C. (1972). The avoidance learning problem. *In*: "The Psychology of Learning and Motivation" (G. H. Bower, Ed.), Vol. 6, 97-145. Academic Press, London, New York

Bolles, R. C. and Grossen, N. E. (1969). Effects of an informational stimulus on the acquisition of avoidance behaviour in rats. *J. Comp. Physiol. Psychol.* 68, 90-99.

Bolles, R. C., Rapp, H. M. and White, G. C. (1968). Failure of sexual activity to reinforce female rats. *J. Comp. Physiol. Psychol.* 65, 311-313.

Bolles, R. C., Stokes, L. W. and Younger, M. S. (1966). Does CS termination reinforce avoidance behaviour? *J. Comp. Physiol. Psychol.* 62, 201-207.

Booth, D. A. (1972). Conditioned satiety in the rat. *J. Comp. Physiol. Psychol.* 81, 457-471.

Bower, G. and Grusec, J. (1964). Effects of prior Pavlovian discrimination training upon learning an operant discrimination. *J. Exp. Anal. Behav.* 7, 401-404.

Broadhurst, P. L. (1957). Emotionality and the Yerkes-Dodson Law. *J. Exp. Psychol.* 54, 345-352.

Brodal, A. (1969). "Neurological Anatomy in Relation to Clinical Medicine" Oxford University Press, New York.

Brown, J. S. (1961). "The Motivation of Behaviour" McGraw Hill, New York.

Brown, P. L. and Jenkins, H. M. (1967). Conditioned inhibition and excitation in operant discrimination learning. *J. Exp. Psychol.* 75, 255-266.

Brown, P. L. and Jenkins, H. M. (1968). Auto-shaping of the pigeon's key-peck. *J. Exp. Anal. Behav.* 11, 1-8.

Brown, R. T. and Wagner, A. R. (1964). Resistance to punishment and extinction following training with shock or non-reinforcement. *J. Exp. Psychol.* 68, 503-507.

Bruce, R. H. (1937). An experimental investigation of the thirst drive in rats with especial reference to the goal gradient hypothesis. *J. Gen. Psychol.* 17, 49-62.

Budgell, P. (1971). Behavioural thermoregulation in the Barbary dove (*Streptopelia risoria*). *Anim. Behav.* 19, 524-531.

Bugelski, R. (1938). Extinction with and without sub-goal reinforcement. *J. Comp. Psychol.* 26, 121-133.

Bunyatyan, G. K. L. (1952). Conditioned internal inhibition and its role in metabolism. *Izv. Akad. Nauk. Arm. SSR*, 5(1). Yerevan.

Bunyatyan, G. K. L., Gasparyan, M. G. and Mkheyan, E. Ye. (1952). The active nature of conditioned internal inhibition. *In:* "Symposium on Problems of Higher Nervous Activity" (Voprosy Vysshei Nervnoi Deyatelnosti), Vol. 1. Yerevan: *Akad. Nauk. Arm. SSR.*

Bush, R. R. and Mosteller, F. (1955). "Stochastic Models for Learning", Wiley, New York.

Butler, R. A. (1957). The effect of deprivation of visual incentives on visual exploration motivation in monkeys. *J. Comp. Physiol. Psychol.* 50, 171-179.

Butter, C. M. and Thomas, D. R. (1958). Secondary reinforcement as a function of the amount of primary reinforcement. *J. Comp. Physiol. Psychol.* 51, 346-348.

Carlin, J. S., Bicknell, E. A. and Sperling, D. S. (1953). Establishment of a conditioned drive based on the hunger drive. *J. Comp. Physiol. Psychol.* 46, 173-175.

Capaldi, E. J. (1967). A sequential hypothesis of instrumental learning. *In:* "The Psychology of Learning and Motivation" (K. W. Spence and J. T. Spence, Eds.), Vol. 1, 67-156. Academic Press, New York, London.

Capaldi, E. J. and Spalding, D. L. (1971). Amobarbital and the partial reinforcement effect in rats: isolating frustrative control over instrumental responding. *J. Comp. Physiol. Psychol.* 74, 467-477.

Charlesworth, W. R. and Thompson, W. R. (1957). Effect of lack of visual stimulus variation on exploratory behaviour in the adult white rat. *Psychol. Rep.* 3, 509-512.

Chi, C. C. (1965). The effect of amobarbital sodium on conditioned fear as measured by the potentiated startle response in rats. *Psychopharmacologia* 7, 115-122.

Chorazyna, H. (1962). Some properties of conditioned inhibition. *Acta. Biol. Exp.* 22, 5-13.

Church, R. M., Wooten, C. L. and Matthews, T. J. (1970). Discriminative punishment and the conditioned emotional response. *Learning Motiv.* 1, 1-17.

Coons, E. E. and Grice, J. A. F. (1968). Lateral hypothalamus: food and current intensity in maintaining self-stimulation hunger. *Science, N.Y.* 159, 1117-1119.

Cravens, R. W. and Renner, K. E. (1970). Conditioned appetitive drive states: empirical evidence and theoretical status. *Psychol. Bull.* 73, 212-220.

Crespi, L. P. (1942). Quantitative variation of incentive and performance in the white rat. *Amer. J. Psychol.* 55, 467-517.

Dally, P. J. (1969). "Anorexia Nervosa", Heinemann, London.

Daly, H. B. (1969). Learning of a hurdle-jump response to escape cues paired with reduced reward or frustrative nonreward. *J. Exp. Psychol.* 79, 146-157.

De Bold, R. C., Miller, N. E. and Jensen, D. D. (1965). Effect of strength of drive determined by a new technique for appetitive classical conditioning of rats. *J. Comp. Physiol. Psychol.* 59, 102-108.

De Molina, A. F. and Hunsperger, R. W. (1962). Organization of the subcortical system governing defence and flight reactions in the cat. *J. Physiol.* 160, 200-213.

Denny, M. R. (1971). Relaxation theory and experiments. *In*: "Aversive Conditioning and Learning" (F. R. Brush, Ed.), 235-295, Academic Press, New York, London.

Denti, A. and Epstein, A. (1972). Sex differences in the acquisition of two kinds of avoidance behaviour in rats. *Physiol. Behav.* 8, 611-615.

Deutsch, J. A. (1964a). Behavioural measurement of the neural refractory period and its application to intracranial self-stimulation. *J. Comp. Physiol. Psychol.* 58, 1-9.

Deutsch, J. A. (1964b). "The Structural Basis of Behaviour", Cambridge University Press, Cambridge.

Di Cara, L. V., Braun, J. J. and Pappas, B. A. (1970). Classical conditioning and instrumental learning of cardiac and gastrointestinal responses following removal of neocortex in the rat. *J. Comp Physiol. Psychol.* 73, 208-216.

Dinsmoor, J. A. (1950). A quantitative comparison of the discriminative and reinforcing functions of a stimulus. *J. Exp. Psychol.* 40, 458-472.

Dollard, J. C. and Miller, N. E. (1950). "Personality and Psychotherapy", McGraw Hill, New York.

Domino, E. F., Caldwell, D. F. and Henke, R. (1965). Effects of psychoactive agents on acquisition of conditioned pole jumping in rats. *Psychopharmacologia* 8, 285-289.

Doty, R. W. and Giurgea, C. (1961). Conditioned reflexes established by coupling electrical excitations of two cortical areas. *In*: "Brain Mechanisms and Learning" (J. F. Delafresnaye, Ed.), 133-151. Blackwell, Oxford.

Douglas, R. J. (1967). The hippocampus and behaviour. *Psychol. Bull.* 67, 416-442.

Drewett, R. F. (1972). Motivational properties of the oestrous cycle. Unpublished D.Phil. thesis, Oxford University.

Drewett, R. F. (1973). Sexual behaviour and sexual motivation in the female rat. *Nature (Lond.)* 242, 476-477.

Dudderidge, H. J., Gray, J. A. and de Wit, H. (in preparation). The influence of amylobarbitone sodium on the partial reinforcement extinction effect with a 24-hour intertrial interval.

Duffy, E. (1951). The concept of energy mobilization. *Psychol. Rev.* 58, 30-40.

Duffy, E. (1957). The psychophysiological significance of the concept of arousal or activation. *Psychol. Rev.* 64, 265-275.

Duffy, E. (1962). "Activation and Behaviour". Wiley, London.

Ehrlich, A. (1959). Effects of past experience on exploratory behaviour in rats. *Canad. J. Psychol.* **13**, 248-254.

Egger, M. D. and Miller, N. E. (1963). When is reward reinforcing? An experimental study of the information hypothesis. *J. Comp. Physiol. Psychol.* **56**, 132-137.

Epstein, A. N., Fitzsimmons, J. T. and Simons, B. J. (1970). Drinking caused by the intracranial injection of angiotensin *J. Physiol.* **210**, 457-474.

Estes, W. K. (1948). Discriminative conditioning. II. Effect of a Pavlovian conditioned stimulus upon a subsequently established operant response. *J. Exp. Psychol.* **38**, 173-177.

Estes, W. K. (1949). Generalization of secondary reinforcement from the primary drive. *J. Comp. Physiol. Psychol.* **42**, 286-295

Estes, W. K. and Burke, C. J. (1953). A theory of stimulus variability of learning. *Psychol. Rev.* **60**, 276-286.

Estes, W. K. and Skinner, B. F. (1941). Some quantitative properties of anxiety. *J. Exp. Psychol.* **29**, 390-400.

Eysenck, H. J. (1967). "The Biological Basis of Personality". Thomas, Springfield, Illinois.

Ferrari, E. A., Todorov, J. C. and Graeff, F. G. (1973). Nondiscriminated avoidance of shock by pigeons pecking a key. *J. Exp. Anal. Behav.* **19**, 211-218.

Ferster, C. B., Appel, J. B. and Hiss, R. A. (1962). The effects of drugs on a fixed-ratio performance suppressed by a pre-time-out stimulus. *J. Exp. Anal. Behav.* **5**, 73-88.

Fitzgerald, R. D. (1966). Some effects of partial reinforcement with shock on classically conditioned heart-rate in dogs. *Amer. J. Psychol.* **79**, 242-249.

Fitzgerald, R. D., Vardaris, R. M. and Teyler, T. J. (1966). Effects of partial reinforcement followed by continuous reinforcement on classically conditioned heart rate in the dog. *J. Comp. Physiol. Psychol.* **62**, 483-486.

Fowler, H. (1967). Satiation and curiosity. *In*: "The Psychology of Learning and Motivation" (K. W. Spence, and J. T. Spence, Eds), Vol. 1, 157-227. Academic Press, New York, London.

Fowler, H. (1971). Implications of sensory reinforcement. *In "The Nature of Reinforcement"* (R. Glaser, Ed.), 151-195. Academic Press, New York, London.

Fox, S. S. (1962). Self-maintained sensory input and sensory deprivation in monkeys. *J. Comp. Physiol. Psychol.* **55**, 438-444.

Freedman, P. E. and Rosen, A. J. (1969). The effects of psychotropic drugs on the double alley frustration effect. *Psychopharmacologia* **15**, 39-47.

Freeman, G. L. (1948). "The Energetics of Human Behaviour", Cornell University Press, Ithaca.

French, D., Fitzpatrick, D. and Thomas, O. L. (1972). Operant investigation of mating preference in female rats. *J. Comp. Physiol. Psychol.* **81**, 226-232.

Fried, P. A. (1973). The septum and hyper-reactivity: a review. *Brit. J. Psychol.* **64**, 267-275.

Friedman, H. and Guttman, N. (1965). Further analysis of the various effects of discrimination training on stimulus generalization gradients. *In* "Stimulus Generalization". (D. I. Mostofsky, Ed.), 255-267. Stanford University Press Stanford.

Gallup, G. G. (1965). Aggression in rats as a function of frustrative nonreward in a straight alley. *Psychon. Sci.* 3, 99-100.

Garcia, J., Kimeldorf, D. J. and Kuelling, R. A. (1955). Conditioned aversion to saccharin resulting from exposure to gamma radiation. *Science, N.Y.* 122, 157-158.

Garcia, J., McGowan, B. K. and Green, K. F. (1972). Biological constraints on conditioning. *In*: "Classical Conditioning II: Current Research and Theory" (A. H. Black and W. F. Prokasy, Eds), 3-27. Appleton-Century-Crofts, New York.

Giurgea, C. and Raiciulesco, N. (1959). Etude électroencéphalographique du réflexe conditionnel à l'excitation électrique corticale directe. *In: Proc. 1st Int. Congress Neurol. Sci.*, Brussels, Vol. 3: EEG, Clinical Neurophysiology and Epilepsy, 156-176. London: Pergamon Press.

Gleitman, H., Nachmias, J. and Neisser, U. (1954). The S-R reinforcement theory of extinction. *Psychol. Rev.* 61, 23-33.

Glickman, S. E. and Schiff, B. B. (1967). A biological theory of reinforcement. *Psychol. Rev.* 74, 81-109.

Goldberg, J. M. and Greenwood, D. D. (1966). Response of neurones of the dorsal and posteroventral cochlear nuclei of the cat to acoustic stimuli of long duration. *J. Neurophysiol.* 29, 72-93.

Gonzalez, R. C., Eskin, R. M. and Bitterman, M. E. (1963). Further experiments on partial reinforcement in the fish. *Amer. J. Psychol.* 76, 366-375.

Gonzalez, R. C., Milstein, S. and Bitterman, M. E. (1962). Classical conditioning in the fish: Further studies of partial reinforcement. *Amer. J. Psychol.* 75, 421-428.

Goodrich, K. P. (1959). Performance in different segments of an instrumental response chain as a function of reinforcement schedule. *J. exp. Psychol.* 57, 57-63.

Gormezano, I. (1965). Yoked comparisons of classical and instrumental conditioning of the eyelid response; and an addendum on "voluntary responders". *In*: "Classical Conditioning" (W. F. Prokasy, Ed.), 48-70, Appleton-Century-Crofts, New York.

Gorska, T. and Jankowska, E. (1961). The effect of deafferentation on instrumental (Type II) conditioned reflexes in dogs. *Acta Biol Exp.* 21, 219-234.

Gorska, T., Jankowska, E. and Kozak, W. (1961). The effect of deafferentation on instrumental (Type II) clearing reflex in cats. *Acta Biol. Exp.* 21, 209-218.

Granit, R. (1955). "Perception and Sensory Reception". Oxford University Press, Oxford.

Gray, J. and Lissman, H. W. (1940). The effect of deafferentation upon locomotive activity of amphibian limbs. *J. Exp. Biol.* 17, 227-235.

Gray, J. and Lissman, H. W. (1946). Further observations on the effect of deafferentation of the locomotor activity of amphibian limbs. *J. Exp. Biol.* 23, 121-132.

Gray, J. A. (1964a). Strength of the nervous system as a dimension of personality in Man: a review of work from the laboratory of B. M. Teplov. *In*: "Pavlov's Typology" (J. A. Gray, Ed.), 157-288. Pergamon Press, Oxford.

Gray, J. A. (1964b). Strength of the nervous system and levels of arousal: a reinterpretation. *In*: "Pavlov's Typology" (J. A. Gray, Ed.), 289-366. Pergamon Press, Oxford.

Gray, J. A. (1965a). Stimulus intensity dynamism. *Psychol. Bull.* 63, 180-196.

Gray, J. A. (1965b). Relation between stimulus intensity and operant response rate as a function of discrimination training and drive. *J. Exp. Psychol.* 69, 9-24.

Gray, J. A. (1967). Disappointment and drugs in the rat. *Advancement of Science* 23, 595-605.

Gray, J. A. (1969). Sodium amobarbital and effects of frustrative nonreward. *J. Comp. Physiol. Psychol.* 69, 55-64.

Gray, J. A. (1970a). The psychophysiological basis of introversion-extraversion. *Behav. Res. Therapy* 8, 249-266.

Gray, J. A. (1970b). Sodium amobarbital, the hippocampal theta rhythm and the partial reinforcement extinction effect. *Psychol. Rev.* 77, 465-480.

Gray, J. A. (1971a). "The Psychology of Fear and Stress", Weidenfeld and Nicolson, London; and McGraw Hill, New York.

Gray, J. A. (1971b). Sex differences in emotional behaviour in mammals including Man: endocrine bases. *Acta Psychol.* 35, 29-46.

Gray, J. A. (1972a). Learning theory, the conceptual nervous system and personality. *In*: "The Biological Bases of Individual Behaviour" (V. D. Nebylitsyn and J. A. Gray, Eds), 372-399. Academic Press, New York, London.

Gray, J. A. (1972b). The structure of the emotions and the limbic system: a theoretical model. *In*: "Physiology, Emotion and Psychosomatic Illness" (R. Porter and J. Knight, Eds), 87-120. Ciba Foundation Symposium, 8 (new series). Associated Scientific Publishers, Amsterdam

Gray, J. A. (1972c). The psychophysiological basis of introversion-extraversion: a modification of Eysenck's theory. *In*: "The Biological Bases of Individual Behaviour" (V. D. Nebylitsyn and J. A. Gray, Eds), 182-205. Academic Press, New York, London.

Gray, J. A. (1973). Causal theories of personality and how to test them. *In*: "Multivariate Analysis and Psychological Theory" (J. R. Royce, Ed.), 409-463. Academic Press, London, New York.

Gray, J. A. and Ball, G. G. (1970). Frequency-specific relation between hippocampal theta rhythm, behavior and amobarbital action. *Science, N.Y.,* 168, 1246-1248.

Gray, J. A. and Drewett, R. F. (in press). The physiological basis of personality traits as illustrated by the study of sex differences. *In*: "Handbook of Modern Personality Theory" (R. B. Cattell and R. M. Dreger, Eds), Appleton-Century-Crofts, New York.

Gray, J. A. and Dudderidge, H. (1971). Sodium amylobarbitone, the partial reinforcement extinction effect and the frustration effect in the double runway. *Neuropharmacology* 10, 217-222.

Gray, J. A. and Smith, P. T. (1969). An arousal-decision model for partial reinforcement and discrimination learning. *In*: "Animal Discrimination Learning" (R. Gilbert and N. S. Sutherland, Eds), 243-272. Academic Press, London, New York. Reprinted as Appendix to this volume.

Grice, G. R. (1948). The relation of secondary reinforcement to delayed reward in visual discrimination learning. *J. Exp. Psychol.* 38, 633-642.

Grossen, N. E., Kostansek, D. J. and Bolles, R. W. (1969). Effects of appetitive discriminative stimuli on avoidance behaviour. *J. Exp. Psychol.* 81, 340-343.

Grossman, S. P. (1967). "A Textbook of Physiological Psychology", Wiley, New York.

Grusec, T. (1968). The peak shift in stimulus generalisation: equivalent effects of errors and noncontingent shock. *J. Exp. Anal. Behav.* 11, 239-249.

Guttman, N. (1965). Effects of discrimination formation on generalization measured from a positive-rate baseline. *In*: "Stimulus Generalization" (D. I. Mostofsky, Ed.), 210-217. Stanford University Press, Stanford.

Guttman, N. and Kalish, H. I. (1956). Discriminability and stimulus generalisation. *J. Exp. Psychol.* 51, 79-88.

Haggard, D. F. (1959). Acquisition of a simple running response as a function of partial and continuous schedules of reinforcement. *Psychol. Rep.* 9, 11-18.

Hammond, L. J. (1966). Increased responding to CS in differential CER. *Psychon. Sci.* 5, 337-338.

Hanson, H. M. (1959). The effects of discrimination training on stimulus generalization. *J. Exp. Psychol.* 58, 321-334.

Haude, R. H. and Ray, O. S. (1967). Visual exploration in monkeys as a function of visual incentive duration and sensory deprivation. *J. Comp. Physiol. Psychol.* 64, 332-336.

Hearst, E. (1965). Approach, avoidance and stimulus generalization. *In*: "Stimulus Generalization" (D. I. Mostofsky, Ed.), 331-355. Stanford University Press, Stanford.

Hearst, E. (1969). Aversive conditioning and external stimulus control. *In*: "Punishment and Aversive Behavior" (B. A. Campbell and R. M. Church, Eds). 235-277. Appleton-Century-Crofts, New York.

Hearst, E., Besley, S. and Farthing, W. G. (1970). Inhibition and the stimulus control of operant behavior. *J. Exp. Anal. Behav.* 14, 373-409.

Hebb, D. O. (1949). "The Organization of Behavior". Wiley, New York.

Hebb, D. O. (1955). Drives and the C. N. S. (conceptual nervous system). *Psychol. Rev.* 62, 243-254.

Hebert, J. A. and Krantz, D. L. (1965). Transposition: a re-evaluation. *Psychol. Bull.* 63, 244-257.

Hendry, D. P. and Rasche, R. H. (1961). Analysis of a new non-nutritive positive reinforcer based on thirst. *J. Comp. Physiol. Psychol.* 54, 477-483.

Henton, W. W. and Brady, J. V. (1970). Operant acceleration during a pre-reward stimulus. *J. Exp. Anal. Behav.* **13**, 205-209.

Herrnstein, R. J. (1969). Method and theory in the study of avoidance. *Psychol. Rev.* **76**, 49-69.

Hilgard, E. R. and Marquis, D. G. (1940). "Conditioning and Learning", Appleton-Century-Crofts, New York.

Hilton, A. (1969). Partial reinforcement of a conditioned emotional response in rats. *J. Comp. Physiol. Psychol.* **69**, 253-260.

Hinde, R. A. (1970). "Animal Behaviour", 2nd Ed. McGraw Hill, New York.

Hinde, R. A. and Stevenson–Hinde, J. (Eds.) (1973). "Constraints on Learning", Academic Press, London.

Holmes, J. D. and Gormezano, I. (1970). Classical appetitive conditioning of the rabbit's jaw movement response under partial and continuous reinforcement schedules. *Learn. Motiv.* **1**, 110-120.

Hoebel, B. G. and Teitelbaum, P. (1962). Hypothalamic control of feeding and self-stimulation. *Science, N.Y.*, **135**, 375-377.

Honig, W. K. (1962). Prediction of preference, transposition, and transposition-reversal from the generalization gradient. *J. Exp. Psychol.* **64**, 239-248.

Horn, G. (1967). Neuronal mechanisms of habituation. *Nature (Lond.)* **215**, 707-711.

Horn, G. (1970). Changes in neuronal activity and their relationship to behaviour. *In:* "Short-Term Changes in Neural Activity and Behaviour" (G. Horn and R. A. Hinde, Eds), 567-606. Cambridge University Press, Cambridge.

Horn, G. and Hinde, R. A. (Eds) (1970). "Short-Term Changes in Neural Activity and Behaviour", Cambridge University Press, Cambridge.

Hull, C. L. (1932). The goal-gradient hypothesis and maze learning, *Psychol. Rev.* **39**, 25-43.

Hull, C. L. (1934). The rat's speed-of-locomotion gradient in the approach to food. *J. Comp. Psychol.* **17**, 393-422.

Hull, C. L. (1943). "Principles of Behavior", Appleton-Century-Crofts, New York.

Hull, C. L. (1952). "A Behavior System", Yale University Press, New Haven.

Hurwitz, H. M. B. (1956). Conditioned responses in rats reinforced by light. *Brit. J. Anim. Behav.* **4**, 31-33.

Hurwitz, H. M. B. and James, R. E. (1970). Deferment of intracranial reinforcement: incentive power of I.C.S. *Physiol. Behav.* **5**, 1309-1312.

Huston, J. P. and Borbely, A. A. (1973). Operant conditioning in forebrain ablated rats by use of rewarding hypothalamic stimulation. *Brain Res.* **50**, 467-472.

Hutchinson, R. R. and Renfrew, J. W. (1966). Stalking attack and eating behaviour elicited from the same sites in the hypothalamus. *J. Comp. Physiol. Psychol.* **61**, 360-367.

Hyde, T. S., Trapold, M. A. and Gross, D. M. (1968). Facilitative effect of a CS for reinforcement upon instrumental responding as a function of reinforcement magnitude: a test of incentive-motivation theory. *J. Exp. Psychol.* **73**, 423-428.

Ilina, G. N. (1959). Extinction and differential inhibition as shown in "reactions of the reverse sign". In: "Typological Features of Higher Nervous Activity in Man" (B. M. Teplov, Ed.), (Tipologicheskiye osobennosti vysshei nervnoi deyatelnosti cheloveka), Vol. 2. Moscow: Akad. Pedagog. Nauk RSFSR.

Ison, J. R. (1964). Acquisition and reversal of a spatial response as a function of sucrose concentration. J. exp. Psychol. 67, 495-496.

Ison, J. R., Daly, H. B. and Glass, D. H. (1967). Amobarbital sodium and the effects of reward and nonreward in the Amsel double runway. Psychol. Rep. 20, 491-496.

Ison, J. R. and Northman, J. (1968). Amobarbital sodium and instrumental performance changes following an increase in reward magnitude. Psychon. Sci. 12, 185-186.

Ison, J. R. and Pennes, E. S. (1969). Interaction of amobarbital sodium and reinforcement schedule in determining resistance to extinction of an instrumental running response. J. Comp. Physiol. Psychol. 68, 215-219.

Ison, J. R. and Rosen, A. J. (1967). The effects of amobarbital sodium on differential instrumental conditioning and subsequent extinction. Psychopharmacologia 10, 417-425.

Jankowska, E. (1959). Instrumental scratch reflex of the deafferentated limb in cats and rats. Acta Biol. Exp. 19, 233-247.

Jenkins, H. M. and Moore, B. R. (1973). The form of the autoshaped response with food or water reinforcers. J. Exp. Anal. Behav. 20, 163-182.

Jouvet, M. and Michel, F. (1959). Aspects électroencéphalographiques de l'habituation de la réaction d'éveil. J. Physiol., Paris 51, 489-490.

Julesz, B. (1964). Binocular depth perception without familiarity cues. Science, N.Y. 145, 356-362.

Kamano, D. K., Martini, L. K. and Powell, B. J. (1966). Avoidance response acquistion and amobarbital dosage levels. Psychopharmacologia 8, 319-323.

Kamin, L. J. (1956). The effects of termination of the CS and avoidance of the US on avoidance learning. J. Comp. Physiol. Psychol. 49, 420-424.

Kamin, L. J. (1957). The gradient of delay of secondary reward in avoidance learning. J. Comp. Physiol. Psychol. 50, 445-449 .

Kamin, L. J. (1968). "Attention-like" processes in classical conditioning. In: "Miami Symposium on the Prediction of Behaviour: Aversive Stimulation" (M. R. Jones, Ed.), 9-31. University of Miami Press, Miami.

Kamin, L. J. (1969). Predictability, surprise, attention and conditioning. In: "Punishment and Aversive Behaviour" (R. Church and B. Campbell, Eds), 279-296. Appleton-Century-Crofts, New York.

Kamin, L. J., Brimer, C. J. and Black, A. H. (1963). Conditioned suppression as a monitor of fear of the CS in the course of avoidance training. J. Comp. Physiol. Psychol. 56, 497-501.

Kendrick, D. C. (1958). Inhibition with reinforcement (conditioned inhibition). J. Exp. Psychol. 56, 313-318.

Kimble, G. A. (Ed.) (1961). "Hilgard and Marquis' Conditioning and Learning", Appleton-Century-Crofts, New York.

Kimble, G. A., Mann, L. I. and Dufort, R. H. (1955). Classical and instrumental eyelid conditioning. *J. Exp. Psychol.* **49**, 407-417.

King, A. R. (1970). Drive related effects of amylobarbitone and chlorpromazine on appetitive and aversively controlled behaviour in the rat. *Physiol. Behav.* **5**, 1365-1371.

Kinsman, R. A. and Bixenstine, V. E. (1968). Secondary reinforcement and shock termination. *J. Exp. Psychol.* **76**, 62-68.

Konorski, J. (1948). "Conditioned Reflexes and Neuron Organization", Cambridge University Press, Cambridge.

Konorski, J. (1967). "Integrative Activity of the Brain", Chicago University Press, Chicago.

Kremer, E. F. (1971). Truly random and traditional control procedures in CER conditoning in the rat. *J. Comp. Physiol. Psychol.* **76**, 441-448.

Kremer, E. F. and Kamin, L. J. (1971). The truly random control procedure: associative or nonassociative effects in rats. *J. Comp. Physiol. Psychol.* **74**, 203-210.

Kumar, R. (1971). Extinction of fear. I. Effects of amylobarbitone and dexamphetamine given separately and in combination on fear and exploratory behaviour in rats. *Psychopharmacologia* **19**, 163-187.

Lawler, E. E. (1965). Secondary reinforcement value of stimuli associated with shock reduction. *Quart J. Exp. Psychol.* **17**, 57-62.

Leitenberg, H., Bertsch, G. J. and Coughlin, R. C. (1968). "Time-out from positive reinforcement" as the UCS in a CER paradigm with rats. *Psychon. Sci.* **13**, 3-4.

Le Magnen, J. (1968). Eating rate as related to deprivation and palatability in normal and hyperphagic rats. Reported at *Third International Conference on the Regulation of Food and Water Intake.*

Le Magnen, J. (1971). Advances in studies on the physiological control and regulation of food intake. *In:* "Progress in Physiological Psychology" (E. Stellar and J. M. Sprague, Eds), Vol. 4, 203-261. Academic Press, New York, London.

Leslie, J. C. and Ridgers, A. (in preparation). Autoshaping and omission training in rats.

Lettvin, J. Y., Maturana, H. R., Pitts, W. H. and McCulloch, W. S. (1961). Two remarks on the visual system of the frog. *In:* "Sensory Communication" (W. Rosenblith, Ed.), Wiley and M.I.T. Press, New York.

Lewis, D. J. (1960). Partial reinforcement: a selective review of the literature since 1950. *Psychol. Bull.* **57**, 1-28.

Lints, C. E. and Harvey, J. A. (1969). Altered sensitivity to footshock and decreased brain content of senotonin following brain lesions in the rat. *J. Comp. Physiol. Psychol.* **67**, 23-32.

Lisina, M. I. (1958). The role of orientation in converting involuntary to voluntary responses. *In:* "The Orienting Reflex and Exploratory Behaviour" (Orientirovochnyi Refleks i orientirovochno-issledovatelskaya Deyatelnost) (L. G. Voronin *et al.*, Eds), 339-344. *Akad. Pedagog. Nauk RSFSR,* Moscow.

Lockard, J. S. (1963). Choice of a warning signal or no warning signal in an unavoidable shock situation. *J. Comp. Physiol. Psychol.* 56, 526-530.

Logan, F. (1954). A note on stimulus intensity dynamism (*V*). *Psychol. Rev.* 61, 77-80.

Logan, F. (1968). Incentive theory and change in reward. *In*: "The Psychology of Learning and Motivation" (K. W. Spence and J. T. Spence, Eds), Vol. 2, 1-30, Academic Press, New York, London.

LoLordo, V. M. (1969). Positive conditioned reinforcement from aversive situations. *Psychol. Bull.* 72, 193-203.

LoLordo, V. M. (1971). Facilitation of food-reinforced responding by a signal for response-independent food. *J. Exp. Anal. Behav.* 15, 49-55.

LoLordo, V. M. and Rescorla, R. A. (1966). Protection of the fear-eliciting capacity of a stimulus from extinction. *Acta Biol. Exp.* 26, 251-258.

Longo, N., Milstein, S. and Bitterman, M. E. (1962). Classical conditioning in the pigeon: exploratory studies of partial reinforcement. *J. Comp. Physiol. Psychol.* 55, 983-986.

Lorenz, K. (1950). The comparative method in studying innate behaviour patterns. *Symp. Soc. Exp. Biol.* 4, 221-268.

Lubow, R. E. and Moore, A. U. (1959). Latent inhibition: the effect of non-reinforced pre-exposure to the conditioned stimulus. *J. Comp. Physiol. Psychol.* 52, 415-419.

Lynch, V. A., Aceto, M. C. G. and Thomas, R. K. (1960). Effects of certain psychopharmacological drugs on conditioning in the rat: I. Avoidance–escape conditioning. *J. Amer. Pharmaceut. Ass.* 49, 205-210.

Lynn, R. (1966). "Attention, Arousal and the Orientation Reaction", Pergamon Press, Oxford.

Mabry, P. D. and Peeler, D. F. (1972). Effect of septal lesions on response to frustrative nonreward. *Physiol. Behav.* 8, 909-913.

McAllister, D. E. and McAllister, W. R. (1964). Second-order conditioning of fear. *Psychon. Sci.* 1, 383-384.

McAllister, W. R. and McAllister, D. E. (1972). Behavioral measurement of conditioned fear. *In*: "Aversive Conditioning and Learning" (F. R. Brush, Ed.), 105-179, Academic Press, New York.

McCleary, R. A. (1966). Response-modulating functions of the limbic system: initiation and suppression. *In*: "Progress in Physiological Psychology" (E. Stellar and J. M. Sprague, Eds), Vol. 1, 209-272. Academic Press, New York, London.

McFarland, D. J. (1965). Flow graph representation of motivational systems. *Brit. J. Math. Stat. Psychol.* 18, 25-43.

McFarland, D. J. (1966). On the causal and functional significance of displacement activities. *Zeits. Tierpsychol.* 23, 217-235.

McFarland, D. J. (1969). Separation of satiating and rewarding consequences of drinking. *Physiol. Behav.* 4, 987-989.

McFarland, D. J. (1971). "Feedback Mechanisms in Animal Behaviour". Academic Press, London.

McFarland, D. J. (1973). Stimulus relevance and homeostasis. *In*: "Constraints on Learning" (R. A. Hinde and J. Stevenson-Hinde, Eds), 141-153. Academic Press, London.

McFarland, D. J. (1974). Experimental investigation of motivational state. *In*: "Motivational Control Systems Analysis" (D. J. McFarland, Ed.), Academic Press, London, New York. (In press).

McFarland, D. J. and McFarland, F. J. (1968). Dynamic analysis of an avian drinking response. *Med. Biol. Engineer.* 6, 659-668.

McFarlane, D. A. (1930). The role of the kinesthesis in maze learning. *Calif. Univ. Publ. Psychol.* 4, 277-305.

McGonigle, B., McFarland, D. J. and Collier, P. (1967). Rapid extinction following drug-inhibited incidental learning. *Nature (Lond.)* 214, 531-532.

McHose, J. H. (1966). Incentive reduction: simultaneous delay increase and magnitude reduction and subsequent responding. *Psychon. Sci.* 5, 215-216.

McHose, J. H. and Ludvigson, H. W. (1965). Role of reward magnitude and incomplete reduction of reward magnitude in the frustration effect. *J. exp. Psychol.* 70, 490-495.

Mackinnon, J. R. (1967). Interactive effects of the two rewards in a differential magnitude of reward discrimination. *J. Exp. Psychol.* 75, 329-338.

Mackintosh, N. J. (1973). Stimulus selection: learning to ignore stimuli that predict no change in reinforcement. *In*: "Constraints on Learning" (R. A. Hinde and J. T. Stevenson-Hinde, Eds), 75-96. Academic Press, London, New York.

MacMillan, A. St. C., Gray, J. A. and Ison, J. R. (1973). An apparent new instance of stimulus intensity dynamism during discrimination of duration of repeating auditory stimuli. *Quart. J. Exp. Psychol.* 25, 62-70.

Magoun, H. W. (1963). "The Waking Brain", 2nd Ed. Thomas, Springfield Illinois.

Margules, D. L. and Stein, L. (1968). Facilitation of Sidman avoidance behaviour by positive brain stimulation. *J. Comp. Physiol. Psychol.* 66, 182-184.

Margulies, S. (1961). Response duration in operant level, regular reinforcement, and extinction. *J. Exp. Anal. Behav.* 4, 317-321.

Meehl, P. E. (1950). On the circularity of the law of effect. *Psychol. Bull.* 47, 52-75.

Mendelson, J. (1966). Role of hunger in T-maze learning for food by rats. *J. Comp. Physiol. Psychol.* 62, 341-349.

Mendelson, J. (1970). Self-induced drinking in rats: the qualitative identity of drive and reward systems in the lateral hypothalamus. *Physiol. Behav.* 5, 925-930.

Miczek, K. A. and Grossman, S. P. (1971). Positive conditioned suppression: effects of CS duration. *J. Exp. Anal. Behav.* 15, 243-247.

Miles, R. C. and Wickens, D. D. (1953). Effect of a secondary reinforcer on the primary hunger drive. *J. Comp. Physiol. Psychol.* 46, 77-79.

Millenson, J. R. and MacMillan, A. St. C. (in press). Abortive responding During punishment of bar holding. *Learn. Motiv.*

Miller, N. E. (1948). Studies of fear as an acquirable drive: I. Fear as motivation and fear-reduction as reinforcement in the learning of new responses. *J. Exp. Psychol.* 38, 89-101.

Miller, N. E. (1951). Learnable drives and rewards. *In:* "Handbook of Experimental Psychology" (S. S. Stevens, Ed.), 435-472. Wiley, New York.

Miller, N. E. (1955). Shortcomings of food consumption as a measure of hunger: results from other behavioral techniques. *Ann. N.Y. Acad. Sci.* 63, 141-143.

Miller, N. E. (1959). Liberalization of basic S-R concepts: extensions to conflict behavior, motivation and social learning. *In:* "Psychology: A Study of a Science" (S. Koch, Ed.), Study 1, Vol. 2, 196-292. McGraw Hill, New York.

Miller N. E. (1964). The analysis of motivational effects illustrated by experiments on amylobarbitone. *In:* "Animal Behaviour and Drug Action" (H. Steinberg, Ed.), 1-18. Churchill, London.

Miller, N. E. (1969). Learning of visceral and glandular responses. *Science, N.Y.* 163, 434-445.

Miller, N. E. (1971). "Selected Papers", Aldine-Atherton, New York.

Miller, N. E. and Carmona, A. (1967). Modification of visceral response, salivation in thirsty dogs, by instrumental training with water reward. *J. Comp. Physiol. Psychol.* 63, 1-6.

Miller, N. E., DiCara, L. K. and Wolf, G. (1968). T-maze learning induced by manipulating antidiuretic hormone. *Amer. J. Physiol.* 215, 684-686.

Miller, N. E. and Kessen, M. L. (1952). Reward effects of food via stomach fistula compared with those of food via mouth. *J. Comp. Physiol. Psychol.* 45, 555-564.

Mischel, T. (1969). "Human Action", Academic Press, New York, London.

Mogenson, G. J. and Morgan, C. W. (1967). Effects of induced drinking on self-stimulation of the lateral hypothalamus. *Exp. Brain Res.* 3, 111-116.

Montgomery, K. C. and Zimbardo, P. G. (1957). Effect of sensory and behavioral deprivation upon exploratory behavior in the rat. *Percept. Mot. Skills* 7, 223-229.

Moore, B. R. (1973). The role of directed Pavlovian reactions in simple instrumental learning in the pigeon. *In:* "Constraints on Learning" (R. A. Hinde and J. Stevenson-Hinde, Eds), 159-186. Academic Press, London, New York.

Morgan, C. T. and Fields, P. E. (1938). The effect of variable preliminary feeding upon the rat's speed-of-locomotion. *J. Comp. Physiol. Psychol.* 26, 331-348.

Morgan, M. J. (1974). Resistance to satiation. *Anim. Behav.* 22, 449-466.

Morris, R. G. M. (1973). The acquisition and maintenance of avoidance behaviour. Unpublished Ph.D. thesis, Sussex University.

Moruzzi, G. and Magoun, H. W. (1949). Brain stem reticular formation and activation in the EEG. *Electroenceph. Clin. Neurophysiol.* 1, 455-473.

Mowrer, O. H. (1947). On the dual nature of learning: a re-interpretation of "conditioning" and "problem-solving". *Harv. Educ. Rev.* 17, 102-148.

Mowrer, O. H. (1954). Ego psychology, cybernetics, and learning theory. *In:* "Learning Theory, Personality Theory, and Clinical Research: The Kentucky Symposium", 81-90. Wiley, New York.

Mowrer, O. H. (1960). "Learning Theory and Behavior", Wiley, New York.

Mowrer, O. H. and Aiken, E. G. (1954). Contiguity vs. drive-reduction in conditioned fear: temporal variations in conditioned and unconditioned stimulus. *Amer. J. Psychol.* 67, 26-38.

Mowrer, O. H. and Solomon, L. N. (1954). Contiguity vs. drive-reduction in conditioned fear: the proximity and abruptness of drive-reduction. *Amer. J. Psychol.* 67, 15-25.

Myer, J. S. (1971). Some effects of noncontingent aversive stimulation. *In*: "Aversive Conditioning and Learning" (F. R. Brush, Ed.), 469-536. Academic Press, New York, London.

Myers, A. K. and Miller, N. E. (1954). Failure to find a learned drive based on hunger; evidence for learning motivated by exploration. *J. Comp. Physiol. Psychol.* 47, 428-436.

Neuringer, A. J. (1969). Delayed reinforcement versus reinforcement after a fixed interval. *J. Exp. Anal. Behav.* 12, 375-384.

Nevin, J. A. and Shettleworth, Sara J. (1966). An analysis of contrast effects in multiple schedules. *J. Exp. Anal. Behav.* 9, 305-315.

Nicholson, J. N. and Gray, J. A. (1972). Peak shift, behavioural contrast and stimulus generalization as related to personality and development in children. *Brit. J. Psychol.* 63, 47-62.

Notterman, J. M. (1959). Force emission during bar pressing. *J. Exp. Psychol.* 58, 341-347.

Notterman, J. M., Schoenfeld, W. N. and Bersh, P. J. (1952). Conditioned heart rate response in human beings during experimental anxiety. *J. Exp. Psychol.* 45, 1-8.

Novin, D. and Miller, N. E. (1962). Failure to condition thirst reduced by feeding dry food to hungry rats. *J. Comp. Physiol. Psychol.* 55, 373-374.

Oakley, D. A. and Russell, I. S. (1972). Neocortical lesions and Pavlovian conditioning. *Physiol. Behav.* 8, 915-926.

Oatley, K. and Dickinson, A. (1970). Air drinking and the measurement of thirst. *Anim. Behav.* 18, 259-265.

Obrist, P. A., Wood, D. M. and Perez-Reyes, M. (1965). Heart rate during conditioning in humans: effects of UCS intensity, vagal blockade and adrenergic block of vasomotor activity. *J. Exp. Psychol.* 70, 32-42.

Olds, J. and Olds, M. (1965). Drives, rewards and the brain. *In*: "New Directions in Psychology", Vol. 2, 329-410. Holt, Rinehart and Winston, New York.

Olds, M. and Olds, J. (1962). Approach-escape interactions in rat brain. *Amer. J. Physiol.* 203, 803-810.

Overmier, J. B., Bull, J. A. and Pack, K. (1971). On instrumental response interaction as explaining the influence of Pavlovian CS[+]S upon avoidance behavior. *Learn. Motiv.* 2, 103-112.

Overmier, J. B. and Payne, R. J. (1971). Facilitation of instrumental avoidance learning by prior appetitive Pavlovian conditioning to the cue. *Acta Neurobiol. Exp.* 31, 341-349.

Pavlov, I. P. (1927). "Conditioned Reflexes", Trans. G. V. Anrep. Oxford University Press, London.

Pavlov, I. P. (1928). "Lectures on Conditioned Reflexes", Trans. W. H. Gantt. Liverwright, New York.

Pavlov, I. P. (1956). The conditioned reflex. "Great Soviet Encyclopaedia", 2nd ed., Vol. 44, 373-380. Moscow: Gosudarstvennoye Nauchnoye Izdatelstvo. (In Russian).

Peckham, R. H. and Amsel, A. (1967). The within-S demonstration of a relationship between frustration and magnitude of reward in a differential magnitude of reward discrimination. *J. Exp. Psychol.* 73, 187-195.

Perin, C. T. (1943). A quantitative investigation of the delay-of-reinforcement gradient. *J. Exp. Psychol.* 32, 37-51.

Perkins, C. C. Jnr. (1953). The relation between conditioned stimulus intensity and response strength. *J. Exp. Psychol.* 46, 225-231.

Perkins, C. C. Jnr. (1968). An analysis of the concept of reinforcement. *Psychol. Rev.* 75, 155-172.

Perkins, C. C. Jnr., Seymann, R. G., Levis, D. J. and Spencer, H. R. Jnr. (1966). Factors affecting preferences for signal-shock over shock-signal. *J. Exp. Psychol.* 72, 190-196.

Pert, A. and Bitterman, M. E. (1970). Reward and learning in the turtle. *Learn. Motiv.* 1, 121-128.

Pinto-Hamuy, T., Santibañez, H. G. and Rojas, J. A. (1963). Learning and retention of a visual conditioned response in neodecorticate rats. *J. Comp. Physiol. Psychol.* 56, 19-24.

Plotkin, H. C. and Russell, I. S. (1969). The hemidecorticate learning deficit: evidence for a quantitative impairment. *Physiol. Behav.* 4, 49-55.

Powell, D. R. Jnr. and Perkins, C. C. Jnr. (1957). Strength of secondary reinforcement as a determiner of the effects of duration of goal response on learning. *J. Exp. Psychol.* 53, 106-112.

Pratt, C. C. (1948). "The Logic of Modern Psychology", Macmillan, New York.

Premack, D. (1965). Reinforcement theory. *In*: "Nebraska Symposium on Motivation" (D. Levine, Ed.), 123-180. University of Nekraska Press, Lincoln, Nebraska.

Premack, D. (1971). Catching up with common sense or two sides of a generalization: reinforcement and punishment. *In*: "The Nature of Reinforcement" (R. Glaser, Ed.), 121-150. Academic Press, New York, London.

Premack, D. and Collier, G. (1962). Analysis of non-reinforcement variables affecting response probability. *Psychol. Monogr.* 76, No. 5 (Whole No. 524).

Razran, G. (1957). The dominance-contiguity theory of the acquisition of classical conditioning. *Psychol. Bull.* 54, 1-46.

Razran, G. (1971). "Mind in Evolution", Houghton Mifflin, Boston.

Reiss, S. and Wagner, A. R. (1972). CS habituation produces a "latent inhibition effect" but no active "conditioned inhibition". *Learn, Motiv.* 3, 237-245.

Rescorla, R. A. (1967). Pavlovian conditioning and its proper control procedures. *Psychol. Rev.* 74, 71-80.

Rescorla, R. A. (1968). Probability of shock in the presence and absence of CS in fear conditioning. *J. Comp. Physiol. Psychol.* 66, 1-5.

Rescorla, R. A. (1969). Pavlovian conditioned inhibition. *Psychol. Bull.* 72, 77-94.

Rescorla, R. A. (1969). Establishment of a positive reinforcer through contrast with shock. *J. Comp. Physiol. Psychol.* 67, 260-263.

Rescorla, R. A. (1972). Informational variables in Pavlovian conditioning. *In*: "The Psychology of Learning and Motivation" (G. H. Bower, Ed.), Vol. 6, 1-46. Academic Press, New York, London.

Rescorla, R. A. (1973). Effect of US habituation following conditioning. *J. Comp. Physiol. Psychol.* 82, 137-143.

Rescorla, R. A. and LoLordo, V. M. (1965). Inhibition of avoidance behaviour. *J. Comp. Physiol. Psychol.* 59, 406-412.

Rescorla, R. A. and Skucy, J. C. (1969). Effect of response-independent reinforcers during extinction. *J. Comp. Physiol. Psychol.* 67, 712-726.

Rescorla, R. A. and Solomon, R. L. (1967). Two process learning theory: relationships between Pavlovian conditioning and instrumental learning. *Psychol. Rev.* 74, 151-182.

Rescorla, R. A. and Wagner, A. R. (1972). A theory of Pavlovian conditioning: variations in the effectiveness of reinforcement and nonreinforcement. *In*: "Classical Conditioning II: Current Research and Theory" (A. H. Black and W. F. Prokasy, Eds), 64-99. Appleton-Century-Crofts, New York.

Revusky, S. H. (1968). Aversion to sucrose produced by contingent X-irradiation—temporal and dosage parameters. *J. Comp. Physiol. Psychol.* 65, 17-22.

Revusky, S. H. and Garcia, J. (1970). Learned associations over long delays. *In*: "The Psychology of Learning and Motivation" (G. H. Bower, Ed.), Vol. 4, 1-84. Academic Press, New York, London.

Reynolds, G. S. (1961). Behavioral contrast. *J. Exp. Anal. Behav.* 4, 57-71.

Reynolds. G. S. (1963). Some limitations on behavioral contrast and induction during successive discrimination. *J. Exp. Anal. Behav.* 6, 131-139.

Ridgers, A. and Gray, J. A. (1973). Influence of amylobarbitone on operant depression and elation effects in the rat. *Psychopharmacologia* 32, 265-270.

Riess, D. and Farrar, C. H. (1973). US duration, conditioned acceleration, multiple CR measurement, and Pavlovian R–R laws in the rat. *J. Comp. Physiol. Psychol.* 82, 144-151.

Rizley, R. C. and Rescorla, R. A. (1972). Associations in second-order conditioning and sensory preconditioning. *J. Comp. Physiol. Psychol.* 81, 1-11.

Robbins, D. (1971). Partial reinforcement: a selective review of the alleyway literature since 1960. *Psychol. Bull.* 76, 415-431.

Roberts, A. E. and Hurwitz, H. M. B. (1970). The effect of a pre-shock signal on a free-operant avoidance response. *J. Exp. Anal. Behav.* 14, 331-340.

Roberts, W. W. (1958). Rapid escape learning without avoidance learning motivated by hypothalamic stimulation in cats. *J. Comp. Physiol. Psychol.* 51, 391-399.

Roberts, W. W. and Keiss, H. O. (1964). Motivational properties of hypothalamic aggression in cats. *J. Comp. Physiol. Psychol.* 58, 187-193.

Rodnick, E. H. (1937). Does the interval of delay of conditioned responses possess inhibitory properties? *J. Exp. Psychol.* 20, 507-527.

Rosen, A. J. (1966). Incentive-shift performance as a function of magnitude and number of sucrose rewards. *J. Comp. Physiol. Psychol.* 62, 487-490.

Rosen, A. J., Glass, D. H. and Ison, J. R. (1967). Amobarbital sodium and instrumental performance following reward reduction. *Psychon. Sci.* 9, 129-130.

Ross, D. M. (1965). The behaviour of sessile coelenterates in relation to some conditioning experiments. *Anim Behav., Supplement* 1, 43-53.

Russell, I. S. (1966). The differential role of the cerebral cortex in classical and instrumental conditioning. *In*: "Biological and Physiological Problems of Psychology", XVIII Internat. Cong. Psychol. Moscow.

Russell, I. S., Plotkin, H. C. and Kleinman, D. (1970). Task difficulty and lateralization of learning in the functional split-brain rat. *Physiol. Behav.* 5, 469-478.

Saavedra, M., Garcia, E. and Pinto-Hamuy, J. (1963). Acquisition of auditory conditioned responses in normal and neodecorticate rats. *J. Comp. Physiol. Psychol.* 56, 31-35.

Saltzman, I. J. (1949). Maze learning in the absence of primary reinforcement: a study of secondary reinforcement. *J. Comp. Physiol. Psychol.* 42, 161-173.

Samuels, I. (1959). Reticular mechanisms and behaviour. *Psychol. Bull.* 56, 1-25.

Schachter, S. (1967). Cognitive effects on bodily functioning: studies of obesity and eating. *In*: "Neurophysiology and Emotion" (D. C. Glass, Ed.), 117-144. Rockefeller University Press, New York.

Schwartz, B. and Williams, D. R. (1972). Two different kinds of key peck in the pigeon: some properties of responses maintained by negative and positive response-reinforcer contingencies. *J. Exp. Anal. Behav.* 18, 201-216.

Sclafani, A. and Grossman, S. P. (1969). Hyperphagia produced by knife cuts between the medial and lateral hypothalamus in the rat. *Physiol. Behav.* 4, 533-537.

Scobie, S. R. (1972). Interaction of an aversive Pavlovian conditioned stimulus with aversively and appetitively motivated operants in rats. *J. Comp. Physiol. Psychol.* 79, 171-188.

Scobie, S. R. (1973). The response-shock interval and conditioned suppression of avoidance in rats. *Anim. Learn. Behav.* 1, 17-20.

Seligman, M. E. P., Maier, S. F. and Solomon, R. L. (1971). Unpredictable and uncontrollable aversive events. *In*: "Aversive Conditioning and Learning" (F. R. Brush, Ed.), 347-400. Academic Press, New York, London.

Seligman, M. E. P., Mineka, S. and Fillit, H. (1971). Conditioned drinking produced by procaine, NaCl, and angiotensin. *J. Comp. Physiol. Psychol.* 77, 110-121.

Sheffield, F. D. (1965). Relation between classical conditioning and instrumental learning. *In*: "Classical Conditioning" (W. F. Prokasy, Ed.), 302-322. Appleton-Century-Crofts, New York.

Sheffield, F. D. and Roby, T. B. (1950). Reward value of a nonnutritive sweet taste. *J. Comp. Physiol. Psychol.* 43, 471-481.

Sheffield, F. D., Roby, T. B. and Campbell, B. A. (1954). Drive reduction versus consummatory behaviour as determinants of reinforcement. *J. Comp. Physiol. Psychol.* 47, 349-354.

Sidman, M. (1953). Avoidance conditioning with brief shock and no extero-ceptive warning signal *Science, N.Y.* 118, 157-158.

Sidman, M., Herrnstein, R. J. and Conrad, D. G. (1957). Maintenance of avoid-ance behavior by unavoidable shock. *J. Comp. Physiol. Psychol.* 50, 553-557.

Siegel, P. S. and Brantley, J. J. (1951). The relationship of emotionality to the consummatory response of eating. *J. Exp. Psychol.* 42, 304-306.

Siegel, P. S. and Siegel, H. S. (1949). The effect of emotionality on the water intake of the rat. *J. Comp. Physiol. Psychol.* 42, 12-16.

Singh, S. D. and Eysenck, H. J. (1960). Conditioned emotional response in the rat: III. Drug antagonism. *J. Gen. Psychol.* 63, 275-285.

Skinner, B. F. (1938). "The Behavior of Organisms", Appleton-Century, New York.

Skinner, B. F. (1948). Superstition in the pigeon. *J. Exp. Psychol.* 38, 168-172.

Sokolov, Ye. N. (1960). Neuronal models and the orienting reflex. *In*: "The Central Nervous System and Behaviour" (M. A. B. Brazier, Ed.), 3rd Conference, 187-276. Josiah Macy Jnr. Foundation, New York.

Sokolov, Ye. N. (1963a). "Perception and the Conditioned Reflex". Pergamon Press, Oxford.

Sokolov, Ye. N. (1963b). Higher nervous functions: the orienting reflex. *Ann. Rev. Physiol.* 25, 545-580.

Sokolov, Ye. N. (1966). Neuronal mechanisms of the orienting reflex. *18th Internat. Cong. Psychol., Moscow, Symposium No. 5: Orienting Reflex, Alterness and Attention*, 31-36.

Solomon, R. L. (1964). Punishment. *Amer. Psychologist* 19, 239-253.

Soltysik, S. (1960). Studies on the avoidance conditioning: III. Alimentary conditioned reflex model of the avoidance reflex. *Acta. Biol. Exp.* 20, 183-192.

Soltysik, S. (1964). Inhibitory feedback in avoidance conditioning. *In*: "Feed-back Systems Controlling Nervous Activity" (A. Escobar, Ed.), (First Conference on Neurobiology), 316-331. Sociedad Mexicana de Ciencias Fisiologicas, Mexico.

Soltysik, S. and Jaworska, K. (1962). Studies on the aversive classical conditioning, 2: On the reinforcing role of shock in the classical leg flexion conditioning. *Acta Biol. Exp.* 22, 181-191.

Soltysik, S. and Kowalska, M. (1960). Studies on the avoidance conditioning: I. Relations between cardiac (type I) and motor (type II) effects in the avoidance reflex. *Acta Biol. Exp.* 20, 157-170.

Spence, J. T. and Spence, K. W. (1966). The motivational components of manifest anxiety. *In*: "Anxiety and Behaviour" (C. D. Spielberger, Ed.), 291-326. Academic Press, New York, London.

Spence K. W. (1937). The differential response in animals to stimuli varying within a single dimension. *Psychol. Rev.* 44, 430-444.

Spence, K. W. (1956). "Behavior Theory and Conditioning", Yale University Press, New Haven.

Spence, K. W. (1966). Cognitive and drive factors in the extinction of the conditioned eye blink in human subjects. *Psychol. Rev.* 73, 445-458.

Spence, K. W., Platt, J. R. and Matsumoto, R. (1965). Intertrial reinforcement and the partial reinforcement effect as a function of number of training trials. *Psychon. Sci.* 3, 205-206.

Staddon, J. E. R. and Simmelhag, V. L. (1971). The "superstition experiment": a re-examination of its implications for the principles of adaptive behavior. *Psychol. Rev.* 78, 3-43.

Starzl, T. E., Taylor, C. W. and Magoun, H. W. (1951). Collateral afferent excitation of reticular formation of brain stem *J. Neurophysiol.* 14, 479-496.

Stein, L. (1964). Reciprocal action of reward and punishment mechanisms. *In:* "The Role of Pleasure in Behaviour" (R. G. Heath, Ed.), pp. 113-139. Harper and Row, New York.

Stein, L. (1965). Facilitation of avoidance behaviour by positive brain stimulation. *J. Comp. Physiol. Psychol.* 60, 9-19.

Strongman, K. T. (1965). The effect of anxiety on food intake in the rat. *Quart. J. Exp. Psychol.* 17, 255-260.

Stumpf, Ch. (1965). Drug action on the electrical activity of the hippocampus. *Internat. Rev. Neurobiol.* 8, 77-138.

Swanson, A. M. and Isaacson, R. L. (1969). Hippocampal lesions and the frustration effect in rats. *J. Comp. Physiol. Psychol.* 68, 562-567.

Sutherland, N. S. (1966). Partial reinforcement and breadth of learning. *Quart. J. Exp. Psychol.* 18, 289-301.

Sutherland, N. S. and Mackintosh, N. J. (1971). "Mechanisms of Animal Discrimination Learning", Academic Press, London, New York.

Taub, E. and Berman, A. J. (1968). Movement and learning in the absence of sensory feedback *In:* "The Neuropsychology of Spatially Oriented Behaviour" (S. J. Freedman, Ed.), 173-192. Dorsey Press, Homewood, Illinois.

Taylor, C. (1964). "The Explanation of Behaviour", Routledge and Kegan Paul, London.

Tchilingaryan, L. I. (1963). Changes in excitability of the motor area of the cerebral cortex during extinction of a conditioned reflex elaborated to direct electrical stimulation of that area. *In:* "Central and Peripheral Mechanisms of Motor Functions" (E. Gutmann and P. Hnik, Eds), 167-175. Czechoslovak Academy of Sciences, Prague.

Teplov, B. M. (1964). Problems in the study of general types of higher nervous activity in man and animals. *In:* "Pavlov's Typology" (J. A. Gray, Ed.), 3-153. Pergamon Press, Oxford.

Terhune, J. G. and Premack, D. (1970). On the proportionality between the probability of not-running and the punishment effect of being forced to run. *Learn. Motiv.* 1, 141-149.

Terrace, H. S. (1963a). Discrimination learning with and without errors. *J. Exp. Anal. Behav.* 6, 1-27.

Terrace, H. S. (1963b). Errorless transfer of a discrimination across two continua. *J. Exp. Anal. Behav.*, 6, 223-232.

Terrace, H. S. (1966a), Stimulus control. *In:* "Operant Behavior: Areas of Research and Application" (W. K. Honig, Ed.), 271-344. Appleton-Century-Crofts, New York.

Terrace, H. S. (1966b). Behavioral contrast and the peak shift: effects of extended discrimination training. *J. Exp. Anal. Behav.* 9, 613-617.

Terrace, H. S. (1971). Escape from S-. *Learn. Motiv.* 2, 148-163.

Terrace, H. S. (1972a). "Active" and "passive" inhibition during successive discrimination learning. *Abstract Guide of 20th Internat. Cong. Psychol., Tokyo.*

Terrace, H. S. (1972b). Conditioned inhibition in successive discrimination learning. *In*: "Inhibition and Learning" (R. A. Boakes and M. S. Halliday, Eds), 99-199. Academic Press, London, New York.

Thomas, E. (1972). Excitatory and inhibitory processes in hypothalamic conditioning. *In*: "Inhibition and Learning" (R. A. Boakes and M. S. Halliday, Eds), 359-380. Academic Press, London, New York.

Thomas, E. and Wagner, A. R. (1964). Partial reinforcement of the classically conditioned eyelid response in the rabbit. *J. Comp. Physiol. Psychol.* 58, 157-158.

Thompson, R. F. and Spencer, W. A. (1966). Habituation. *Psychol. Rev.* 73, 16-43.

Thompson, T. and Bloom, W. (1966). Aggressive behavior and extinction-induced response-rate increase. *Psychon. Sci.* 5, 335-336.

Thompson, T. I. and Sturm T. (1965). Classical conditioning of aggressive display in Siamese fighting fish. *J. Exp. Anal. Behav.* 8, 397-403.

Thor, D. H. and Hoats, D. L. (1968). A circadian variable in self-exposure to light. *Psychon. Sci.* 12, 1-2.

Thorpe, W. H. (1963). "Learning and Instinct in Animals", Methuen, London.

Trapold, M. A. (1962). The effect of incentive motivation on an unrelated reflex response. *J. Comp. Physiol. Psychol.,* 55, 1034-1039.

Trapold, M. A., Lawton, G. W., Dick, R. A. and Gross, D. M. (1968). Transfer of training from differential classical to differential instrumental conditioning. *J. Exp. Psychol.* 76, 568-573.

Trapold, M. A. and Overmier, J. B. (1972). The second learning process in instrumental learning. *In*: "Classical Conditioning II: Current Research and Theory" (A. H. Black and W. F. Prokasy, Eds), 427-452. Appleton-Century-Crofts, New York.

Trapold, M. A. and Winokur, S. (1967). Transfer from classical conditioning and extinction to acquisition, extinction and stimulus generalization of a positively reinforced instrumental response. *J. Exp. Psychol.* 73, 517-525.

Tugendhat, B. (1960a). The normal feeding behaviour of the three-spined stickleback (*Gasteosteus aculeatus L*). *Behaviour* 15, 284-318.

Tugendhat, B. (1960b). The disturbed feeding behaviour of the three-spined stickleback: I. Electric shock is administered in the food area. *Behaviour* 16, 159-187.

Turner, L. H. and Solomon, R. L. (1962). Human traumatic avoidance learning; theory and experiments on the operant-respondent distinction and failures to learn. *Psychol. Monogr.* 76. No. 40 (Whole No. 559).

Ulrich, R. E. (1967). Pain-agression. *In*: "Foundations of Conditioning and Learning" (G. A. Kimble, Ed.), 600-622. Appleton-Century-Crofts, New York.

Vandaris, R. M. and Fitzgerald, R. D. (1969). Effects of partial reinforcement on a classically conditioned eyeblink response in dogs. *J. Comp. Physiol. Psychol.* 67, 531-534.

Vinogradova, O. S. (1961). "The Orienting Reflex and its Neurophysiological Mechanisms (Orientirovchny Refleks i yego Neirofiziologicheskiye Mekhanizmy)". Akad. pedagog. Nauk RSFSR, Moscow.

Vinogradova, O. S. (1966). Investigation of habituation in single neurons of different brain structures with special reference to the hippocampus. *18th Internat. Cong. Psychol., Moscow, Symposium No. 5: Orienting Reflex, Alertness and Attention,* 55-58.

Vinogradova, O. S. (1970). Registration of information and the limbic system. *In:* "Short-term Changes in Neural Activity and Behaviour" (G. Horn and R. A. Hinde, Eds), 95-140. Cambridge University Press, Cambridge.

Wagner, A. R. (1959). The role of reinforcement and non-reinforcement in an "apparent frustration effect". *J. Exp. Psychol.* 57, 130-136.

Wagner, A. R. (1961). Effects of amount and percentage of reinforcement and number of acquisition trials on conditioning and extinction. *J. Exp. Psychol.* 62, 234-242.

Wagner, A. R. (1963a). Conditioned frustration as a learned drive. *J. Exp. Psychol.* 66, 142-148.

Wagner, A. R. (1963b). Sodium amytal and partially reinforced runway performance. *J. Exp. Psychol.* 65, 474-477.

Wagner, A. R. (1966). Frustration and punishment. *In:* "Current Research on Motivation" (R. M. Haber, Ed.), 229-239. Holt, Rinehart and Winston, New York.

Wagner, A. R. and Rescorla, R. A. (1972). Inhibition in Pavlovian conditioning: application of a theory. *In:* "Inhibition and Learning" (R. A. Boakes and M. S. Halliday, Eds), 301-336. Academic Press, London, New York.

Wagner, A. R., Siegel, L. S. and Fein, G. G. (1967a). Extinction of conditioned fear as a function of percentage of reinforcement. *J. Comp. Physiol. Psychol.* 63, 160-164.

Wagner, A. R., Thomas, E. and Norton, T. (1967b). Conditioning with electrical stimulation of motor cortex: evidence of a possible source of motivation. *J. Comp. Physiol. Psychol.* 64, 191-199.

Warren, J. A. Jnr. and Bolles, R. C. (1967). A re-evaluation of a simple contiguity interpretation of avoidance learning. *J. Comp. Physiol. Psychol.* 64, 179-182.

Webb, W. E. and Goodman, I. J. (1958). Activating role of an irrelevant drive in absence of the relevant drive. *Psychol. Rep.* 4, 235-238.

Weisman, R. G. and Litner, J. S. (1969). Positive conditioned reinforcement of Sidman avoidance behavior in rats. *J. Comp. Physiol. Psychol.* 68, 597-603.

Weiss, P. (1941). Self-differentiation of the basic patterns of coordination. *Comp. Psychol. Monog.* 17, 1-96.

Wiepkema, P. R. (1971). Positive feedbacks at work during feeding. *Behaviour* 39, 266-273.

Wike, E. L. and Casey, A. (1954). The secondary reinforcing value of food for thirsty animals. *J. Comp. Physiol. Psychol.* 47, 240-243.

Williams, D. R. and Williams, H. (1969). Auto-maintenance in the pigeon: sustained pecking despite contingent non-reinforcement. *J. Exp. Anal. Behav.* 12, 51-520.

Williams, J. L., Treichler, F. R. and Thomas, D. R. (1964). Satiation and recovery of the "air-drinking" response in rats. *Psychon. Sci.* 1, 49-50.

Woodworth, R. S. and Schlosberg, H. (1954). "Experimental Psychology", Methuen, London.

Yamaguchi, H. G. (1952). Gradients of drive stimulus (S_D) intensity generalization. *J. Exp. Psychol.* 43, 298-304.

Yeatman, F. R. and Hirsch, J. (1971). Attempted replication of, and selective breeding for, instrumental conditioning of *Drosophila Melanogaster. Anim. Behav.* 19, 454-462.

Zener, K. (1937). The significance of behavior accompanying conditioned salivary secretion for theories of the conditioned response. *Amer. J. Psychol.* 50, 384-403.

Ziff, P. R. and Capaldi, E. J. (1971). Amytal and the small trial partial reinforcement effect: stimulus properties of early trial nonrewards. *J. Exp. Psychol.* 87, 263-269.

ADDITIONAL REFERENCES ADDED IN PROOF

Amsel, A. (1967). Partial reinforcement effects on vigor and persistence. *In* "The Psychology of Learning and Motivation" (K. W. Spence and J. T. Spence, Eds), Vol 1, 2-65. Academic Press, New York.

Capaldi, E. J. (1971). Memory and learning: a sequential viewpoint. *In* "Animal Memory" (W. K. Honig and P. H. R. James, Eds), 115-154. Academic Press, New York.

Egger, M. D. and Miller, N. E. (1962). Secondary reinforcement in rats as a function of information value and reliability of the stimulus. *J. exp. Psychol.* 64, 97-104.

Hearst, E. (1967). Oscillatory behavior during approach-avoidance conflict. *J. exp. Anal. Behav.* 10, 75-84.

Miller, N. E. (1961). Implications for theories of reinforcement. *In* "Electrical Stimulation of the Brain" (D. Sheer, Ed.), 575-581. University of Texas Press, Austin, Texas.

Mowrer, O. H. and Lamoreaux, R. R. (1946). Fear as an intervening variable in avoidance conditioning. *J. comp. Psychol.* 39, 29-49.

Oatley, K. (1967). A control model for the physiological basis of thirst. *Med. biol. Engin.* 5, 225-237.

Reiss, S. and Wagner, A. R. (1973). CS habituation produces a "latent inhibition effect" but no active "conditioned inhibition". *Learn. Motiv.* 3, 237-245.

Tinbergen, N. (1951). *The Study of Instinct.* Oxford University Press, Oxford.

Author Index

Numbers in italics are those pages on which references are listed.

Subject Index

Numbers in *italics* indicate pages where definitions of some important terms may be found. A full explanation of the notation used for primary instrumental reinforcement will be found on pp. 133-135, and for secondary instrumental reinforcement on pp. 238-230.